A Conceptual Modeling Approach to Design of
Catalogs and Cataloging Rules

A Conceptual Modeling Approach to Design of
Catalogs and Cataloging Rules

Shoichi Taniguchi

Hituzi Syobo Publishing

Copyright © Shoichi Taniguchi 2007
First published 2007

Author: Shoichi Taniguchi

All rights reserved. Except for the quotation of short passages for the purposes of criticism and review, no part of this publication may be reduced, stored in a retrieval system, or transmitted in any form or by any means, electronic, mechanical, photocopying, recording or otherwise, without the written prior permission of the publisher.
In case of photocopying and electronic copying and retrieval from network personally, permission will be given on receipts of payment and making inquiries. For details please contact us through e-mail. Our e-mail address is given below.

Book Design © Hirokazu Mukai (glyph)

Hituzi Syobo Publishing
5-21-5 Koishikawa Bunkyo-ku Tokyo, Japan 112-0002

phone +81-3-5684-6871 fax +81-3-5684-6872
e-mail: toiawase@hituzi.co.jp
http://www.hituzi.co.jp/
postal transfer 00120-8-142852

ISBN978-4-89476-332-6
Printed in Japan

Contents

List of Figures	x
List of Tables	xiv
Preface	xv
Acknowledgments	xix

Chapter 1 Introduction — 1
1.1 Catalogs and Their Design — 1
1.2 Conceptual Design and Modeling in Systems Development — 4
1.3 Design Methodology for Catalogs and Cataloging Rules — 7

Chapter 2 Literature Review — 13
2.1 Objectives and Functions of Catalogs — 13
2.2 Modeling of Bibliographic Universe and Records — 16
  2.2.1 Discussions Preceding and Affecting Modeling — 16
  2.2.2 Models That Have Been Proposed — 18
2.3 Analysis and Modeling of Bibliographic Relationships — 27
2.4 Objectives for Construction of Cataloging Codes — 30
2.5 Modeling of Cataloging Process — 32

Chapter 3 A Conceptual Model Giving Primacy to Text-level Bibliographic Entity — 37
3.1 What Are 'Text' and 'Expression'? — 37
3.2 Significance of Models Giving Primacy to Text-level Entity — 40
3.3 Examining Typical Models Containing Text-level Entity — 41
  3.3.1 Two Methods of Defining Bibliographic Entity — 41
  3.3.2 Modeling Current Practice at Conceptual Level — 43
  3.3.3 IFLA Study Group's FRBR Model — 48
  3.3.4 Taniguchi's Three-layered Model — 50

3.4 Defining Text-level Entity and Other Entities ... 52
  3.4.1 Entities Forming Model Giving Primacy to Text-level Entity ... 52
  3.4.2 Implications of Proposed Framework ... 54
  3.4.3 Correlation With Other Relevant Models ... 60
3.5 Associating Attributes with Text-level Entity ... 64
  3.5.1 Titles and Statements of Responsibility that Appear in Item ... 64
  3.5.2 Method Shown in FRBR Model—
      Associating Attributes With Manifestation-level Entity ... 64
  3.5.3 Method for Text-prioritized Model—
      Associating Attributes With Text-level Entity ... 68
  3.5.4 Examples of Other Attributes Associated With Text-level Entity ... 71
3.6 Defining Relationships Between Instances of Text-level Entity ... 72
  3.6.1 Relationships Defined in FRBR Model ... 72
  3.6.2 Relationships in Text-prioritized Model ... 74
3.7 Creating Scenario on How Bibliographic Entities Are Used ... 75
  3.7.1 What Is Scenario? ... 75
  3.7.2 Scenario Deduced from Modeling of Current Practice ... 76
  3.7.3 Scenario for FRBR Model ... 77
  3.7.4 Scenario for Text-prioritized Model ... 79
3.8 Showing Examples of Bibliographic Records in Line with Text-prioritized Model ... 80
  3.8.1 Premises for Showing Examples ... 80
  3.8.2 Case 1: Book ... 81
  3.8.3 Case 2: Book ... 89
  3.8.4 Case 3: Sound Recording ... 93
  3.8.5 Case 4: Electronic Resource ... 99
3.9 Chapter Conclusion ... 103

Chapter 4 Conceptual Modeling of Component Parts of Bibliographic Resources ... 107

4.1 Significance of Modeling Component Parts and Types of Component Parts ... 107
4.2 Modeling of Component Parts in FRBR ... 108
  4.2.1 Case of Content Parts in FRBR ... 108

4.2.2 Case of Document Parts in FRBR	112
4.3 Modeling of Component Parts in Text-prioritized Model	113
4.3.1 Case of Content Parts in Text-prioritized Model	113
4.3.2 Case of Document Parts in Text-prioritized Model	115
4.4 Examples of Bibliographic Records of Component Parts in Line with Text-prioritized Model	116
4.5 Modeling of Resources at Aggregate Level	124
4.6 Discussion on Consistency in Conceptual Models	128
4.7 Chapter Conclusion	129

Chapter 5 Trial on Creation of Text-level Entity Records from Pre-existing MARC Records — 131

5.1 Two Methods of Creating Bibliographic Records in Accordance with Text-prioritized Model	131
5.2 Outline of Conversion Procedure from MARC Bibliographic Records	133
5.3 Dividing MARC Bibliographic Records	134
5.3.1 Problems Involved in Dividing MARC Records	134
5.3.2 Work level Records	143
5.3.3 Expression level Records	144
5.3.4 Manifestation and Item level Records	147
5.4 Merging Divided Records and Developing Relationships	148
5.5 Prototype System for Retrieving and Displaying Records	160
5.5.1 An Example of System Use	161
5.5.2 Another Example of System Use	170
5.5.3 Extended Search Mode	180
5.6 Chapter Conclusion	186

Chapter 6 Relevant Projects and Discussions — 189

Chapter 7 Analysis of Requirements of Cataloging Rules by Use of Orientedness — 201

7.1 What Is 'Orientedness'?	201

7.1.1	Aim of Introducing a New Concept	201
7.1.2	Definition of Orientedness	202
7.1.3	Orientedness Corresponding to Objectives of Bibliographic Description	204
7.1.4	Other Categories of Orientedness	207
7.1.5	Orientedness Involved in Choosing Access Points and Building Headings	208
7.1.6	Relationships Between Orientedness and User Tasks and Between Orientedness and Objectives for Construction of Cataloging Codes	209

7.2 Assessment of Principles of Description in Terms of Orientedness   212
   7.2.1 Assessment of Description Principles   212
   7.2.2 Assessment of Bibliographic Elements   216
7.3 Assessment of Principles of Access Points and Headings in Terms of Orientedness   219
7.4 Investigation of Orientedness in AACR2 Descriptive Rules   222
7.5 Identification of Alternative Rules for AACR2 Descriptive Rules with Their Orientedness   226
   7.5.1 Identification of Possible Alternatives   226
   7.5.2 Identification of Possible Sets of Rules   228
7.6 Chapter Conclusion   233

Chapter 8 Design of Cataloging Rules Using Conceptual Modeling of Cataloging Process   235

8.1 Outline of Conceptual Design Procedure for Cataloging Rules   235
8.2 Phase 0: Specifying Requirements and Defining Cataloger Tasks   239
   8.2.1 Specifying Requirements by Use of Orientedness   239
   8.2.2 Defining Cataloger Tasks   240
8.3 Phase 1: Building Core Model   241
   8.3.1 Specifying Basic Event and Action Patterns Under Task 'Specify Source of Values'   242
   8.3.2 Specifying Basic Event and Action Patterns Under Other Tasks   249
8.4 Phase 2: Propagating Core Model and Defining Propagated Model by Choosing Event-Action Pairs   260

8.4.1	Step 1: Propagating Core Model	260
8.4.2	Step 2: Defining Propagated Model by Choosing Event-Action Pairs	267
8.5	Chapter Conclusion	269

Chapter 9 Application of Proposed Design Method: Issue of Recording Evidence in Bibliographic Records 271

9.1	Aim of Recording Evidence	271
9.2	Phase 0: Specifying Requirements in Terms of Orientedness Involved in Recording Evidence	272
9.3	Phase 1: Modifying Core Model by Adding Actions of Recording Evidence	273
9.3.1	Enumerating Action Patterns Based on Classes of Evidence	273
9.3.2	Assessing Orientedness among Evidence Classes	275
9.3.3	Levels to Which Evidence Recording is Applied	277
9.3.4	Phase 2: Propagating Core Model and Defining Propagated Model by Choosing Event-Action Pairs	278
9.4	Examples of Recording Evidence	279
9.4.1	Examples from Pre-existing Records and Rules	279
9.4.2	Examples of Recording Evidence in Bibliographic Records	280
9.5	Possible Usage of Recorded Evidence	291
9.5.1	Identification and Distinction of Resources	291
9.5.2	Transformation of Data Values	293
9.6	Chapter Conclusion	294

Chapter 10 Conclusion 297

References 301

Index 313

Figures

Figure 3-1. Bibliographic entities defined in the two methods. 53
Figure 3-2. Bibliographic entities and their relationships in the proposed model. 54
Figure 3-3. Mapping of bibliographic entities in the other models to those in the proposed model. 62
Figure 3-4. Mapping attributes to user tasks in the FRBR model. 65
Figure 3-5. Mapping attributes to user tasks in the proposed model. 69
Figure 3-6. A scenario derived from the modeling of current practice. 77
Figure 3-7. A scenario for the FRBR model. 79
Figure 3-8. A scenario for the proposed model. 80
Figure 3-9-1. Case 1-1. MARC bibliographic record for a book. 84
Figure 3-9-2. Case 1-2. An example of a set of records for the book in line with the proposed model. 85
Figure 3-9-3. Case 1-3. Another example of a set of records for the book in line with the proposed model. 87
Figure 3-9-4. Case 1-4. An example of a set of records for the book in line with the FRBR model. 89
Figure 3-9-5. Case 1-5. An example of a set of records for the book in line with the three-layered model. 89
Figure 3-10. Case 2. An example of a set of records for another book in line with the proposed model. 92
Figure 3-11-1. Case 3-1. MARC bibliographic record for a sound recording. 95
Figure 3-11-2. Case 3-2. An example of a set of records for the sound recording in line with the proposed model. 96
Figure 3-11-3. Case 3-3. Another example of a set of records for the sound recording in line with the proposed model. 98
Figure 3-11-4. Case 3-4. An example of a set of records for the sound recording in line with the FRBR model. 99

Figure 3-12-1. Case 4-1. MARC bibliographic record for an electronic resource. 101
Figure 3-12-2. Case 4-2. An example of a set of records for the electronic resource in line with the proposed model. 103
Figure 4-1. Modeling of a content part in the FRBR model. 109
Figure 4-2. Modeling of a document part in the FRBR model. 113
Figure 4-3. Modeling of a content part in the text-prioritized model. 114
Figure 4-4. Modeling of a document part in the text-prioritized model. 115
Figure 4-5-1. Case 1-1. MARC bibliographic record for an item at the integral unit level. 118
Figure 4-5-2. Case 1-2. An example of a set of records for a content part. 120
Figure 4-6. Case 2. Another example of a set of records for a content part. 122
Figure 4-7. Case 3. An example of a set of records for a document part. 124
Figure 4-8. Modeling of a resource at the aggregate level in the FRBR model. 126
Figure 4-9. Modeling of a resource at the aggregate level in the text- prioritized model. 126
Figure 4-10. Modeling of a serial in the FRBR model. 127
Figure 4-11. Modeling of a serial in the text-prioritized model. 127
Figure 5-1. An example of a set of records created through the MARC record division. A case of book. 139
Figure 5-2. An example of a set of records created through the MARC record division. A case of sound recording. 141
Figure 5-3. An example of a set of records created through the MARC record division. Another case of sound recording. 143
Figure 5-4. A merged record at the *work* level. 152
Figure 5-5. Another merged record at the *work* level. Case of musical work. 153
Figure 5-6. Another merged record at the *work* level. Case of musical work. 155
Figure 5-7. Merged records at the *expression* level. 157
Figure 5-8. *Work* level records having relationships with the record in Figure 5-4. 159
Figure 5-9. *Work* level records having relationships among them. 160
Figure 5-10. Initial search screen. 163
Figure 5-11-1. The result of a search showing hit records in a brief form (the top part). 163
Figure 5-11-2. The result of a search showing hit records in a brief form (the bottom part). 164

Figure 5-12-1. The screen showing a selected *work* record (the top part). 164
Figure 5-12-2. The screen showing a selected *work* record (the middle part). 165
Figure 5-12-3. The screen showing a selected *work* record (the bottom part). 165
Figure 5-13-1. The screen showing a selected *expression* record (the top part). 166
Figure 5-13-2. The screen showing a selected *expression* record (the bottom part). 166
Figure 5-14-1. The screen showing a selected pair of *expression* and *manifestation* records (the top part). 167
Figure 5-14-2. The screen showing a selected pair of *expression* and *manifestation* records (the bottom part). 167
Figure 5-15. The screen showing another pair of *expression* and *manifestation* records. 168
Figure 5-16. The screen showing another *expression* record. 168
Figure 5-17. The screen showing a *manifestation* record linked to the *expression*. 169
Figure 5-18-1. The screen showing a different *work* record (the top part). 169
Figure 5-18-2. The screen showing a different *work* record (the bottom part). 170
Figure 5-19-1. The result of another search showing hit records (the top part). 172
Figure 5-19-2. The result of another search showing hit records (the bottom part). 172
Figure 5-20-1. The screen showing a musical *work* record (the top part). 173
Figure 5-20-2. The screen showing a musical *work* record (the second part) 173
Figure 5-20-3. The screen showing a musical *work* record (the third part). 174
Figure 5-20-4. The screen showing a musical *work* record (the bottom part). 174
Figure 5-21-1. The screen showing an *expression* linked to the musical *work* (the top part). 175
Figure 5-21-2. The screen showing an *expression* linked to the musical *work* (the bottom part). 175
Figure 5-22-1. The screen showing the first *expression-manifestation* pair (the top part). 176
Figure 5-22-2. The screen showing the first *expression-manifestation* pair (the bottom part) 176
Figure 5-23. The screen showing the second *expression-manifestation* pair. 177
Figure 5-24. The screen showing the third *expression-manifestation* pair. 177
Figure 5-25. The screen showing a different musical *work* record. 178
Figure 5-26. The screen showing a different expression record. 178
Figure 5-27-1. The screen showing a *manifestation* that contains more than one *expression* (the top part). 179

Figure 5-27-2. The screen showing a *manifestation* that contains more than one *expression* (the bottom part). 179
Figure 5-28. The screen showing another *expression* contained in the *manifestation*. 180
Figure 5-29. The screen showing a search in the extended mode. 183
Figure 5-30-1. The result of an extended mode search (the top part). 183
Figure 5-30-2. The result of an extended mode search (the bottom part). 184
Figure 5-31. The screen showing an *expression* record matched in the extended search mode. 184
Figure 5-32. A search result with the same query in the standard mode. 185
Figure 5-33. The result of another search in the standard mode. 185
Figure 5-34. A search result with the same query in the extended mode. 186
Figure 7-1. Relationships between the categories of orientedness and the user tasks. 211
Figure 7-2. Orientedness involved in the bibliographic elements in ISBD and AACR2. 219
Figure 8-1. Outline of conceptual design procedure for cataloging rules. 239
Figure 8-2. A diagram showing state transitions under the task 'Specify Source of Values.' 247
Figure 8-3. A diagram showing state transitions under the task 'Choose Values.' 254
Figure 8-4. A diagram showing state transitions under the task 'Establish Form of Values.' 258
Figure 9-1. An example of recording evidence in a bibliographic record. 287
Figure 9-2. Another example of recording evidence in a bibliographic record. 291

Tables

Table 5-1. Mapping of data elements in line with the text-prioritized model to MARC21 data elements.   136

Table 7-1. Summary of possible sets of rules when each category of orientedness is maximized.   232

Table 8-1. Summary of the categories of orientedness involved in the event-action pairs under the task 'Specify Source of Values.'   248

Table 8-2. Basic event and action patterns under the task 'Choose Values.'   252

Table 8-3. Summary of the categories of orientedness involved in the event-action pairs under the task 'Choose Values.'   255

Table 8-4. Basic event and action patterns under the task 'Establish Form of Values.'   256

Table 8-5. Summary of the categories of orientedness involved in the event-action pairs under the task 'Establish Form of Values.'   259

Table 8-6. Part of propagated event and action patterns on the 'date of publication, distribution, etc.' under the task 'Choose Values.'   263

Table 8-7. Part of propagated event and action patterns on the 'date of publication, distribution, etc.' under the task 'Establish Form of Values.'   266

PREFACE

This book examines the application of conceptual modeling to the design of catalogs and cataloging rules, with the aim of utilizing the valuable characteristics of that modeling approach.

Conceptual modeling of the bibliographic universe is crucial for designing catalogs, and if we use the entity-relationship model as a modeling language, then the model is made up of bibliographic and other entities, their attributes and relationships. In the first half of the book, a conceptual model is proposed which gives primacy to the text-level (in other words, expression-level) bibliographic entity. First, a viewpoint on the case in which the bibliographic entity is given primacy in a model is introduced, and is used to examine certain models. Second, a new model is proposed that gives primacy to the text-level entity, chiefly by indicating differences from the IFLA Study Group's *Functional Requirements for Bibliographic Records* (FRBR) model, which gives primacy to the manifestation-level entity. The text-level entity, its main attributes, relationships between instances of the entity, and a scenario of how entities are used by users are clarified. Third, the FRBR model and the newly proposed model are examined in modeling component parts of resources. Further, to investigate the feasibility of creating bibliographic records in accordance with the proposed model, MARC bibliographic records are converted into those structured under the hierarchical records approach. In addition, a prototype system is developed for retrieving and displaying the structured records in order to demonstrate their usefulness.

In the latter half of the book, a method of designing cataloging rules at the conceptual level is proposed, which attains consistent and scalable design. Cataloging rules in this case indicate those instructing how to create bibliographic record(s) for bibliographic resource(s) in a way that reflects the entities established in a conceptual model of the bibliographic universe, or specifically how to deal with and record each data element of the bibliographic record. First, a new concept of 'orientedness' is introduced, to analyze cataloging rules and thus to represent functional and non-functional requirements in the cataloging process. Second, a method is proposed of designing cataloging rules by utilizing conceptual modeling of the cataloging process while applying the concept of orientedness. A general model for the cataloging process is also proposed as part of the design method. Additionally, to show the validity and usefulness of the method, the design method is applied to the new issue of recording evidence in bibliographic records.

This work was conducted as my doctoral dissertation which was submitted to Keio University in June 2004 and approved in March 2005. The dissertation has been published as this book with only minor additions and modifications. Thus, this work does not reflect research findings in this field more recent than 2004.

The dissertation is based on the following existing papers:

Taniguchi, S. An analysis of orientedness in cataloging rules. *Journal of the American Society for Information Science*. vol. 50, no. 5, 1999, pp. 448-460. Copyright © 1999 Wiley Periodicals, Inc.

Taniguchi, S. Design of cataloging rules using conceptual modeling of cataloging process. *Journal of the American Society for Information Science and Technology*. vol. 55, no. 6, 2004, pp. 498-512. Copyright © 2004 Wiley Periodicals, Inc.

Taniguchi, S. Recording evidence in bibliographic records and descriptive metadata. *Journal of the American Society for Information Science and Technology*. vol. 56, no. 8, 2005, pp. 872-882. Copyright © 2005 Wiley Periodicals, Inc.

Taniguchi, S. A conceptual model giving primacy to expression-level bibliographic entity in cataloging. *Journal of Documentation*. vol. 58, no. 4, 2002, pp. 363-382. Copyright © 2002 MCB UP Ltd.

Taniguchi, S. Conceptual modeling of component parts of bibliographic resources in cataloging. *Journal of Documentation*. vol. 59, no. 6, 2003, pp. 692-708. Copyright © 2003 MCB UP Ltd.

Taniguchi, S. Expression-level bibliographic entity records: a trial on creation from pre-existing MARC records. *Cataloging & Classification Quarterly*. vol. 38, no. 2, 2004, pp. 33-59. Copyright © 2004 The Haworth Press, Inc.

I have engaged in research on information organization, and cataloging in particular, for more than fifteen years. At the outset, I did not imagine that this pursuit would continue for such a long time and that I would become so deeply involved in such research.

In 1990, as my first research result, I proposed a three-layered model to understand the implications of critical issues involved in current cataloging practice and to seek a possible alternative framework for resolving those issues. To me, it seemed crucial to differentiate critical issues from others and also to differentiate individual critical issues from each other, with a proper and stable framework. I proposed a model for that objective by referring to research works by Patrick Wilson and others. However, the initial model did not clearly differentiate conceptual-level arguments from those at the implementation level, and it thus contained both conceptual modeling of a resource and a practical record structure representing the resource. During several years after proposing the initial model, I have struggled to elaborate and extend the model in various ways by myself, but did not succeed sufficiently.

The draft version of FRBR was made public by the IFLA Study Group in 1996. Having seen the model represented in the draft, I was astonished, and also shocked, at its comprehensiveness—that was the model that I had sought for several years. After seeing FRBR, I changed my research strategy and pursued the implications of the major different characteristics of the two models: the three-layered model gives primacy to the text-layer (i.e., a text-level entity) so as to cope with some major issues that have developed in cataloging, such as the treatment of reproductions and electronic resources. Finally, I was able to propose a model that gives primacy to the text-level entity, which occupies half of this book.

Meanwhile, I also have pursued a method of designing cataloging rules by utilizing conceptual modeling of the cataloging process. It seemed to me that there had been no formalized design methodology for rules and thus a more logical and systematic way to design those rules was required. At first, I was keenly aware of the necessity of a proper concept to explain the diversity among cataloging rules and the difference among possible alternative rules or sets of rules. With this recognition, in 1997 I introduced and set up the new concept of 'orientedness' that can be used for such objective, and tried to apply the concept to existing cataloging rules like AACR; it was the first result of my research on this topic. Finally, I was able to propose a step-by-step method of designing rules at the conceptual design stage, by utilizing a general model for the cataloging process and also applying the concept of orientedness. This subject occupies the second half of this book.

I am still conducting research on cataloging and will never complete it, but I wished to draw a line by publishing this book—an interim report of my research—and was fortunate to receive a grant for its publication. The publication of this book was supported in part by a Grant-in-Aid for Publication of Scientific Research Results from the Japan Society for the Promotion of Science.

ACKNOWLEDGMENTS

First and foremost, I wish to express my thanks to Takaaki Kuroiwa, Emeritus Professor at the University of Library and Information Science, for initially inviting me to the university as a Research Associate eighteen years ago. He gave me the chance to engage in research and education in academia, and has continuously encouraged me in my research and other activities.

I also wish to express my gratitude to Professor Shuichi Ueda of Keio University for his continuing encouragement during the preparation of my doctoral thesis. It took more than five years to complete my thesis after deciding to write one and asking him to be my advisor, and during those years he has waited patiently for its completion. Without his continuous encouragement, my thesis would not have seen the light of day.

I am deeply indebted to a number of my colleagues at the Graduate School of Library, Information and Media Studies, University of Tsukuba—especially Professor Nobuyuki Midorikawa—for their cooperation in support of my research.

Special thanks are also due to Dr. Barbara B. Tillett, Library of Congress, for helpful comments and suggestions on some of the manuscripts of the papers constituting the thesis. I could not have made my contribution in the cataloging field if I had not met her, and she has been a role model for me.

I am also indebted to Hituzi Syobo Publishing—in particular, President Isao Matsumoto, and Takashi Moriwaki—for taking on the publication of my work. I respect their enthusiasm for scholarly publishing.

Finally, I would like to thank my wife, Shukuko, for her unwavering support and patience during these eighteen years.

July 2006
Shoichi Taniguchi

Chapter 1

Introduction

1.1 Catalogs and Their Design

The environment within which catalogs are built and cataloging is conducted has changed dramatically during these thirty or forty years. We are in a situation where the volume and complexity of resources to be bibliographically controlled continue to grow. The emergence of new forms of electronic publishing is a typical example. At the same time, we are also under pressure to curb both cataloging costs and efforts as well as to adapt cataloging codes and practices to a more computerized environment. We also need to respond more effectively to an increasingly broad range of user expectations and needs.

We have coped with the situation, mainly through the introduction and ongoing development of automated systems for the creation and processing of bibliographic data, and through the growth of large-scale databases and shared cataloging. These responses to the situation have been effective, and have to some extent succeeded. However, catalogs, cataloging codes, and cataloging practices, must continue changing to keep up with the environmental changes.

A catalog (catalogue) is defined in *Anglo-American Cataloguing Rules, 2nd ed., 2002 revision* (in short, AACR2, 2002 revision) as, "a list of library materials contained in a collection, a library, or a group of libraries, arranged according to some definite plan,"[1] and has always been an essential tool provided to users. A catalog consists of 'entries' and 'references.' An 'entry' is "a record of an item in a catalogue,"[2] and contains bibliographic data (including subject data) and holdings data about an item being catalogued. The entry is also called a 'bibliographic record' (or merely a 'record'), particularly when it is machine-readable. However, the term 'catalog record' has not been used.

The entry is made up of a 'bibliographic description' (or merely 'description'), 'access points/headings,' and 'holdings.' The bibliographic description is "to bring out all aspects of the item being described, including its content, its carrier, its type of publication, its bibliographic relationships, and whether it is published or unpublished."[3] On the other hand, a heading refers to "a name, word, or phrase placed at the head of a catalogue entry to provide an access point."[4] It is not, however, necessary that it be placed at the head of an entry unless a catalog is implemented as a card catalog. An access point is "a name, term, code, etc., under which a bibliographic record may be searched and identified,"[5] which contains the heading in definition.

Subject data about an item is expressed through part of description, such as summary notes, and through headings, such as classification codes and subject headings. The 'holdings' describe holdings and administrative data on an item such as its call number, location mark, and details of the library's holdings of a multipart item or a continuing resource.

Catalogs are usually implemented as databases, with sophisticated interfaces for catalogers and users. We call such a database system for catalogers an 'online catalog,' and that for users an 'OPAC' (online public access catalog) although the latter can also be called an 'online catalog.' An online catalog for catalogers usually has the function of authority control and thus contains, or can access, authority records for name and subject headings.

The current framework of bibliographic records, together with current practice based on that framework, are basically defined in cataloging codes, MARC formats, and other guidelines. The value and importance of standardization is widely recognized, and thus the basic framework and practice defined in cataloging codes and others are to some extent standardized all over the world.

However, there has been no formalized design methodology which is independent of, and applicable to, any situation or issue in designing catalogs and cataloging codes. Determining a way to deal with an individual issue has been done on an ad-hoc basis while referring chiefly to accumulated experience. We need a more logical and systematic way to design catalogs and cataloging codes so as to cope more effectively and efficiently with the current situation, complicated as it is by technological innovation, budgetary constraints, and increasing user needs.

Moreover, existing cataloging codes and individual rules are not necessary well-formed, and have ambiguity. Some researchers, such as Hjerppe and Olander,[6] and I,[7] have pointed out this fact, referring to investigations of the structure of the codes and rules. For instance, I proposed and developed a prototype system to analyze the ambiguity and complexity of cataloging rules in the hope of contributing toward quality control of cataloging standards. This system is capable of analyzing the internal structure of each rule and also inter-rule relationships, although it can handle only a restricted range of rules.

Over the last decade, on the other hand, several researchers have explored ways to apply conceptual modeling techniques to address issues in the cataloging field. To put it more precisely, they have endeavored to develop models for catalogs at the conceptual (or logical) level, in order to re-examine the current framework of bibliographic records and the current practice based on that framework, and then to propose an alternative framework. The reason why they have adopted a modeling approach is that it naturally leads to a re-examination at the most fundamental level and thus may bring effective results. Of course, a modeling approach has been commonly used in other fields such as systems development and database construction, and this constitutes another reason for its adoption. Results of research into the modeling approach to catalogs and related issues now attract much interest from researchers and practitioners in the cataloging field.

The most prominent among those results is the conceptual model that has been developed by the IFLA (International Federation of Library Associations and Institutions) Study Group on the Functional Requirements for Bibliographic Records (FRBR)[8]. This is also the most comprehensive and detailed model in almost all respects, being designed to serve as a framework for relating bibliographic data to user needs by using the entity-relationship analysis technique. There are several other models that have been proposed by other researchers; all of these are brief but have their own significance.

The conceptual modeling approach is expected to be one of the more useful and effective approaches to coping with the current situation. Put simply, it begins by recognizing the issues we are facing at the conceptual level, next trying to find a way of resolving some of these issues at that level, and lastly trying to implement the solution at the practical level. To be precise, through conceptual modeling of the bibliographic universe which information resources and their users build, we can recognize an issue clearly and find a way for resolving it. We should pursue this approach further, in reconceptualizing records and restructuring them in terms of addressing user needs.

Paralleling these efforts, we should try to apply conceptual modeling to the cataloging process, to design optimal cataloging codes and rules which would result from some of the useful characteristics of the approach. Very few attempts have been made at approaching the cataloging process through conceptual modeling, and no model for the process has ever been developed. To put it more precisely, we have no general models which are applicable to any situation or system, although there might be models dependent on a specific situation, such as operational models for certain cataloging systems.

1.2 Conceptual Design and Modeling in Systems Development

'Conceptual design' (or 'conceptual system design') can be defined in several ways. One definition of the term can be found in the international standard ISO/IEC 2382-20 as, "a system design activity concerned with specifying the logical aspects of the system organization, its processes, and the flow of information through the system."[9] Another is a narrower definition, such as, "a process that uses a modeling technique to create a model of an information system structure or a database structure that represents the universe of discourse." This latter is my own definition, compiled by reference to several others.

The process of conceptual design is usually carried out through creating a model, as described in the second definition, and thus is also called 'conceptual modeling (modelling).' The model created is therefore a 'conceptual model,' of which the definition is, "a representation of the characteristics of a universe of discourse by means of entities and entity relationships."[10]

Similarly, Thayer and Thayer define a conceptual model as, "in system/software system engineering, a requirements model of the system/software system to be developed, its internal components, and the behavior of both the system and its environment."[11] Loucopoulos and Karakostas define conceptual modeling as, "the activity of formally defining aspects of the physical and social world around us for the purpose of understanding and communication."[12] Also, Rolland and Prakash define it as aiming at "abstracting the specification of the required information system, i.e., the conceptual schema, from an analysis of the relevant aspects of the Universe of Discourse about which the user community needs information."[13] We can find various, but similar definitions.

'Conceptual schema' is sometimes used as a synonym, since the result of conceptual modeling is a specification of an information system and such a specification is also called a 'schema.' However, this term has a particular meaning in the context of the ANSI/SPARC three-level database architecture. I therefore do not use it in the present study.

Key characteristics of conceptual design and modeling can be summarized as (a) implementation independence and (b) formality. Implementation independence leads to differentiating conceptual design from the detailed design of a system, which should take its implementation into consideration. Similarly, it enables us to differentiate conceptual design from the logical and physical design of a database, which depends on a data model supported in a given database management system and its configuration. On the other hand, formality imposes to use of a modeling language and its associated analysis technique.

Based on a survey of prior research results, Loucopoulos & Karakostas comprehensively specify 'a set of requirements for a conceptual schema' (i.e., conceptual specification) as: "implementation independence, abstraction, formality, constructability, ease of analysis, traceability, executability, and minimality."[14] All of these requirements would be valid, but implementation independence and formality are worthy of being focused upon.

The usefulness and significance of conceptual design and modeling are currently well and widely recognized. However, according to Loucopoulos & Karakostas, "In information systems, conceptual modelling has been traditionally associated with the task of database design. In recent years, however, it has been recognized that conceptual modelling can and should be used for specifying the four major domains of information systems, …, namely the subject world, the usage world, the system world, and the development world."[15]

In addition, conceptual design and modeling are variously positioned in the systems development life cycle (SDLC), depending on systems development methodologies and others. Referring to several frameworks of SDLC that have been so far proposed, I adopt in the present study the following simple framework: (a) requirements analysis and determination, (b) conceptual design, namely, conceptual modeling, and (c) detailed design of a system, or logical and physical design of a database. In this framework, requirements analysis and determination precedes conceptual design, with requirements being represented in any form. On the other hand, detailed design of a system and logical and physical design of a database follow their conceptual design, which is independent of any data model or other implementation considerations.

Valacich, George, and Hoffer shows an example of an SDLC which consists of four phases: Phase 1: systems planning and selection, Phase 2: systems analysis, Phase 3: systems design, and Phase 4: systems implementation and operation[16]. Systems analysis, in Phase 2, is further divided into sub-phases: requirements determination, requirements structuring, and alternative generation and selection. The second sub-phase 'requirements structuring' includes 'process modeling' and 'conceptual data modeling.' Process modeling involves "graphically representing the processes, or actions, that capture, manipulate, store, and distribute data between a system and its environment and among components within a system."[17] In contrast, conceptual data modeling builds "a detailed model that shows the overall structure of organizational data while being independent of any database management system or other implementation considerations."[18] Both of these techniques are conceptual modeling that I intend to adopt in the present study. Based on the results of such modeling, the systems design in Phase 3 must be conducted within its SDLC. The design phase here consists of designing the human interface and designing a database, that is, the logical and physical design of a database.

Likewise, Shelly, Cashman, and Rosenblatt illustrate a similar SDLC of which the systems analysis phase includes requirements modeling, data and process modeling, object modeling (i.e., object-oriented modeling), and transition to systems design[19]. In this SDLC, data and process modeling and object modeling are alternative ways to view and model the system requirements, and thus are the conceptual modeling that I have adopted here.

In the field of database design, on the other hand, Whittington shows 'a development model for database systems' which consists of five stages: conceptual analysis, logical design, structured design, physical design, and implementation[20]. In his framework, conceptual analysis "involves formulating the data objects of the universe of discourse in terms of a data-modelling formalism, to produce a specification of what it is that the required database is to represent."[21] This corresponds to the conceptual modeling adopted in the present study.

Similarly, Teory demonstrates 'a database life cycle' consisting of five steps: Step 1: requirements analysis, Step 2: logical design, Step 3: physical design, Step 4: data distribution, and Step 5: database implementation, monitoring, and modification[22]. If we follow the relational data model, the logical design step is divided into the following sub-steps: entity-relationship (E-R) modeling, view integration, transformation of the E-R model to SQL tables, and normalization of tables. E-R modeling is the conceptual modeling adopted here.

Conceptual modeling employs a modeling language and its associated analysis technique. Widely used languages and analysis techniques are the E-R model and the object-oriented models.

The basic E-R model consists of three classes of constructs: entities, relationships, and attributes. Each entity, relationship, and attribute, respectively indicate a set of things of the same kind, a type of association among one or more entities, and a set of characteristics of entities. Particular occurrences of an entity, a relationship, and an attribute, are respectively called an entity instance, a relationship instance, and an attribute value. Some extended models have also been proposed.

Object-oriented models involve concepts similar to the E-R model. They use a class (or an object class), an attribute, and an association, each of which respectively corresponds to an entity, an attribute, and a relationship in the E-R model. A single instance of a class or an association is called, respectively, an object (or an object instance) and a link. In addition, an operation for a class and its implementation—'a method'—for an object, which are the behavior aspects of the class and the object, are involved in the object-oriented models. Furthermore, the object-oriented approach generally includes several additional unique concepts such as abstraction, inheritance, polymorphism, and encapsulation. There have been several variations in object-oriented models and thus their integration has been intended. The UML (Unified Modeling Language), by the Object Management Group, is the most significant example of such integration.

1.3 Design Methodology for Catalogs and Cataloging Rules

By applying the process framework of systems analysis and design, which I outlined in the preceding section, to the design of catalogs and cataloging rules, we can attain the two process frameworks: that of designing catalogs and that of designing cataloging rules.

The process of designing catalogs proceeds in the following order:

1) Requirements analysis and determination, including specification of the objectives and functions of catalogs.
2) Conceptual modeling of the bibliographic universe, created by information resources and their users, while reflecting the requirements determined.
3) Logical design of records, including specification of data elements, record structure, etc., based on the conceptual model.

Logical and physical design of catalog databases follows the above process if we implement catalogs as databases under certain data models.

We need to design cataloging rules in addition to designing catalogs. Cataloging rules contain decisions or instructions on how to create bibliographic record(s) for bibliographic item(s) in a way that reflects the entities/objects established in the model above, or specifically how to deal with and record each attribute of the entities/objects and each type of relationship/association between them. These matters are not included in the modeling of the bibliographic universe.

The process of designing cataloging rules consists of the following phases:

1) Requirements analysis and determination, involving restrictions and conditions on the cataloging (i.e., data creation) process.
2) Conceptual design of rules, including the modeling of the cataloging process.
3) Detailed design of rules, including transformation into rule expressions which are intelligible and comprehensible for catalogers.

By following the process in the frameworks, the valuable characteristics of conceptual design and modeling would be utilized.

The present study has two aims, in line with these two process frameworks. One aim is to propose a conceptual model for catalogs (and cataloging) which gives primacy to a text-level bibliographic entity. Several models have been proposed so far, including the model by the IFLA Study Group and another that I previously proposed[23]. Therefore I will try to propose a new one which will bring some additional benefits, while referring to the extant models.

The other aim is to propose a general model for the cataloging process at the conceptual level, and also to propose a method of designing cataloging rules by utilizing the model and applying a new concept 'orientedness.' I do not intend to propose a model and a method which can be applied only to the conceptual model giving primacy to a text-level bibliographic entity; I propose a general model and a method applicable to any conceptual model for catalogs.

Chapter 2 reviews prior research results related to the conceptual design and modeling of catalogs and cataloging rules. In particular, research and discussions are reviewed concerning the objectives and functions of catalogs, modeling of the bibliographic universe, analysis of bibliographic relationships, principles of the construction of cataloging codes, and modeling of the cataloging process.

In Chapter 3, a conceptual model giving primacy to text-level bibliographic entity is proposed with the aim of approaching critical issues in cataloging, such as the so-called 'format variations' and 'content versus carrier' issues. Although several models proposed so far contain a text-level entity (or object), the role and function of the entity in each model is not clear. In this chapter, first, a viewpoint is introduced on which entity is to be given primacy among bibliographic entities in a model, and is applied to the examination of certain models. Second, a new model that gives primacy to text-level entity is proposed using the E-R modeling language.

Chapter 4 examines the differences between two conceptual models in modeling component parts of bibliographic resources. These are the model by the IFLA Study Group, and that proposed in Chapter 3. The two models are examined from the viewpoint of modeling component parts when each part in itself is a resource to be described. The examination is done on two types of component parts: a content part and a document part, which are different in terms of whether they are physically independent.

Chapter 5 reports on a trial to investigate the feasibility of creating bibliographic records in accordance with the model proposed in Chapter 3, carried out through an attempt at converting existing MARC records. First, methods of creating records are examined in terms of their structure. A method that explicitly shows the structure of the model on which records are based is then selected. Second, a trial is conducted to convert MARC bibliographic records into those structured according to the method selected, by developing programs to facilitate conversion. Third, a prototype system to use the structured records is developed in order to demonstrate the usefulness of such records.

Chapter 6 examines projects and discussions that would be relevant to the model proposed in Chapter 3. Examples are (a) those proposing and adopting record structures different from those of the current style and (b) those adopting the same record structure as that of the current style but proposing different ways of dealing with resources.

In Chapters 7-9, it is attempted to accomplish the second aim of the present study. Chapter 7 introduces and sets up a new concept 'orientedness' that can be used to represent the functional and non-functional requirements of cataloging rules (or, to be precise, the cataloging process or the output of the process). The extent to which each individual cataloging rule can be explained in terms of orientedness is investigated in respect of each of the rules in AACR2, 2002 revision. Furthermore, possible alternatives to each existing rule are shown, along with the difference in orientedness among those alternatives.

Chapter 8 proposes a method to design cataloging rules by utilizing conceptual modeling of the cataloging process, and also by applying the concept of orientedness set out in Chapter 7. It also proposes a general model for the cataloging process at the conceptual level, which is independent of any situation, system, or cataloging code. The design method is made up of several phases involving the development of the general model, thus providing consistent and scalable design.

Chapter 9 tries to apply the design method proposed in Chapter 8 to the new issue of recording evidence which explains why and how the data values are recorded for elements. Recording evidence is beyond the scope of conventional cataloging practice and rules. However, it is shown that, by following the design method, proper rules for recording evidence are obtained.

Chapter 10 summarizes the whole results of the present study.

Notes

1 Joint Steering Committee for Revision of AACR (2002, p. Appendix.D-2)
2 Joint Steering Committee for Revision of AACR (2002, p. Appendix.D-3)
3 Joint Steering Committee for Revision of AACR (2002, p. Part I.2)
4 Joint Steering Committee for Revision of AACR (2002, p. Appendix.D-4)

5 Joint Steering Committee for Revision of AACR (2002, p. Appendix.D-1)
6 Hjerppe and Olander (1998)
7 Taniguchi (1995, 1996)
8 IFLA Study Group on the FRBR (1997)
9 ISO/IEC 2382-20 (1990, p. 7)
10 ISO/IEC 2382-17 (1999, p. 6)
11 Thayer and Thayer (1990, p. 615)
12 Loucopoulos and Karakostas (1995, p. 72)
13 Rolland and Prakash (2000)
14 Loucopoulos and Karakostas (1995, p. 77)
15 Loucopoulos and Karakostas (1995, p. 73)
16 Valacich, George, and Hoffer (2001)
17 Valacich, George, and Hoffer (2001, p. 146)
18 Valacich, George, and Hoffer (2001, p. 186)
19 Shelly, Cashman, and Rosenblatt (2001)
20 Whittington (1988)
21 Whittington (1988, p. 232)
22 Teory (1999)
23 Taniguchi (1990, 1993b, 1997a)

Chapter 2

Literature Review

This chapter aims at reviewing literatures and research results that would be related to requirements definition/analysis and conceptual modeling of catalogs and cataloging. I take up discussions on (a) objectives and functions of catalogs, (b) modeling of the bibliographic universe, (c) analysis and modeling of bibliographic relationships, (d) objectives for (or principles of) the construction of cataloging codes, and (e) modeling of the cataloging process, in this order.

2.1 Objectives and Functions of Catalogs

Requirements definition on catalogs has traditionally been discussed as an issue of defining objectives and/or functions of catalogs. The objectives (and functions) have been formulated roughly as two objectives. The first objective is conventionally called 'finding objective,' which assumes a user having in hand author, title, or other information on a resource is looking for that resource. The second objective is called 'collocating objective,' which assumes a user comes with similar information but needs a set of resources, such as the set of all resources by a given author, or a given work.

The statement on objectives and functions of catalogs adopted at the International Conference on Cataloging Principles held in Paris in 1961 contains the following:

> The catalogue should be an efficient instrument for ascertaining
> 1. whether the library contains a particular book specified by
>   (a) its author and title, or
>   (b) if the author is not named in the book, its title alone, or
>   (c) if author and title are inappropriate or insufficient for identification, a suitable substitute for the title; and

2. (a) which works by a particular author and
(b) which editions of a particular work are in the library[1].

The statement was obviously based on Lubetzky's objectives in 1960[2] and also Cutter's in 1904[3]. Those two objectives, namely, finding and collocating objectives, have been widely accepted in the cataloging field. However, their meanings have not been more clarified. One main reason would be ambiguities involved in the terms 'book' and 'work,' which are traditional bibliographic entities in the cataloging field—this issue will be touched shortly later. Another would come from the limited scope of the Paris Principles, which intentionally excluded an objective governing organization by subject. Some people therefore interpreted that there should be the third objective governing subject organization, whereas others thought that such an objective was inherently covered by the collocating objective.

Meanwhile, the IFLA Study Group on the Functional Requirements for Bibliographic Records (FRBR) made public a comprehensive conceptual model for bibliographic records in 1997. For representing the user needs of bibliographic records, they defined "generic tasks that are performed by users when searching and making use of national bibliographies and library catalogues."[4] The tasks defined are 'find,' 'identify,' 'select,' and 'obtain.' Those seem to be identified as a result of the articulation of the process carried out by users when searching and making use of bibliographic records—a user generally performs first finding resources (or more formally, entities) that correspond to her/his stated search criteria, and then either identifying resources or selecting resources that are appropriate to her/his needs, and finally obtaining access to the resources being identified or selected.

The study group probably intended to reformulate the objectives of catalogs by combining these tasks with bibliographic entities that they define, instead of the conventional two objectives, so as to provide clearly defined, structured objectives.

Likewise, as part of conceptual design of full-scale bibliographic databases (of course, including catalogs), Green presented functions of such databases—"identification of bibliographic items, selection of appropriate bibliographic items, showing the availability of bibliographic items, and showing relationships between bibliographic items."[5] These functions, except the last, correspond properly to the user tasks 'identify,' 'select,' and 'obtain,' respectively.

Svenonius recently reexamined both the traditional formulation of objectives and the user tasks introduced by IFLA Study Group and provided a new formulation of objectives[6]. Her main criticism to the formulation with the user tasks was that the task 'find' "diminishes the importance of the concept of collocation."[7] Therefore she decomposed the task into two: "to find a singular entity" and "to locate sets of entities representing all documents belonging to the same work, all documents belonging to the same edition, all documents by a given author, all documents on a given subject, …"[8] Furthermore, she introduced a new objective 'navigation objective,' which is "to navigate a bibliographic database (that is, to find works related to a given work by generalization, association, and aggregation; to find attributes related by equivalence, association, and hierarchy)."[9]

For discussions under the Joint Steering Committee for Revision of AACR (Anglo-American Cataloguing Rules), Tillett[10] tried to paraphrase Svenonius's objectives. And more recently, on the basis of the prior discussions, IFLA Meeting of Experts on an International Cataloguing Code in 2003 has approved the draft of the 'Statement of International Cataloguing Principles,' which include the formulation of objectives/functions of catalogs:

3. Functions of the Catalogue
The functions of the catalogue are to enable a user:
3.1. to 'find' bibliographic resources in a collection (real or virtual) as the result of a search using attributes or relationships of the resources:
3.1.1. to 'locate' a single resource
3.1.2. to 'locate' sets of resources representing
—all resources belonging to the same work, …
3.2. to 'identify' a bibliographic resource or agent…
3.3. to 'select' a bibliographic resource that is appropriate to the user's needs…
3.4. to 'acquire' or 'obtain' access to an item described…
3.5. to 'navigate' a catalogue…[11]

2.2 Modeling of Bibliographic Universe and Records

2.2.1 Discussions Preceding and Affecting Modeling

Bibliographic records in catalogs must represent both the intellectual/artistic properties and the physical properties of bibliographic resources. Recognition about such a matter can be traced back to 18th or 19th century, according to Verona[12]. That recognition requires that any resource should be viewed from both the intellectual/artistic aspect and the physical aspect and also it is important to distinguish these two aspects.

In the statement on objectives/functions of catalogs adopted at the International Conference on Cataloging Principles, which has been quoted above, 'a book' and 'a work' represent a resource viewed from the physical aspect and that from the intellectual/artistic aspect, respectively. The statement itself and also the distinction between these two aspects were inherited directly from those by Lubetzky and Cutter. Other terms such as 'document' and 'publication,' instead of 'book,' have been sometimes used as those being opposed to 'work'. However, the concepts of 'book' (including alternative terms) and 'work' have been used vaguely, sometimes confused, and have never been clearly defined, as Hoffman and Carpenter have pointed out[13]. Even Lubetzky pointed out the problem, stating that: "Because the material *book* embodies and represents the intellectual *work*, the two have come to be confused, and the terms are synonymously used not only by the layman but also by the cataloger himself."[14] Hagler covers this 'work versus book/document' issue rather thoroughly in his books[15].

In addition to discussions about work-book distinction, there have been other discussions preceding and directly affecting the modeling of bibliographic resources and the bibliographic universe. These are as follows.

1) Which objective should be prioritized under the main entry system? This choice implies the selection of either 'book' or 'work' as the basis for the main entry. Verona argued that main entries should focus on book, and thus work should be identified and collocated through added entries[16]. Conversely, Lubetzky insisted that we should give precedence to work, not book[17]. Wilson argues, again, that a reordering of the relative priorities of the two objectives is preferable; that is, the collocating objective should receive first priority, in the context of the current technological environment[18].

2) What is a 'work'? There has been a variety of usage of the term 'work.' Domanovszky tried to enumerate typical usages of the term[19]. He, and also Wilson[20], investigated records actually collocated by main and added entry headings within catalogs, to clarify its meaning. On the other hand, a close examination of the concept shows that, even within the history of AACR, the concept of 'work' has been interpreted in various ways[21].

3) What is an 'edition'? The term 'edition' as used in the Paris Principles seems to represent a concept intermediate between 'work' and 'book.' In other cases, however, the term has been used as synonymous with 'book.' Defining the term raises other questions about (a) what makes the distinction between it and 'printing' (or 'issue'), and (b) what differences between two books (or documents) are significant enough to justify treating them as different editions—that is, to create a new bibliographic record. Jones and Kastner provided a detailed review of the edition-printing distinction[22].

4) What is a 'text'? Wilson is probably the first researcher in the cataloging field to introduce the term 'text' to describe something independent from both an intellectual/artistic content that he called a 'work,' and its physical manifestation that he called an 'exemplar.'[23] He stated that, "A text, a sequence of words and auxiliary symbols, is an abstract entity, like the words of which it is composed."[24] He pursued an examination of the treatment of text in AACR by observing entries collocated by main and added entries within catalogs[25].

These issues are closely related to the 'work versus book' issue, and sometimes make the latter more complicated.

We need another term 'item.' This is referred to in AACR2, 2002 revision, as "A document or set of documents in any physical form, published, issued, or treated as an entity, and as such forming the basis for a single bibliographic description."[26] The point of this term is to indicate a given bibliographic resource (or set of resources) which forms "the basis for a single bibliographic description" when catalogers try to create a description (and thus a bibliographic record). In other words, an 'item' is the starting point of making a bibliographic record, since we make a record (in particular, a description) by referring to this physical exemplar. However, it has sometimes been used as synonymous with 'book'/'document,' without consideration for the distinction between them.

2.2.2 Models That Have Been Proposed

In the following, I review models and equivalents that have so far been proposed for catalogs and bibliographic records. Those lacking any formal modeling language are included. They are in chronological order.

1) *O'Neil and Visine-Goetz's model* (1989)[27]

O'Neil and Visine-Goetz presented their model at a 1987 conference, of which the proceedings were published in 1989. They defined necessary 'bibliographic entities' while limiting their discussion to monographs. Those entities are named as *work, text, edition, printing,* and *book*, which are defined in a hierarchical way. It would be the first example of an attempt to build a model with 'bibliographic entities' in a discussion about cataloging, although they did not call their result a model.

The *book* was defined as "An individual physical manifestation of a bibliographic entity"[28] and also described as "the bibliographic entity at the lowest level of the hierarchy and the only one which corresponds to a physical object."[29] It corresponds to 'item.'

The definitions of the other entities are:

Work A set of related texts with a common origin and content.
Text A set of editions with the same content.
Edition A set of printings produced from substantially the same type image.
Printing A set of books printed at one time or printed at different times containing no more than slight variations[30].

O'Neil and Visine-Goetz stated that they introduced the entity 'text' by referring to the study by Wilson, and also borrowed the edition-printing distinction by referring to the discussions by Wanninger[31], and Jones and Kastner. They further explained each of the entities to some extent, including some attributes or properties of the entities. However, it was not a clear discussion. At the same time, they examined hierarchical bibliographic relationships between the entities.

2) *Svenonius's model* (1992)[32]

In a 1990 seminar, whose proceedings were published in 1992, Svenonius presented a study to emphasize the importance of the modeling approach to bibliographic records and the bibliographic universe. She argued that some fundamental issues and problems in cataloging should be addressed by clarifying bibliographic entities, their attributes, and the relationships among them. She also emphasized that examination of the use of bibliographic records by users (i.e., modeling of record usage by users) is necessary, and should be combined with the other modeling.

She showed a tentative model of the bibliographic universe for 'book-like items,' with the aim of illustrating an example of models. The model is illustrated using E-R modeling language. In addition to *items* that imply "individual physical items,"[33] the model contains the following bibliographic entities:

(1) impressions (the set of all items emanating from a single typesetting, published by one publisher, or a set of joint publishers, on one date), (2) editions (the set of all items emanating from a "single act of typographic composition"), (3) texts (the set of all items manifesting essentially the same content), (4) works (the set of all manifestations of an original text and all manifestations derived from that original by translation or revision), and (5) superworks (the set of all manifestations of an original work and all manifestations derived from it)[34]. [The underlines are added.]

These entities constitute a hierarchy, beginning with *items* and ending with *superworks*. Other types of entities are only listed, i.e., "people, places, organizations and subjects," with neither definition nor explanation. In addition, the importance of relationships among bibliographic entities was noted and some were listed: "the set-subset (hierarchical) relationship, the vertical (part-whole) relationship, the chronological (successive edition) relationship, and the derivative relationship."[35] Again, neither definition nor explanation was provided.

3) *Taniguchi's three-layered model* (1990-1997)[36]

Since 1990, I have been proposing a three-layered model to understand the implications of critical issues involved in current practice and to seek a possible alternative framework for resolving those issues. Initially, the model did not clearly differentiate conceptual level arguments from those at the implementation level, thus containing both the conceptual modeling of a resource and a practical record structure representing the resource[37]. After proposing the initial model, I realized that the two or more levels of arguments had to be differentiated. I consequently proposed a model focusing only on conceptual level modeling[38], following examination of some other models including the draft version of FRBR by the IFLA Study Group. In addition, I have tried to compare bibliographic records in catalogs, and those in abstracting-and-indexing services, by applying the model to both records so as to clarify the differences between them.

As its name indicates, from its initial stage the three-layered model conceptualizes a resource with a three-layer structure: *work*, *text*, and *medium*. In other words, a resource can be divided into these three layers.

The work-layer denotes what is the intellectual or artistic content of a resource; thus, it is equivalent to the definition of the concept in other models or arguments. The text-layer corresponds to a text defined by Wilson; the concept was borrowed from him. It is, however, considered not to involve a work, but just to be interrelated with a work; *text* expresses *work*. The medium-layer denotes what corresponds to a physical manifestation having had the text removed from it—the physical medium or carrier itself.

These imply that every layer of this model is constructed to be mutually exclusive. The model did not use any formal conceptual modeling language and thus the role of a layer would be somewhat ambiguous. Moreover, the model did not contain a layer corresponding to an individual item below the medium-layer.

The chief attributes of each layer have been enumerated. For example, the work-layer accepts the name headings of the authors or creators of a work and a uniform title for a work, if any. On the other hand, some label information, such as titles, statements of responsibility, and edition designations that appear in an item, but not label information related only to the physical medium or physical embodiment of a text, is associated with the text-layer not the medium-layer. The remaining information, such as names of publisher, distributor, etc., and physical description, in addition to label information not associated with the text-layer, is associated with the medium-layer.

Regarding relationships among instances assigned to individual layers, I[39] listed them by referring to the categories of bibliographic relationships established by Tillett[40]. For example, relationships among instances of *text* are associated with the categories 'equivalence,' 'derivative,' and 'descriptive.' Relationships among combined instances of *text* and *medium* are the categories 'accompanying' and 'sequential.'

One of the major characteristics of the model was the aim of making a bibliographic description of an item which gives primacy to the text-layer (i.e., a text-level entity), by applying the three-layer structure to an item. From the beginning, I have intended to give primacy to the text-layer so as to cope with some major issues that have developed in cataloging, such as the treatment of reproductions and electronic resources.

4) *Leazer's conceptual schema* (1993)[41]

Leazer tried to analyze the data elements defined in the USMARC Format for Bibliographic Data (currently, MARC21 Format for Bibliographic Data) in order to design a conceptual schema of bibliographic databases, including catalogs. As necessary bibliographic entities, he used the dichotomy of *work* and *item*—the latter was adopted instead of 'book,' but with the same meaning, as he noted. He stated that "Catalogs have two kinds of objects to control: items and works,"[42] whose definitions were borrowed from prior studies. He also introduced non-bibliographic entities: *people* and *corporate body*. His study, however, did not cover other USMARC formats, such as that for authority data.

Specifying the attributes of each individual entity makes the core result of his study as follows:

Attributes of *work*: title, edition, bibliographic relationships, series information, intellectual content, intellectual form, date, language, topical content, geographic information, audience, historical information about the work, miscellaneous, historical contribution to the development of a discipline, and critical assessment of the work's aesthetic values. 'Bibliographic relationships' here indicates information about those relationships.

Attributes of *item*: title of item, bibliographic relationships, series information, frequency of publication, details of publication, publisher, place of publication, date of publication, lending and access, physical description, extent, physical form, pagination, physical size, special equipment required to use the item ... <u>Attributes of non-bibliographic entities</u>: author/creator name and historical information about the author/creator.

Using these bibliographic and non-bibliographic entities, a comprehensive mapping of data elements in the MARC format relating to the entities and their attributes was generated.

Furthermore, the taxonomies of bibliographic relationships developed by others such as Tillett were applied to the entities above. Consequently, for instance, (a) *work*-to-*work* relationships include accompanying, derivative, descriptive, sequential, and whole-part relationships, (b) *work*-to-*item* relationships cover containment, descriptive, and equivalence relationships, and (c) *item*-to-*item* relationships, are identified as accompanying, equivalence, and whole-part relationships.

5) *Heaney's object-oriented cataloging model* (1995)[43]

Heaney reanalyzed a bibliographic record in an approach based on object-oriented modeling, in order to demonstrate the advantages to be gained thereby. Using an object-oriented modeling approach, inheritance of attributes from upper-level objects to those lower, and encapsulation of an object and its associated operations—which are called 'methods' in object-oriented modeling—can be utilized.

He established the necessary bibliographic classes of objects: *text, publication*, and *copy*.

"Texts are strings of sentences. They have titles and they are in a language. They can be subjected to various operations, including translation, revision, and aggregation with other texts."[44] The class *text* thus has attributes such as title and language, and operations like translation, revision, and aggregation. In the examples demonstrated in his paper, main entry heading, uniform title, title proper, and some added entry headings, are associated with this class. In addition, a derived class of 'derived text' is defined, which has attributes similar to derived title and derived language, as well as to title and language.

Publication: This can be divided into several media subclasses, like *book, film*, etc. It has several attributes, such as extent, dimension, packaging, and identification number, and operations like reformatting and republication. In his examples as demonstrated, title proper and almost all other descriptive elements not associated with *text* are associated with *publication*.

Copy: This class has attributes such as call number, location, and binding quality, and operations such as loan, reservation, and sending for binding.

He has focused, for convenience, on written works and published texts, resulting in the use of the terms *text* and *publication*. He also suggested that "In a more generalized formulation, it may be more appropriate to use the terms that are now coming to be widely used, and to call them the 'Work model' and the 'Manifestation model.'"[45] These mean *work* and *manifestation*, respectively.

He shows another class, *Agent*, which has associations with the classes *text*, *publication*, and *copy*.

6) *Green's conceptual model* (1996)[46]

Green presented a conceptual design of a full-scale bibliographic database (including bibliographic, authority, holdings, and classification data) using E-R modeling language. She enumerated a total of 37 bibliographic and non-bibliographic entities to constitute the model. Attributes of entities and relationships among entities, including their cardinalities, were also listed.

The entities *uniform work*, *work*, *bibliographic set*, and *bibliographic copy*, are bibliographic entities in a strict or narrower sense, and the entity *bibliographic unit* was introduced as a meta-level entity to cover those and others.

Uniform work: "an abstract, virtual intellectual product (e.g., a text in all its versions)."[47] Its attributes are: uniform title, variant title, parallel title, reports-successful-procedure/methodology indicator, and summary.

Work: "a more-or-less fixed version (e.g., edition, translation, paraphrase, condensation) of an intellectual product."[48] Its attributes are: pair of rating type and rating, pair of language role (e.g., sung, spoken, written) and language, nature, scope, artistic form, and intended audience.

Bibliographic set: "the set of copies produced under essentially the same circumstances."[49] The attributes are: pair of title proper and title script/alphabet, alternative title, pair of parallel title and sequence indicator, and others. Most bibliographic data elements constituting a description are associated with this entity.

Bibliographic copy: "an individual physical entity."[50] The attributes are: master copy indicator; note statement; circulation status; condition; restriction on use statement; composite of classification scheme, prefix, class number, suffix, and copy number; and pair of action type and action date.

By referring to their definitions, it is obvious that each of the four bibliographic entities above respectively corresponds to *work, text, edition*, and *book*, in O'Neil and Visine-Goetz's model.

Relationships among these bibliographic entities are categorized into two types: 'is-related-to' and 'has-part.' The former relationship has its attributes such as relationship type (e.g., edition, translation, supplement, etc.) and relationship modifier (e.g., sequence indicator, date, language). The latter, 'has-part,' has attributes like type indicator, sequence value, and first/middle/last indicator. However, all relationships are modeled as being among *bibliographic units*, and not assigned to specific entities like *uniform work* and *work*.

Some of the other entities defined in the model are: *visual material, aural material, tactile material*, and so on—the so-called 'class of material' that includes form of expression, recording mode, form of carrier, and others. Other categories of entities are (a) body and its subordinate entities like *person, corporate body, meeting, collection*, and *government body*, (b) *performance unit, uniform performance*, and *performance/event*, which are used to represent performance of a play, opera, ballet, etc., and (c) *concept, concept name, class number*, and others, to represent the subject dealt with in *bibliographic unit*.

7) *IFLA Study Group's Functional Requirements for Bibliographic Records* (1997)[51]

The IFLA Study Group on the FRBR released the Draft Report for World-Wide Review in 1996, and then themselves published the Final Report in 1997. The latter report was also published by a publisher in 1998.

In their study, the study group has developed a conceptual model for bibliographic records—in other words, the bibliographic universe. As previously mentioned, this model is the most comprehensive and detailed in almost all respects. The model uses E-R modeling language, and defines four bibliographic entities, which they call 'Group 1 entities.'

Work: "a distinct intellectual or artistic creation."[52]

Expression: "the intellectual or artistic realization of a *work* in the form of alpha-numeric, musical, or choreographic notation, sound, image, object, movement, etc., or any combination of such forms."[53]

Manifestation: "the physical embodiment of an *expression* of a *work*."[54]

Item: "a single exemplar of a *manifestation*."[55]

These entities are defined in a hierarchical way as their definitions show clearly. Each of the entities respectively corresponds to *work, text, edition,* and *book,* in O'Neil and Visine-Goetz's model. The model also enumerates comprehensively the attributes of each entity, and demonstrates the mapping of the attributes to ISBD (International Standard Bibliographic Description), GARE (Guidelines for Authority and Reference Entries), and GSARE (Guidelines for Subject Authority and Reference Entries) data elements.

Relationships among these entities are also enumerated comprehensively. They are divided into two: (a) those between different entities, like *work*-to-*expression* relationships, and (b) those between the same entities, like *work*-to-*work* relationships. The model shows a comprehensive taxonomy of relationships for each bibliographic entity level, while probably considering prior research results by Tillett and others.

The model defines other groups of entities in addition to Group 1. The second group is *person* and *corporate body*, which have 'responsibility' relationships with Group 1 entities. Similarly, the third group entities represent "an additional set of entities that serve as the subjects of *works*" and are "*concept* (an abstract notion or idea), *object* (a material thing), *event* (an action or occurrence), and *place* (a location)."[56] It is worth noting that 'subject' relationships exist between *work* and any entities in the first and second groups; that is, "a *work* may have as its subject one or more than one *work, expression, manifestation, item, person,* and/or *corporate body*."[57]

At the same time, the model defines four generic user tasks that are performed by users when searching and making use of bibliographic records, as mentioned in the preceding section. Using these tasks, the model tries to assess the relative significance of each attribute and relationship in supporting a task being performed by users.

As a result, this model seems to be the most prominent and influential. It has been attracting wide interest in the conceptual modeling of the bibliographic universe, and has had a big impact on research methods in the cataloging field. It has caused many discussions and trials. Le Boeuf comprehensively reviewed articles, reports, and projects related to the model[58].

8) *Delsey's analysis of the logical structure of AACR* (1998-1999)[59]

Delsey attempted to apply an approach used in the study by the IFLA Study Group to the current AACR2, in order to "develop a formalized schema to reflect the internal logic of the AACR."[60] He first outlined his analysis of the logical structure of AACR2 at a 1997 conference[61]. After his paper received general approval, he tried to present an exhaustive schema (i.e., model) for bibliographic resources and their universe being dealt with in AACR2 Part I (description) and Part II (headings, uniform titles, and references), by using the E-R analysis technique. The resulting model is fairly complicated, so that it fully reflects the complexities involved in AACR2—in other words, how the current AACR2 views and deals with the bibliographic universe.

Item and *work* are the most basic entities constituting the schema, by reflecting their treatment in AACR2. In AACR2 Part I, the entity 'item' is a key construct. Delsey noted that "item is defined relative to the cataloguer's decision in choosing an entity as the object of description" and "the item may equate to any one of a number of candidate entities: *document, document part, copy, content part*, or *collection*."[62] *Item* in his model is thus defined as an entity that contains the characteristics of both the book/document-level and copy-level, and at the same time can be regarded as either level entity, depending on the class of materials or situation. It would be better to say that *item* is defined as an entity resulting from selection as the object of bibliographic description.

Various additional bibliographic entities are defined in the model. For example, when *item* equates to *document*, the entities *content, infixion, physical carrier*, and *container* are additionally introduced, resulting from the subdivision of *document*.

In addition, entities external to *item* are established: (a) *person* and *corporate body*, (b) *production, creation*, and *ownership*, (c) *manufacture, release, copy, impression, issue, edition*, and *collection*, (d) *series, subseries, class of materials, type of publication*, and *chief source of information*, and (e) others, like *equipment*. He calls the entity *item* and the group (d) entities like *series*, 'bibliographic' ones, whereas the others are designated 'real world.' The 'bibliographic' entities in his schema "are used to structure the rules, and the relationships between those entities."[63]

For each entity and relationship among entities, comprehensive attributes and their definitions are shown, as well as bibliographic data elements found in AACR2 and corresponding to the attributes.

AACR2 Part II was similarly analyzed and modeled. Additional 'bibliographic' entities, such as *work, heading, bibliographic identity, uniform title, reference*, and *description*, are introduced in the analysis of Part II. In addition, some 'real world' entities are introduced, like *modification, performance, compiling/editing, emanation*, and *other association*.

9) *Svenonius's review of bibliographic entities* (2000)[64]

Svenonius discussed the function of basic entities mandated by the bibliographic objectives and the problems that attend their definition. She made distinction between conceptual and operational definitions for entities and adopted the latter. The necessity of an operational definition expressed in set-theoretic terms is emphasized for uniformity and precision. For an example of such definition, a work W_i was defined as "the set of all documents that are copies of (equivalent to) a particular document a_w (an individual document chosen as emblematic of the work, normally its first instance) or related to this individual by revision, update, abridgment, enlargement, or translation."[65]

The entities *document, work, superwork, edition, subedition, version, author*, and *subject*, are fully discussed. Others, like *text, impression, imprint, archive*, and *collection*, are only briefly addressed.

She does not, however, seem to intend to replace other models—including that proposed by the IFLA Study Group—with these entities or, in other words, does not intend to provide a complete, alternative model.

2.3 Analysis and Modeling of Bibliographic Relationships

Bibliographic relationships between items are modeled as relationships between instances of bibliographic entities (usually, instances of the same entity) at the conceptual level. To be exact, each relationship between given items is actually unique in an individual case. It is thus important to study how to categorize them into logical types of relationships that can operate between instances of the same entity class.

Several very useful studies have been undertaken by scholars to show such relationship types, independent of the studies on modeling of the bibliographic universe and records reviewed in the preceding section. Of course, some models for the bibliographic universe, like those by the IFLA Study Group and Green, actually include taxonomy of relationship types, since they need such types to delineate the relationships among the entities/objects they defined. To put it another way, bibliographic relationship analysis not accompanying modeling of bibliographic resources would be based on the current framework of bibliographic records.

I here cover studies not reviewed in the preceding section.

1) *UNIMARC Format's categories of relationships* (1977, 1980)[66]

The first significant attempt to define bibliographic relationships was probably done in the UNIMARC Format published by the IFLA. The format identified three main categories of relationships:

1. Vertical – the hierarchical relationships of the whole to its parts, and the parts to a whole, ...
2. Horizontal – the relationship between versions of an item in different languages, formats, media, etc. ...
3. Chronological – the relationship in time between issues of an item, ...[67]

Each category is divided into more-specific types of relationships. These categories, however, were not exhaustive, and also did not contain the degree of detail necessary to categorize all types of more complex relationships.

2) *Goossens and Mazur-Rzesos's relationship analysis* (1982)[68]

The second attempt was an analysis by Goossens and Mazur-Rzesos. They limited their examination to 'hierarchical' relationships, which is equal to 'vertical' as defined by UNIMARC. They introduced a schematic representation for hierarchical relationships to express simple and complex tree structures; it works well for strict hierarchy resources like series and subseries. However, the tree structure does not work so well when expressing supplementary and accompanying resources. Thus, their analysis has limitations on this point.

3) *Tillett's taxonomy of relationships* (1987)[69]

Tillett conducted a comprehensive and detailed study of bibliographic relationships, which became a landmark study. The research results were first presented in her doctoral dissertation in 1987, and then published as a series of articles in 1991-92[70]. She presented a taxonomy of relationships discovered by examining twenty-four different cataloging codes. Seven categories of relationships were identified in this taxonomy: equivalence, derivative, descriptive, whole-part, accompanying, sequential, and shared characteristics. The derivative, whole-part, and sequential relationships are respectively equivalent to the horizontal, vertical, and chronological relationships in UNIMARC.

Furthermore, through examining various cataloging codes, Tillett identified the various types of linking devices used to establish each type of relationship of bibliographic records. She also conducted an empirical study designed to examine the extent of bibliographic relationships as reflected in their frequencies of occurrence in the MARC records of the Library of Congress.

4) *Smiraglia's taxonomy of derivative relationships* (1992)[71]

Smiraglia investigated the derivative relationships and broke them down into several subcategories: simultaneous derivations, successive derivations, translations, amplifications, extractions, adaptations, and performances. In addition, he conducted an empirical study to show the proportion of resources exhibiting derivative relationships by examining the resources themselves beyond the catalog. As a result of his study, he found that a large percentage, i.e., about 50 percent of the works contained in the resources he examined exhibited such relationships.

5) *Vellucci's analysis of relationships among musical resources* (1995, 1997)[72]

Another study was conducted by Vellucci, focusing on bibliographic relationships that exist among musical resources. The basis for the study was a sample of music scores drawn from the catalog of a university. She applied the taxonomy developed by Tillett to music and identified subgroups within each category of relationships that reflect the nature of musical resources. She found a considerable degree of musical resources having at least one relationship, stemming from the inherent nature of music. Her research results was first presented in her doctoral dissertation in 1995, and then published as a monograph in 1997 after some chapters had been restructured and expanded.

6) *Smiraglia and Leazer's analyses of derivative relationships* (1996-2002)[73]

Smiraglia and Leazer have been conducting a series of empirical analyses of derivative relationships among works. Smiraglia also examines relationships among theological works.

Their research has adopted the simple schema that *work* and *item* basically construct the bibliographic universe and, based on this schema, has tried to quantitatively and qualitatively clarify various relationships among works. Although they succeed in showing the complexities of relatedness among resources, it would be difficult to apply their research results to a conceptual model of the bibliographic universe with the aim of refining the model, simply because of the schema they adopted.

7) *Tillett's re-categorization of bibliographic relationships* (2001)[74]

Tillett re-examined her taxonomy of bibliographic relationships and proposed a new one. To summarize the new taxonomy, there are: (a) primary relationships at the same bibliographic entity levels, (b) content relationships, including equivalence, derivative, and descriptive relationship, (c) whole-part and part-to-part relationships, the latter including accompanying and sequential relationships, and (d) shared characteristic relationships. She also added 'responsibility' relationships and 'subject' relationships defined in the model by the IFLA Study Group.

2.4 Objectives for Construction of Cataloging Codes

Requirements definition for the cataloging process has not been discussed explicitly nor formally. In other words, the requirements of catalogs, including the cataloging process, have conventionally been discussed only as objectives of catalogs. Recently, however, objectives for (or principles of) the construction of cataloging codes—also called 'principles of bibliographic description and access'—are being recognized and discussed as distinct from the above objectives. This distinction is valid, and both types of objectives should be used as part of requirements.

Svenonius, who first recognized the significance of such objectives/principles, proposed a set of them: (a) General design principles, which are Principle of sufficient reason and Principle of parsimony, and (b) Principles of bibliographic description and access, which are Principle of user convenience, Principle of common usage, Principle of representation, Principle of sufficiency and necessity, Principle of standardization, and Principle of integration[75].

The JSC for Revision of AACR has been examining the adoption of these objectives/principles for the Introduction to AACR after paraphrasing them a little[76]. Paralleling this examination, the IFLA Meeting of Experts on an International Cataloguing Code in 2003 has approved the draft of a 'Statement of International Cataloguing Principles,' which contain Objectives for the Construction of Cataloguing Codes:

Convenience of the user of the catalogue. Decisions taken in the making of descriptions and controlled forms of names for access should be made with the user in mind.

Common usage. Normalized vocabulary used in descriptions and access should be in accord with that of the majority of users.

Representation. Entities in descriptions and controlled forms of names for access should be based on the way an entity describes itself.

Accuracy. The entity described should be faithfully portrayed.

Sufficiency and necessity. Only those elements in descriptions and controlled forms of names for access that are required to fulfill user tasks and are essential to uniquely identify an entity should be included.

Significance. Elements should be bibliographically significant.

Economy. When alternative ways exist to achieve a goal, preference should be given to the way that best furthers overall economy (i.e., the least cost or the simplest approach).

Standardization. Descriptions and construction of access points should be standardized to the extent and level possible. ...

Integration. The descriptions for all types of materials and controlled forms of names of entities should be based on a common set of rules, to the extent possible[77].

2.5 Modeling of Cataloging Process

Very few attempts have been made at approaching the cataloging process with modeling, and no conceptual model for the process has ever been developed. Exceptions are studies of 'cataloger tasks' and the categorization of cataloging rules.

The cataloging process contains a wide variety of tasks performed by catalogers, from creating a record (and a database) to maintaining the record (and the database). Le Boeuf enumerated several tasks, such as transcribe, describe, make identifiable, link, manage, and convey information relevant to rights management[78]. These tasks were mapped into the typology of data in bibliographic and/or authority records: transcription data, description data, identification data, data giving access to other data, management data, and rights management data. However, he did not provide any explanation or discussion.

Significant parts of the cataloging process have been specified in and formulated as cataloging rules independent of any situation or system. Therefore, studies on the categorization of cataloging rules, in particular, in respect of the functions they perform, are related to modeling of the process.

There have to date been several classifications of cataloging rules. Fidel and Crandall investigated the AACR2 rules using E-R modeling for a generalized database design[79]. Their results indicated that each rule in AACR2 belonged to at least one of six types: content; establishing entities, relationships, or attributes; authorized sources; domain; format; and access points. This classification is a mixture of that from the viewpoint of rule form and that from the viewpoint of rule function.

Another classification was proposed by Jeng, being made up of definition, description, organization, source of information, identification, and transcription[80]. This categorization overlaps Fidel and Crandall's results, but it focuses more on the functions that rules perform.

Meanwhile, Molto and Svenonius have proposed another classification, which is made up of Source: "to specify a source from which the data element is to be taken"; Choice: "to specify choice of a data element when more than one, or possibly none, is appropriate"; Form: "to specify the form in which the data element is to be recorded"; and Definition: "to define a term used in a rule."[81] This categorization approaches modeling of the process while overlaping the other results.

Notes

1. International Conference on Cataloguing Principles (1963, pp. 91-92.)
2. Lubetzky (1960)
3. Cutter (1904)
4. IFLA Study Group on the FRBR (1997, p. 8)
5. Green (1996, p. 209)
6. Svenonius (2000, Chapter 2)
7. Svenonius (2000, p. 17)
8. Svenonius (2000, pp. 18, 20)
9. Svenonius (2000, p. 20)
10. Tillett (2001b)
11. IFLA Meeting of Experts on an International Cataloguing Code (2004)
12. Verona (1959)
13. Hoffman (1981), Carpenter (1981)
14. Lubetzky (1969, p. 11)
15. Haglar (1991, 1997)
16. Verona (1959, p. 59)
17. Lubetzky (1963, p. 141)
18. Wilson (1989a, 1989b)
19. Domanovszky (1975)
20. Wilson (1989a)
21. Yee (1994b, 1994c, 1995a, 1995b, 1998)
22. Jones and Kastner (1983)
23. Wilson (1968)
24. Wilson (1968, p. 7)
25. Wilson (1968, 1989a)
26. Joint Steering Committee for Revision of AACR (2002, p. Appendix.D-4)

27 O'Neil and Visine-Goetz (1989)
28 O'Neil and Visine-Goetz (1989, p. 172)
29 O'Neil and Visine-Goetz (1989, p. 173)
30 O'Neil and Visine-Goetz (1989, p. 172)
31 Wanninger (1982)
32 Svenonius (1992)
33 Svenonius (1992, p. 5)
34 Svenonius (1992, pp. 5-6)
35 Svenonius (1992, p. 7)
36 Taniguchi (1990, 1993a, 1993b, 1993c, 1997a)
37 Taniguchi (1990, 1993a, 1993b, 1993c)
38 Taniguchi (1997a, 1999b)
39 Taniguchi (1993c)
40 Tillett (1987, 1991a, 1991b)
41 Leazer (1993)
42 Leazer (1993, p. 18)
43 Heaney (1995)
44 Heaney (1995, p. 140)
45 Heaney (1995, p. 152)
46 Green (1996)
47 Green (1996, p. 215)
48 Green (1996, p. 215)
49 Green (1996, p. 215)
50 Green (1996, p. 210)
51 IFLA Study Group on the FRBR (1996, 1997)
52 IFLA Study Group on the FRBR (1997, p. 16)
53 IFLA Study Group on the FRBR (1997, p. 18)
54 IFLA Study Group on the FRBR (1997, p. 20)
55 IFLA Study Group on the FRBR (1997, p. 23)
56 IFLA Study Group on the FRBR (1997, p. 16)
57 IFLA Study Group on the FRBR (1997, p. 16)
58 Le Boeuf (2001)
59 Delsey (1998b, 1999)
60 Delsey (1998b, p. 1)

61 Delsey (1998a)
62 Delsey (1998b, Table.1-1)
63 Delsey (1998b, p. 4)
64 Svenonius (2000, Chapter 3)
65 Svenonius (2000, p. 37)
66 IFLA Working Group on Content Designators (1977, 1980)
67 IFLA Working Group on Content Designators (1977, p. 58; 1980, p. 54)
68 Goossens and Mazur-Rzesos (1982)
69 Tillett (1987)
70 Tillett (1991a, 1991b, 1992a, 1992b)
71 Smiraglia (1992)
72 Vellucci (1995, 1997)
73 Leazer and Smiraglia (1996, 1999), Smiraglia and Leazer (1999), Smiraglia (2002)
74 Tillett (2001a)
75 Svenonius (2000, Chapter 5)
76 Tillett (2001b)
77 IFLA Meeting of Experts on an International Cataloguing Code (2004)
78 Le Boeuf (2001)
79 Fidel and Crandall (1988)
80 Jeng (1991)
81 Molto and Svenonius (1998, p. 8)

Chapter 3

A Conceptual Model Giving Primacy to Text-level Bibliographic Entity[1]

3.1 What Are 'Text' and 'Expression'?

The term 'text' has had several meanings even in the cataloging field. Wilson was probably the first researcher to introduce the term to describe something independent from both an intellectual/artistic content that he called a 'work,' and its physical manifestation that he called an 'exemplar.'[2] His intention was to provide a clearer view of the bibliographic universe, which had until then been discussed using the concepts 'work' and 'book'/'document.' He described his recognition using a practical example as follows:

[H]e has composed or invented a *work*, a poem or letter or report; he has ordered certain words into a certain sequence and so produced a *text*; he has produced marks or inscriptions on some material that constitute an *exemplar* of the text. The three descriptions are not independent, for he could have produced no work without producing some text, and could have produced no text without producing some permanent or transitory exemplar of that text. But the descriptions are by no means equivalent, for the work produced is not the text produced, nor is the text produced the exemplar produced. The three descriptions mention items of quite distinct varieties[3].

Based on this recognition, a new development has begun. He defined the term 'text' by stating that "a sequence of words and auxiliary symbols, is an abstract entity, like the words of which it is composed."[4] Since his introduction of the term, however, it has been used in several different meanings. One usage is to be almost interchangeable with the term 'work.' For example, Cockshutt et al. pointed out that the term was used as synonymous with 'work' in some cases, while being differentiated from 'work' in other cases, even within AACR2 Chapter 21[5].

Another example can be found in the *ALA Glossary of Library and Information Science*[6]. The glossary shows the following five definitions of the term 'text':

1. The words of the author, or the signs and symbols used in place of words by the author, in a written or printed work.
2. The body of a book, exclusive of the headlines, notes, illustrations, and other elements of a page.
3. A term used as a general material designation to designate printed material accessible to the naked eye (e.g., a book, a pamphlet, or a broadside). (AACR2)
4. The words of a song, song cycle, or, in the plural, a collection of songs. (AACR2)
5. In data transmission, the body of a message[7].

The first definition above comes from that of Wilson, and there is little gap between it and the definition of 'work' in the same glossary: "Bibliographically defined, a specific body of recorded information in the form of words, numerals, sounds, images, or any other symbols, as distinct from the substance on which it is recorded."[8] In the present study, the term 'text' is used with those two similar definitions.

Instead of 'text,' another term, 'expression,' has recently been introduced so as to be fit for non-alpha-numeric notation, like sound and image, as well as for alpha-numeric notation. Additionally, adoption of that term by the IFLA Study Group on the FRBR influences its popularity. FRBR defines 'expression' as "the intellectual or artistic realization of a work in the form of alpha-numeric, musical, or choreographic notation, sound, image, object, movement, etc., or any combination of such forms."[9] The term 'work' in this case means an intellectual or artistic creation itself (i.e., an abstract entity).

In the present study, I will use the two terms 'text' and 'expression' as being synonymous, simply because the difference between them is not important for the study.

In conceptual modeling following a given modeling language, an entity or object corresponding to 'text'/'expression' as defined above can be set up. This is the text-level entity or object. It is easy to find such an entity or object in the models that have been proposed so far. Some models call it 'text,' but others give it another appellation, as we have seen in Chapter 2.

Re-examining the current cataloging framework at the conceptual level, and seeking an alternative desirable framework at that level, inevitably imposes on us a structural view of a resource, which is a basic constituent of the bibliographic universe. As a natural consequence of a structural view of a resource, various models have introduced a text-level entity or object as one of the bibliographic entities or objects within the models.

It is not necessarily clear, however, what role or function the text-level entity/object has (or is expected to have), and what relative position the entity/object has vis-à-vis others in a model.

The aim of this chapter is first to introduce a viewpoint regarding which entity/object (or entities/objects) is to be given primacy among bibliographic entities/objects in a conceptual model. Another aim is to show an outline of a conceptual model in which text-level entity/object takes priority. Let us give the name 'a model giving primacy to text-level entity' (or, in short, 'a text-prioritized model') to such a model. Broadly speaking, such models imply that the text is regarded as being more substantial than ever, and the bibliographic description of an item is made mainly based on the text, or at least on both the text and the physical medium of the item.

First, I re-examine the FRBR model from the viewpoint of giving primacy to text-level entity. At the same time, I show the outline of a new model giving primacy to that entity, by chiefly indicating differences from the FRBR model in (a) defining the entity and (b) associating attributes with the entity. The FRBR model as a whole is inclined to give primacy to manifestation-level entity, as will be shown later. Second, by applying the concept of 'user tasks' found in the FRBR model to the new model outlined in this study, I create a scenario on how entities are used by users. Third, some examples of bibliographic record equivalents in line with the new model are shown.

No conceptual models have ever been developed with careful attention to which entity is prioritized, let alone giving primacy to text-level entity. Rather, the core of this viewpoint could be found in discussions on records structures, attributed to matters concerning the logical design or implementation level subsequent to the conceptual design level—for example, discussion by Howarth[10] and Multiple

Versions Forum[11], which will be addressed in Chapter 6.

In this study, the entity-relationship (E-R) model is used as a modeling language and analysis technique. The reason why the E-R model is adopted here is that (a) it is widely used, as shown by the fact that the FRBR model adopted it—the model is the most prominent and comprehensive and thus the examination in this chapter will proceed by indicating differences from it—and (b) it can if necessary be easily converted to representations with an object-oriented modeling language like UML.

3.2 Significance of Models Giving Primacy to Text-level Entity

The significance or necessity of a model giving primacy to text-level entity are as follows:

1) An identical text appears frequently in more than one medium or form—reproductions or others. This has imposed critical problems in current cataloging practice; we make a new record for a new text, and do the same (i.e., make a new record) for the same text in a different format. As a result, we choose to communicate to users the difference in manifestation rather than the identity in text. Users are often perplexed to encounter very similar records (in some cases, a large number of similar records), whose interrelations are not clear. We have called it the 'format variations' or 'multiple versions' issue.

Within the current framework, there have been numerous efforts to solve this problem; for instance, Multiple Versions Forum in 1989, the development of *Guidelines for Bibliographic Description of Reproductions*[12] by ALCTS CCS CC: DA (Association for Library Collections and Technical Services. Cataloging and Classification Section. Committee on Cataloging: Description and Access) in 1995, etc. However, no sufficient solutions have yet been found nor implemented. By contrast, a model giving primacy to text-level entity should be capable of providing a complete solution, since it makes us grasp each individual item at its text level and thus represent items sharing an identical text at that level, with the result of sufficient control of those items. Consequently, users will be able to have an OPAC which generates a display of the bibliographic data of those items in a form being intelligible to them.

2) It has been pointed out numerous times that almost all users are usually

concerned with a text or a work (i.e., the intellectual/artistic aspect of a resource) and not a physical manifestation (i.e., the physical aspect). For instance, in three main working papers prepared for the International Conference on Cataloguing Principles in 1961, Lubetzky[13], Verona[14], and Jolley[15] all agreed on this point, whereas they had different opinions on the matter that which objective should be prioritized under the main entry system. A method of providing more detailed information on the text and work involved in an item is required. A model of this type will have the capability of satisfying such a requirement—at least a requirement toward a text—in a straightforward manner.

3) There exist a wide variety of texts derived from a single text. Reflecting user needs for representing relationships among texts and/or works, in recent years there has been renewed interest in analyzing and categorizing those relationships, as seen in Chapter 2. A method is needed for indicating such relationships in catalogs. A model of that kind would also be capable of meeting this requirement.

4) Electronic resources on a network (typically on the Internet) force us to neglect the physical medium in which they are fixed—their physicality is minimized. There is little need to provide information on the medium/carrier in their bibliographic descriptions. Similarly, electronic resources fixed with a format in a medium would force us to focus on the text and its format, not the medium. Such resources would require a more text-level oriented approach than before.

Moreover, these resources are dealt with in cataloging and also in the field of metadata. It would be feasible to connect discussions on cataloging with those on metadata (in particular, descriptive metadata), which is defined here as structured (descriptive) data about a resource, provided we adopt a strategy of shifting from physical manifestations to texts. It would also be feasible to have interoperability, to some extent, between bibliographic data made by following the model of this type and metadata created in agreement with one of the proposed schema, like Dublin Core.

3.3 Examining Typical Models Containing Text-level Entity

3.3.1 Two Methods of Defining Bibliographic Entity

According to the FRBR model, entities forming a conceptual model are divided into three groups. The first group comprises "the products of intellectual or artistic endeavour that are named or described in bibliographic records."[16] The entities belonging to this group are usually called 'bibliographic entities.' If we focus on these entities, we realize that there are two methods of defining an entity: the hierarchical way and the parallel way[17]. It is thus necessary to review these methods in brief before examining existing models and proposing a new one.

One method is to define an entity in a hierarchical manner—a lower-level entity encapsulates its upper-level one. This method implies that each entity—except the top in a hierarchy—involves the properties of its upper-level entity and those of its own. At the same time, this method involves viewing an item from the aspect of an instantiation process; an item in hand is understood to result from the stepwise instantiation process from an idea itself that is the most abstract to a physical item. For example, it is possible to assume that, to begin with, a person has composed or invented an idea itself, next she/he has ordered certain words into a certain sequence, and lastly she/he has produced marks and inscriptions on a given medium that produces a physical manifestation. If in accordance with this view, an item can be modeled with entities such as a work-level, a text-level, and a physical manifestation-level entity, each of which is defined as being inclusive of the preceding. A sort of 'is-a' relationship exists between an entity and its subordinates. We call this method of defining an entity the 'hierarchical way.' A typical example of the adoption of this method is the FRBR model.

The other method is to define a bibliographic entity in a mutually exclusive manner—entities do not share anything. This method implies that we can conceptualize an item in hand with mutually exclusive entities. It also leads to the view from an item's structural aspect. It allows us to model an item with entities such as a work-level, a text-level, and a medium-level entity, each of which is defined as being mutually exclusive. A 'part-of' relationship therefore exists between an item and each of the defined entities, if the whole item is regarded as one entity; in object-oriented modeling with UML, this is called 'aggregation.' We call this method the 'parallel way.' A typical example of this method can be found in the 'three-layered model' and a partial example is found in Delsey's model of the logical structure of AACR.

These two methods of defining an entity are not contradictory. Although it seems impossible to apply these methods together, it is possible at least to combine them in a model. Or rather, both aspects on which the methods are based are required in order to grasp and represent an item more completely; the methods are only different in which aspect takes precedence over the other. They should therefore be considered complementary to each other[18].

The 'cardinality' of a relationship between entities refers to the maximum (and sometimes also the minimum) number of instances of one entity associated with a single instance of the other entity, and thus describes a constraint on the relationship. It is also sometimes called 'connectivity' or 'multiplicity.' According to the hierarchical way, entity instances construct a tree structure from the top-level instance to the bottom-level ones—the cardinality is one-to-many. Many-to-many cardinality also occurs in entities defined in the hierarchical way, when more than one tree of entity instances share the identical node (i.e., the same instance). But with such cases, there is a need to confirm the validity in a bibliographical sense of applying the many-to-many cardinality to entities. On the contrary, with the parallel way where entities are defined as being exclusive, there is no constraint on the number of entity instances that are associated through the relationship. This indicates a bipartite structure and its cardinality is many-to-many.

Attention should also be paid to the 'inheritance' characteristic of entities defined by either method. Defining entities in the hierarchical way presupposes in principle the inheritance of attributes from an entity to its subordinates. Defining entities in the parallel way, on the other hand, does not provide any view on the inheritance of attributes between entities; it is necessary to define attributes at each entity repeatedly where the sharing of attributes among entities is required.

3.3.2 Modeling Current Practice at Conceptual Level

Before examining existing models containing the text-level entity, it would be better to roughly conceptualize current cataloging practice represented, typically, by ISBD, AACR2, and MARC formats like MARC21, while also introducing a viewpoint regarding which entity is to be given primacy among the bibliographic entities.

Actual practice embraces complexities with many exceptional treatments—Delsey's analysis of AACR2 manifests such circumstances. It is therefore possible to construct several models for current practice, while at the same time it is difficult for any single such model to cover the whole range of current practice. The simplest, and thereby the most fundamental, model would be to better understand the practice, especially in an initial stage of the examination.

Current practice is conceptualized most simply by the entities *work* and *book/document*, being derived from the traditional distinction between them which was mentioned in Chapter 2. This model, however, is still at the same level as the traditional discussion and cannot proceed beyond that point.

Therefore, it would be better to adopt a model with three bibliographic entities—*work, manifestation*, and *item*—and other types of entities such as *person* and *corporate body*. The most important difference between these two models is that the latter introduces a distinction between *manifestation* and *item*.

The entity *work* can be defined as "a distinct intellectual or artistic creation," as shown by the FRBR model, whereas both AACR2[19] in 1978 and its latest edition, the 2002 revision, do not contain any formal definition of the term. Through a close examination of the 'work' concept, it can be realized that it has been interpreted in various ways even within the history of AACR[20]. Part of the complexities and ambiguity of 'work' derive from the fact that it has not been clearly differentiated from the concept of 'text.'

Let us argue the relative weight of the entity *work* in current cataloging practice by referring to the current record framework. *Work* apparently does not perform a key role in describing an item being cataloged, although its existence is supposed to be a prerequisite in making a bibliographic description. By contrast, *work* is the key presupposition in selecting and assigning headings for an item. Almost all of the headings, however, do not represent *work* itself.

Work itself is only represented with a uniform title and its corresponding authority record that contains some data elements assisting in catalogers' judgment on works. It is important to stress that uniform titles are optional and applied not to all items but to restricted ones, although their application depends finally on the policy of a cataloging agency. Current AACR2, for example, does not allow for assigning a uniform title when it is the same as the title proper; it seems to be an economical decision in card catalogs not in current OPACs. Or, it is possible to consider that, in addition to a uniform title and its authority record, *work* is manifested in a 'name-title added entry' heading and a 'name-title reference,' where the title in these cases usually indicates the title proper, not a uniform title. Such a heading and reference are also used in restricted cases. All these things clarify that (a) a work-level entity instance is not necessarily created for every item, (b) few properties of *work* can be recorded in a bibliographic record, and hence (c) *work* is not given primacy in the model for current practice.

The second entity is *manifestation*. It is usually defined as the "physical embodiment of a *work*", this being a slightly modified definition of that in the FRBR model[21]. When a *work* is realized in a form of text, the resulting text is embodied finally in a medium—this is a *manifestation*. In current practice, it is evident that an item is captured and described mainly at this manifestation-level; (a) every bibliographic record is created for a new manifestation, not for an item (i.e., a copy), except unpublished items, as will be seen later, and (b) most of data elements constituting a bibliographic description are related to *manifestation*. Hence *manifestation* seems to be predominant for bibliographic description, conforming to the above examination of *work*.

This argument is valid at least in AACR2, more precisely, in AACR 1st ed. (AACR1)[22] after it adopted the first ISBD and was revised in 1974[23]. Before then, the role and relative position of *work* was more significant than that in current practice, as Howarth pointed out[24]. Strictly speaking, current practice in itself has a wide range of variations, and the weight of *work* depends on a particular cataloging code.

It should also be added that in current practice the text of an item is usually dealt with as being contained in either *work* or *manifestation*. Cockshutt et al. found that the 'text' is sometimes used as being synonymous with 'work' in AACR2 Chapter 21[25]. Another example is Delsey's analysis of AACR2; his model contains the entity 'content,' which would correspond to 'text,' as one of entities constituting the entity 'document' or others. To put it another way, in some cases a text is regarded as the concrete aspect of *work*, and in other cases it is dealt with as the intellectual or artistic aspect of *manifestation*. A text-level entity independent of the above two therefore is not required for modeling current practice.

The third entity *item* is defined as "a single exemplar of a *manifestation*,"[26] this definition being borrowed from the FRBR model. Similarly, AACR2, 2002 revision defines it as "a document or set of documents in any physical form, published, issued, or treated as an entity, and as such forming the basis for a single bibliographic description."[27] As being understood with these definitions, *item* appears as a physical piece in hand that serves as a starting point for cataloging.

However, two slightly different meanings are embedded in the definitions. One is to regard *item* as the whole entity that contains a work, its text, its medium, and others. The other is to see it as distinct from *manifestation* in containing characteristics that separately identify an individual copy of the manifestation. In this sense, the entity can instead be called 'copy,' as suggested by Vellucci[28]. These two meanings can be drawn from either of the two methods of defining an entity and hence they do not conflict with the methods.

In the case of published resources where all copies are produced from the same master copy and which occupy principal position in cataloging, properties peculiar to the entity *item* (i.e., the characteristics of a copy) are usually represented only in the note area of the bibliographic description and other data elements like a location mark. Or, in some systems, all information on a copy is recorded in a holdings or item record separate from a bibliographic record. Although the entity *item* is a starting point for making a bibliographic description and thus a bibliographic record, the description is made mainly based on not *item* but *manifestation*, and the relative weight of *item* in cataloging practice is less than that of *manifestation*.

Jonsson, who is an exception that consciously touched an issue of 'the basis for a record,' described as follows, by referring to the rule 0.24 of AACR2 and FRBR.

> Although a cataloguer normally works from one single Item of a Manifestation, the normal approach is to assume that this Item, this copy in hand, represents a class of Manifestations, so that you describe the Manifestation rather than the Item, the edition rather than the copy.—Now, it isn't possible to map Manifestation to edition only, but a Manifestation of which there are multiple Items clearly corresponds to edition at a principle level. We are not in the habit of making separate records for every Item of a Manifestation, that would be absurd, and 0.24 has not been interpreted to mean that[29].

This explanation is basically matched with our interpretation, although his interest was put on not conceptual modeling but record creation at the implementation level.

These three bibliographic entities seem to be defined in the hierarchical way mentioned above. A *work* may be embodied in one or more than one *manifestation*; likewise a *manifestation* may embody one or more than one *work*. A *manifestation*, in turn, may be exemplified by one or more than one *item*. The diagrammatic representation on these is:

| work | ←← is embodied in →→ | manifestation |
| manifestation | ← is exemplified by →→ | item |

The '←' and '→' in the diagram indicate '1' cardinality; the '←←' and '→→' indicate 'many.'

It would be possible, at the same time, to re-define these entities as those by the parallel way and to conceptualize current practice with redefined entities. The reason is that *work* is just an abstract entity and thus there is no substantial difference between *manifestation* that includes *work* and *manifestation* after the *work* is removed from it. An additional reason is that the two meanings of *item* do not conflict with either of the two ways of defining an entity, including the parallel way as already mentioned.

The above conceptualization of current practice can be roughly associated with the current records structure; the entities *work*, *manifestation*, and *item* correspond respectively to the uniform title authority record, bibliographic record, and holdings record.

Regarding non-bibliographic entities, it is better to introduce at least those such as either *author* or *person* and *corporate body*. These are represented by (a) data elements in the bibliographic description like statements of responsibility and notes on the statements, (b) author headings (i.e., personal name headings, corporate name headings, etc.), and (c) name authority records that contain several data elements assisting in catalogers' judgment on the identification of persons and corporate bodies. These entities are associated with *work* through 'responsibility' relationships at the conceptual level. In contrast, in the current records structure, name authority records are linked to bibliographic records, not to uniform title authority records. The reason is that uniform titles are applied only to restricted cases or types of resources.

It follows, from what has been said in this section, that any conceptual model following current practice does not have any necessity to introduce a text-level entity, whereas some other models which try to propose a different structure and practice might introduce such an entity.

3.3.3 IFLA Study Group's FRBR Model

The FRBR model, as we have seen in Chapter 2, contains four bibliographic entities defined in the hierarchical way—*work, expression, manifestation*, and *item*. The model called them 'Group 1 entities.' The diagrammatic representation of the entities and relationships among them is:

work	← is realized through →→	expression
expression	←← is embodied in →→	manifestation
manifestation	← is exemplified by →→	item

First, it is worth noting that an independent text-level entity named *expression* is introduced. Its definition was quoted at the beginning of this chapter. FRBR noted that defining and introducing *expression* brings us the following three benefits: (a) "Defining *expression* as an entity in the model gives us a means of reflecting the distinctions in intellectual or artistic content that may exist between one realization and another of the same *work*," (b) "Defining expression as an entity also enables us to draw relationships between specific *expressions* of a *work*," and (c) "We can also use the entity defined as *expression* to indicate that the intellectual or artistic content embodied in one *manifestation* is in fact the same as that embodied in another *manifestation*."[30] Consequently, such a model would enable us to accomplish more elaborate bibliographic control by inserting the new entity between *work* and *manifestation*, both of which are already set up in modeling current practice. Therefore, FRBR and some of its preceding models tried to incorporate such an entity, as has been seen in Chapter 2.

Regarding the cardinality of relationships between *expression* and the other entities, the model specifies that (a) a one-to-many relationship exists between *work* and *expression* and (b) a many-to-many relationship exists between *expression* and *manifestation*. This means that, in addition to that an *expression* instance may be embodied in one or more *manifestations*, a *manifestation* instance may embody one or more *expressions*, which is called 'collection' in the current AACR2. There is no mention of the inheritance issue of attributes in FRBR.

We should also notice that this model keeps in principle the framework of current cataloging practice; *manifestation* occupies the predominant position and the bibliographic description of an item is made mainly based on *manifestation*, whereas *work* and *expression* are subordinate to *manifestation*. That is to say, *expression*, as being similar to *work*, can be interpreted as an intermediary entity leading users to *manifestation*, and is not expected to play a major role in identifying and describing an item.

Such an interpretation is derived from some evidences.

1) In this model, it is not obvious, or at least not declared explicitly, whether an *expression* instance exists for every item. The model does not in fact touch on the minimum cardinality on the *expression* side of the relationship, neither between it and *work* nor between it and *manifestation*. Such an issue is also called 'existence' of the entity in relationships; the existence is specified as either 'mandatory' or 'optional.' An additional indication is that almost all discussions following FRBR, including those by ALCTS CCS CC:DA[31] and JSC for Revision of AACR[32], have not presupposed the mandatory existence of *expression*.

2) Another evidence is that all label information including titles, statements of responsibility, and edition designations that all appear in an item, is associated with *manifestation* and none of that information is associated with *expression*—the role of label information will be discussed later.

3) At the same time, the model is not able to show what the title of *expression* means in practice (i.e., to identify properly the title with any known data element), although that title is set up for the entity.

We may note, in passing, that the model enumerates exhaustively the inherent characteristics of a text as the attributes of *expression* and lists many sorts of relationships between *expressions*, as will be seen later. This fact may imply that the model has features to lead to a model giving primacy to a text-level entity.

The model defines non-bibliographic entities: 'Group 2 entities' and 'Group 3 entities.' Group 2 represents entities "responsible for the intellectual or artistic content, the physical production and dissemination, or the custodianship of the entities in the first group."[33] This group consists of "*person* (an individual) and *corporate body* (an organization or group of individuals and/or organizations)"[34] and these entities have 'responsibility' relationships with each of the bibliographic entities. It is shown that these entities cover publishers, owners, borrowers, etc. beyond the so-called authors and creators.

The entities in Group 3 represent "an additional set of entities that serve as the subjects of *works*" and are: "*concept* (an abstract notion or idea), *object* (a material thing), *event* (an action or occurrence), and *place* (a location)."[35] 'Subject' relationships exist between these entities and the entity *work*. The same relationships also exist between *work* and the entities in the first and second groups; it indicates that "a *work* may have as its subject one or more than one *work*, *expression, manifestation, item, person*, and/or *corporate body*."[36]

3.3.4 Taniguchi's Three-layered Model

As described in Chapter 2, I have been proposing a three-layered model since 1990. At its beginning I did not clearly differentiate conceptual level arguments from those at the implementation level[37], thus later having proposed a model focusing only on conceptual level modeling[38].

The model conceptualizes a resource with a three-layer structure: work, text, and medium. In other words, an item can be decomposed into these three layers. The text-layer corresponds to a text defined at the beginning of this chapter. It is however considered not to involve a work, but just to be interrelated with a work, which is the intellectual or artistic content of an item; the text expresses the work. The medium-layer denotes what corresponds to a physical manifestation, but after the text has been removed from it—the physical medium or carrier itself. These imply that every layer of this model is constructed to be mutually exclusive, i.e., in the parallel way. No problems will occur if we consider each layer of the model to be an entity in E-R modeling, although the model did not use any formal conceptual modeling language at its beginning and thus the role of a layer would be somewhat ambiguous. With this assumption, it is possible to reveal the model with the following diagrammatic representation of the entities and relationships among them.

| *work* | ←← is expressed in →→ | *text* |
| *text* | ←← is fixed in →→ | *medium* |

One of the major characteristics of the model is the aim of making a bibliographic description of an item which gives primacy to the text-layer (i.e., a text-level entity), by applying the three-layer structure to an item. This can be explained by several reasons. One reason is that some label information, such as titles, statements of responsibility, and edition designations that appear in an item, but not label information related only to the physical medium or physical embodiment of a text, is associated with the text-layer not the medium-layer. Another reason is that every layer, including the text-layer, has an instance of its own in every item. The preceding reason causes the mandatory occurrence of a text-layer instance as well as that of the medium-layer, for accepting such label information.

Furthermore, I have intended from the beginning (a) to introduce the text-layer as the key constituent of the model, while conceiving such an idea by referring to the discussion by Wilson, and (b) to give primacy to the text-layer so as to cope with some fundamental issues that have arisen in cataloging, such as the treatment of microform reproduction and electronic resources.

In connection with the work-layer, the layer accepts the name headings of the authors or creators of a work and a uniform title for a work, if any. An instance of the work-layer is thus in principle needed in every item, except resources lacking author headings. Nevertheless, the work-layer is thought to be an intermediary to the text-layer that takes a major role in identifying and describing an item.

The three-layered model, strictly speaking, did not contain any arguments on the cardinality issue of relationships between the layers, but it _did_ contain some discussion on the unit of each layer instance for choosing an appropriate unit, in particular, that for the text-layer—this is indirectly related to the cardinality issue. The conclusion, in short, is that the cardinality of a relationship between two adjacent layers is many-to-many, being consistent with the basic nature of the relationship between the layers (i.e., to be mutually exclusive to each other). A fuller discussion on the cardinality of the relationship between the work-layer (i.e., a work-level entity) and text-layer (i.e., a text-level entity) will be attempted later.

It should also be noted that the model did not contain a layer corresponding to an individual copy below the medium-layer, reflecting current practice where recording copy related information is limited to only some data elements.

The model contained name authority records, in addition to bibliographic records, to represent the bibliographic universe and associate authors with the work-layer. Based on this point, one may say that the model could accept a layer (or an entity) corresponding those authority records, whereas it did not set up such a layer as its constituent.

3.4 Defining Text-level Entity and Other Entities

3.4.1 Entities Forming Model Giving Primacy to Text-level Entity

Requisite entities forming a new conceptual model giving primacy to a text-level entity are proposed next; requisite attributes of the text-level entity and relationships between instances of the entity will be shown in later sections.

Requisite entities can be proposed on the basis of the integration of the FRBR model and the three-layered model. A close look at these two models leads to the conclusion that the new model must consist of four bibliographic entities, two entities involved in 'responsibility' relationships (i.e., *person* and *corporate body*), and some additional ones involved in 'subject' relationships. And it also leads to the conclusion that each bibliographic entity must be constructed according to both methods of defining an entity. It is possible and also necessary to construct each entity in a combined way so that an entity can be viewed from either aspect (i.e., the structural and instantiation aspects), depending on the situation.

The four indispensable bibliographic entities, when defined in the hierarchical way, are identical to those defined in the FRBR model: *work, expression, manifestation*, and *item*. These are built on conforming with the instantiation process from an abstract work to an item in hand. These are depicted in the upper part of Figure 3-1.

At the same time, the entities, when defined in the parallel way, equal those—to be precise, those transferred from the layers—in the three-layered model: *work, text*, and *medium*. We have to add an entity corresponding to the *item* in the former set of entities, for representing characteristics at the level of an individual copy. The entity added is named *copy* here, while it may be called 'copy's characteristics' to be more precise. These entities are built to be resulted from the division of an item into components that are mutually exclusive. These are depicted in the lower part of Figure 3-1.

Chapter 3 A Conceptual Model Giving Primacy to Text-level Bibliographic Entity 53

```
  work
        expression
                manifestation
                          item
  work    text    medium    copy
```

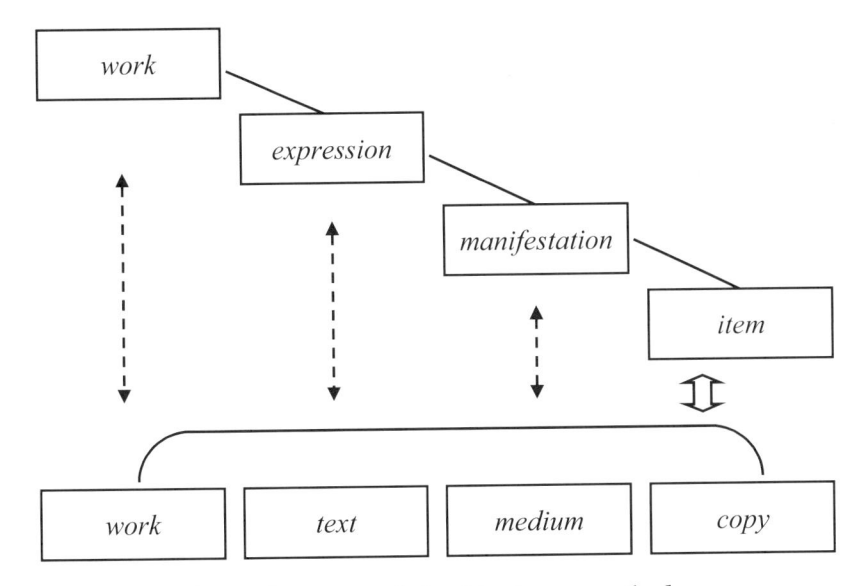

Figure 3-1. Bibliographic entities defined in the two methods.

These two series of entities can be integrated into one series, resulting in the structure shown in Figure 3-2. *Work* is the same if it is defined in either the hierarchical or parallel way. *Expression* is considered to be an entity which combines *work* with *text* defined in the parallel way. *Manifestation*, likewise, is an entity which combines *expression* in the hierarchical way and *medium* in the parallel way. *Item*, in turn, is an entity which joins *manifestation* with *copy*. The resultant entities for the model to be proposed are called, for example, *work*, *expression/text*, *manifestation/medium*, and *item/copy*, respectively, in a convenient manner. The diagrammatic representation of these entities and relationships among them is as follows:

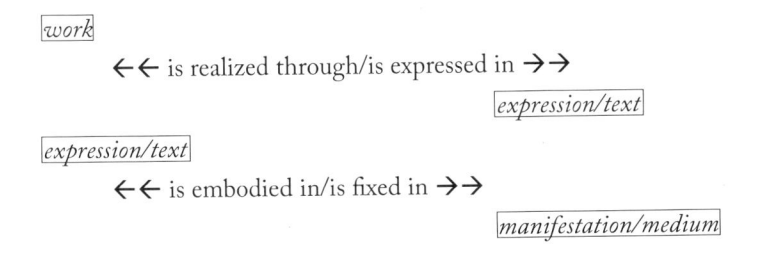

work
  ←← is realized through/is expressed in →→
    expression/text

expression/text
  ←← is embodied in/is fixed in →→
    manifestation/medium

manifestation/medium
⬅⬅ is exemplified by/is complemented with ➡➡
item/copy

These entities as a whole intend to demonstrate a conceptual modeling where the text-level entity *expression/text* is given primacy; this model differs from the FRBR model in this regard. The other bibliographic entities are inevitably subordinate to *expression/text*; *manifestation/medium* is subordinate to *expression/text* and *item/copy*, in turn, is subsidiary to *manifestation/medium*, while *work* is an intermediary to access *expression/text*.

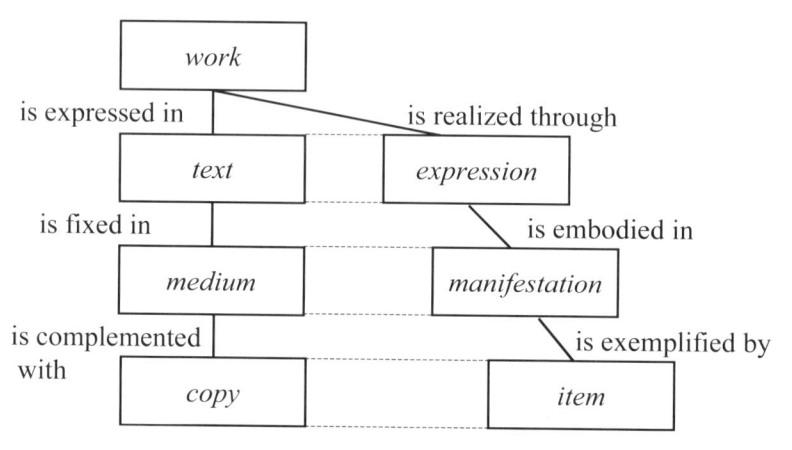

Figure 3-2. Bibliographic entities and their relationships in the proposed model.

3.4.2 Implications of Proposed Framework

This section examines what the proposed framework implies or imposes at the conceptual design (or, in certain cases, logical design or implementation) level.

1) *Two ways of defining the text- and manifestation-level entities*

The text-level entity *expression/text* and the manifestation-level entity *manifestation/medium* are defined, in the parallel way, as that an instance of the former entity can be divided into some parts and then each part is fixed in an instance of the latter, whereas, on the other hand, an instance of the latter can accept more than one instance of the former. Hence, the cardinality between the two entities is many-to-many.

In contrast, in the hierarchical way, the two entities are defined as that a single instance of *expression/text* can be physically embodied on or in different sorts of medium (i.e., can be embodied in different instances of *manifestation/medium*). This is a sort of 'is-a' relationship and its cardinality is one-to-many. At the same time, in the hierarchical way, different instances of the former entity are occasionally embodied in a single instance of the latter (in other words, can share the identical instance of the latter). Hence, the cardinality is many-to-one. Finally, we can get the many-to-many relationship between the two entities, even in the hierarchical way, by combining these two cardinalities.

2) *Existence of the text-level entity*

An instance of the text-level entity *expression/text* is created for every item to be described; this includes the cases where an *expression/text* instance corresponds to more than one item. It is similar to the three-layered model. This matter belongs to the existence issue (or the minimum cardinality issue) on relationships associated with a text-level entity; the existence of the entity is mandatory, in other words, the minimum cardinality is 1 (not zero) on the *expression/text* side of the relationship either between it and *work* or between it and *manifestation/medium*.

This is an inevitable result deduced from the premise that the text-level entity was chosen to be given primacy. It leads to associating necessary attributes that enable us to identify and describe an item at the text level, with a text-level entity; this point will be examined later. It also leads to creating instances of the bibliographic entities below *expression/text* (i.e., *manifestation/medium* and *item/copy*) for every item.

3) *Unit on which a bibliographic description based*

A bibliographic description and also a record must be created based on the unit of the entity *expression/text*, if the policy of creating each record based on one bibliographic entity is adopted. This is also a natural result from the premise that the text-level entity is specified to be predominant. This matter, however, seems to be beyond the scope of conceptual modeling and to be an issue at the logical design or implementation stage.

In contrast, the issue does not arise, when we select another policy of creating a record at every level of bibliographic entities, where the resulting records representing an item as a whole are linked to each other.

4) *Criteria of identity for the text-level entity*

A detailed investigation is required to establish criteria for deciding the unit of (in other words, the boundaries for) *expression/text*. We need such criteria before making a description and also a record based on that entity if we adopt the policy noted above. This issue is equivalent to that on the criteria of identity for a text-level entity (and also a text itself), since that unit consolidates a range of texts that share a certain identity into one text at the conceptual level.

From the conceptual definition of a text and a text-level entity, aspects of physical format such as typeface and page layout are excluded from and irrelevant to the identity of a text and its corresponding entity. Hence verifying the identity between texts should be done by character-by-character comparison. From the viewpoint of operational aspect, on the other hand, it is not feasible to compare texts, character by character, in most cases, except for some electronic resources that are texts in the form of alpha-numeric or other notation (not in the form of sound, image, etc.). Another problem is that, if we adopt the above criteria, each individual physical manifestation will probably be judged as having its own unique text different from all others, except for the cases of facsimile reproduction, microform reproduction, etc. Perfect identical texts but different physical manifestations have seldom occurred in practice, except for certain types of reproduction. Rather, there have been plenty of very similar but slightly different texts—those contain trivial or negligible variation for most users other than bibliographers or textual scholars.

It follows from what has been said that it would be practical and valid to suppose that texts are identical unless some clues external to, and accompanied to, the texts show their differences. This recognition would be in accordance to some extent with the following description found in FRBR.

> On a practical level, the degree to which bibliographic distinctions are made between variant *expressions* of a *work* will depend to some extent on the nature of the *work* itself, and on the anticipated needs of users. ... Variations that would be evident only from a more detailed analysis and comparison of

expressions (e.g., variations between several of the early texts of Shakespeare's *Hamlet*) would normally be reflected in the data only if the nature or stature of the *work* warranted such analysis, and only if it was anticipated that the distinction would be important to users[39].

We need to elaborate proper criteria of identity for a text-level entity, while considering balance between the desirable granularity of identity and the applicability of the criteria; this is beyond the scope of conceptual modeling.

There is one other thing that should be touched on in relation to this matter. Some standard identifiers for texts have been discussed and defined by the ISO (International Standardization Organization). According to Le Boeuf[40], the ISWC (International Standard Work Code), ISRC (International Standard Recording Code), ISAN (International Standard Audiovisual Number), and ISTC (International Standard Textual Work Code) are identifiers for texts. I, however, do not want to dwell on the matter, since those identifiers would be defined in accordance with the demands of the so-called rights management community, including the publishing and music industries, and such identifiers do not necessarily accord with our needs and discussions.

5) Definition of the manifestation-level entity

If we want to adapt more properly the proposed framework to electronic resources, it is probably reasonable to decompose the manifestation-level entity *manifestation/medium* into a format-level and a carrier-level entity. The 'format' here indicates the formatting of a text, including typeface and page layout. It also indicates the so-called 'logical format' independent from physical carriers in which a text is fixed and stored. On the other hand, the 'carrier' is a physical medium itself, excluding the above 'format,' but involving the so-called 'physical format' dependent on a medium. Adopting these two entities, instead of the manifestation-level entity, leads to the conclusion that for networked resources only the format-level entity is applicable but the carrier-level entity is not.

It must be noted that the definition and names of these new entities would represent the adoption of the parallel way to define them, although it is still unclear. Hence, we need to define these entities in each of the two ways (at least, the hierarchical way) and assign proper names to them for reflecting the way adopted.

6) *Cardinality of the relationship between the text- and work-level entities*

The cardinality of the relationship between *work* and *expression/text* should be considered to be many-to-many, not one-to-many, since these entities are defined in the parallel way as well as in the hierarchical way. The many-to-many cardinality allows the creation of *work* instances in a flexible manner; for example, more than one *work* instance can be created against a single *expression/text*, when necessary. I have argued that, in the course of discussion on the three-layered model, it is sometimes difficult to create an instance of the work-layer (i.e., the entity *work*) in such a manner that general consensus is obtained on it, since creating a *work* instance depends on a cataloging code being adopted and ultimately on the individual cataloger's judgment on works[41]. A considerable number of studies have been made on the concept 'work'; nevertheless, we have not arrived yet at a consensus on it.

Furthermore, the following passage is found in the description of the FRBR model:

> Because the notion of a *work* is abstract, it is difficult to define precise boundaries for the entity. The concept of what constitutes a *work* and where the line of demarcation lies between one *work* and another may in fact be viewed differently from one culture to another. Consequently the bibliographic conventions established by various cultures or national groups may differ in terms of the criteria they use for determining the boundaries between one *work* and another[42].

From this passage one may say that it is difficult to create *work* instances in a stable and widely accepted way covering "various cultures or national groups," or sometimes even within a culture or a nation. Meanwhile, one may say that it is necessary to permit the creation of various *work* instances against the identical text, if we take into account from the beginning the possibility of the exchange or sharing of bibliographic information among "various cultures or national groups." Reflecting these makes the cardinality of the relationship between *work* and *expression/text* many-to-many.

7) Existence of the work-level entity

We may, in addition to the point just mentioned above, note that existence of *work* should be considered to be either mandatory or optional, that is, the minimum cardinality on the *work* side of the relationship from it to *expression/text* should be considered to be either 1 or zero. This means that the proposed framework should also permit to create a *work* instance for every item, or alternatively to create a *work* in limited cases. In other words, I postulate that a *work* instance can be created in a flexible manner.

In cases where the existence is mandatory (i.e., the minimum cardinality is 1), one *work* instance at least must be created for every item. It does not contradict the argument that the *work* is not chosen to be predominant. It intends to provide users with some information on *work* but not with core information to identify and describe an item. *Work* may accept some attributes, such as the name headings of the authors or creators of a work, and a uniform title assigned to a work or the title proper of an item containing the work if no uniform title is assigned. It is in accord with the fact that some researchers have insisted that uniform titles must be constructed and applied consistently for all works so as to expand the role of uniform titles in OPACs of the future[43].

If the existence is optional (i.e., the minimum cardinality is zero), it means to create a *work* in limited cases. According to the current AACR2, and thus, in modeling this current practice, for example, uniform title authority records apply to restricted cases or types of resources, a *work* instance is created in restricted cases.

The important point to note is that the existence of the work-level entity, and the cardinality between the text- and work-level entities addressed here, do not affect conceptual modeling where the text-level entity is given primacy.

8) Cardinality of the relationship between the manifestation- and item-level entities

The cardinality issue of the relationship between *manifestation/medium* and *item/copy* is worth a passing mention. In FRBR, the cardinality is one-to-many; more than one *item* exemplifies the same *manifestation*. This is a view taken from the aspect of an instantiation process; in other words, a definition in the hierarchical way. In contrast, the newly proposed model specified that the cardinality is many-to-many. Such cardinality comes from combining that in the hierarchical way and that in the parallel way. In the parallel way, a *manifestation/ medium* can be split into some instances of *item/copy* by intention, and at the same time different *manifestation/medium* instances can be physically bound together in a single *item/copy*. This leads to the many-to-many cardinality. FRBR views such reconfiguration as one type of relationship between *items*[44], not the cardinality of the relationship between *manifestation* and *item*. However, this view is improper, since an *item* that exists independently before the reconfiguration involving it occurs does not exist unchanged after the reconfiguration, and hence it is impossible to associate a reconfiguration relationship with *items*.

On the other hand, if we limit our discussion to unpublished resources, the cardinality of the relationship between the two entities is one-to-one.

9) *Section conclusion*

What has been said in this section about the cardinality and existence of the four bibliographic entities should be concluded as follows, with the notation in UML:

```
work  0..*  ——  1..*  expression/text
expression/text  1..*  ——  1..*  manifestation/medium
manifestation/medium  1..*  ——  1..*  item/copy
```

'0..*' indicates the range from zero to many, and likewise '1..*' indicates the range from one to many.

In the following sections, to simplify the appellation, I will use the entity names *expression*, *manifestation*, and *item* for respectively indicating the entities *expression/ text*, *manifestation/medium*, and *item/copy* of the proposed model.

3.4.3 Correlation With Other Relevant Models

1) *Other conceptual models*

As we have seen in Chapter 2, several other models have incorporated and defined a text-level entity or its equivalent. This seems to be the natural result of an attempt to view in a more structured way an item to be catalogued. All those models, however, have been only briefly described in their studies and do not give any viewpoint on which entity is to be given primacy, much less giving primacy to a text-level entity. Based on my interpretation of those models, I present Figure 3-3, which illustrates mappings among entities set up in those models. The models included are those by O'Neill and Visine-Goetz, Svenonius, Leazer, Heaney, and Green[45].

The figure shows at the extreme left the four bibliographic entities in the model proposed in the present study. It shows at the second from the left the entities proposed by O'Neill and Visine-Goetz, and their mapping to those in the proposed model. The entities *work, text,* and *book,* are clearly mapped, respectively, into the *work, expression,* and *item* entities of the proposed model. The entities *edition* and *printing*, on the other hand, are mapped into the same entity, *manifestation*. This means that the proposed model does not differentiate between these two entities nor designate the difference the entities represent. Likewise, from the third column onward to the right, (a) the entities set up in each of the other models, and also (b) the mapping from those entities in each model to those in the proposed model (not that to their immediate left) are shown. The dotted line used in Leazer's model indicates that *item* in his model might be mapped to *item*, in addition to *manifestation*, of the proposed model.

If we observe these models from the aspect of ways of defining entities, one may say that they, except Leazer's, adopt the hierarchical way to define their entities.

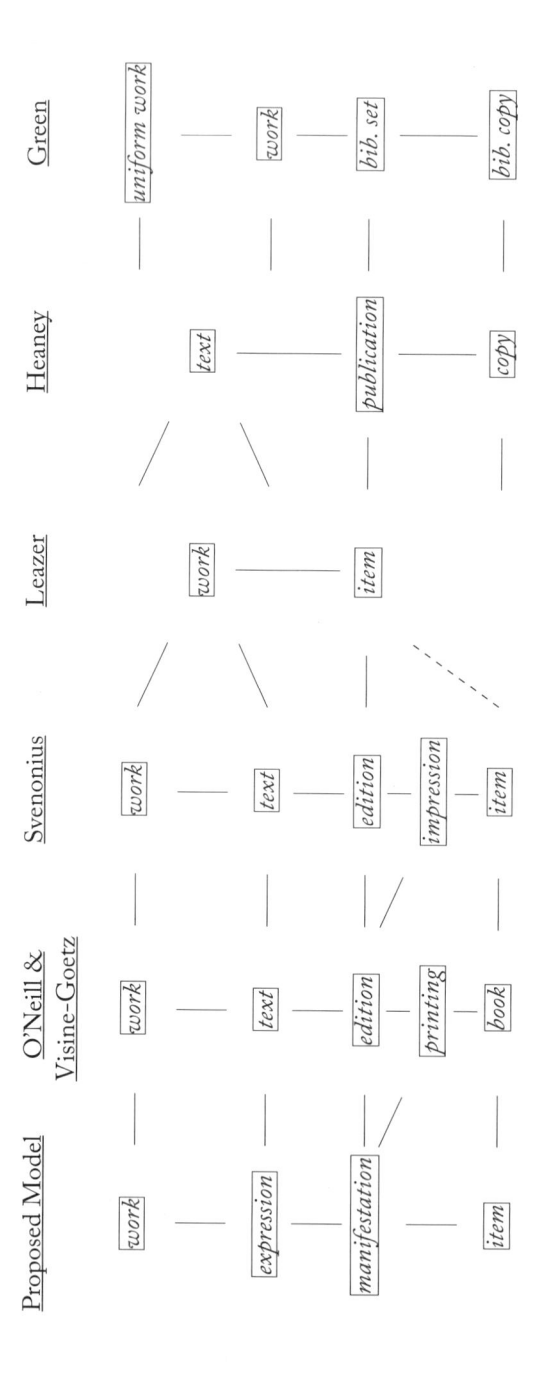

Figure 3-3. Mapping of bibliographic entities in the other models to those in the proposed model.

2) Delsey's model on the logical structure of AACR2

Delsey attempted to apply an approach used in FRBR to the current AACR2 in order to "develop a formalized schema to reflect the internal logic of the AACR,"[46] as we have seen in Chapter 2. What has to be noticed in his model are the following:

1) He noted that "item is defined relative to the cataloguer's decision in choosing an entity as the object of description" and "the item may equate to any one of a number of candidate entities: *document, document part, copy, content part*, or *collection*."[47] The *item* in his model is thus defined as an entity that contains the characteristics of both the manifestation-level and copy-level, and at the same time can be regarded as either level entity, depending on the class of materials or situation. It would be better to say that *item* is defined as an entity resulting from selection as the object of bibliographic description.

This definition of *item* would be more proper if we emphasize the ability of reflecting current practice. However, the present study intends to pursue modeling in a simpler and more coherent manner and thus such a definition of *item* is not adopted here.

2) Various additional bibliographic entities are defined in his model. For example, when *item* equates to *document* (which is a manifestation-level entity), entities *content, infixion, physical carrier*, and *container* are additionally introduced, resulting from the decomposition of *document*. They are considered to be defined in the parallel way and correspond to a text-level, a format-level, a carrier-level, and a container-level entity, respectively; but we have not defined any container-level entity in the present study.

From this point one may say that his model shows some features deduced from the combination of the FRBR model and the three-layered model, thus providing a possible pathway to the model proposed in the present study. It contains some bibliographic entities defined in the hierarchical way and others in the parallel way. It is however important to bear in mind that his model pursues the modeling of the internal structure of the current AACR2 (and current practice) not the modeling of its alternatives, including a way which gives primacy to a text-level entity.

3.5 Associating Attributes with Text-level Entity

3.5.1 Titles and Statements of Responsibility that Appear in Item

It is very important to consider how to associate titles and statements of responsibility that appear in an item with any of the bibliographic entities defined in a conceptual model. In this study I have already used this point as one of clues to judge which entity is given primacy or whether a text-level entity is given primacy. The reason why these elements are important is that they play a significant role in finding and identifying an item; namely, they are the most useful and are actually used for that purpose. Of course, the elements contribute sometimes, for example, to indicate the scope and contents of an item and to provide information on an item's bibliographic relationships to others, although such functions cannot be satisfied with those elements alone.

There are at least two methods of associating those elements with entities as attributes of an entity: one is to associate them with a manifestation-level entity and the other is to associate them with a text-level one. Although it seems to be natural and valid to associate the elements (or a major part of them) with an entity given primacy in a model, we will examine each method in depth respectively and characterize a proper method for our text-prioritized model.

Before examining each method, it is useful to confirm that the FRBR model indicates the relative significance of each attribute (and also data element) in supporting a task being performed by users. Defining tasks and assessing the relative significance of attributes with the tasks are very unique to FRBR; those matters are not involved in usual E-R modeling and object-oriented modeling. I will use them demonstrated in FRBR in the course of examining the validity of the methods. In the FRBR model, there are 14 sub-tasks in total extracted from the combination of the four tasks 'find,' 'identify,' 'select,' and 'obtain,' and the four bibliographic entities; the task 'obtain' is applicable only to instances of the entities *manifestation* and *item*, which are physical entities.

3.5.2 Method Shown in FRBR Model—Associating Attributes With Manifestation-level Entity

The first method is to associate such titles and statements of responsibility with a manifestation-level entity as its attributes. This method is conformable with both the model for current practice and that of Delsey's analysis of AACR2. The FRBR model also adopts this method, and it is taken as a typical example of showing the method. Figure 3-4 sketches out at the left the method in the model. All titles that appear in an item, except ones that are uniquely associated with an individual copy, and all statements of responsibility, regardless of entity levels to which persons or corporate bodies represented in those statements have actually contributed, are associated with *manifestation*. These titles, for example, are then mapped to data elements like the title proper, parallel titles, and other title information, according to a cataloging code such as AACR2 or to the ISBD.

Attribute and its data element

work — [title] uniform title, or title proper → find, identify, and select *work* (**User tasks**)

expression — [title] (none) ┄┄► find, identify, and select *expression*

manifestation — [title] title that appears in an item / [statement of responsibility] statement that appears in an item → find, identify, select, and obtain *manifestation*

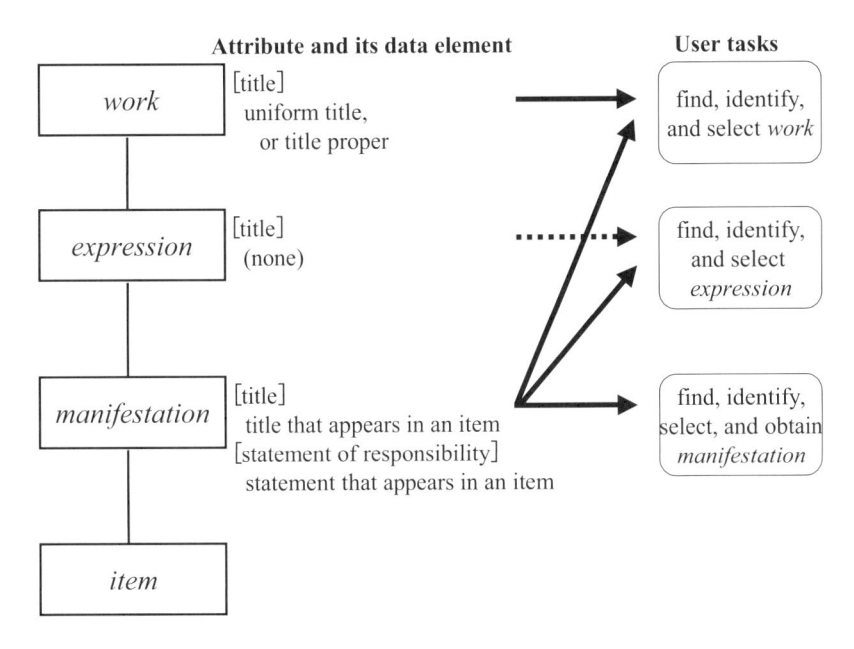

item

Figure 3-4. Mapping attributes to user tasks in the FRBR model.

In the FRBR model an attribute 'title of the *expression*' is defined to the entity *expression*, but no substantial content of that attribute is indicated—there is no ISBD or GARE data element which can be mapped to the attribute, according to the explanation in the model itself[48]. At the *work* level, on the other hand, an attribute 'title of the *work*' is defined, being mapped to a uniform title heading (assigned by a cataloger) or the title proper (found on an item) if a uniform title is not applied.

The figure exhibits at the right user tasks (to be precise, sub-tasks) that would be attained with the above attributes—in other words, user tasks for which the attributes are assessed to be important. It shows, with the arrows from the attributes of entities to user tasks, that the attribute 'title' associated with each entity (except *item*) is assessed to be significant for supporting the user tasks of each entity level. We should, at the same time, remember that the 'title' of *expression* has no substantial content; an arrow with a dotted line in the figure denotes this. It also indicates that the attributes 'title' and 'statement of responsibility' of *manifestation* are needed to fulfill user tasks related to *work* and *expression*, while these attributes are of course significant for supporting user tasks of *manifestation*[49]. To put it more precisely, several other attributes of *manifestation*, like edition designation, place of publication/distribution, etc., are also assessed to be requisite attributes to fulfill some user tasks related to *work* and *expression*[50]; this is not depicted in the figure because of its complexity.

Regarding the attribute 'statement of responsibility,' it must be noted that (a) the FRBR model develops other non-bibliographic entities (e.g., *person* and *corporate body*) for persons and corporate bodies recorded in the attribute 'statement of responsibility' of *manifestation* and (b) the model links those entities to the bibliographic ones in question (e.g., *work* or *expression*) through relationships such as 'is created by' or 'is realized by.' Moreover, the entities *person* and *corporate body* have an attribute to record their names (e.g., 'name'), which can record more than one name and form of name that probably include names described in the 'statement of responsibility' of *manifestation*.

The points to observe are the following:

1) At first glance, the whole structure shown in the figure appears to be complicated rather than simple. This is caused by what I will call 'upward pseudo-assignment' of attribute values of *manifestation*–i.e., 'title' and 'statement of responsibility'—to the upper-level entities *expression* and *work*. The inheritance of attribute values from an upper-level to a lower-level entity can easily be understood, but the converse, and pseudo-assignment of attribute values, is more complex. This conclusion comes from the following:

1-a) No function involved in E-R modeling nor in object-oriented modeling is able to represent properly such a mechanism. Hence, it is difficult to manifest such a mechanism beyond any possibility of misunderstanding. However, in FRBR, it is shown only in a table indicating the assessment of the importance of each attribute to tasks, and there is no additional explanation.

1-b) It is not clear, when a single *manifestation* instance contains more than one *expression*, what titles (titles for *expressions*, the collective title for the whole *manifestation*, or both) are 'upward pseudo-assigned' to *work* and *expression*. At the same time, it is also not clear, when a single *expression* instance is embodied in different *manifestations* that have titles different from each other, which titles (all different titles or only limited titles) are 'upward pseudo-assigned' to *work* and *expression*.

1-c) Such 'upward pseudo-assignment' makes the distinction vague between the fulfillment of tasks related to *manifestation* with these attribute values and that of *work* or *expression* with the same attribute values. In the case of the task 'find,' in particular, the distinction cannot be made if only these attributes are used to carry out the task. In the case of the tasks 'identify' and 'select,' it is possible to distinguish those of different levels since they need other attributes in addition to these—in other words, they could not be accomplished without attributes other than these.

2) If we focus on the text-level entity *expression*, it is evident that the task 'find' *expression* has no sufficient basis to carry out that task and depends heavily on the attributes of *manifestation*. According to the explanation in the FRBR model[51], some other attributes are useful for supporting this task, such as language and other distinguishing characteristics, which are attributed to *expression*. They can, however, be expected only to complement the major data elements, like the title and statement of responsibility 'upward pseudo-assigned' from *manifestation*. On the other hand, although the tasks 'identify' and 'select' *expression* can be accomplished using various attributes of that entity, they have to be carried out subsequent to tasks related to other entities (i.e., *manifestation* or *work*), since the task 'find' *expression* is not self-attainable as mentioned above.

3) User tasks related to *manifestation* are fully accomplished with the attributes of the entity itself without any support from the attributes of other level entities. This is consistent with the point that the FRBR model gives primacy to *manifestation*.

3.5.3 Method for Text-prioritized Model—Associating Attributes With Text-level Entity

The second method is to associate titles and statements of responsibility that appear in an item with a text-level entity. This method implies that in most cases without any problem such titles and statements of responsibility can be regarded and dealt with as the attribute values of the title and responsibility designation of a text-level entity as they are. In only the cases where this supposition is not appropriate, we need additional treatment as will be touched on later. Also, the method corresponds to the fact that in most cases users are not aware of the difference between titles and statements of responsibility to be attributed to a text-level entity and those to be attributed to a manifestation-level entity.

This method can be observed in the three-layered model. In that model, those elements (except statements of responsibility which are only related to the medium-layer) are associated with the text-layer. Edition statements (except ones relating only to a difference in form) are also associated with the text-layer. On the other hand, data elements such as place of publication, name of publisher, date of publication, etc., are all attributed to the medium-layer.

Next an appropriate method for the entities proposed in the present study is characterized, while referring to the method shown in the three-layered model. This method must result in giving primacy to a text-level entity; for example, all tasks related to a text-level entity must be accomplished with attributes of that entity. It also must be able to solve issues involved in the method for the FRBR model. Figure 3-5 demonstrates the method for our text-prioritized model in a manner similar to Figure 3-4.

The figure shows that titles, statements of responsibility, and edition statements that appear in an item are associated with the text-level entity *expression*, excepting edition statements that are related only to *manifestation*. The elements not associated with *expression* are consequently associated with *manifestation*, together with other elements like place of publication, name of publisher, etc. On the other hand, the entity *work* has its title, such as a uniform title or a title proper when a uniform title is not applied.

```
              Attribute and its date element                 User tasks

              [title]
   work         uniform title, or title proper          ──▶  find, identify,
                [responsibility designation                   and select work
                  name heading that pertains to work

              [title]
  expression    title that appears in an item           ──▶  find, identify,
                [responsibility designation]                  and select
                  statement that appers in an item           expression
                  name heading that pertains to expression
                [edition designation]
                  statement that appears in an item

 manifestation [edition designation]                    ──▶  [find], identify,
                  statement on difference in form            select, and obtain
                                                             manifestation

   item
```

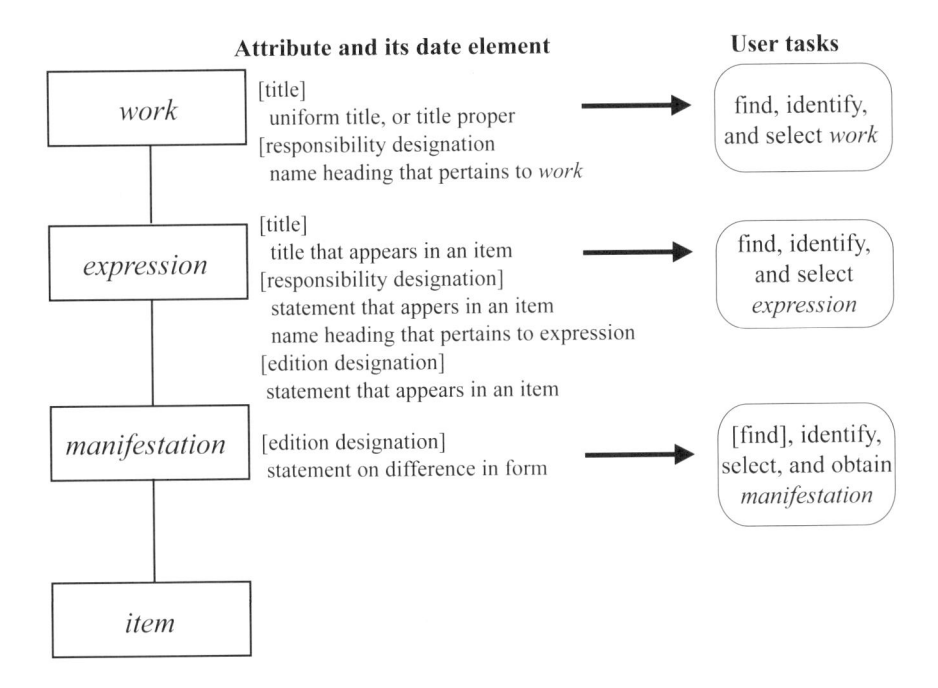

Figure 3-5. Mapping attributes to user tasks in the proposed model.

The method demonstrated in the figure requires some further explanation.

1) If we focus on tasks related to *expression*, it is concluded that these tasks, including 'find,' can be accomplished with attributes and data elements associated with the entity, assuming that several other attributes characterizing the entity (e.g., form, date, language) are also assigned to it. The reason for this conclusion is that sufficient data elements to accomplish the tasks are assigned to *expression*; it is evident if we compare the method with that shown in Figure 3-4.

2) We know the fact that there are some manifestations with the same text but different titles from each other—different titles may be assigned by the same or different publishers. According to our text-prioritized model, in such cases a single instance of *expression* is created for those manifestations, thus accepting more than one title that appear in them as its 'title' attribute values. That seems not to cause any problem in conceptual models including ours. We can deal with it in any convenient way at the implementation stage. For example, if necessary, we can choose one title from those as the 'title proper' attribute value of the

expression instance. Furthermore, we can also record any of titles not chosen as the 'title proper' value of the *expression* instance in each individual instance of *manifestation* that corresponds to that title.

3) Let us think about the cases where a *manifestation* instance embodies more than one *expression*. When an item corresponding to such a *manifestation* does not bear a collective title that covers the whole item, each *expression* instance should have a 'title' value for its own text, usually extracted from titles that appear in the item. On the other hand, if an item bears a collective title in the above case, each *expression* instance would have that collective title as well as a title corresponding to its own text.

4) Consistent with the preceding points, the task 'find' *manifestation* is not accomplished with only data elements associated with the entity, since those elements are not enough for finding tasks. That task is enclosed in square brackets in the figure so as to indicate this. This fact implies that we usually reach a *manifestation* instance only through an *expression* when we attribute the item's title and statement of responsibility to the latter entity.

5) With respect to the attribute 'title' of *work*, we assigned it a uniform title or the title proper if no uniform title is applied to the work; the title proper means in this case a title that is selected from titles appearing in an item according to the instructions in a cataloging code. This title and other characterizing data elements, like form, date, etc., associated with *work* would be enough to attain tasks related to the entity. Moreover, we assume that in our model the entities *person* and *corporate body* are developed and linked to bibliographic entities including *work*, as is the same as that in the FRBR model. In addition, it is assumed provisionally that *work* has an attribute 'responsibility designation' represented with name headings (or their equivalents) of *person* and *corporate body* linked to *work* in question; the figure contains this attribute and its data element.

The FRBR model, on the contrary, regards titles and statements of responsibility that appear in an item as vital data elements to attain tasks related to *work*, as we have seen earlier. It is not certain which of the two methods is valid for the work-level tasks. We need further investigation, but this matter does not affect at all any model giving primacy to text-level entity.

6) We arrive at the conclusion that the whole structure of mapping attributes and data elements to user tasks, shown in the figure, is simple, on the grounds that

user tasks at each entity level are in principle satisfied with the attributes of the entity's own.

3.5.4 Examples of Other Attributes Associated With Text-level Entity

It is obviously necessary to associate several other attributes, in addition to the title, responsibility designation, and edition designation that we examined in the preceding sections, with the entity *expression*, in order to designate fully the characteristics of texts and support the user tasks of that entity level. The FRBR model, for example, listed relatively comprehensive attributes (and also data elements) of *expression*, whereas it lacks some crucial ones if seen from the viewpoint of giving primacy to the text-level entity, as discussed. It is thus possible to show an example of an attribute set that should be associated with a text-level entity, referring to the conclusion in the preceding section and the FRBR model.

The following are logical attributes (not data elements defined in cataloging codes or others) that are expected to be associated with *expression* and be generally applicable to any kind of text. Asterisks indicate those attributes are borrowed from the FRBR model.

title of *expression*
responsibility designation
edition designation (when not pertaining to format/medium)
series designation
form of *expression**
date of *expression**
language of *expression**
other distinguishing characteristic*
extensibility of *expression**
revisability of *expression**
extent of *expression**
summarization of content*
context for *expression**
critical response to *expression**
use restrictions on *expression**

Attributes applicable only to a specific type of text are: sequencing pattern (serial), expected regularity of issue (serial), expected frequency of issue (serial), type of score (musical notation), medium of performance (musical notation or recorded sound), scale (cartographic image/object), projection (cartographic image/object), presentation technique (cartographic image/object), representation of relief (cartographic image/object), geodetic, grid, and vertical measurement (cartographic image/object), recording technique (remote sensing image), special characteristic (remote sensing image), technique (graphic or projected image). All of these attributes are listed in FRBR, and therefore the model would make much more of the text-level entity at this point.

3.6 Defining Relationships Between Instances of Text-level Entity

3.6.1 Relationships Defined in FRBR Model

FRBR identifies the following categories of relationship types between instances of the text-level entity *expression*: (a) whole/part relationships, (b) abridgement, revision, translation, and musical arrangement, between *expression* instances of the same *work* instance, and (c) successor, supplement, complement, summarization, adaptation, transformation, and imitation, between *expression* instances of different *work* instances. For each type of relationships, a list of examples that would be typically involved in the relationship type is provided.

1) Whole/part relationships at the level of *expression* are defined as the same as those at the level of *work*. Only some typical examples listed at the *expression* level are different from those at the *work* level.

FRBR states that: "The specific kinds of parts recognized as components of the *expression*, ..., will differ somewhat from those recognized as components of the *work*. For example, a table of contents, list of references, or index, would be viewed as parts of the *expression* inasmuch as they normally entail reference to the particulars of the *expression*."[52] This would be a valid recognition, and listing examples based on such recognition would also be valid.

On the other hand, regarding the *work* level, the model states that: "Segmental parts are discrete components of a *work* whose content exists as a distinct identifiable segment within a whole. Among discrete components of *works* would be included prefaces, chapters, sections, parts, and so on."[53] However, prefaces, chapters, etc., are not included among components of *expressions*. Why are such segments not recognized as examples of relationship types at the *expression* level? This point is not clear.

2) The second category of relationship types, i.e., abridgement, revision, translation, and musical arrangement, are defined at only the *expression* level, since they occur between *expression* instances of the same *work*, not between *expression* instances of different *works*. In contrast, the third category of types, i.e., successor, supplement, complement, etc., are defined at both the *expression* and *work* levels; they are relationships that occur between *expressions* of different *works* and also between those *works*. Typical examples of these types at the two levels would, of course, be a little different from each other; certain examples would occur at either level.

The second and third categories of relationship types enumerated in FRBR are relatively comprehensive, and would be sufficient for a general class of resources. However, how can these relationship types be identified between given *expressions* and/or *works* unless *expressions* have enough attributes, including titles, statements of responsibility, etc? We need to remind ourselves of the fact that the FRBR model does not define enough attributes for the text-level entity *expression* to 'find,' 'identify,' and 'select' that level of instances, as we have seen in the preceding sections.

Even the third category of relationship types could be identified on the basis of attribute values of *expression* instances; i.e., at the *expression* level. The reason for this is that (a) these relationship types can be seen as part of a continuum of intellectual or artistic content from the original resource, (b) up to a cut-off point, expressions in resources are considered different but works are the same; i.e., different *expressions* of the same *work*, and (c) different *works* are identified for cases beyond that point[54]. In other words, it is impossible to determine whether works are the same without reference to their expressions.

This is coincident with the fact that (a) FRBR additionally defines *expression-to-work* relationships; i.e., relationships that can be drawn between an *expression* of one *work* and a different *work*, and (b) it explains the reason why such relationships are needed as follows:

Drawing the relationship from the *expression* level to the *work* level is done quite commonly, most often because a specific *expression*-to-*expression* relationship cannot be readily determined. For example, it may be difficult to determine the specific text (i.e., *expression*) that was used as the basis for a dramatization or screenplay[55].

Such *expression*-to-*work* relationships would not be needed if (a) the relationships between *works* are determined without reference to their expressions, or (b) the relationships between *works* are determined prior to those between *expressions*.

3.6.2 Relationships in Text-prioritized Model

It is obvious that a comprehensive arrangement is required for relationship types between instances of a text-level entity in the pursuit of a model giving primacy to that entity. As we have seen, the arrangement shown in the FRBR model seems to be relatively comprehensive as a whole, although it has some flaws. I therefore borrow those relationship types arranged in FRBR and apply them to the entity *expression* in our text-prioritized model, with some modifications.

In the text-prioritized model, the three categories of relationship types that FRBR sets out should be defined at the *expression* level: (a) whole/part, (b) abridgement, revision, translation, and musical arrangement, between *expressions* of the same *work*, and (c) successor, supplement, complement, summarization, adaptation, transformation, and imitation, between *expressions* of different *works*.

1) Whole/part relationships at the *expression* level should include (a) all examples enumerated for that level in FRBR and also (b) some of the examples enumerated for the *work* level in FRBR, such as 'chapters, sections, parts, etc.' Consequently, the following examples should be listed for the *expression* level in the text-prioritized model: (a) chapters, sections, parts, etc., (b) volume/issue of serial, (c) table of contents, etc., (d) illustration for a text, (e) sound aspect of a film, (f) amendment, (g) monograph in a series, (h) journal article.

2) Relationship types between *expressions* of the same *work* and between *expressions* of different *works* in the text-prioritized model should be basically identical to those in FRBR. In addition, all examples listed for these relationship types in FRBR should be included. However, I would like to emphasize again that there is an essential difference in associating attributes with the text-level

entity. In the text-prioritized model, attributes sufficient to identify these various relationship types between *expression* instances are associated with the entity *expression*, including titles and statements of responsibility. This is the result of giving primacy to the text-level entity.

3.7 Creating Scenario on How Bibliographic Entities Are Used

3.7.1 What Is Scenario?

As we have seen, the user tasks that the FRBR model defines can be understood as a sequence of actions performed by users—in other words, a process conducted by users—when they are searching and making use of bibliographic records. If we consider the execution order of the sub-tasks (which are tasks defined at each bibliographic entity level) by users in usual cases, we may be able to depict the outline of the whole process conducted by users. I call it a 'scenario,' which represents a possible but main sequence of events that might take place at the conceptual level.

Such a scenario results in showing which bibliographic entity is predominant in a conceptual model, as well as showing the whole process conducted by users. This is because an entity can be regarded as being predominant in a model if the following conditions are satisfied: (a) users begin their search with the entity in most cases, and (b) the entity is necessarily identified or selected in the process.

Any scenario of this type at the conceptual level becomes that of a practical level as it is if we assume that a bibliographic record is created for each instance of bibliographic entities at different levels and the resulting records are linked to each other. At the same time it is necessary to recognize the risk of over-simplification of actual usage process, which would be more complex and inherently trial-and-error (not linear) process. In fact a series of user tasks could be interrupted and ended at any point, or jumps to any other different tasks could happen suddenly.

Any scenario of such type would be represented with 'activity diagram' or 'sequence diagram' in UML; however, we need here only to show an outline of the sequence of actions in order to clarify the main sequence. I therefore use a brief chart proper for this aim.

The scenarios developed below contain the user tasks defined by FRBR. The user tasks redefined by Svenonius or Tillett[56] in the course of rearranging objectives/functions of catalogs can be used instead of those in FRBR, if it is more appropriate. Moreover, the scenarios here do not contain tasks related to either the entities *person* and *corporate body* or those that serve subject searching (e.g., *concept, object*, etc., in the FRBR model) so as to make the scenarios simple. They postulate, however, that these non-bibliographic entities are developed and used in the case of access through authors or subjects; they presuppose the involvement of tasks related to the non-bibliographic entities, such as 'find' *person*, 'identify' *person*, 'select' *person*, etc., in the scenarios.

3.7.2 Scenario Deduced from Modeling of Current Practice

Figure 3-6 demonstrates an abridged scenario of how bibliographic entities developed by modeling current cataloging practice are used in a user's search process. The figure indicates the following:

1) The tasks 'find' *manifestation* and 'find' *work* are first carried out, but the latter task is less frequently performed since *work* instances exist only in the restricted cases as confirmed earlier.

2) After the task 'find' *manifestation* is performed and the resultant set of *manifestation* instances is created, another task 'identify' or 'select' *manifestation* is usually carried out for any of those *manifestation* instances.

3) And then, if one or more *manifestation* instances are 'identified' or 'selected' as being appropriate for the user's needs, they are finally 'obtained' by the user: "e.g., to place a purchase order for a publication, to submit a request for the loan of a copy of a book in a library's collection, …"[57]

4) Or, if one or more appropriate *manifestation* instances are 'identified' or 'selected,' *item* instances linked to any or each of those *manifestation* instances are either 'identified' or 'selected' and finally 'obtained' by the user.

It is reasonable to consider this series of tasks to be the mainstream in using bibliographic entities (and also bibliographic records), as well as to consider the entity *manifestation* to be predominant in the model. Most current OPACs are designed while supposing this series of tasks.

5) After appropriate *manifestation* instances are 'identified' or 'selected,' the user can move to work instances, if any, that are linked to those *manifestation* instances. If a proper *work* instance, as a result, is 'identified' or 'selected,' *manifestation* instances linked to the *work* instance are collocated and thus we will return to the

task 'identify' or 'select' *manifestation*. Some OPACs enable us to carry out such tasks with uniform title authority records linked to bibliographic records.

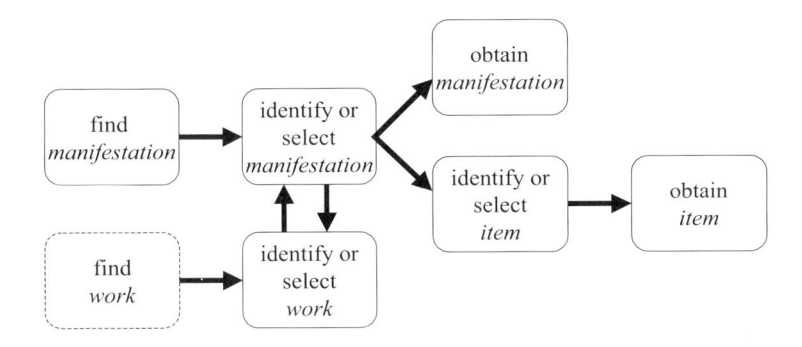

Figure 3-6. A scenario derived from the modeling of current practice.

3.7.3 Scenario for FRBR Model

We can create a scenario of using bibliographic entities defined in the FRBR model as manifested in Figure 3-7. The most important difference between this scenario and that represented in Figure 3-6 is that the tasks 'find' *expression* and 'identify' or 'select' *expression* are inserted in this scenario. This scenario indicates the following:

1) The task 'find' *manifestation* is first carried out; it has solid basis for its accomplishment as confirmed earlier. The tasks 'find' *work* and 'find' *expression*, on the contrary, would be less frequently performed, since (a) it is not clear whether *work* and *expression* instances exist in all items and (b) attributes and data elements associated with the entities and used as clues to find them are very much restricted other than titles and statements of responsibility that are 'upward pseudo-assigned' from *manifestation*. This is obviously true of the task 'find' *expression*; a dotted line enclosing the task shows this point in the figure.

2) After the task 'find' *manifestation* is performed and the resultant set of *manifestation* instances is created, another task 'identify' or 'select' *manifestation* is usually carried out for any of those *manifestations*.

3) And then, if one or more *manifestations* are 'identified' or 'selected' as being appropriate for the user's needs, they are finally 'obtained' by the user.

4) Or, if one or more appropriate *manifestations* are 'identified' or 'selected,' *item*

instances linked to any or each of those *manifestations* are either 'identified' or 'selected' and finally 'obtained' by the user.

The steps from 2 to 4 above are equivalent to those in the scenario for the modeling of current practice. Also, it is reasonable to consider the series of tasks shown at the steps from 1 to 4 (i.e., from 'find' *manifestation* to 'obtain' *manifestation* or *item*) to be the mainstream in using bibliographic entities, as well as to consider *manifestation* to be given priority in the model—this is similar to the scenario for the modeling of current practice.

5) After appropriate *manifestation* instances are 'identified' or 'selected,' the user can move to *works* or *expressions*, if any, that are linked to those *manifestations*. As a result, for example, if a proper *work* is 'identified' or 'selected,' *manifestations* linked to the *work* are collocated, and thus we will return to the task 'identify' or 'select' *manifestation*. Or, if an appropriate *expression* is 'identified' or 'selected,' (a) *manifestations* linked to the *expression* are newly collocated, and then the user returns to the task at *manifestation*, or (b) she/he may proceed further to a *work* linked to the *expression*.

The tasks related to *work* and *expression*, including 'find' *work* and 'find' *expression*, are additional and hence subordinate to the mainstream of tasks from 'find' *manifestation* to 'obtain' *manifestation* or *item*. They play an intermediary function to navigate users to the tasks 'identify' or 'select' *manifestation*.

In this scenario, the problem involved in the 'upward pseudo-assignment' of attribute values could be reduced to the minimum. On the contrary, if we consider another scenario where the task 'find' *work* or 'find' *expression* is first carried out—instead of the task 'find' *manifestation*—as a part of the mainstream of tasks, the problem is critical. That is to say, the distinction among these three tasks of 'find' an entity cannot be made if only attributes like titles and statements of responsibility are used to carry out the tasks. This indicates that users must recognize the distinction among the three tasks of 'find' an entity and specify clearly the entity level that the task 'find' should be performed whenever they search—it would be a difficult premise.

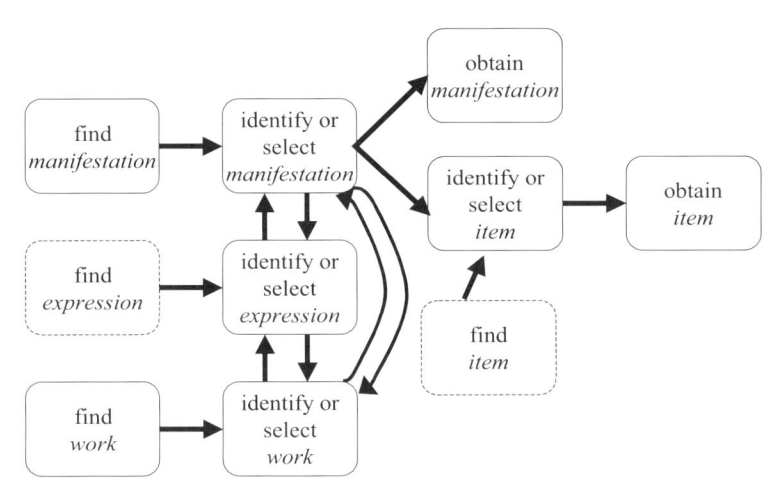

Figure 3-7. A scenario for the FRBR model.

3.7.4 Scenario for Text-prioritized Model

Figure 3-8 illustrates a scenario that harmonizes with the model proposed in the present study. The most important difference between this and the above two can be observed in a series of tasks regarded as the mainstream of using bibliographic entities. In the scenario for our text-prioritized model, a series of tasks thought to be the mainstream begins with the task 'find' *expression* and then 'identify' or 'select' *expression*. After that, one or more *manifestation* instances that are linked to each of those *expression* instances are 'identified' or 'selected' by the user as appropriate. Next, subsequent tasks equivalent to those shown in the above two scenarios are performed in turn. Being consistent with the change that arose in the mainstream of tasks, the task 'find' *manifestation* falls from, and is subordinate to, the mainstream. The tasks 'find' *work* and 'identify' or 'select' *work* remain in principle at the position shown in the scenario for the FRBR model.

It must be emphasized that a new type of OPAC is needed to assist users in performing a series of tasks illustrated on the scenario in Figure 3-8, when bibliographic records are created in line with a structure that consists of the four bibliographic entities.

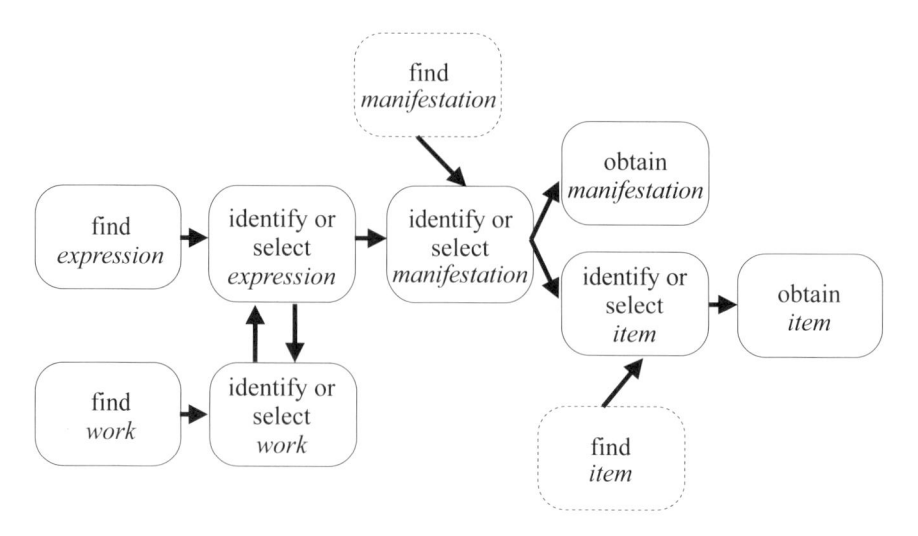

Figure 3-8. A scenario for the proposed model.

3.8 Showing Examples of Bibliographic Records in Line with Text-prioritized Model

3.8.1 Premises for Showing Examples

The following attempts to illustrate several examples of bibliographic records created in line with the model proposed in this study. However, only a conceptual model for catalogs—not a way of cataloging—is proposed in this chapter. It is thus impossible to create records while referring only to the model. For creating records, it may be necessary at least to define a record format at the logical design or implementation level subsequent to the conceptual design level and also to develop a set of rules to record each individual data element. Equivalents of bibliographic records will therefore be illustrated in line with the conceptual model in order to provide a clearer image of this model.

The expedients are adopted of (a) using an existing MARC bibliographic record, (b) transferring the data elements of the MARC record to the attributes of the bibliographic entities, and (c) supplying data values to nearly mandatory attributes (i.e., data elements) if no data value is found in the MARC record. Also adopted is the way of creating an individual bibliographic record for each entity instance and linking the resulting records to each other to show an item

Chapter 3 A Conceptual Model Giving Primacy to Text-level Bibliographic Entity 81

as a whole. Moreover, it is assumed that other kinds of records corresponding to non-bibliographic entities, such as *person* and *corporate body*, must be created and linked to some of the bibliographic records; such records will be additionally shown in some cases of the following examples. Headings assigned to the MARC records, such as personal names (MARC21[58] field tag 700), corporate names (tag 710), subject headings (tag 650), and others, on the other hand, remain as the data elements of the newly created bibliographic records to support their 'identify' and 'select' tasks.

3.8.2 Case 1: Book

Figure 3-9-1 shows the MARC bibliographic record with Library of Congress (LC) control number 97001449, which represents a book *Maxwell's Handbook for AACR2R* published in 1997 being chosen as an item to be cataloged. Each data element is preceded by its MARC tag.

Figure 3-9-2 demonstrates a set of bibliographic records for representing the book in line with the proposed model. The set is composed of five records: a *work*, an *expression*, a *manifestation*, and two *item* records—LC holds two copies of the book. Each record consists of (a) several data elements and their data values transferred from the MARC bibliographic record, and (b) data values supplied for this illustration—they are preceded by '+'.

A single *work* record (i.e., a single instance of the entity *work*) is developed so as to cover the book *Handbook for AACR2* by Margaret Maxwell and its revised editions. Instead, we can create a single *work* record for an individual edition, depending on the policy of developing an instance of *work*. The model proposed in this study can accept either of the ways.

Data element values contained in the *work* record are roughly divided into some groups: (a) titles of *work*, (b) names of persons and corporate bodies responsible for *work* (i.e., some name headings like tags 100, 700), (c) subject terms or codes assigned to *work* (tags 082, 650), and (d) other characteristics of *work*, like date, form, etc.

Data element values in the *expression* record are: (a) titles and statements of responsibility that appear in an item (tags 245, 246), (b) names of persons and corporate bodies responsible for *expression* (i.e., name headings), (c) date and language of *expression* (a part of tag 008), (d) other characteristics (tag 504), and

(e) descriptions of bibliographic relationships (tags 500, 700 with subfield code |t). Subject terms or codes can be assigned to the *expression* record in lieu of the *work*, if we adopt an alternative policy.

Being consistent with the data elements of the *expression* record, the data elements of the *manifestation* record in this example are: (a) publisher, place and date of publication (tag 260), (b) physical medium and extent of the carrier (tag 300), and (c) manifestation identifier like ISBN (tag 020). Each *item* record has only two data fields (i.e., tags 050 and 991); but it could contain some administrative data for the particular copy.

The whole bibliographic family of the above *work* is illustrated as follows:

[W1] Margaret Maxwell's *Handbook for AACR2*, 1980-
  [E1] *Handbook for AACR2* by Margaret Maxwell, 1980
    [M1] book published in 1980
  [E2] *Handbook for AACR2, 1988 revision* by Margaret Maxwell, 1989
    [M1] book published in 1989
  [E3] *Maxwell's handbook for AACR2R* by Robert Maxwell with Margaret Maxwell, 1997
    [M1] book published in 1997

Each line indicates one instance of a bibliographic entity (as well as one bibliographic record in the way adopted for the illustration in Figure 3-9-2), denoting only its brief title, responsibility designation, and date. '[W]' stands for a *work* instance; '[E]' for an *expression*; and '[M]' for a *manifestation*. Accordingly, [W1], its subordinate [E3], and [M1] are entity instances that were illustrated in the figure. There are 'revision' relationships among [E1], [E2], and [E3].

If we combine the set of records shown in Figure 3-9-2 with (a) other records transformed from different MARC bibliographic records corresponding to the pair of [E1] and its [M1] (LC control number 80017667) and the pair of [E2] and its [M1] (LC control number 88036703), and also with (b) those from MARC name authority records corresponding to the two *persons* associated with the *work* and the *expressions* (LC name authority control numbers 80017667 and 95028779), the resultant set of records are obtained as shown in Figure 3-9-3. Newly added records are preceded by an asterisk.

Let us, for the moment, look at additional two examples of bibliographic records in line with other models. First, a set of records representing the same book but in line with the FRBR model are demonstrated in Figure 3-9-4, which is created in a way similar to the preceding two figures. That way of elements assignment is based on the table developed by Delsey for mapping between data elements in the MARC21 format and the entities in FRBR[59]. The fields 082, 500, etc., are not included in the figure, since these fields were not associated with any specific entity in Delsey's mapping table. Moreover, all headings (main and added entry headings) assigned to the MARC record are associated with the entities *work*, *person*, and *concept* (not the bibliographic entities). Hence, relationships between non-bibliographic entities and bibliographic ones (like *work* and *expression*) are presupposed as being developed. There are many differences between Figures 3-9-4 and 3-9-2. The point I wish to emphasize is that the *expression* instance in the FRBR model does not have substantial contents and thus is weak in existence. In contrast, the *manifestation* instance in that model accepts most data values recorded in the current bibliographic record.

Next, a set of records representing the same resource but in line with the three-layered model is demonstrated in Figure 3-9-5. In this example, Figures 3-9-5 and 3-9-2 are almost identical and I have nothing particular to point out regarding differences between them, except that Figure 3-9-5 does not contain copy-level information.

```
000 01518cam 2200337 a 450
001 2123029
005 20010809103647.0
008 970102s1997 ilua b 001 0 eng
035 __ |9 (DLC) 97001449
906 __ |a 7 |b cbc |c orignew |d 1 |e ocip |f 19 |g y-gencatlg
925 0_ |a acquire |b 2 shelf copies |x policy default
955 __ |a pc19 to la00 01-02-97; lk24 01-07-97; lj07 01-15-97; lk46 01-17-97;aa05 01-21-97; CIP ver. pv07 07-29-97
010 __ |a 97001449
020 __ |a 0838907040 (alk. paper)
040 __ |a DLC |c DLC |d DLC
```

050 00 |a Z694.15.A56 |b M393 1997

082 00 |a 025.3/2 |2 21

100 1_ |a Maxwell, Robert L., |d 1957-

245 10 |a Maxwell's handbook for AACR2R : |b explaining and illustrating the Anglo-American cataloguing rules and the 1993 amendments / |c Robert L. Maxwell with Margaret F. Maxwell.

246 30 |a Handbook for AACR2R

260 __ |a Chicago, IL : |b American Library Association, |c 1997.

300 __ |a xii, 522 p. : |b ill. ; |c 26 cm.

500 __ |a Rev. ed. of: Handbook for AACR2, 1988 revision / by Margaret Maxwell.

504 __ |a Includes bibliographical references and index.

630 00 |a Anglo-American cataloguing rules |x Handbooks, manuals, etc.

650 _0 |a Descriptive cataloging |x Rules |x Handbooks, manuals, etc.

700 1_ |a Maxwell, Margaret F., |d 1927-

700 1_ |a Maxwell, Margaret F., |d 1927- |t Handbook for AACR2, 1988 revision.

984 __ |a gsl

991 __ |b c-GenColl |h Z694.15.A56 |i M393 1997 |t Copy 1 |w BOOKS

991 __ |b r-MRR |h Z694.15.A56 |i M393 1997 |t Copy 2 |m Ref Desk |w GenBib

Figure 3-9-1. Case 1-1. MARC bibliographic record for a book.

[*work* record 1]

+title: Handbook for AACR2

700 1_ |a Maxwell, Margaret F., |d 1927-

+date: 1980-

082 00 |a 025.3/2 |2 21

630 00 |a Anglo-American cataloguing rules |x Handbooks, manuals, etc.

650 _0 |a Descriptive cataloging |x Rules |x Handbooks, manuals, etc.

[*expression* record 1]

245 10 |a Maxwell's handbook for AACR2R : |b explaining and illustrating the Anglo-American cataloguing rules and the 1993 amendments / |c Robert L. Maxwell with Margaret F. Maxwell.

246 30 |a Handbook for AACR2R

100 1_ |a Maxwell, Robert L., |d 1957-

700 1_ |a Maxwell, Margaret F., |d 1927-
008 ...s1997 ...eng
504 __ |a Includes bibliographical references and index.
500 __ |a Rev. ed. of: Handbook for AACR2, 1988 revision / by Margaret Maxwell.
700 1_ |a Maxwell, Margaret F., |d 1927- |t Handbook for AACR2, 1988 revision.

[*manifestation* record 1]
260 __ |a Chicago, IL : |b American Library Association, |c 1997.
300 __ |a xii, 522 p. : |b ill. ; |c 26 cm.
020 __ |a 0838907040 (alk. paper)

[*item* record 1]
050 00 |a Z694.15.A56
991 __ |b c-GenColl |h Z694.15.A56 |i M393 1997 |t Copy 1 |w BOOKS

[*item* record 2]
050 00 |a Z694.15.A56
991 __ |b r-MRR |h Z694.15.A56 |i M393 1997 |t Copy 2 |m Ref Desk |w GenBib

Figure 3-9-2. Case 1-2. An example of a set of records for the book in line with the proposed model.

[*work* record 1]
+title: Handbook for AACR2
700 1_ |a Maxwell, Margaret F., |d 1927-
+date: 1980-
082 00 |a 025.3/2 |2 21
630 00 |a Anglo-American cataloguing rules |x Handbooks, manuals, etc.
650 _0 |a Descriptive cataloging |x Rules |x Handbooks, manuals, etc.

*[*expression* record 2]
245 10 |a Handbook for AACR2 : |b explaining and illustrating Anglo-American cataloguing rules, second edition / |c by Margaret F. Maxwell.
100 1_ |a Maxwell, Margaret F., |d 1927-

008 ...s1980 ...eng
504 __ |a Includes bibliographical references and index.

*[*manifestation* record 2]
260 __ |a Chicago : |b American Library Association, |c 1980.
300 __ |a xi, 463 p. ; |c 24 cm.
020 __ |a 0838903010 (pbk.) : |c $8.00 (est.)

*[*expression* record 3]
245 10 |a Handbook for AACR2, 1988 revision : |b explaining and illustrating the Anglo-American cataloguing rules / |c by Margaret Maxwell ; with a new chapter by Judith A. Carter.
100 1_ |a Maxwell, Margaret F., |d 1927-
700 1_ |a Carter, Judith A.
008 ...s1989 ...eng
504 __ |a Includes bibliographical references and index.
500 __ |a Rev. ed. of: Handbook for AACR2.
700 1_ |a Maxwell, Margaret F., |d 1927- |t Handbook for AACR2.

*[*manifestation* record 3]
260 __ |a Chicago : |b American Library Association, |c 1989.
300 __ |a ix, 436 p. : |b ill. ; |c 26 cm.
020 __ |a 0838905056 (alk. paper)

[*expression* record 1]
245 10 |a Maxwell's handbook for AACR2R : |b explaining and illustrating the Anglo-American cataloguing rules and the 1993 amendments / |c Robert L. Maxwell with Margaret F. Maxwell.
246 30 |a Handbook for AACR2R
100 1_ |a Maxwell, Robert L., |d 1957-
700 1_ |a Maxwell, Margaret F., |d 1927-
008 ...s1997 ...eng
504 __ |a Includes bibliographical references and index.
500 __ |a Rev. ed. of: Handbook for AACR2, 1988 revision / by Margaret Maxwell.

700 1_ |a Maxwell, Margaret F., |d 1927- |t Handbook for AACR2, 1988 revision.

[*manifestation* record 1]
260 __ |a Chicago, IL : |b American Library Association, |c 1997.
300 __ |a xii, 522 p. : |b ill. ; |c 26 cm.
020 __ |a 0838907040 (alk. paper)

[*item* record 1]
050 00 |a Z694.15.A56
991 __ |b c-GenColl |h Z694.15.A56 |i M393 1997 |t Copy 1 |w BOOKS

[*item* record 2]
050 00 |a Z694.15.A56
991 __ |b r-MRR |h Z694.15.A56 |i M393 1997 |t Copy 2 |m Ref Desk |w GenBib

*[*person* record 1]
100 10 |a Maxwell, Margaret F., |d 1927-
670 __ |a Her Shaping a library, 1973.
670 __ |a Letter from M. Maxwell, 6/20/80 |b (author's preference: Margaret F. Maxwell)
670 __ |a WW lib. serv., 1966: |b p. 462 (Maxwell, Margaret Finlayson, b. 6/9/27)
678 __ |a librarian; |a Ph.D.; |a Grad. Lib. Sch., Univ. of Ariz., Tucson

*[*person* record 2]
010 __ |a n 95028779
035 __ |a (DLC)n 95028779
040 __ |a DLC |c DLC
100 10 |a Maxwell, Robert L., |d 1957-
670 __ |a In aedibus Aldi, 1995: |b CIP t.p. (Robert L. Maxwell) data sheet (Robert LeGrand Maxwell; b. 12-14-1957)

Figure 3-9-3. Case 1-3. Another example of a set of records for the book in line with the proposed model.

[*work* record 1]

504 __ |a Includes bibliographical references and index.

700 1_ ...|t Handbook for AACR2, 1988 revision.

[*work* record 2]

630 00 |a Anglo-American cataloguing rules

[*expression* record 1]

008 ...eng

[*manifestation* record 1]

008 ...s1997

020 __ |a 0838907040 (alk. paper)

245 10 |a Maxwell's handbook for AACR2R : |b explaining and illustrating the Anglo-American cataloguing rules and the 1993 amendments / |c Robert L. Maxwell with Margaret F. Maxwell.

246 30 |a Handbook for AACR2R

260 __ |a Chicago, IL : |b American Library Association, |c 1997.

300 __ |a xii, 522 p. : |b ill. ; |c 26 cm.

[*item* record 1]

050 00 |a Z694.15.A56

[*person* record 1]

100 1_ |a Maxwell, Robert L., |d 1957-

[*person* record 2]

700 1_ |a Maxwell, Margaret F., |d 1927-

[*concept* record 1]

630 00 ...|x Handbooks, manuals, etc.

[*concept* record 2]
650 _0 |a Descriptive cataloging |x Rules |x Handbooks, manuals, etc.

Figure 3-9-4. Case 1-4. An example of a set of records for the book in line with the FRBR model.

[*work* record 1]
700 1_ |a Maxwell, Margaret F., |d 1927-
082 00 |a 025.3/2 |2 21
630 00 |a Anglo-American cataloguing rules |x Handbooks, manuals, etc.
650 _0 |a Descriptive cataloging |x Rules |x Handbooks, manuals, etc.

[*text* record 1]
245 10 |a Maxwell's handbook for AACR2R : |b explaining and illustrating the Anglo-American cataloguing rules and the 1993 amendments / |c Robert L. Maxwell with Margaret F. Maxwell.
246 30 |a Handbook for AACR2R
100 1_ |a Maxwell, Robert L., |d 1957-
700 1_ |a Maxwell, Margaret F., |d 1927-
008 ...s1997 ...eng
504 __ |a Includes bibliographical references and index.
500 __ |a Rev. ed. of: Handbook for AACR2, 1988 revision / by Margaret Maxwell.
700 1_ |a Maxwell, Margaret F., |d 1927- |t Handbook for AACR2, 1988 revision.

[*medium* record 1]
260 __ |a Chicago, IL : |b American Library Association, |c 1997.
300 __ |a xii, 522 p. : |b ill. ; |c 26 cm.
020 __ |a 0838907040 (alk. paper)

Figure 3-9-5. Case 1-5. An example of a set of records for the book in line with the three-layered model.

3.8.3 Case 2: Book

Figure 3-10 shows another example of a book, that is, 'AACR2' published in 1978. The MARC bibliographic record with LC control number 78013789 was used in this case.

There are several ways of developing *work* records for this example, depending on the policy. One way is to create a single *work* record (i.e., a single instance of the entity *work*) for AACR2 and its additional editions like 1988 revision and 1998 revision—we adopted this way provisionally. Another is, for example, to create a single *work* record for the whole AACR family containing all its editions like AACR1 and AACR2.

In the figure, we developed two *manifestation* records, since hardbound and softbound should be dealt with as different manifestations. It is different from LC's current practice. It is obviously possible to deal with such a book as one *manifestation* in line with LC's practice. We also developed four *item* records, but there is no information in the MARC record about which *manifestation* each *item* is linked to.

The whole bibliographic family of the *work* AACR2 and its preceding family AACR1 are illustrated as follows, assuming that they are different works all derived from the 'superwork' AACR:

[W0] AACR
    [W1] AACR1, 1967-1977
        [E1] North American text, 1967
            [M1] book published in 1967
        [E2] British text, 1967
            [M1] book published in 1967
        [E3] North American text. Chap. 6 revised, 1974
        [E4] British text. Chap. 6 revised, 1974
        [E5] North American text. Chap. 12 revised, 1975
        [E6] ...
    [W2] AACR2, 1978-
        [E1] AACR2, 1978
            [M1] book in hardbound published in 1978
            [M2] book in softbound published in 1978
            [M3] book in binder published in 1978
        [E2] Revisions 1982
            [M1] book published in 1982
        [E3] Revisions 1983

[E4] Chap. 9, draft revision, 1987
[E5] 1988 revision
[E6] Amendments 1993
[E7] ...

Each line indicates one instance of a bibliographic entity (and also one bibliographic record in the figure) in a manner similar to Case 1. [W2], its subordinate [E1], and [M1], [M2] are entity instances that were illustrated in the figure. Regarding *manifestation* instances, all but some [M1] are omitted here. There is a 'successor' relationship between the *work* instances [W1] and [W2]. Likewise, there are 'revision' relationships between "[E1] AACR2, 1978" and each of other *expression* instances under the *work* [W2]. In reality, however, for example, [E2], [E3], and [E4] are updates to parts of the whole work [W2], and thus alternatively they can be viewed and dealt with as separate works in 'whole-part' relationship to the whole work.

[*work* record 1]
+title: Anglo-American cataloguing rules. 2nd ed.
+title: AACR2
710 20 |a American Library Association.
+responsibility: British Library
+responsibility: Canadian Committee on Cataloguing
+responsibility: Library Association
+responsibility: Library of Congress
700 10 |a Gorman, Michael, |d 1941-
700 10 |a Winkler, Paul W. |q (Paul Walter)
+date: 1978-
500 __ |a Originally published (1967) in two versions under the following titles: Anglo-American cataloging rules. North American text; Anglo-American cataloguing rules. British text.
082 00 |a 025.3/2
650 0_ |a Descriptive cataloging |x Rules.

[*expression* record 1]

245 00 |a Anglo-American cataloguing rules / |c prepared by the American Library Association ... [et al.] ; edited by Michael Gorman and Paul W. Winkler.

250 __ |a 2d ed.

008 ...s1978 ...eng

504 __ |a Includes bibliographical references and index.

[*manifestation* record 1]

260 0_ |a Chicago : |b ALA, |c 1978.

300 __ |a xvii, 620 p. ; |c 26 cm.

020 __ |a 083893210X.

[*manifestation* record 2]

260 0_ |a Chicago : |b ALA, |c 1978.

300 __ |a xvii, 620 p. ; |c 26 cm.

020 __ |a 0838932118 |b pbk.

[*item* record 1]

050 00 |a Z694 |b .A5 1978

991 __ |b c-GenColl |h Z694 |i .A5 1978 |t Copy 1 |w BOOKS

[*item* record 2]

050 00 |a Z694 |b .A5 1978

991 __ |b c-GenColl |h Z694 |i .A5 1978 |p 00015187050 |t Copy 8 |w CCF

[*item* record 3]

050 00 |a Z694 |b .A5 1978

991 __ |b r-BusRR |h Z694 |i .A5 1978 |t Copy 11 |w GenBib bi 87-010521

[*item* record 4]

050 00 |a Z694 |b .A5 1978

991 __ |b r-MicRRRef |h Z694 |i .A5 1978 |t x copy |w GenBib bi 87-010521

Figure 3-10. Case 2. An example of a set of records for another book in line with the proposed model.

3.8.4 Case 3: Sound Recording

Figure 3-11-1 shows an example of a musical sound recording; the MARC bibliographic record with LC control number 99583364 was chosen as an example record. Figure 3-11-2 shows a set of records representing that resource in line with the proposed model, using the same manner as that of Case 1 and 2.

In the case of musical sound recordings, a *work* record represents a musical work itself, while an *expression* record represents the performance of the work at a certain point in time (i.e., musical sounds resulting from a performance), and a *manifestation* represents the sound recorded in the given format and carrier. In this example, the *manifestation* contains two different *expressions*, each of which has its corresponding *work*.

If we take some bibliographic records illustrated in Figure 3-11-2 (i.e., the *work* record 1, *expression* 1, and *manifestation* 1), the bibliographic family including the sound recording and some others related to the work 'Ernest Bloch's Schelomo' is depicted as follows, assuming that [W1], its subordinate [E2], and [M1] correspond to the above records, respectively:

> [W1] Ernest Bloch's *Schelomo*
> [E1] a performance by Gregor Piatigorsky, Boston Symphony Orchestra, and Charles Munch recorded in 1958?
> > [M1] recordings released on 33 1/3 rpm sound discs in monaural in 1958 by RCA Victor
> > [M2] recordings released on 33 1/3 rpm sound discs, in stereophonic in 1964 by RCA Victor
> > [M3] ...
>
> [E2] a performance by Mstislav Rostropovich, Orchestre national de France , and Leonard Bernstein recorded in 1977
> > [M1] recordings released on 33 1/3 rpm sound discs in quadraphonic in 1977 by Angel
> > [M2] recordings released on 33 1/3 rpm sound discs in quadraphonic in 1984 by Musical Heritage Society
> > [M3] ...
>
> [E3] ...

If we combine the records shown in Figure 3-11-2 with a name authority record for Ernest Bloch and a name-title authority record for his *Schelomo* (LC name authority control numbers 79150283 and 88610521, respectively), the resultant set of records are illustrated as Figure 3-11-3. The *work* record 1 was expanded and the *person* record 1 was newly added.

In addition, a set of records representing the same resource but in line with the FRBR model are demonstrated in Figure 3-11-4, which is created in a way similar to Figure 3-9-4 based on the mapping developed by Delsey. In this case, there is no data value associated with the *expression* record—the field 500 was not associated with any specific entity in Delsey's mapping, and all composers and performers were associated with *person* and *corporate body*, not with *work* nor *expression*. This is a significant difference between Figures 3-9-2 and 3-9-4 that we should note.

```
000 01286njm 22003371a 450
001 12060954
005 20000618195903.0
007 sdubqme-------
008 921016s1977 xxu n fhi
035 __ |a (OCoLC)ocm26796403
906 __ |a 0 |b cbc |c copycat |d 3 |e ncip |f 19 |g y-soundrec
010 __ |a 99583364
028 02 |a SQ 37256 |b Angel
040 __ |a DLC |c MWalB |d DLC
042 __ |a lcderive
050 00 |a Angel SQ 37256
100 1_ |a Bloch, Ernest, |d 1880-1959.
240 10 |a Schelomo
245 10 |a Schelomo |h sound recording : |b Hebrew rhapsody / |c Bloch. Concerto in A minor, op. 129 / Schumann.
260 __ |a Hollywood, CA : |b Angel, |c p1977.
300 __ |a 1 sound disc : |b analog, 33 1/3 rpm, quad. ; |c 12 in.
511 0_ |a Mstislav Rostropovich, violoncello ; Orchestre national de France ; Leonard Bernstein, conductor.
```

500 __ |a Durations: 22:46 ; 25:25.
500 __ |a Program notes by P. Andry and E. Mason on container.
650 _0 |a Violoncello with orchestra.
650 _0 |a Concertos (Violoncello)
700 1_ |a Rostropovich, Mstislav, |d 1927- |4 prf
700 1_ |a Bernstein, Leonard, |d 1918- |4 prf
700 12 |a Schumann, Robert, |d 1810-1856. |t Concertos, |m violoncello, |n op. 129, |r A minor.
710 2_ |a Orchestre national de France. |4 prf
985 __ |c OCLC |e Claimed Recordings

Figure 3-11-1. Case 3-1. MARC bibliographic record for a sound recording.

[*work* record 1]
100 1_ |a Bloch, Ernest, |d 1880-1959.
240 10 |a Schelomo
650 _0 |a Violoncello with orchestra.

[*work* record 2]
700 12 |a Schumann, Robert, |d 1810-1856. |t Concertos, |m violoncello, |n op. 129, |r A minor.
650 _0 |a Concertos (Violoncello)

[*expression* record 1]
245 10 |a Schelomo : |b Hebrew rhapsody / |c Bloch.
511 0_ |a Mstislav Rostropovich, violoncello ; Orchestre national de France ; Leonard Bernstein, conductor.
008 ...s1977
+form: musical sound
500 __ |a Durations: 22:46.
700 1_ |a Rostropovich, Mstislav, |d 1927- |4 prf
700 1_ |a Bernstein, Leonard, |d 1918- |4 prf
710 2_ |a Orchestre national de France. |4 prf

[*expression* record 2]
245 10 ...Concerto in A minor, op. 129 / Schumann.
511 0_ |a Mstislav Rostropovich, violoncello ; Orchestre national de France ; Leonard Bernstein, conductor.
008 ...s1977
+form: musical sound
500 __ |a Durations: 25:25.
700 1_ |a Rostropovich, Mstislav, |d 1927- |4 prf
700 1_ |a Bernstein, Leonard, |d 1918- |4 prf
710 2_ |a Orchestre national de France. |4 prf

[*manifestation* record 1]
245 10 ... |h sound recording
260 __ |a Hollywood, CA : |b Angel, |c p1977.
300 __ |a 1 sound disc : |b analog, 33 1/3 rpm, quad. ; |c 12 in.
007 sdubqme-------
028 02 |a SQ 37256 |b Angel
500 __ |a Program notes by P. Andry and E. Mason on container.

[*item* record 1]
050 00 |a Angel SQ 37256

Figure 3-11-2. Case 3-2. An example of a set of records for the sound recording in line with the proposed model.

[*work* record 1]
100 1_ |a Bloch, Ernest, |d 1880-1959.
240 10 |a Schelomo
650 _0 |a Violoncello with orchestra.
100 10 |a Bloch, Ernest, |d 1880-1959. |t Schelomo
400 10 |a Bloch, Ernest, |d 1880-1959. |t Solomon
400 10 |a Bloch, Ernest, |d 1880-1959. |t Shelomo
400 1_ |a Bloch, Ernest, |d 1880-1959. |t Hebraic rhapsody
400 1_ |a Bloch, Ernest, |d 1880-1959. |t Hebrew rhapsody
670 __ |a Shostakovich, D.D. Concerto no. 1 for cello and orchestra, op. 107 (1959)

[SR] p1986: |b label (Schelomo = Solomon : Hebraic rhapsody for violoncello and orchestra)
670 __ |a LC data base, 2-22-88 |b (hdg.: Bloch, Ernest, 1880-1959. Schelomo)
670 __ |a New Grove, 2nd ed. |b (Schelomo; vc, orch, 1915-16)

[*work* record 2]
700 12 |a Schumann, Robert, |d 1810-1856. |t Concertos, |m violoncello, |n op. 129, |r A minor.
650 _0 |a Concertos (Violoncello)

[*expression* record 1]
245 10 |a Schelomo : |b Hebrew rhapsody / |c Bloch.
511 0_ |a Mstislav Rostropovich, violoncello ; Orchestre national de France ; Leonard Bernstein, conductor.
008 ...s1977
+form: musical sound
500 __ |a Durations: 22:46.
700 1_ |a Rostropovich, Mstislav, |d 1927- |4 prf
700 1_ |a Bernstein, Leonard, |d 1918- |4 prf
710 2_ |a Orchestre national de France. |4 prf

[*expression* record 2]
245 10 ...Concerto in A minor, op. 129 / Schumann.
511 0_ |a Mstislav Rostropovich, violoncello ; Orchestre national de France ; Leonard Bernstein, conductor.
008 ...s1977
+form: musical sound
500 __ |a Durations: 25:25.
700 1_ |a Rostropovich, Mstislav, |d 1927- |4 prf
700 1_ |a Bernstein, Leonard, |d 1918- |4 prf
710 2_ |a Orchestre national de France. |4 prf

[*manifestation* record 1]
245 10 ... |h sound recording

260 __ |a Hollywood, CA : |b Angel, |c p1977.

300 __ |a 1 sound disc : |b analog, 33 1/3 rpm, quad. ; |c 12 in.

007 sdubqme-------

028 02 |a SQ 37256 |b Angel

500 __ |a Program notes by P. Andry and E. Mason on container.

[*item* record 1]

050 00 |a Angel SQ 37256

*[*person* record 1]

100 1_ |a Bloch, Ernest, |d 1880-1959

400 1_ |a Bloch, Ernst, |d 1880-1959

670 __ |a Pizzetti, I. |b Musicisti contemporanei, 1914.

670 __ |a Baker, 8th ed. |b (Bloch, Ernest; b. July 24, 1880, Geneva; d. July 15, 1959, Portland, Oreg.; Swiss-born American composer)

670 __ |a His Sonate, 1938: |b labels (Ernst Bloch) album cover (Ernest Bloch)

Figure 3-11-3. Case 3-3. Another example of a set of records for the sound recording in line with the proposed model.

[*work* record 1]

240 10 |a Schelomo

[*work* record 2]

|t Concertos, |m violoncello, |n op. 129, |r A minor.

[*expression* record 1]

(none)

[*manifestation* record 1]

007 sdubqme-------

008 ...s1977

028 02 |a SQ 37256 |b Angel

245 10 |a Schelomo |h sound recording : |b Hebrew rhapsody / |c Bloch. Concerto in A minor, op. 129 / Schumann.

260 __ |a Hollywood, CA : |b Angel, |c p1977.
300 __ |a 1 sound disc : |b analog, 33 1/3 rpm, quad. ; |c 12 in.
511 0_ |a Mstislav Rostropovich, violoncello ; Orchestre national de France ; Leonard Bernstein, conductor.

[*item* record 1]
050 00 |a Angel SQ 37256

[*person* record 1]
100 1_ |a Bloch, Ernest, |d 1880-1959.

[*person* record 2]
700 1_ |a Rostropovich, Mstislav, |d 1927- |4 prf

[*person* record 3]
700 1_ |a Bernstein, Leonard, |d 1918- |4 prf

[*person* record 4]
700 12 |a Schumann, Robert, |d 1810-1856.

[*corporate body* record 1]
710 2_ |a Orchestre national de France. |4 prf

[*concept* record 1]
650 _0 |a Violoncello with orchestra.

[*concept* record 2]
650 _0 |a Concertos (Violoncello)

Figure 3-11-4. Case 3-4. An example of a set of records for the sound recording in line with the FRBR model.

3.8.5 Case 4: Electronic Resource

Figure 3-12-1 shows an example of an electronic resource; the MARC bibliographic record with LC control number 96802206 was used. Figure 3-12-2 shows a set of records representing that resource in line with the proposed model, using the same method as those for the above examples.

The resource in this example is the proceedings of a conference, and has been published in three ways: a CD-ROM, a remote access Web site, and an issue of a printed serial. The texts of the proceedings published in the three ways are identical and thus only one *expression* record is developed in Figure 3-12-2. The *work* record is developed for the whole series of the *Proceedings of the International WWW Conference*. Instead, we could create a *work* record for an individual numbered conference (e.g., the 5th conference, in this case).

The whole bibliographic family of the above *work* is illustrated as follows:

> [W1] *Proceedings of the International World-Wide Web Conference*, 1994-
> > [E1] *Proceedings of the 1st International World-Wide Web Conference*, 1994
> > > [M1] Internet Web site opened in 1994
> >
> > [E2] *Proceedings of the 2nd International World-Wide Web Conference*, 1994
> > > [M1] Internet Web site opened in 1994
> >
> > [E3] ...
> >
> > ...
> >
> > [E5] *Proceedings of the 5th International World-Wide Web Conference*, 1996
> > > [M1] CD-ROM published in 1996
> > > [M2] special issue of the serial *Computer networks and ISDN systems* published in 1996
> > > [M3] Internet Web site opened in 1996
> >
> > [E6] ...

[W1], [E5], and its subordinate [M1], [M2], and [M3] are entity instances that were illustrated in Figure 3-12-2.

---

000 01783cmm 2200385 a 450
001 5002131
005 20000531103921.0

```
007 cc ug|
008 961003s1996 ne d eng
035 __ |9 (DLC) 96802206
906 __ |a 7 |b cbc |c orignew |d u |e ncip |f 19 |g y-gencompf
955 __ |a vb24 to MRC 10-03-96; aa11 11-09-99
010 __ |a 96802206
020 __ |a 0444825010
040 __ |a DLC |c DLC |d DLC
050 00 |a TK5105.888
082 00 |a 025.04 |2 21
111 2_ |a International WWW Conference |n (5th : |d 1996 : |c Paris, France)
245 00 |a Proceedings of the 5th International World-Wide Web Conference |h [computer file] : |b May 6-10 1996, Paris, France.
246 30 |a World-Wide Web Conference
256 __ |a Computer data.
260 __ |a Amsterdam : |b Elsevier Science, |c [1996]
300 __ |a 1 computer laser optical disc ; |c 4 3/4 in. + |e 1 insert.
538 __ |a System requirements for IBM: 386SX or higher; 4MB RAM; MSDOS; HTML viewer software (e.g., Netscape); CD-ROM drive.
538 __ |a System requirements for Macintosh: Macintosh; 4MB RAM; System 7.0 or higher; HTML viewer; CD-ROM drive.
500 __ |a Title from disc label.
500 __ |a Also published as a special issue of: Computer networks and ISDN systems (Vol. 28, issues 7-11, 1996).
530 __ |a Also available via the Internet.
520 __ |a Contains 58 HTML-formatted technical papers accepted for presentation at the 5th International World-Wide Web Conference, 7th to 9th of May, 1996, in Paris.
650 _0 |a World Wide Web (Information retrieval system) |v Congresses.
650 _0 |a Internet |v Congresses.
710 2_ |a Elsevier Science Publishers.
730 0_ |a Computer networks and ISDN systems.
856 7_ |u http://www5conf.inria.fr |2 http
991 __ |b c-MRC |h TK5105.888 |i [1996 00558] |t Copy 1 |w CF
```

Figure 3-12-1. Case 4-1. MARC bibliographic record for an electronic resource.

[*work* record 1]

+title: Proceedings of the International World-Wide Web Conference

111 2_ |a International WWW Conference

+date: 1994-

082 10 |a 025.04 |2 21

650 _0 |a World Wide Web (Information retrieval system) |x Congresses.

650 _0 |a Internet (Computer network) |x Congresses.

[*expression* record 1]

111 2_ |a International WWW Conference |n (5th : |d 1996 : |c Paris, France)

008 ...s1996 ...eng

245 10 |a Proceedings of the 5th International World-Wide Web Conference : |b May 6-10 1996, Paris, France.

246 30 |a World-Wide Web Conference

520 __ |a Contains 58 ... technical papers accepted for presentation at the 5th International World-Wide Web Conference, 7th to 9th of May, 1996, in Paris.

500 __ |a Title from disc label.

[*manifestation* record 1]

245 10 |h [computer file]

256 __ |a Computer data.

260 __ |a Amsterdam : |b Elsevier Science, |c [1996]

300 __ |a 1 computer laser optical disc ; |c 4 3/4 in. + |e 1 insert.

538 __ |a System requirements for IBM: 386SX or higher; 4MB RAM; MSDOS; HTML viewer software (e.g., Netscape); CD-ROM drive.

538 __ |a System requirements for Macintosh: Macintosh; 4MB RAM; System 7.0 or higher; HTML viewer; CD-ROM drive.

020 __ |a 0444825010

710 2_ |a Elsevier Science Publishers.

520 __ |a ... HTML-formatted ...

[*manifestation* record 2]

500 __ |a ... published as a special issue of: Computer networks and ISDN systems (Vol. 28, issues 7-11, 1996).

```
730 0_  |a Computer networks and ISDN systems.
710 2_  |a Elsevier Science Publishers.


[ manifestation record 3 ]
245 10  |h [computer file]
256 __  |a Computer data.
530 __  |a Available also through the Internet.
856 7_  |2 http
520 __  |a ... HTML-formatted ...


[ item record 1 ]
050 00  |a TK5105.888
991 __  |b c-MRC |h TK5105.888 |i [1996 00558] |t Copy 1 |w CF


[ item record 2 ]
856 7_  |u http://www5conf.inria.fr
```

Figure 3-12-2. Case 4-2. An example of a set of records for the electronic resource in line with the proposed model.

3.9 Chapter Conclusion

A new viewpoint on whether a text-level entity is given primacy among bibliographic ones in a conceptual model was introduced to examine the role and function of that entity in each model. As a result, it was found that almost all models including the FRBR model do not deal with a text-level entity as a predominant one, with exceptions like the three-layered model.

A new model giving primacy to text-level entity was also proposed using the E-R modeling language. By chiefly indicating differences from the FRBR model, the new model was proposed; it comprises necessary bibliographic entities including that of text-level, their attributes, their relationships, and other entities. The text-level entity, its main attributes, and relationships between instances of the entity were examined in particular. Furthermore, clarification of the implication of that model within the scope of conceptual modeling was attempted as much as possible.

As a result, for example, the following was clarified on the implication of giving primacy to a certain bibliographic entity in a model:

1) An instance of the entity which was given primacy must be created for every item.

2) Bibliographic records must be created based on the unit of the entity given primacy, when adopting the policy of creating each record based on a bibliographic entity.

3) Titles, statements of responsibility, and others that appear in an item (excluding some exceptions) must be associated with the entity given primacy. Other attributes (and also data elements) fully characterizing the entity must be associated with it as well.

4) Important relationships between instances of the entity given primacy must be identified and represented in any manner.

5) User tasks related to the entity given primacy are accomplished with the attributes associated with the entity itself and relationships between instances of the entity. This can be deduced from the above 3 and 4.

6) A scenario showing the whole process conducted by users begins with a task related to the entity given primacy (e.g., 'find' that level entity). Also instances of the entity are necessarily 'identified' or 'selected' in the process shown in the scenario.

Notes

1 Part of this chapter has already been reported as a paper in *Journal of Documentation* and a report. Taniguchi (2002a, 2003b)
2 Wilson (1968)
3 Wilson (1968, p. 6)
4 Wilson (1968, p. 7)
5 Cockshutt et al. (1983)
6 Young (1983)
7 Young (1983, p. 227)
8 Young (1983, p. 243)
9 IFLA Study Group on the FRBR (1997, p. 18)
10 Howarth (1998b)
11 Multiple Versions Forum (1990)

12 ALCTS CCS CC:DA (1995)
13 Lubetzky (1963)
14 Verona (1963)
15 Jolley (1963)
16 IFLA Study Group on the FRBR (1997, p. 12)
17 Taniguchi (1999b)
18 Taniguchi (1999b)
19 American Library Association et al. (1978)
20 Yee (1994b, 1994c, 1995a, 1995b, 1998)
21 IFLA Study Group on the FRBR (1997, p. 20)
22 American Library Association et al. (1967)
23 American Library Association et al. (1974)
24 Howarth (1998a)
25 Cockshutt et al. (1983)
26 IFLA Study Group on the FRBR (1997, p. 23)
27 Joint Steering Committee for Revision of AACR (2002, p. Appendix.D-4)
28 Vellucci (1998)
29 Jonsson (2002, p. 1)
30 IFLA Study Group on the FRBR (1997, p. 20)
31 ALCTS CCS CC:DA (1999), ALCTS CCS CC:DA, Task Force on Recommendation 2 in 4JSC/ALA/30 (2000)
32 Joint Steering Committee for Revision of AACR, Format Variation Working Group (2001, 2002a)
33 IFLA Study Group on the FRBR (1997, p. 13)
34 IFLA Study Group on the FRBR (1997, p. 13)
35 IFLA Study Group on the FRBR (1997, p. 16)
36 IFLA Study Group on the FRBR (1997, p. 16)
37 Taniguchi (1990, 1993a, 1993b)
38 Taniguchi (1997a, 1999b)
39 IFLA Study Group on the FRBR (1997, pp. 19-20)
40 Le Boeuf (2001)
41 Taniguchi (1990, 1993a, 1993b, 1997a)
42 IFLA Study Group on the FRBR (1997, p. 16)
43 Hagler (1998), Ridley (1998), Vellucci (1998)

44 IFLA Study Group on the FRBR (1997, pp. 79-80)
45 O'Neill and Visine-Goetz (1989), Svenonius (1992), Leazer (1993), Heaney (1995), Green (1996)
46 Delsey (1998b, 1999)
47 Delsey (1998b, Table.1-1)
48 IFLA Study Group on the FRBR (1997, p. 120)
49 IFLA Study Group on the FRBR (1997, p. 93)
50 IFLA Study Group on the FRBR (1997, p. 93)
51 IFLA Study Group on the FRBR (1997, p. 90)
52 IFLA Study Group on the FRBR (1997, p. 73)
53 IFLA Study Group on the FRBR (1997, p. 69)
54 Tillett (2001a)
55 IFLA Study Group on the FRBR (1997, p. 74)
56 Svenonius (2000, Chapter 2), Tillett (2001b)
57 IFLA Study Group on the FRBR (1997, p. 9)
58 Library of Congress (1999b)
59 Delsey (2002)

Chapter 4

Conceptual Modeling of Component Parts of Bibliographic Resources[1]

4.1 Significance of Modeling Component Parts and Types of Component Parts

I have introduced in Chapter 3 a viewpoint regarding which entity is to be given primacy among bibliographic entities in a conceptual model, with the aim of clarifying the role and function of text-level entity. I also outlined a model giving primacy to text-level entity, by chiefly indicating differences from the FRBR model, which does not deal with the entity as being prioritized. More studies are needed to investigate the feasibility and usefulness of this model.

The aim of the present chapter is to examine differences in modeling component parts of bibliographic resources (chapters of books, articles in serials, etc.) in the comparison between the FRBR model and that proposed in Chapter 3.

Component parts of resources are closely related to text-level entity, since they can be viewed as forming the logical content structure of their host items (i.e., resources at the integral unit level) and also the entity is expected to undertake to show the detailed logical structure of resources. However, no studies on conceptual models, except FRBR, have ever touched on issues concerning the modeling of component parts. Moreover, if we take into consideration the fact that FRBR does not view the text-level entity *expression* as being prioritized and is inclined to give primacy to *manifestation*, a question arises: Is FRBR able to deal properly with and model component parts?

First, I re-examine the FRBR model from the viewpoint of modeling component parts when each part in itself is a resource to be described. I examine the way in the model (a) to define entities at the component level corresponding to component parts, (b) to associate attributes with those entities, and (c) to assign whole/part relationships between entities at the component level and those at the integral unit level. Consequently, it will be clarified whether entities at the component level can operate in the same way as entities at the integral unit level. This is part of the verification of consistency within the model. Second, by applying the identical viewpoint to the text-prioritized model proposed in Chapter 3, I examine the methods adopted in the model to show its characteristic. Additionally, I examine the modeling of resources at the aggregate level.

Guidelines for the Application of the ISBDs to the Descriptions of Component Parts defines a 'component part' as "A part of a publication (a chapter of a book, an article in a serial, a band on a sound recording, etc.) that for purposes of bibliographic identification or access is dependent upon the identification of the publication in which it is contained."[2] I use the term 'component part' in this sense. The guidelines also terms "The publication (book, serial, sound recording, etc.) in which a component part is contained"[3] a 'host item.'

From the viewpoint on whether it is physically independent, the component part can be divided into two types: document part and content part—I borrowed the terms from Delsey[4]. The 'document part' is defined as "a physically separate component of a document."[5] The 'document' in this definition refers to "an object that comprises intellectual and/or artistic content and is conceived, produced, and/or issued as an entity"[6]—it implies a resource at the integral unit level. The document part includes "Each physically separate component of a multipart document," "Any component issued with and intended to be used with a document (accompanying material)," and "An individual issue of a serial."[7] On the other hand, the 'content part' indicates "an individual component of the intellectual or artistic content of a document or document part"[8] and, of course, is not physically independent. This includes an article in a serial, a chapter/section/part of a resource, illustration for a text, sound aspect of a film, and so on. If a journal article is physically independent (that is the case of offprint), however, the article in itself becomes a document part, not a content part. I use these types when examining the two models.

4.2 Modeling of Component Parts in FRBR

4.2.1 Case of Content Parts in FRBR

Before examining the way of modeling component parts in the FRBR model, I confirm a few points on the modeling of host items.

Chapter 4 Conceptual Modeling of Component Parts of Bibliographic Resources   109

1) A host item is a resource to be dealt with as independent in all aspects, and thus any conceptual model assumes it a basic (and default) type of resource to be modeled. The FRBR model represents the bibliographic entities—*work, expression, manifestation*, and *item*—primarily as integral units, which correspond to host items.

2) The entity *expression* has an attribute 'summarization of content,' which indicates "an abstract, summary, synopsis, etc., or a list of chapter headings, songs, parts, etc. included in the *expression*."[9] This attribute is closely related to component parts, since "a list of chapter headings, songs, parts, etc." shows actually the titles and others of component parts contained in the host item.

Next, I turn to the case of content parts in FRBR. Figure 4-1 illustrates at the left the modeling of a host item, i.e., a resource at the integral unit level. The instances of the entities *work, expression, manifestation*, and *item* are shown with only some attributes (and also examples of their values) that are closely related to this discussion. The upward pseudo-assignment of attribute values is indicated with an arrow on a dotted line.

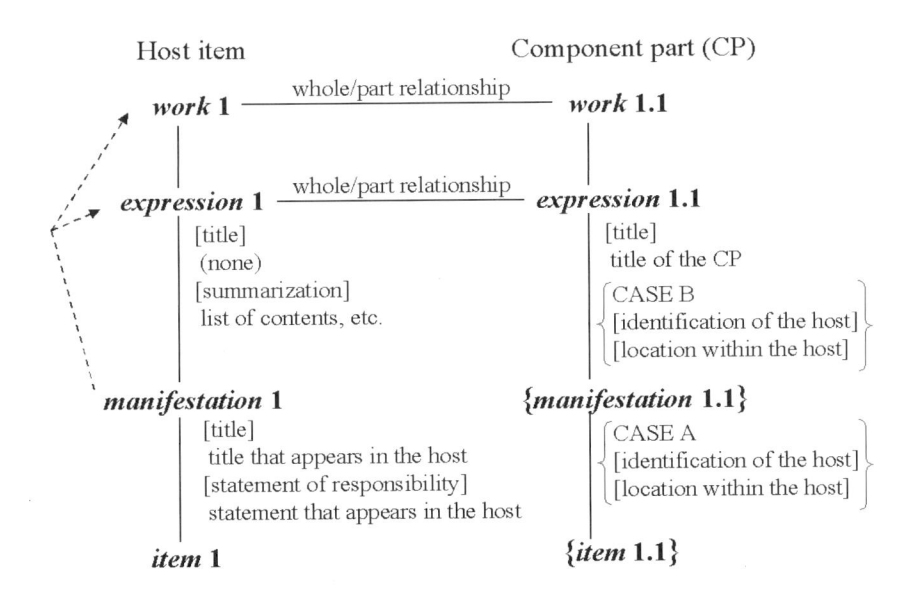

```
Host item                                        Component part (CP)

   work 1   ——whole/part relationship——   work 1.1

   expression 1  ——whole/part relationship——  expression 1.1
     [title]                                    [title]
     (none)                                     title of the CP
     [summarization]                            ⎡ CASE B                         ⎤
     list of contents, etc.                     ⎨ [identification of the host]   ⎬
                                                ⎣ [location within the host]    ⎦

   manifestation 1                              {manifestation 1.1}
     [title]                                    ⎡ CASE A                         ⎤
     title that appears in the host             ⎨ [identification of the host]   ⎬
     [statement of responsibility]              ⎣ [location within the host]    ⎦
     statement that appears in the host

   item 1                                       {item 1.1}
```

Figure 4-1. Modeling of a content part in the FRBR model.

The modeling of a content part contained in the host item is illustrated at the right of the figure, showing a structure different from that for the host item.

The instance *work*1.1 is developed corresponding to the intellectual or artistic content of the content part. There are at least two ways to develop *work* instances as discussed in Chapter 3; one is to create an instance for every item, while the other is to create it in limited cases. This is not essential for the discussion on modeling component parts and thus I assume that a *work* instance is created for every item in the discussion of the present chapter.

The *expression*1.1 is created to represent principally the content part; namely, *expression*, not *manifestation*, is a main entity to correspond to and represent the content part. The reasons are as follows:

1) The unit of (in other words, the boundaries for) a content part is obviously based on *expression* as can be deduced from the definition of a content part—it is not physically independent. The unit of (and also the boundaries for) *manifestation*, on the other hand, must be based on physicality and it is difficult to view *manifestation* as an entity mainly corresponding to a content part. If we consider some examples of content parts, like illustration for a text and sound aspect of a film, these can be easily understood.

2) Referring to the FRBR model, Delsey developed a formalized and detailed schema to reflect the internal logic of AACR2[10], which specifies the current cataloging practice. We can regard that schema as basically an expansion of FRBR.

According to his schema, when an item to be described is a content part, only the content part itself makes up of the item and any other constituent is not involved. Constituents external to the content part are infixion, physical carrier, and container—the infixion refers to "the formatting of intellectual or artistic content"[11] and thus the content part is 'set as' infixion. Those are, together with the content part, surely included in *manifestation* in FRBR. *Expression* should therefore be a main entity corresponding to the content part and playing a role to represent it.

Furthermore, the schema shows relationships between constituents; document (and also document part) 'consists of' content, and then content 'contains' content part. Document and document part obviously correspond to *manifestation* in

FRBR, while content and content part do to *expression*. Also, content and content part coincide with the instance *expression*1 and *expression*1.1 in Figure 4-1, respectively.

It follows from what has been said that an *expression* instance is always created for a content part and the title, statement of responsibility, and others that appear in the content part are associated with the entity. It must be noted that at that time the title and others are not upward pseudo-assigned to *work*—only attribute values of *manifestation* can be dealt with in such a way. An attribute 'summarization' of *expression* for a content part itself indicates the content summarization of the content part.

It is not clear in FRBR whether an instance of *manifestation* is developed for a content part to be described. Hence, we need to assume both cases. First, we take up the case where the instance is developed. In this case, some attributes are associated with *manifestation*; one is the location of the content part within the host item and another is the identification of the host item. Figure 4-1 shows the instance *manifestation*1.1 with brace and its attributes as Case A. Next, it is the case where the *manifestation* instance is not created and thus necessary attributes above are associated with *expression*. The figure denotes this as Case B.

Any instance of the entity *item* for a content part should not be usually developed; the instance would be developed only when characteristics need to be described which are unique to the content part itself of the particular copy *item*1. The *item*1.1 is denoted with brace in the figure.

What has to be noticed here is that the modeling of a content part results in different structure from that for its host item, even if it is assumed that *manifestation* and *item* instances are created for the content part itself. The major difference in the resultant structures is which entity (i.e., *expression* or *manifestation*) is associated with the title and others that appear in the content part. It seems to be a critical problem that the resultant structures vary depending on the type of resource described.

It should also be added that in the FRBR model relationships between content parts and their host items are recognized as whole/part relationships mainly at the *work* and *expression* levels, although those at the two levels differ somewhat from each other. 'Intellectual part of a multipart work,' 'journal article,' 'illustration for a text,' and 'sound aspect of a film,' which are actually content parts of a host item, are enumerated as examples of the whole/part relationships at both levels. In contrast, 'chapter, section, part, etc.,' which is categorized as 'segmental parts' in the model, is assigned only to the *work* level; I addressed this matter in Chapter 3.

4.2.2 Case of Document Parts in FRBR

Next, I examined the case where a resource to be described is a document part. A document part, which is physically independent of its host item, can be dealt with in a similar manner for the host item, although its identification is dependent on the identification of the host item. A *manifestation* instance is always developed for a document part, since it principally corresponds to and represents the document part. Figure 4-2 illustrates at the right the instance *manifestation*1.1 for a document part. In Delsey's schema, when an item described is a document part, the item consists of several constituents: content (or content part), infixion, and physical carrier. They are surely included in the *manifestation* in FRBR.

Titles, statements of responsibility, and edition designation of a document part are all associated with *manifestation*. These attribute values should be upward pseudo-assigned to the upper level instances *work* and *expression*, as in the same way as that for a host item. The figure shows this with an arrow on a dotted line. The location of a document part within the host item and the identification of the host are also associated with *manifestation*.

The *item*1.1 should be developed, since we necessarily have a copy of a document part at hand according to the premise for the case of document parts. In contrast, it is not sure whether an *expression* instance is always created for a document part—it is the same for a host item. *Expression* lacks the solid and stable basis for its own existence, even if it is the case of a document part. In the figure, the *expression*1.1 is enclosed with brace for indicating this point. Whether an *item* instance for a host item is developed depends on the situation if one holds the host item itself in addition to the document part.

Whole/part relationships between document parts and their host items are assigned to the *work* and *expression* levels—it is equal to the case for content parts. Volume/issue of serial, for example, is shown as a relationship type at both levels.

Chapter 4 Conceptual Modeling of Component Parts of Bibliographic Resources 113

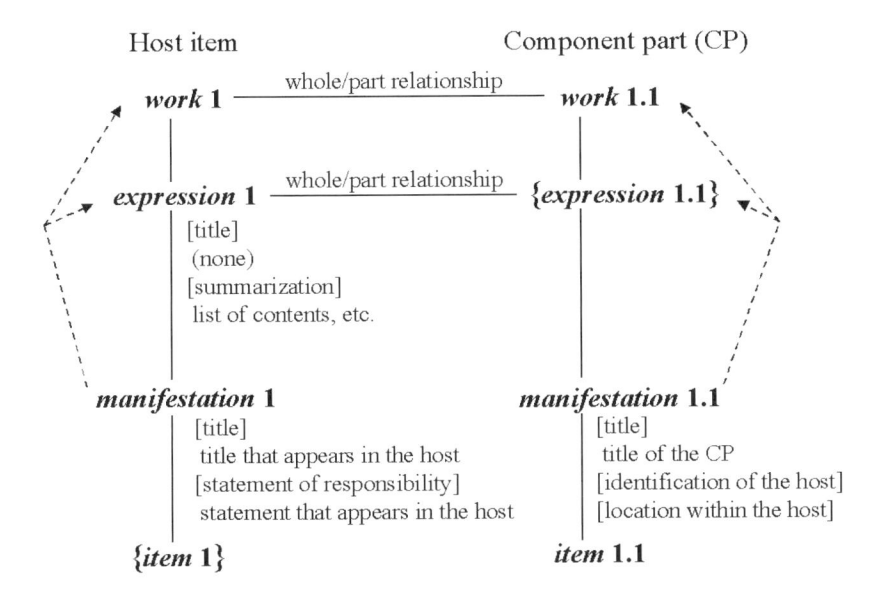

```
       Host item                          Component part (CP)
                     whole/part relationship
      work 1  ──────────────────────  work 1.1

        │                                    │
                     whole/part relationship
      expression 1  ──────────────────  {expression 1.1}
        │ [title]                            │
          (none)
          [summarization]
          list of contents, etc.

        │                                    │
      manifestation 1                    manifestation 1.1
        │ [title]                            │ [title]
          title that appears in the host       title of the CP
          [statement of responsibility]        [identification of the host]
          statement that appears in the host   [location within the host]

      {item 1}                            item 1.1
```

Figure 4-2. Modeling of a document part in the FRBR model.

4.3 Modeling of Component Parts in Text-prioritized Model

4.3.1 Case of Content Parts in Text-prioritized Model

Figure 4-3 illustrates at the left the modeling of a host item in the text-prioritized model, with bibliographic entities and some of their attributes. The figure also illustrates at the right the modeling of a content part of the host. Titles, responsibility designation, and edition designation of a content part are all associated with an *expression* instance for the content part. This is done irrelevant to whether a resource is physically independent, since the model focuses on a resource chiefly at the text-level.

```
              Host item                    Component part (CP)
          work 1  ──whole/part relationship──  work 1.1
            │                                    │
       expression 1 ──whole/part relationship── expression 1.1
            │  [title]                            │  [title]
            │  title that appears in the host    │  title of the CP
            │  [responsibility designation]      │  [identification of the host]
            │  statement that appears in the host│  ⎧CASE A                        ⎫
            │  [summarization]                   │  ⎨[location within the host]    ⎬
            │  list of contents, etc.            │  ⎩                              ⎭
       manifestation 1                        manifestation 1.1
            │                                    │  ⎧CASE B                        ⎫
            │                                    │  ⎨[location within the host]    ⎬
            │                                    │  ⎩                              ⎭
            │                                    │
          item 1                              {item 1.1}
```

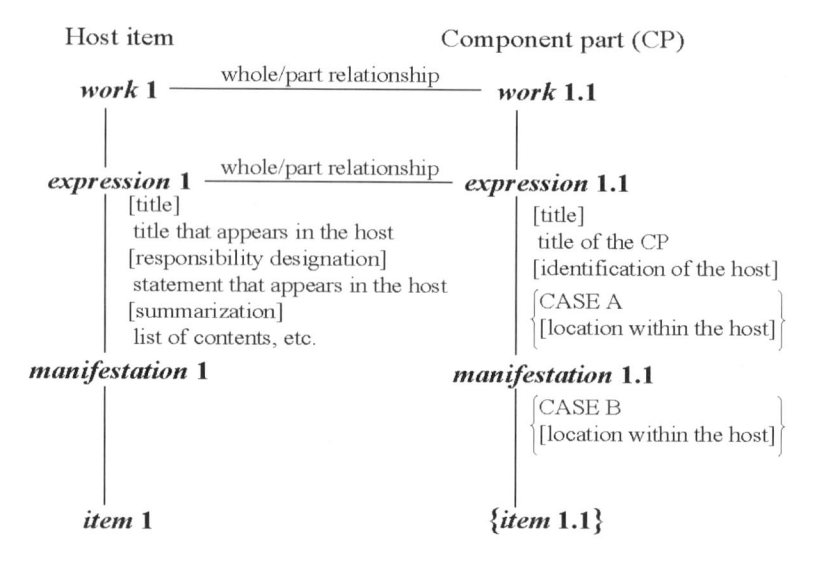

Figure 4-3. Modeling of a content part in the text-prioritized model.

In addition to these attributes, the identification of the host item is associated with *expression*. To put it more specifically, this becomes the identification of the host *expression*. It corresponds to the matter that the attribute 'series designation' is associated with *expression*.

There would be two ways of associating the location within the host item with entity. One is to associate it with *expression*. In this case, the attribute would be the location within the host *expression*; the figure denotes this as Case A. The other is to associate it with *manifestation*, indicating that the attribute would be the location within the host *manifestation* (shown as Case B in the figure). If the location is expressed in terms of inclusive pagination (e.g., p. 12-25), it would be proper to deal with it as Case B.

An instance *item*1.1 is enclosed with brace in the figure because of the same reason as that discussed in the case for FRBR.

Relationships between content parts and their host items are assigned mainly to the *work* and *expression* levels as whole/part relationships; this is equivalent to that for FRBR. It is necessary to add a type of whole/part relationship 'chapter, section, part, etc.' to the *expression* level, although the type is assigned to only the *work* level in FRBR.

4.3.2 Case of Document Parts in Text-prioritized Model

When a document part is a resource to be described in the text-prioritized model, the resultant structure from the modeling is basically the same as that in the case of a content part illustrated in Figure 4-3. Figure 4-4 shows the resultant structure. Titles, responsibility designation, and edition designation of a document part are all associated with an *expression* instance for the document part. Also, the identification of the host item is associated with the *expression* for the document part. The reason for these results is that the text-prioritized model views and represents a resource chiefly at the *expression* level and thus the model is relatively independent of resource's physical condition and characteristic.

A few changes were made in Figure 4-3 so as to make it proper for a document part and produce Figure 4-4. The brace enclosing the *item* for a component part was removed. It means that for a document part the instance is always created. The *item* for a host item, in contrast, was enclosed with brace; a copy of a host item is not necessary held in a given organization.

```
Host item                                    Component part (CP)
work 1  ──── whole/part relationship ────   work 1.1
  │                                            │
  │        whole/part relationship             │
expression 1 ────────────────────────  expression 1.1
  [title]                                    [title]
  title that appears in the host             title of the CP
  [responsibility designation]               [identification of the host]
  statement that appears in the host         ⎰CASE A                         ⎱
  [summarization]                            ⎱[location within the host]⎰
  list of contents, etc.
manifestation 1                              manifestation 1.1
                                             ⎰CASE B                         ⎱
                                             ⎱[location within the host]⎰
  │                                            │
{item 1}                                     item 1.1
```

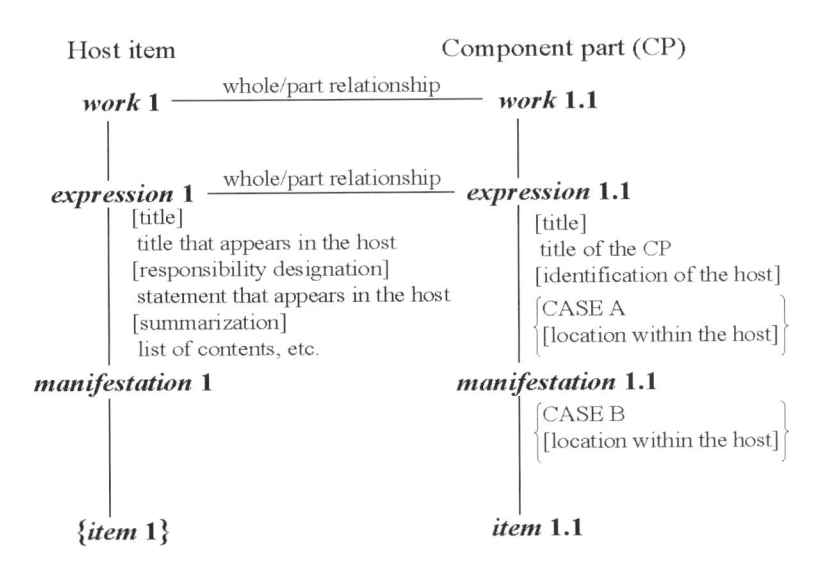

Figure 4-4. Modeling of a document part in the text-prioritized model.

4.4 Examples of Bibliographic Records of Component Parts in Line with Text-prioritized Model

The following attempts to illustrate a few examples of bibliographic records of component parts created in line with the text-prioritized model. To be precise, equivalents of bibliographic records are illustrated, since discussion only at the conceptual level has been attempted in this chapter.

The expedients are adopted of (a) using an existing MARC bibliographic record, (b) transferring the data elements of the MARC record to the attributes of the bibliographic entities, and (c) supplying data values to nearly mandatory attributes (i.e., data elements) if no data value is found in the MARC record. Also adopted is the way of creating an individual record for each entity instance and linking the resulting records to each other to show an item as a whole. These are the same as those adopted in Chapter 3.

1) *Case 1: a content part*

Figure 4-5-1 shows the MARC bibliographic record with LC control number 99568013 was chosen as a base record. The resource described in the MARC record is a musical sound recording. On the other hand, Figure 4-5-2 demonstrates a set of bibliographic records representing two content parts and their host item, which are transformed from the MARC record. In the case of musical sound recordings, a *work* record represents a musical work itself, while an *expression* represents the performance of the work at a certain point in time (i.e., musical sounds resulting from a performance), and a *manifestation* represents the sound recorded in the given format and carrier. Each record consists of (a) several data elements and their data values transferred from a MARC record—they are preceded by the MARC tags—and (b) data values supplied for this illustration—they are preceded by '+'.

In this example, each content part is represented with an *expression* and a *work*. *Works* are developed based on analytical added entries (tag 700 and its second indicator value is '2'), which contain a title and responsibility designation. Two *expressions* are developed, each of which corresponds to a *work*. Data element values in the *expressions* are mostly extracted from the MARC record; (a) a title from the contents note (tag 505), (b) responsibility designation from tags 511,

700, and 710, (c) date from tags 033 and 518, and (d) extent, i.e., duration from tags 306 and 500. Only the form of the *expression* and the identification of the host are supplied for the *expressions*; the identification is indicated in a brief way. *Manifestations* and *items* for the content parts are not created, because of the lack of its necessity in this case.

For the host item, an *expression*, a *manifestation*, and an *item* are developed in the same way as those adopted in Chapter 3. In the *expression*, data values shown in the *expressions* for the content parts are shown again. Any *work* for the host item is not developed; instead, it is possible to create one, if we adopt an alternative policy.

Whole/part relationships between each *expression* for the content parts and that for the host are established, although they are not depicted in Figure 4-5-2.

```
000 01541cjm 22003731 450
001 12043278
005 20000615184233.0
007 sdubmmenn-----
008 780112q19701977caucon
035 __ |a (OCoLC)ocm03554354
906 __ |a 0 |b cbc |c copycat |d 3 |e ncip |f 19 |g y-soundrec
010 __ |a 99568013
028 03 |a IGI 335 |b Educational Media Assoc.
033 1_ |a 1942---- |a 1936----
040 __ |a DLC |c PPT |d OCoLC |d InU |d DLC
042 __ |a lcderive
050 00 |a Educational Media Assoc. IGI 335
245 00 |a Adolf Busch in memoriam. |h Sound recording
260 __ |b [Educational Media Assoc.] |c [197-?]
300 __ |a 1 disc. |b 33 1/3 rpm. mono. |c 12 in.
306 __ |a 003130 |a 003125
511 0_ |a Adolf Busch, violin; Philharmonic; Fritz Busch, conductor (in the 1st work); Concertgebouw; Bruno Walter, conductor (in the 2nd work)
518 __ |a The 1st work recorded in 1942; the 2nd work recorded in 1936.
500 __ |a Durations: 31 min., 30 sec.; 31 min., 25 sec.
```

505 0_ |a Beethoven, L. Violin concerto in D, op. 61.--Busoni, F. Violin concerto in D, op. 35a.

590 __ |a 262 conversion.

590 __ |a 305 conversion.

650 _0 |a Concertos (Violin)

700 1_ |a Busch, Adolf, |d 1891-1952. |4 prf

700 1_ |a Walter, Bruno, |d 1876-1962. |4 prf

700 12 |a Beethoven, Ludwig van, |d 1770-1827. |t Concertos, |m violin, orchestra, |n op. 61, |r D major.

700 12 |a Busoni, Ferruccio, |d 1866-1924. |t Concertos, |m violin, orchestra, |n op. 35a, |r D major.

710 2_ |a Concertgebouworkest. |4 prf

985 __ |c OCLC |e Claimed Recordings

Figure 4-5-1. Case 1-1. MARC bibliographic record for an item at the integral unit level.

Component Part

[*work* record 1.1]

700 12 |a Beethoven, Ludwig van, |d 1770-1827. |t Concertos, |m violin, orchestra, |n op. 61, |r D major.

650 _0 |a Concertos (Violin)

[*expression* record 1.1]

505 0_ |a Beethoven, L. Violin concerto in D, op. 61

511 0_ |a Adolf Busch, violin; Philharmonic; Fritz Busch, conductor (in the 1st work)

700 1_ |a Busch, Adolf, |d 1891-1952. |4 prf

033 1_ |a 1942----

518 __ |a The 1st work recorded in 1942

+form: musical sound

306 __ |a 003130

500 __ |a Durations: 31 min., 30 sec.

+identification of the host: 245 00 |a Adolf Busch in memoriam.

[*work* record 1.2]
700 12 |a Busoni, Ferruccio, |d 1866-1924. |t Concertos, |m violin, orchestra, |n op. 35a, |r D major.
650 _0 |a Concertos (Violin)

[*expression* record 1.2]
505 0_ |a ... Busoni, F. Violin concerto in D, op. 35a.
511 0_ |a Adolf Busch, violin; Concertgebouw; Bruno Walter, conductor (in the 2nd work)
700 1_ |a Busch, Adolf, |d 1891-1952. |4 prf
700 1_ |a Walter, Bruno, |d 1876-1962. |4 prf
710 2_ |a Concertgebouworkest. |4 prf
033 1_ |a 1936----
518 __ |a the 2nd work recorded in 1936.
+form: musical sound
306 __ |a 003125
500 __ |a Durations: 31 min., 25 sec.
+identification of the host: 245 00 |a Adolf Busch in memoriam.

Host Item
[*expression* record 1]
245 00 |a Adolf Busch in memoriam.
511 0_ |a Adolf Busch, violin; Philharmonic; Fritz Busch, conductor (in the 1st work); Concertgebouw; Bruno Walter, conductor (in the 2nd work)
700 1_ |a Busch, Adolf, |d 1891-1952. |4 prf
700 1_ |a Walter, Bruno, |d 1876-1962. |4 prf
710 2_ |a Concertgebouworkest. |4 prf
033 1_ |a 1942---- |a 1936----
518 __ |a The 1st work recorded in 1942; the 2nd work recorded in 1936.
+form: musical sound
306 __ |a 003130 |a 003125
500 __ |a Durations: 31 min., 30 sec.; 31 min., 25 sec.
505 0_ |a Beethoven, L. Violin concerto in D, op. 61.--Busoni, F. Violin concerto in D, op. 35a.

> [*manifestation* record 1]
> 245 00 ... |h Sound recording
> 028 03 |a IGI 335 |b Educational Media Assoc.
> 007 sdubmmenn-----
> 008 ....q19701977
> 260 __ |b [Educational Media Assoc.] |c [197-?]
> 300 __ |a 1 disc. |b 33 1/3 rpm. mono. |c 12 in.
>
> [*item* 1]
> 050 00 |a Educational Media Assoc. IGI 335

Figure 4-5-2. Case 1-2. An example of a set of records for a content part.

2) *Case 2: a content part*

Another example of a content part (in this case, a paper in a proceedings) and its host (i.e., the whole proceedings) is shown in Figure 4-6. The MARC record with LC control number 98034562 was used for illustrating the proceedings.

One paper entitled *Modeling the logic of AACR* by Delsey was chosen as a content part to be described. A *work* and an *expression* record are created to show the paper. All of the attribute values of these entity instances are supplied, since the MARC record does not contain any. The title and the name of the author are needed as attribute values of the *work* and *expression*. Also, the identification of the host and the location within the host are supplied to the *expression* in a brief manner. No attribute value is supplied to the *manifestation* and *item* for the content part. Whole/part relationships at the *work* and *expression* levels are supposed (but, not depicted) between the content part and its host.

> **Component Part**
> [*work* record 1.1]
> +title: Modeling the logic of AACR
> +responsibility: Tom Delsey
> +date: 1997
>
> [*expression* record 1.1]
> +title: Modeling the logic of AACR

+responsibility: Tom Delsey
+date: 1997
+language: English
+identification of the host: 245 14 |a The principles and future of AACR : |b proceedings of the International Conference on the Principles and Future Development of AACR, Toronto, Ontario, Canada, October 23-25, 1997 / |c Jean Weihs, editor.
+location within the host: p. 1-16.

Host Item
[*work* record 1]
111 2_ |a International Conference on the Principles and Future Development of AACR |d (1997 : |c Toronto, Ont.)
245 14 |a The principles and future of AACR
082 00 |a 025.3/2 |2 21
630 00 |a Anglo-American cataloguing rules |x Congresses.
650 _0 |a Descriptive cataloging |z United States |x Rules |x Congresses.
650 _0 |a Descriptive cataloging |z Great Britain |x Rules |x Congresses.
650 _0 |a Descriptive cataloging |z Canada |x Rules |x Congresses.
650 _0 |a Descriptive cataloging |z Australia |x Rules |x Congresses.

[*expression* record 1]
111 2_ |a International Conference on the Principles and Future Development of AACR |d (1997 : |c Toronto, Ont.)
245 14 |a The principles and future of AACR : |b proceedings of the International Conference on the Principles and Future Development of AACR, Toronto, Ontario, Canada, October 23-25, 1997 / |c Jean Weihs, editor.
246 3_ |a Principles and future of Anglo-American cataloguing rules
504 __ |a Includes bibliographical references and indexes.
700 1_ |a Weihs, Jean Riddle.

[*manifestation* record 1]
260 __ |a Ottawa : |b Canadian Library Association ; |a Chicago : |b American Library Association, |c 1998.

300 __ |a xi, 272 p. : |b ill. ; |c 28 cm.

[*item* record 1]
050 00 |a Z694.15.A5 |b I55 1997
991 __ |b c-GenColl |h Z694.15.A5 |i I55 1997 |t Copy 1 |w BOOKS

Figure 4-6. Case 2. Another example of a set of records for a content part.

3) *Case 3: a document part*

An example of a document part (in this case, an issue of a serial) and its host (i.e., the serial as a whole) is demonstrated in Figure 4-7. In this case, an issue of a serial has its own title different from the serial's title and thus alternatively it can be viewed as an example of a monograph and the monographic series containing that monograph.

The MARC bibliographic record with LC control number 54062638 was used for illustrating the serial; a large number of fields probably not essential for this discussion are omitted.

The issue vol. 36, no. 1 of the serial was chosen as a document part to be described. A *work*, an *expression*, a *manifestation* and an *item* record are created to show the issue of the serial. Referring to the record illustrated in *Maxwell's Handbook for AACR2R*[12], most of the attribute values are supplied, since the MARC record does not contain any. The title and editor of that issue become attribute values of the *work* and *expression*. Also, the identification of the host and the location within the host are supplied to the *expression* in a brief manner. No attribute value is supplied to the *item* for the document part; we do not have any information on a particular copy. Whole/part relationships at the *work* and *expression* levels are supposed (but, not depicted) between the document part and its host.

If an issue of a serial does not have any title and others of its own, title and others of the *work* and *expression* for the document part do not have any value. Only date, the identification of the host, the location within the host, etc. will be represented in the *work* and *expression* in that case.

Component Part
[*work* record 1.1]
+title: Recent trends in rare book librarianship
+responsibility: Cloonan, Michele Valerie, 1955-
+date: 1987

[*expression* record 1.1]
+title: Recent trends in rare book librarianship
+responsibility: Michele Valerie Cloonan, issue editor.
+date: 1987
+note: Title from cover.
+note: Includes bibliographical references.
+identification of the host: 245 00 |a Library trends.
+location within the host: Vol. 36, no. 1

[*manifestation* record 1.1]
710 2_ |a University of Illinois at Urbana-Champaign. |b Graduate School of Library and Information Science.
+date: 1987
+extent: 256 p. ; 23 cm.

[*item* record 1.1]
(none)

Host Item
[*work* record 1]
245 00 |a Library trends.
710 2_ |a University of Illinois (Urbana-Champaign campus). |b Library School.
710 2_ |a University of Illinois (Urbana-Champaign campus). |b Graduate School of Library Science.
710 2_ |a University of Illinois at Urbana-Champaign. |b Graduate School of Library Science.
710 2_ |a University of Illinois at Urbana-Champaign. |b Graduate School of Library and Information Science.

```
008 ...c19529999
082 __ |a 020.5
650 _0 |a Library science |x Periodicals.


[ *expression* record 1 ]
245 00 |a Library trends.
310 __ |a Quarterly
362 0_ |a Vol. 1, no. 1 (July 1952)-
008 ...c19529999...qr...eng
500 __ |a Each issue is concerned with one aspect of librarianship, and is planned by an invited guest editor.
500 __ |a Title from cover.
510 1_ |a Library literature |x 0024-2373


[ *manifestation* record 1 ]
260 __ |a Urbana, Ill. : |b University of Illinois Library School, |c 1952-
550 __ |a Issued by: University of Illinois Library School, 1952- ; University of Illinois Graduate School of Library Science; <1961>-fall 1980; University of Illinois Graduate School of Library and Information Science, 1981-
300 __ |a v. ; |c 24 cm.
022 0_ |a 0024-2594


[ *item* record 1 ]
050 00 |a Z671 |b .L6173
991 __ |b c-GenColl |h Z671 |i .L6173 |w SERIALS
```

Figure 4-7. Case 3. An example of a set of records for a document part.

4.5 Modeling of Resources at Aggregate Level

The logical structure of models representing resources at the aggregate level and those at the integral unit level that belong to the aggregate resources is in principle equivalent to the structure of models representing document parts and their host items. The reasons are that (a) a document part is a physically independent resource as its definition shows, and thus is viewed as a resource at the integral unit level, and (b) the host item of a document part is either a single physical object (for example, an offprint of a journal article and its host the issue of the journal containing the article) or more than one physical object (an issue of a journal and its host the whole journal).

Figure 4-8 illustrates the structure for such cases being modeled with the FRBR model. At the left in the figure, a resource at the aggregate level is represented with some attributes. Titles, statements of responsibility, and other attributes of the resource are attributed to *manifestation*. These attribute values are upward pseudo-assigned to the *work* and *expression* instances; this is indicated with an arrow on a dotted line. The *item* is enclosed with braces, since an *item* instance for the resource at that level is not necessary developed. At the right in the figure, a resource at the integral unit level is illustrated; this scheme is equivalent to that for a host item in Figures 4-1 and 4-2. Titles, statements of responsibility, and other attributes of a resource at the integral unit level are associated with *manifestation*. Series statement, which is the only attribute providing information on resources at the aggregate level, is also associated with *manifestation*. However, a series statement is not upward pseudo-assigned to the *work* and *expression* instances, according to FRBR[13]. Moreover, whole/part relationships are assigned to the *work* and *expression* instances, not *manifestation*. We may, at the same time, recall that the *expression* instance lacks a solid and stable basis for its own existence.

In contrast, Figure 4-9 illustrates the structure for those cases when modeled in the text-prioritized model. At the left in the figure, a resource at the aggregate level is represented with some attributes. Titles, statements of responsibility, and others of the resource are associated with *expression*. At the right in the figure, a resource at the integral unit level is represented with some attributes. Both (a) titles, statements of responsibility, and others of a resource at the integral unit level and (b) a series statement, providing information on a resource at the aggregate level, are associated with *expression*. In addition, whole/part relationships are assigned to the *work* and *expression* instances, based on the attributes associated with these entities.

If the structure shown in Figures 4-8 and 4-9 is applied to a case in which a resource at the aggregate level is a serial and that at the integral unit level is either an offprint of an article or an issue of the serial, Figures 4-10 and 4-11 will be obtained.

```
aggregate level                      integral unit level
         whole/part relationship
  work 1 ─────────────────────  work 1.1
    │                                 │
    │        whole/part relationship  │
    expression 1 ──────────────  expression 1.1
    [title]                           [title]
    (none)                            (none)


    manifestation 1                   manifestation 1.1
    title of the resource             title, etc. of the resource
    at the aggregate level            at the integral unit level
    statement of responsibility       series statement
    of the resource at the            (title, etc. of the resource
    aggregate level                    at the aggregate level)
    {item 1}                          item 1.1
```

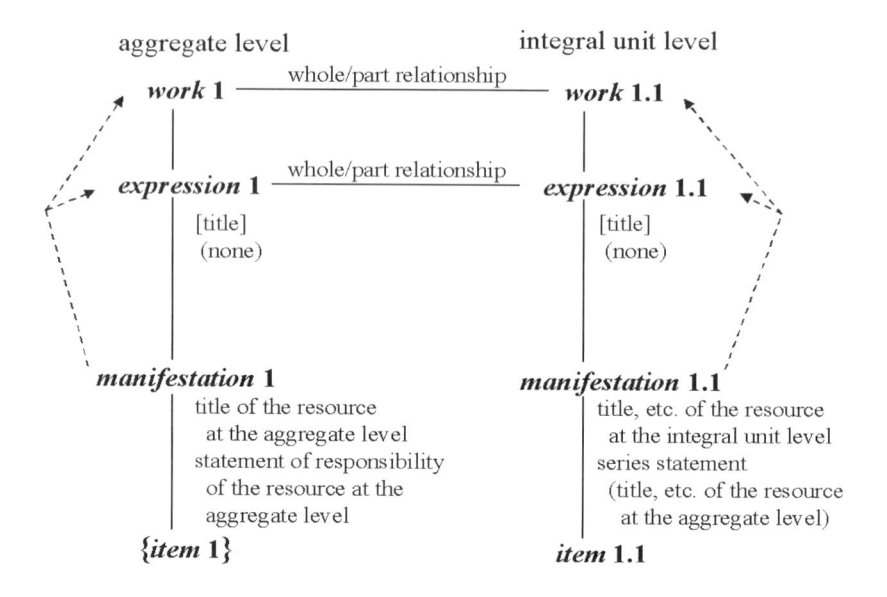

Figure 4-8. Modeling of a resource at the aggregate level in the FRBR model.

```
aggregate level                      integral unit level
            whole/part relationship
    work 1 ─────────────────────  work 1.1
      │  intended termination          │
      │                                │
    expression 1 ──whole/part relationship── expression 1.1
    title of the resource             title, etc. of the resource
    at the aggregate level            at the integral unit level
    statement of responsibility       series statement
    of the resource at the            (title, etc. of the resource
    aggregate level                    at the aggregate level)

    manifestation 1                   manifestation 1.1

    {item 1}                          item 1.1
```

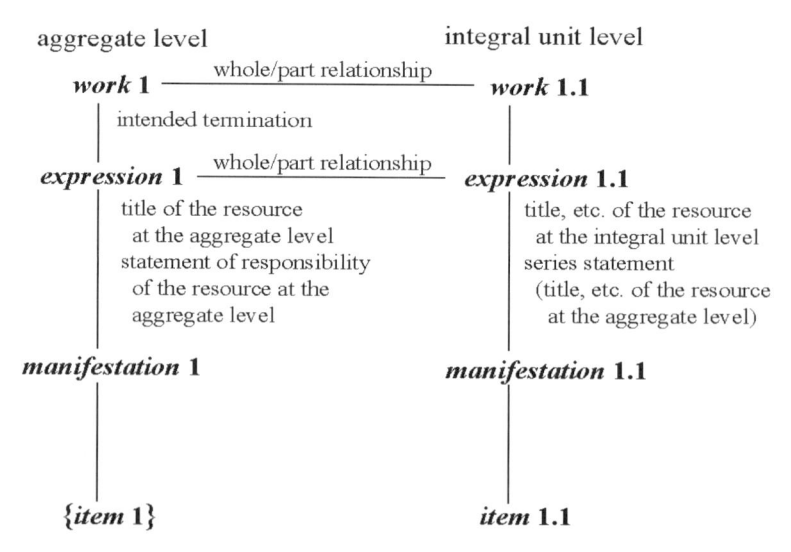

Figure 4-9. Modeling of a resource at the aggregate level in the text- prioritized model.

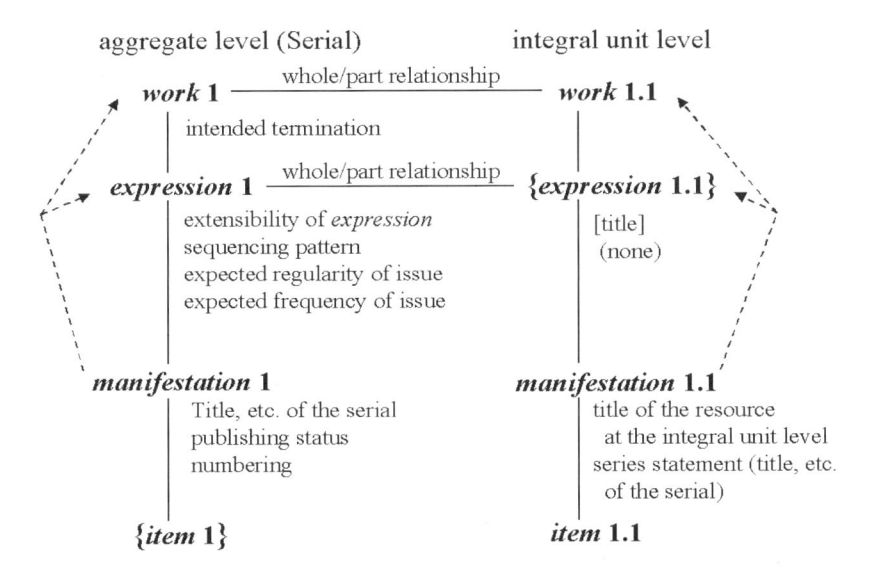

```
aggregate level (Serial)           integral unit level
        whole/part relationship
  work 1 ─────────────────────  work 1.1
     │ intended termination          │
     │      whole/part relationship  │
  expression 1 ─────────────────  {expression 1.1}
     │ extensibility of expression   │ [title]
     │ sequencing pattern            │ (none)
     │ expected regularity of issue  │
     │ expected frequency of issue   │
     │                               │
  manifestation 1                 manifestation 1.1
     │ Title, etc. of the serial     │ title of the resource
     │ publishing status             │ at the integral unit level
     │ numbering                     │ series statement (title, etc.
     │                               │   of the serial)
     │                               │
  {item 1}                        item 1.1
```

Figure 4-10. Modeling of a serial in the FRBR model.

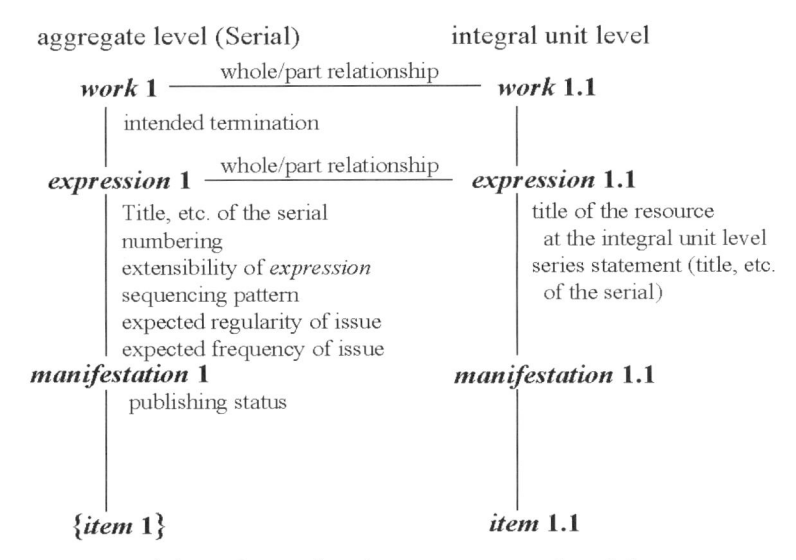

```
aggregate level (Serial)           integral unit level
        whole/part relationship
  work 1 ─────────────────────  work 1.1
     │ intended termination          │
     │      whole/part relationship  │
  expression 1 ─────────────────  expression 1.1
     │ Title, etc. of the serial     │ title of the resource
     │ numbering                     │ at the integral unit level
     │ extensibility of expression   │ series statement (title, etc.
     │ sequencing pattern            │   of the serial)
     │ expected regularity of issue  │
     │ expected frequency of issue   │
  manifestation 1                 manifestation 1.1
     │ publishing status             │
     │                               │
     │                               │
  {item 1}                        item 1.1
```

Figure 4-11. Modeling of a serial in the text-prioritized model.

4.6 Discussion on Consistency in Conceptual Models

FRBR contains the following description:

> The structure of the model, ..., permits us to represent aggregate and component entities in the same way as we would represent entities that are viewed as integral units. ... For the purposes of the model, entities at the aggregate or component level operate in the same way as entities at the integral unit level; they are defined in the same terms, they share the same characteristics, and they are related to one another in the same way as entities at the integral unit level[14].

However, in reality, a content part was modeled as being different from a document part and a host item, i.e., a resource at the integral unit level, as we have seen above.

Loucopoulos and Karakostas have pointed out that 'external consistency' is a desirable property in conceptual models, in addition to 'internal consistency.'[15] Internal consistency (or consistency, merely) has been pointed out many times and widely understood, but external consistency has not. They defined the external consistency as "the agreement between what is stated in the requirements model and what is true in the problem domain"[16]; requirements model here equals a conceptual one.

It is hard to say that the FRBR model violates definitely such external consistency. However, it would be undesirable that different types of resources result in different structures of modeling. I would therefore like to expand the scope of the external consistency to a little extent so as to cover the above issue; different types of resources should be modeled in the same (or, at least, a similar) way.

It would also become a crucial problem when records based on the model are gathered and integrated into a database; an identical expression (i.e., text) could be a content part and, in another case, be a document part, and in a further case, be a document itself.

From the investigations carried out in the present and preceding chapters, we may say the following:

1) The FRBR model, like other models giving primacy to *manifestation*, views

manifestation as the integral (and also inseparable) combination of the intellectual content and the physical form. This view is weak in structuring a resource to be modeled. It is therefore a little difficult for the model to deal with component parts, which are closely related to the structural aspect of a resource, in particular, the intellectual content of a resource at the integral unit level. Actually, *expression* in the model is expected to take a role to control *manifestation* together with *work* and not to 'describe' (e.g., characterize) a resource at that level.

2) The text-level entity *expression* in a model giving primacy to the entity undertakes to describe the structural aspect of the intellectual content, namely, the logical content structure of a resource. *Work* undertakes the semantic aspect of the intellectual content, i.e., abstract intellectual content itself. On the other hand, *manifestation* in the model describes the structural aspect of the physical form, i.e., the physical structure of a resource. Therefore, such a model can deal well with component parts without any difficulties.

4.7 Chapter Conclusion

Two models were examined from the viewpoint of modeling component parts of resources. One is the FRBR model and the other is the text-prioritized model proposed in Chapter 3. As a result, the following was clarified:

1) It is useful and necessary to examine a conceptual model in terms of two types of component parts: a content part and a document part. It is also necessary to compare the resultant structure from modeling a component part with that from a resource at the integral unit level in each model. We can consequently validate consistency of the model.

2) In the FRBR model, a document part and a resource at the integral unit level are modeled basically in the identical way. However, a content part is modeled in a different way from that for the above two types.

3) In the text-prioritized model, those three types of resources are modeled in basically the same manner. This shows an advantage of the model.

It follows from what has been said that (a) bibliographic records for component parts can be created in a consistent manner independent of types of component parts in line with the text-prioritized model, and thus (b) users would be able to have access and use component parts in a more consistent and intelligible manner by means of those records. In other words, the text-prioritized model would provide a solution to issues such as the 'format variations' or 'multiple versions' issue and the 'content versus carrier' issue related to component parts, as well as their host items.

Notes

1 Part of this chapter has already been reported as a paper in *Journal of Documentation*. Taniguchi (2003a)
2 IFLA (1988, p. 2)
3 IFLA (1988, p. 2)
4 Delsey (1998b)
5 Delsey (1998b, p. 8)
6 Delsey (1998b, p. 8)
7 Delsey (1998b, Table.8-1)
8 Delsey (1998b, p. 8)
9 IFLA Study Group on the FRBR (1997, p. 37)
10 Delsey (1998b, 1999)
11 Delsey (1998b, p. 8)
12 Maxwell and Maxwell (1997, p. 300)
13 IFLA Study Group on the FRBR (1997, p. 93)
14 IFLA Study Group on the FRBR (1997, p. 28)
15 Loucopoulos and Karakostas (1995)
16 Loucopoulos and Karakostas (1995, p. 128)

Chapter 5

Trial on Creation of Text-level Entity Records from Pre-existing MARC Records[1]

This chapter aims to investigate the feasibility of creating bibliographic records in accordance with the text-prioritized model, by attempting conversion of existing records. Implementation of the model takes place in two aspects: (a) to create records for newly accepted resources and (b) to convert existing records according to the model. These two aspects, of course, have many features in common; however, the record conversion has usually more difficulties than the other. It is thus worth examining the conversion procedure and also clarifying issues that occur in the conversion process.

First, in this chapter I categorize the methods of creating bibliographic records in terms of the structure of records and then adopt a method that seems to be best for the model. Second, I report on a trial to convert MARC bibliographic records into those structured according to the method adopted, by developing programs to facilitate the conversion. Third, I demonstrate a prototype system to use these structured records after conversion in order to show the usefulness of such records.

5.1 Two Methods of Creating Bibliographic Records in Accordance with Text-prioritized Model

If all possible methods of creating bibliographic records in accordance with the text-prioritized model are taken into account, in terms of the structure under which records are constructed, these methods can be categorized generally into two: (a) single bibliographic record approach and (b) hierarchical multiple records approach. The single record approach aims to create records at the text-level (i.e., the *expression* level) as well as at the work-level, and to include all data elements corresponding to the manifestation in the *expression* level records—in this chapter, the term 'expression level,' instead of 'text level,' is used in order to harmonize with the entity's name 'expression.' This approach does not create separate records for multiple manifestations of the same text and is thus called the single record approach. In contrast, the hierarchical records approach intends to create records at both *expression* and *manifestation* levels, in addition to the *work* level.

For both approaches, the *work* level records are equivalent to uniform title (and name-title) authority records in the current framework. This study does not touch on whether an *item* level record is created corresponding to a holdings record in the current framework—if it is not created, data elements at the *item* level are included in the immediate upper-level record.

A major advantage of the single record approach is it "avoid[s] the creation of full catalog records for each manifestation"[2]. "This is potentially a great time-and money-saver for libraries, especially when the library's clientele is not primarily concerned with the bibliographic details of each manifestation in a library's collection."[3] Another advantage is it "provide[s] very clear displays for users who see all manifestations on the same record display."[4] It "provide[s] an easy way to group (collocate) information about closely related items in a collection, such as known reproductions."[5]

At the same time, several disadvantages of this approach (namely, issues to be resolved) at different levels can be pointed out as follows:

1) Criteria for deciding the unit of (in other words, the boundaries for) the text-level entity *expression* is newly required, since records must be created based on the unit of the entity. The criteria are equivalent to that of the identity for the entity. They must be practical and implementable.

2) Resolve the issue on cardinality between *expression* and *manifestation*, in relation to the aforementioned point. The cardinality between the two is many-to-many and thus, for example, it should be determined how to deal with cases where a single manifestation contains more than one text.

3) Use of available physical objects is required to arrive at a general text description (i.e., information on text) that applies to all manifestations containing identical texts. The gap between levels, in other words, between what is actually available and what is to be described should be wider than before and subject to further revisions and extra cataloging work as subsequent manifestations appear.

4) Expect difficulties with exchanging and sharing records. Libraries do not always have all manifestations of a given text. Automatic merging of records containing data element values representing only some of the manifestations of a

certain text, for example, would be difficult in some cases.

5) Dysjunction between existing records and those newly created occur, if automatic conversion of existing records proves difficult.

On the other hand, advantages and disadvantages of the hierarchical multiple records approach are similar to those of the single record approach, but differences exist:

1) The issue described in 2 above does not apply, since records are created at both the *expression* and *manifestation* levels and thus there is no need to compromise between the units at the two levels.

2) The issue in 4 above also does not apply. In the hierarchical records approach, data element values characterizing each manifestation make an individual *manifestation* level record, which is linked to the *expression* level record. This structure certainly facilitates the exchange and sharing of records; automatic merging, for example, can be implemented more easily.

3) A new issue regarding complexity in managing records by catalogers and systems is added. Also, complexity in the use of records by general users increases when the combination of records at different levels is incorporated.

By comparing these two approaches, I adopted the hierarchical multiple records approach in the trial reported in this chapter, in order to show explicitly the structure of the model on which bibliographic records are based.

Moreover, it was assumed in this trial that it is possible to judge whether texts/expressions are the same by referring to their titles, statements of responsibility, edition statements, and others represented within existing records. In other words, I adopted the criteria of identity for *expression* where two texts/expressions are judged as identical when those data values are basically identical. Creating *work* records is assumed to be optional in this trial; namely, *work* records are created as comprehensive as possible, but in some cases they are not.

5.2 Outline of Conversion Procedure from MARC Bibliographic Records

I conducted a trial to convert existing MARC bibliographic records into those structured under the hierarchical records approach, by developing programs to facilitate this conversion. The aim of the trial was to: (a) clarify the procedure of converting them as automatically as possible, including identifying steps that need to be carried out by human, and (b) identify possible alternatives in each step of the conversion.

Several researches have been conducted on converting existing records or extracting *work* and/or *expression* records from existings[6], although all of these researches were done in the context of FRBR implementation, adopting different records structures from the structure in the present study.

3,705 MARC bibliographic records were obtained from the Library of Congress (LC) Online Catalog with an author search by the heading "Beethoven, Ludwig van, 1770-1827." The intention was to obtain records related to each other in a variety of ways instead of obtaining proper samples statistically. Records coded in the MARC21 format were first converted with the utility software in Perl called 'marc.pl' to text representations that each MARC datafield makes a line.

The records were converted in the following steps:

1) Division of each MARC record into *work*, *expression*, *manifestation*, and *item* level records in accordance with the model.

2) Identification of records at the *work* and *expression* levels which represent the same work or expression and then merging those records.

3) Identification of certain types of relationships between records at the same entity-level and then linking those records.

Programs in Perl were developed to facilitate and support these conversion steps. In the present study, records corresponding to non-bibliographic entities, like *person, corporate body, concept, object*, etc. were not developed; only records corresponding to bibliographic entities were created.

5.3 Dividing MARC Bibliographic Records

5.3.1 Problems Involved in Dividing MARC Records

Dividing MARC records requires mapping of data elements specified in the MARC21 bibliographic format to the entities defined in the model. Such mapping was performed with reference to the efforts by Delsey[7] and LC[8] and, of course, the format specification itself[9].

Delsey carried out a comprehensive study of functional analysis of the current MARC21 bibliographic and holdings formats while being commissioned by LC. The study correlates the MARC data elements with the entities specified in

FRBR and also his analysis on the logical structure of AACR2. Based on Delsey's study, LC made a specification for displaying bibliographic records for multiple manifestations of the same work in a hierarchical manner. The mapping scheme proposed by Delsey and LC, however, was developed in the context of the FRBR model, and thus a full re-examination of the mapping scheme was needed to adapt it to the text-prioritized model.

A general problem in defining the mapping is that the MARC format itself is not based on any conceptual model including FRBR, and there is ambiguity among the four bibliographic entities to be mapped for the many elements specified in the format. This has been pointed out even in the research on FRBR implementation[10]. The mapping in the present study was finally defined after looking into actual data values recorded in individual MARC fields in question. For example, 'date of a work' (tag 700/710/711 subfield code |f) was correlated with *work* in the mapping by Delsey and LC according to its explanation in the format specification. The actual data of most cases, however, were dates when musical works had been performed; it should be mapped to *expression*.

Another problem is the existence of data errors or variations probably caused by changes in rules that instruct manners of recording data values; this is an inevitable problem. For instance, there were many records where no 'relator code' (700/710 |4) was recorded for performers of musical works. There were also many cases where 'type of record' (position 06 in the record leader) and/or 'category of material' (position 00 in tag 007) were not properly coded.

Table 5-1 illustrates the mapping of the data elements of each entity level record to those specified in the MARC21 format when adopting the text-prioritized model. The left column of the table lists, under each entity level record, data elements that were developed basically corresponding to logical attributes defined in the model. The right shows MARC21 field tags and subfield codes (if necessary) that were correlated with the data element on the left.

Figures 5-1, 5-2, and 5-3 demonstrate records created by dividing the MARC records with a program facilitating the mapping shown in Table 5-1. The MARC record with LC control number 09018573 was chosen and divided into multiple records in Figure 5-1—a book, in this case. One record was created at each entity level. In this example, there is no need to modify data values after record division using the program. Each data value mapped to either record is shown with the data element label and the MARC21 field tag, indicator, and subfield code. The record identifier—w-no, e-no, m-no, or i-no—was automatically assigned to individual records created through the MARC record division. This identifier was used for linking records, e.g., the 'linked w-no: w02629' in the *expression* level record whose e-no is e00617 indicates the link between the *expression* and the *work* having that w-no.

Figure 5-2 demonstrates another example using the MARC record with LC control number 00587344, which is a sound recording. The style in the figure is the same as that in Figure 5-1. In this case, there however are several data values that need to be modified manually; asterisks preceding data element labels indicate such values in the figure. Figure 5-3 also demonstrates another example of sound recordings, of which LC control number is 99592154.

Table 5-1. Mapping of data elements in line with the text-prioritized model to MARC21 data elements.

Data element in line with the model	MARC21 data element
Work	
Title	Main work: 130/240/243 |a, |n, |p, |m, |r, |k, |s or 245 |a, |n, |p (except musical work) Additional work: 700/710/711 |t, |n, |p, |m, |r, |k, |s 730(indicator02=2) |a, |t, |n, |p, |m, |r, |k, |s 740(indicator02=2) |a, |n, |p
Responsibility	Main work: 100/110/111 Additional work: 700/710/711 (excluding |t, |n, |p, |m, |r, |k, |s)
Date	Main work: 045
Form	Main work: 047, 048, LDR/06, Music:008/18-19
Coordinates	Main work: 034 (excluding |b, |c, |h), 255 |c, |e
Subject	Main work: 080, 082, 6XX

Chapter 5 Trial on Creation of Text-level Entity Records from Pre-existing MARC Records   137

Expression	
Title	245 (excluding |c)
	242, 246, 247, 730/740(indicator02 ≠ 2)
Responsibility	245/242 |c, 511
	100/110/111 (unless main work is developed)
	700/710/711 (unless additional work is developed)
Edition	250
Date	008:06-14, 033, 518, 130/240/243 |d, |f
Form	LDR/06
	047, 048, LDR/06, Music:008/18-19 (unless main work is developed)
Language	130/240/243 |l, 546, 041, 008/35-37
Score type	254, Music:008/20
Other characteristics	130/240/243/ |o
Summarization	505, 520
Series	440, 490, 800, 810, 811, 830
Extent	256, 306, 500
Scale	034 |b, |c, |h, 255 (excluding |c, |e)
Numbering (serial)	362
Others	500, 501, 502, 504, 507, 508, 510, 513, 514, 515, 516, 521, 522, 525, 545, 547, 555, 556, 567, 580, 584, 586
Subject	080, 082, 6XX (unless main work is developed)
Manifestation	
Publisher	260 |a, |b, |e, |f
Date	260 |c, |g
Form	245 |h, LDR/06
Extent	007, 300
Identifier	020, 022, 024, 027, 028, 030, 074
Others	500, 506, 524, 530, 533, 534, 535, 536, 538, 540, 550, 565, 581
Item	
Identifier	050, 051
Others	541, 544, 561, 562, 583, 585

[*work* record 1]

w-no: w02629

LCCN: 010 |a   09018573

title: 240 10|aCorrespondence.

responsibility: 100 1 |aBeethoven, Ludwig van,|d1770-1827.

subject: 600 10|aBeethoven, Ludwig van,|d1770-1827|xCorrespondence.

subject: 650 0|aComposers|zAustria|xCorrespondence.

[*expression* record 1]

e-no: e00617

linked w-no: w02629

LCCN: 010 |a   09018573

title: 245 10|aBeethoven's letters :|ba critical edition

responsibility: 245 10|cwith explanatory notes by A.C. Kalischer ; translated with preface by J.S. Shedlock.

responsibility: 700 1 |aKalischer, Alfred Christlieb,|d1842-1909.

responsibility: 700 1 |aShedlock, J. S.|q(John South),|d1843-1919.

date: 008/06-14 s1909

form: LDR/06 a{alpha-numeric notation}

language: 240 10|lEnglish

language: 008/35-37 eng

language: 041 1 |aeng|hger

[*manifestation* record 1]

m-no: m00583

linked e-no: e00617

LCCN: 010 |a   09018573

publisher: 260 |aLondon :|bJ.M. Dent ;|aNew York :|bE.P. Dutton,

date: 260 |c1909.

form: LDR/06 a{book}

extent: 300 |a2 v. :|bill. ;|c24 cm.

others: 500 |aIncludes indexes.

[*item* record 1]
i-no: i00583
linked m-no: m00583
LCCN: 010 |a 09018573
identifier: 050 00|aML410.B4|bA23.S5 1909

Figure 5-1. An example of a set of records created through the MARC record division. A case of book.

[*work* record 1]
w-no: w02747
LCCN: 010 |a 00587344
title: 240 10|aConcertos,|mpiano trio, orchestra,|nop. 56,|rC major.
responsibility: 100 1 |aBeethoven, Ludwig van,|d1770-1827.
form: LDR/06 j{musical work}
form: 008/18-19 co
subject: 650 0|aConcertos (Piano trio)
*subject: 650 0|aConcertos (Violin and violoncello)

[*work* record 2]
w-no: w02746
LCCN: 010 |a 00587344
title: 700 12|tConcertos,|mviolin, violoncello, orchestra,|nop. 102,|rA minor.
responsibility: 700 12|aBrahms, Johannes,|d1833-1897.
form: LDR/06 j{musical work}

[*expression* record 1]
e-no: e00685
*linked w-no: w02746
linked w-no: w02747
LCCN: 010 |a 00587344
title: 245 10|aConcerto en do maj., op. 56.
responsibility: 245 10|cBeethoven.
responsibility: 511 0 |aHenryk Szeryng, violinist ; Fournier, violoncellist ; Megaloff, pianist (1st work) ; Orchestre del la Suisse Romande ; Samuel Baud-Bovy, conductor.

responsibility: 700 1 |aSzeryng, Henryk.|4prf
responsibility: 700 1 |aFournier, Pierre,|d1906-|4prf
responsibility: 700 1 |aBaud-Bovy, Samuel,|d1906-|4cnd
responsibility: 710 2 |aOrchestre de la Suisse romande.|4prf
responsibility: 710 2 |aRadio Suisse romande.
date: 008/06-14 s1968
date: 518 |aOriginally recorded for Radio Suisse romande, probably in 1968.
form: LDR/06 j{musical sound}
extent: 306 |a003406
extent: 500 |aDurations: 34:06.

[*expression* record 2]
e-no: e00686
linked w-no: w02746
*linked w-no: w02747
LCCN: 010 |a 00587344
title: 245 10Concerto en la min, op. 102.
responsibility: 245 10Brahms.
*responsibility: 511 0 |aHenryk Szeryng, violinist ; Fournier, violoncellist ; Megaloff, pianist (1st work) ; Orchestre del la Suisse Romande ; Samuel Baud-Bovy, conductor.
responsibility: 700 1 |aSzeryng, Henryk.|4prf
responsibility: 700 1 |aFournier, Pierre,|d1906-|4prf
responsibility: 700 1 |aBaud-Bovy, Samuel,|d1906-|4cnd
responsibility: 710 2 |aOrchestre de la Suisse romande.|4prf
responsibility: 710 2 |aRadio Suisse romande.
date: 008/06-14 s1968
date: 518 |aOriginally recorded for Radio Suisse romande, probably in 1968.
form: LDR/06 j{musical sound}
extent: 306 |a003106
extent: 500 |aDurations: 31:06.

[*manifestation* record 1]
m-no: m00646
linked e-no: e00685

Chapter 5 Trial on Creation of Text-level Entity Records from Pre-existing MARC Records   141

linked e-no: e00686
LCCN: 010 |a 00587344
publisher: 260 |a1968.
form: LDR/06 j{musical sound recording}
form: 245 10|h[sound recording]
extent: 007 ss|l|njlbunnue
extent: 300 |a1 sound cassette :|banalog.
others: 524 |aHenryk Szeryng Audio Materials (Library of Congress).
*others: 533 |aPlayback copy.|bWashington, D.C. :|cLibrary of Congress Recording Laboratory,|d2000.|eOn 1 sound cassette : digital.
*others: 533 |aPreservation master.|bWashington, D.C. :|cLibrary of Congress Recording Laboratory,|d2000.|eOn 1 sound tape reel : analog, 7 1/2 ips, 2 track, mono. ; 10 in.

[*item* record 1]
i-no: i00646
linked m-no: m00646
LCCN: 010 |a 00587344
identifier: 050 00|aRYI 3951
identifier: 050 00|aRGA **** (playback copy)
identifier: 050 00|aRW* **** (preservation master)
others: 541 |aTransferred from the Library of Congress Music Division, Nov. 16, 1992.

Figure 5-2. An example of a set of records created through the MARC record division. A case of sound recording.

[*expression* record 1]
e-no: e04100
LCCN: 010 |a 99592154
title: 245 00|aClassical hits
responsibility: 110 2 |aOrpheus Chamber Orchestra.
responsibility: 511 0 |aOrpheus Chamber Orchestra.
responsibility: 700 1 |aHaydn, Joseph,|d1732-1809.
responsibility: 700 1 |aGluck, Christoph Willibald,|bRitter von,|d1714-1787.

responsibility: 700 1 |aHaydn, Michael,|d1737-1806.
responsibility: 700 1 |aBoccherini, Luigi,|d1743-1805.
responsibility: 700 1 |aMozart, Wolfgang Amadeus,|d1756-1791.
responsibility: 700 1 |aBeethoven, Ludwig van,|d1770-1827.
responsibility: 700 1 |aMendelssohn-Bartholdy, Felix,|d1809-1847.
responsibility: 700 1 |aSchubert, Franz,|d1797-1828.
responsibility: 710 2 |aPolyGram Records.
date: 008/06-14 s1993
form: LDR/06 j{musical sound}
summarization: 505 0 |aString Quartet in F major, Hob. III:17 : (1) Andante cantabile ("Serenade") (3:16) / Joseph Haydn -- Orphee et Eurydice : (2) Dance of the Furies (4:04) ; (3) Dance of the Blessed Spirits (6:10) / Christoph Willibald Gluck -- Notturno in F major : (4) Adagio (6:48) / Michael Haydn -- String Quintet in E major, G 281 : (5) Menuetto (3:24) / Luigi Boccherini -- Eline kleine Nachtmusik in G major : (6) Romance (5:46) / Wolfgang Amadeus Mozart -- The creatures of Prometheus, op. 43 : (7) Finale (6:28) / Ludwig van Beethoven -- A midsummer night's dream : (8) Intermezzo (3:21) ; (9) Notturno (5:59) / Felix Mendelssohn -- Rosamunde, D 797 : (10) No. 5 Entr'acte (6:32) ; (11) No. 6 Shepherd's melodies (1:29) ; (12) No. 9 Ballet II (6:27) ; (13) No. 2 Ballet (part 2) (3:49) / Franz Schubert.
subject: 650 0|aOrchestral music.

[*manifestation* record 1]
m-no: m03481
linked e-no: e04100
LCCN: 010 |a 99592154
publisher: 260 |aHamburg :|bDeutsche Grammophon,
date: 260 |c1993.
form: LDR/06 j{musical sound recording}
form: 245 00|h[sound recording]
extent: 007 sdufzngnn-----
extent: 300 |a1 sound disc (63:33) :|bdigital ;|c4 3/4 in.
identifier: 028 01|a437 782-2|bDeutsche Grammophon
others: 500 |aProgram notes included on insert.
others: 538 |aCompact disc (DDD).

[*item* record 1]
i-no: i03481
linked m-no: m03481
LCCN: 010 |a 99592154
identifier: 050 00|aDeutsche Grammophon 437 782-2

Figure 5-3. An example of a set of records created through the MARC record division. Another case of sound recording.

5.3.2 Work level Records

It is worth discussing extraction and development of *work* level records in detail, since they affect those of *expressions*.

A main *work* represented as the main entry heading in an individual MARC record was usually extracted and developed as a *work* record if tag 130 (main entry—uniform title) appeared, or if tag 100/110/111 (main entry—name heading) together with tag 240/243 (uniform title) or 245 (title proper, etc.) appeared. In the case of tag 245, it was used only when 240/243 did not appear. In case of musical work, however, tag 245 was not used for developing a *work* record; namely, if tag 240/243 did not appear, such a *work* record was not created. The reason was that almost all cases lacking tag 240/243 seemed to be collections of various musical works and therefore were not worth developing *work* records. Both examples of Figures 5-1 and 5-2 are cases of having tags 240 and 100. In contrast, the example of Figure 5-3 is a case of not creating any *work* record.

It is, of course, possible to not use tag 245 in any case. Collocating *expression* level records, however, will not be achieved in this case, since comprehensive development of *work* records and the merging of those records enable collocation of *expressions* via links between a *work* and its *expressions* under the records structure adopted in this study. In contrast, another alternative is to develop a *work* record in all cases; a *work* record is created with a title and a statement of responsibility in the field of tag 245, when any main entry heading, i.e., a name or a uniform title does not appear.

Data values comprising a *work* title were limited to the subfields listed in Table 5-1 and the others were omitted. Data values of other elements such as date and form were extracted from the record leader (its position 06), a fixed coded field (tag 008), and some variable datafields (045, 047, 048). Classification codes (tags 050

|a, 080, 082) and subject headings (tag 6XX) were mapped to the element 'subject' of a *work* record developed according to the above policy. When such a *work* was not developed, form and subject data values were assigned to an *expression* level record, as shown in Figure 5-3.

In addition to a *work* record based on the main entry heading, additional *work* records were developed, by extracting from added entry headings in the same MARC record. The condition for creating such records was: (a) appearance of tag 700/710/711 (added entry—name heading) containing subfield |t (title), or (b) tag 730/740 (added entry—title) with a second indicator value of 2. If the MARC format specification is followed rigidly for the former case, only tag 700/710/711 with second indicator 2 will be an analytical entry, which means a *work* independent of the main *work* extracted from the same MARC record. The proposal by LC[11] follows this specification. However, actual data observed in either field with second indicator blank (i.e., not 2) is apparently viewed as analytical entries without any problem. Therefore, the above policy was adopted. Furthermore, any relationship, such as whole/part or others, was not developed between the additional *works* and main *work* extracted from the same MARC record.

Figure 5-2 shows an example of such an additional *work* record developed using tag 700. Additional *works* had limited data elements like title, responsibility designation, and form. The element 'subject' was not assigned, since it is impossible to judge mechanically which classification code(s) and subject heading(s) is proper for each additional *work*. In the example shown in the figure, the second subject element with tag 650 in the main *work* should be moved to the additional *work* according to the meaning that the subject heading represents; the asterisk indicates this point.

5.3.3 Expression level Records

The most significant difference between mapping in Table 5-1 and those by Delsey and LC is found in mapping for *expression* and *manifestation* level records. It is derived directly from the difference between the text-prioritized model and FRBR. Titles, statements of responsibility, etc., that appear in an item were attributed to the *expression* record in accordance with the text-prioritized model, whereas they were correlated with the *manifestation* in FRBR. Table 5-1 indicates that tags 242, 245, 246, and 247 are titles and responsibility designations in an *expression*.

The mapping of other data elements is:

1) Edition statement (tag 250) was mapped to the *expression* record, including improper cases where a statement indicated only a difference in form—it is difficult to distinguish such cases from others in a mechanical manner.

2) Date of *expression* was extracted from various fields like tags 008 (positions 06-14), 033, 518, and 130/240/243 |d and |f. In case of musical work, date from these fields was the date of performance or arrangement of a musical work. Language was also extracted from various fields.

3) Form of *expression* was extracted from the record leader (position 06) in a similar way to that for the form of *work*.

4) Summarization was correlated with the formatted contents note (tag 505) and the summary, etc. note (520).

5) Series statement (tags 440, 490) and series added entry (800, 810, 811, 830) were assigned to the *expression* record in line with the model.

6) Extent of *expression* included computer file characteristics (tag 256) and playing time (306). General note (tag 500) of which value began with a word 'duration' was also extracted as the extent of *expression*.

7) An element 'others' was developed to accommodate various data values that should be attributed to the *expression* record but are not mapped to the other elements of the *expression*. At the current stage, more than half of 5XX fields were tentatively mapped to the element 'others,' as shown in Table 5-1. General note (500) whose value contained a keyword like 'title from,' 'recorded,' or 'performed' was also assigned to the element.

8) All data values discussed on *work* records were assigned to *expression* records, when the main *work* record was not developed.

Another significant difference between this study and others so far is the attempts on division of a MARC record into multiple *expressions* in certain cases. All other studies need not attempt this, since they adopted FRBR, which gives primacy to *manifestation*, and existing MARC records are made usually based on the unit of *manifestation*. In contrast, if the text-prioritized model is followed, the unit of *expression* should be adopted as the unit for generating an *expression* level record. Furthermore, in this study, it was assumed that *expressions* are identical unless some clues external to, and accompanying, the *expressions* show their differences. In other words, it is possible to extract and divide *expressions* with reference to such clues.

The boundaries for *expression*, however, are represented in several but not obvious ways in MARC records. A method to divide a MARC record of which tag 245 contains more than one title proper (and corresponding statement of responsibility, if any) and develop an *expression* record corresponding to an individual title proper was adopted. This is a case of an item without a collective title. That division was carried out using a program that interprets occurrence patterns of punctuation marks specified in the cataloging rules. Actual patterns however were relatively complex; the field consists of several subfields (e.g., parallel title, other title information) and also patterns change vastly depending on whether those expressions within an item were realized by the same person(s) or body(bodies), or by different ones. Moreover, errors in punctuation usage were involved in some cases.

The MARC record used in Figure 5-2 was an example of which tag 245 contained two pairs of a title and a statement of responsibility. The original data value in the field was "245 10|aConcerto en do maj., op. 56|h[sound recording] /|cBeethoven. Concerto en la min, op. 102 / Brahms." The figure shows two *expressions* developed through the record division with a program.

Other element values, except for duration from tags 306 and 500, were not divided and were all assigned to each individual *expression* created from the same MARC record. The reason is that it was extremely difficult to divide those values properly and to identify mechanically a corresponding *expression* for each individual value after the division. Such data values therefore require manual modification. For example, in Figure 5-2, the responsibility designation from tag 511 in the second *expression* record contains the name of a pianist irrelevant to the *expression*.

Besides, such division based on tag 245 leads to another issue; there is a need for each individual *expression* after the division to identify a corresponding *work* among those created from the same MARC record and then to link them. It is too difficult to implement this procedure as a program, since titles and others are usually different in form between the field 245 and the main and added entry headings. In the example of Figure 5-2, each *expression* contains two link indications to a *work* record, namely, 'linked w-no:' which the program assigned automatically in the process of record division. Improper link indications need to be deleted in manual operations.

Alternative (or additional) ways to divide a MARC record into multiple *expressions* would be to use the formatted contents note (tag 505) and/or 'with' note (501). However, in practice, information on each individual expression (e.g., date, extent, etc.) extracted from such fields is usually not recorded sufficiently in a MARC record. An example of the formatted contents note is shown in Figure 5-3.

5.3.4 Manifestation and Item level Records

The mapping scheme for *expression* level records discussed above necessarily defines fields to be mapped to *manifestation* records. Data elements mapped to *manifestation* were limited to those such as publisher/distributor (tag 260 |a, |b, |e, |f), date of publication/distribution (260 |c, |g), form of carrier (245 |h, position 06 in the record leader), extent of carrier (007, 300), and identifier (020, 022, etc.). Such limited mapping is significantly different from those by Delsey and LC. In addition to these fields, various 5XX note fields except for those assigned to *expression* were mapped to *manifestation*.

A *manifestation* record was developed for each MARC record, since an individual MARC record is supposed to be created at the *manifestation* level, namely, on the unit of *manifestation*.

Likewise, only some fields in a MARC record were mapped to *item* level records—tags 050 and 051 for identifier and some of 5XX for the element 'others.' In some cases a MARC record contained description for more than one item (i.e., copy). For example, tags 533 and 050 in Figure 5-2—the former tag was mapped to *manifestation* and the latter to *item*–indicate the holdings of two other copies in LC—one is a playback copy and the other a preservation master. Such data values may be modified and multiple *item* level records also developed, if necessary.

As a result of dividing 3,705 MARC bibliographic records with the program, 11,328 *work* level records, 4,372 *expressions*, 3,705 *manifestations*, and 3,705 *items* were obtained. It can thus be said that the program achieved reasonable success in dividing MARC records but it still needs to be elaborated.

5.4 Merging Divided Records and Developing Relationships

The second step of the conversion from MARC records is to merge records at the *work* and *expression* levels that were created through MARC record division and represent the same *work* or *expression*. This step consists of the following four sub-steps:

Sub-step 1: A key for finding candidate records to be merged was assigned to individual *work* and *expression* level records with a program. The key for a *work* record was constructed by concatenating a primary author with a primacy title after normalization. The primary author was assumed to be one that appeared first among responsibility designations in the record. The primary title was also assumed in a similar way. The author and title chosen were normalized according to NACO Authority File Comparison Rules[12] to delete content designators, punctuation marks, diacritics, etc. They are controlled as headings (or part of headings) except titles from tag 245 and therefore finding candidate records by comparing keys was useful and successful.

The followings are examples of the assigned key for a *work* record; the key for the *work* shown in Figure 5-1 and the keys for the two *works* in Figure 5-2, respectively:

[w02629]: beethoven, ludwig van. correspondence.
[w02747]: beethoven, ludwig van. concertos, pianotrio, orchestra, op. 56, c major.
[w02746]: brahms, johannes. concertos, violin, violoncello, orchestra, op. 102, a minor.

For *expression* records, in contrast, it is relatively difficult to automate the finding of candidate records. The key for an *expression* was constructed by concatenating a title that appeared first in the record (usually a title proper in tag 245) with all responsibility designations (including 245 |c and 511), and edition designation (250) if any. That key was normalized in the same way as that for the key for a *work*. Tag 511 was included since, in many cases, 245 |c did not contain the names of performers in sound recording. Tags 700 and 710, instead of 511, could be used if those tags including subfield |4 (relator code) are comprehensively recorded. Titles and others extracted from those fields chosen were all free-text descriptions, including transcription from the prescribed source of information. The keys based on these descriptions therefore were not suitable for algorithmic record grouping and were used only for listing nearby records.

The followings are the assigned keys for the *expressions* in Figures 5-1, 5-2, and 5-3, respectively:

[e00617]: beethovens letters : a critical edition / with explanatory notes by
   a.c. kalischer ; translated with preface by j.s. shedlock.
[e00685]: concerto en do maj, op. 56 / beethoven. henryk szeryng, violinist ;
   fournier, violoncellist ; megaloff, pianist (1st work) ; orchestre del
   la suisse romande ; samuel baud-bovy, conductor.
[e00686]: concerto en la min, op. 102 / brahms. henryk szeryng, violinist ;
   fournier, violoncellist ; megaloff, pianist (1st work) ; orchestre del
   la suisse romande ; samuel baud-bovy, conductor.
[e04100]: classical hits / orpheus chamber orchestra.

Sub-step 2: Lists showing possible candidate records to be merged were compiled through mechanical sorting with keys. Other lists also showed all *works* and *expressions* in a brief manner after sorting them with their keys, thereby showing nearby records. Other types of lists can be compiled if necessary.

Sub-step 3: These lists were checked manually to determine whether the candidate records were suitable for merger. Indication of addition of records to be merged and deletion of records from the candidates was added to the list files.

Sub-step 4: The record merge was carried out using a program while referring to the list files that had been validated and modified manually. During the merge, data values were unified which were the same including tag, indicator, and subfield code in the merged records. Data values of which only certain parts of these content designators were different remained as different values. The intention was to show all occurrence patterns of data values, thereby validating the record division and merge. Examples of *work* records after the merge are shown in Figures 5-4, 5-5, and 5-6; the first example is the record after merging the *work* in Figure 5-1, the second is that incorporating the first *work* in Figure 5-2, and the third is a different example of musical work that merged many records. Likewise, examples of *expression* records after the merge are shown in Figure 5-7—the first example in the figure is the record after merging the *expression* in Figure 5-1. After loading records into a database, it is of course possible to merge records individually with a function of the database management system.

As a result of the record merge, the number of *work* records decreased to 5,008 and that of *expressions* also decreased to 4,248; but I am still in the process of finding records to be merged.

The third step of the conversion from MARC records is to develop relationships among records at the same level and link them. This step was manually done; no program to support finding relationships among records has been developed yet. It would be relatively difficult to develop such a program, since clues to find records related to each other are scattered over most data elements including 'others' within a record and also shown in various styles in an individual element. Figure 5-8 shows two *work* records that were identified as those having relationships with the record shown in Figure 5-4. Similarly, Figure 5-9 shows four *work* records that have relationships among them.

---

w-no: w02627

other w-no: w02522

other w-no: w02523

other w-no: w02538

other w-no: w02539

other w-no: w02620

other w-no: w02628

...

LCCN: 010 |a 03016279

LCCN: 010 |a 03024854

LCCN: 010 |a 04005589

LCCN: 010 |a 05015883

LCCN: 010 |a 07030417

LCCN: 010 |a 07030418

...

title: 240 00|aCorrespondence.

title: 240 10|aCorrespondence.

title: 245 00|aBeethoven's letters.

title: 245 00|aBeethovens sämtliche briefe.
title: 245 00|aBriefe Beethovens.
title: 245 00|aBriefe.
title: 245 00|aDrei und achtzig neu aufgefundene Original-Briefe Ludwig van Beethoven's an den Erzherzog Rudolph. Cardinalerzbieshof von Olmütz K.H.
title: 245 00|aLetters.
title: 245 00|aLudwig van Beethovens sämtliche Briefe und Aufzeichnungen.
title: 245 00|aNeue briefe Beethovens.
title: 245 00|aNew Beethoven letters.
title: 245 10|aBeethoven intimo.
title: 245 10|aBeethoven letters in America.
title: 245 10|aBeethoven-Briefe an Nicolaus Simrock, F. G. Wegeler, Eleonore v. Breuning und Ferf. Ries.
title: 245 10|aBeethoven-Briefe.
title: 245 10|aBeethovens Briefe.
title: 245 10|aNeue Beethovenbriefe.
title: 245 13|aLe lettere di Beethoven.
title: 245 14|aDer Briefwechsel mit dem Verlag Schott.
title: 700 1 |tLetter [1825 Aug., Baden, Austria] to Karl Holz [Vienna] [from old catalog]
responsibility: 100 1 |aBeethoven, Ludwig van,|d1770-1827.
responsibility: 700 1 |aBeethoven, Ludwig van,|d1770-1827.
subject: 082 |a927.8
subject: 082 00|a780/.92/4
subject: 082 00|a780/.92/4|219
subject: 082 00|a780/.92/4|aB
subject: 082 00|a780/.924
subject: 082 00|a780/.924|aB
subject: 082 00|a780/.92|aB|221
subject: 600 00|aRudolph,|cArchduke of Austria, Abp. of Olmütz,|d1788-1831.
subject: 600 00|aRudolph,|cArchduke of Austria,|d1788-1831|xCorrespondence.
subject: 600 10|aBeethoven, Ludwig van,|d1770-1827.
subject: 600 10|aBeethoven, Ludwig van,|d1770-1827|xCorrespondence.
subject: 610 20|aB. Schott's Söhne (Mainz, Rhineland-Palatinate, Germany)

subject: 650 0|aComposers|xCorrespondence.
subject: 650 0|aComposers|zAustria|xCorrespondence.

Figure 5-4. A merged record at the *work* level.

w-no: w02747
other w-no: w02765
other w-no: w02770
other w-no: w02771
other w-no: w02772
other w-no: w02774
other w-no: w03306
...
LCCN: 010 |a 00587344
LCCN: 010 |a 00718135
LCCN: 010 |a 85750698
LCCN: 010 |a 86754225
LCCN: 010 |a 86754876
LCCN: 010 |a 88750099
...
title: 240 00|aConcertos,|mpiano trio, orchestra,|nop. 56,|rC major.
title: 240 10|aConcertos,|mpiano trio, orchestra,|nop. 56,|rC major.
title: 700 12|tConcertos,|mpiano trio, orchestra,|nop. 56,|rC major.
responsibility: 100 1 |aBeethoven, Ludwig van,|d1770-1827.
responsibility: 700 12|aBeethoven, Ludwig van,|d1770-1827.
date: 045 0 |bd1804
form: 008/18-19 co
form: 008/18-19 mu
form: 047 |aco|aft
form: 048 |bka01|aca06|aoa
form: 048 |bka01|bsa01|bsc01|aoa
form: 048 |bsa01|bsc01|bka01|aoa
form: 048 |bva01|bvb01|bvc01|bvd01|bve01|bvf01|bka01|aca04|aoa
form: LDR/06 c{musical work}
form: LDR/06 j{musical work}

subject: 650 0|aChoruses, Secular (Mixed voices) with orchestra.
subject: 650 0|aChoruses, Secular (Mixed voices) with orchestra|vScores.
subject: 650 0|aConcertos (Piano trio)
subject: 650 0|aConcertos (Piano trio)|vScores.
subject: 650 0|aConcertos (Piano trio)|xScores.
subject: 650 0|aConcertos (Piano trio)|xSolos with piano.
subject: 650 0|aConcertos (Violin and violoncello)
subject: 650 0|aConcertos (Violin)
subject: 650 0|aConcertos (Violoncello)
subject: 650 0|aPiano with orchestra.
subject: 650 0|aPiano with orchestra|vScores.

Figure 5-5. Another merged record at the *work* level. Case of musical work.

w-no: w00460
other w-no: w00346
other w-no: w00949
other w-no: w01588
other w-no: w02416
other w-no: w02742
other w-no: w02803
...
LCCN: 010 |a 00716341
LCCN: 010 |a 00716520
LCCN: 010 |a 00717529
LCCN: 010 |a 00727787
LCCN: 010 |a 68130324
LCCN: 010 |a 70751173
...
title: 240 00|aConcerto, piano, mo. 4, op. 58, G major. [from old catalog]
title: 240 00|aConcerto, piano, no. 4, op. 58, G major. [from old catalog]
title: 240 00|aConcerto, piano, no. 4. op. 58. G major. [from old catalog]
title: 240 00|aConcerto,|mpiano,|nno. 4, op. 58,|rG major [from old catalog]
title: 240 00|aConcerto,|mpiano,|nno. 4, op. 58,|rG major. [from old catalog]
title: 240 10|aConcertos,|mpiano, orchestra,|nno. 4, op. 58,|rG major.

title: 700 1 |tConcerto, piano, no. 4, op. 58, G major.

title: 700 1 |tConcerto, piano, no. 4, op. 58, G major. [from old catalog]

title: 700 1 |tConcerto, piano, no. 4, op. 58. G major. [from old catalog]

title: 700 1 |t[Concerto, piano no. 4, op. 58, G major. [from old catalog]

title: 700 12|tConcerto, piano, no. 4, op. 58, G major. [from old catalog]

title: 700 12|tConcerto,|mpiano,|nno. 4, op. 58,|rG major.

title: 700 12|tConcertos,|mpiano, orchestra,|nno. 4, op. 58,|rG major.

responsibility: 100 1 |aBeethoven, Ludwig van,|d1770-1827.

responsibility: 100 1 |aBeethoven, Ludwig van,|d1770-1827. [from old catalog]

responsibility: 700 1 |aBeethoven, Ludwig van,|d1770-1827.

responsibility: 700 1 |aBeethoven, Ludwig van,|d1770-1827.|h[Sound recording] [from old catalog]

responsibility: 700 1 |aBeethoven, Ludwig,|cvan,|d1770-1827.

responsibility: 700 12|aBeethoven, Ludwig van,|d1770-1827.

responsibility: 700 12|aBeethoven, Ludwig van,|d1770-1827. [from old catalog]

date: 045 0 |bd1806

date: 045 1 |bd1805|bd1845

form: 008/18-19 co

form: 008/18-19 m

form: 008/18-19 mu

form: 008/18-19 uu

form: 048 |bka01|aoa

form: LDR/06 a{musical work}

form: LDR/06 c{musical work}

form: LDR/06 j{musical work}

subject: 650 0|aConcertos (Piano)

subject: 650 0|aConcertos (Piano) [from old catalog]

subject: 650 0|aConcertos (Piano)|x2-piano scores.

subject: 650 0|aOvertures. [from old catalog]

subject: 650 0|aPiano music. [from old catalog]

subject: 650 0|aRondos (Piano with orchestra) [from old catalog]

subject: 650 0|aRondos (Piano) [from old catalog]

subject: 650 0|aSonatas (Piano) [from old catalog]

subject: 650 0|aSymphonies.

subject: 650 0|aVariations (Piano)
subject: 650 0|aVariations (Piano) [from old catalog]

Figure 5-6. Another merged record at the *work* level. Case of musical work.

e-no: e00617
other e-no: e00618
linked w-no: w02629
linked w-no: w02630
LCCN: 010 |a   09018573
LCCN: 010 |a   74102225
title: 245 00|aBeethoven's letters;|ba critical edition with explanatory notes,
title: 245 10|aBeethoven's letters :|ba critical edition
responsibility: 245 00|cby Alf C. Kalischer. Translated with pref. by J. S. Shedlock.
responsibility: 245 10|cwith explanatory notes by A.C. Kalischer ; translated with preface by J.S. Shedlock.
responsibility: 700 1 |aKalischer, Alfred Christlieb,|d1842-1909.
responsibility: 700 1 |aShedlock, J. S.|q(John South),|d1843-1919,|etr.
responsibility: 700 1 |aShedlock, J. S.|q(John South),|d1843-1919.
date: 008/06-14 r19691909
date: 008/06-14 s1909
form: LDR/06 a{alpha-numeric notation}
language: 008/35-37 eng
language: 041 1 |aengger
language: 041 1 |aeng|hger
language: 240 10|lEnglish
series: 490 0 |aSelect bibliographies reprint series

e-no: e00616
other e-no: e00615
linked w-no: w02627
linked w-no: w02628
LCCN: 010 |a   76022344
LCCN: 010 |a   77114868
title: 245 00|aBeethoven's letters (1790-1826) from the collection of Dr. Ludwig

Nohl,|balso his letters to the Archduke Rudolph, Cardinal-Archbishop of Olmqdz, K. W., from the collection of Dr. Ludwig Ritter von K · hel.

title: 245 10|aBeethoven's letters (1790-1826) from the collection of Dr. Ludwig Nohl :|balso his letters to the Archduke Rudolph, Cardinal-Archbishop of Olmqdz, K. W., from the collection of Ludwig, Ritter von K · hel

responsibility: 245 00|cTranslated by Lady Wallace.

responsibility: 245 10|ctranslated by Grace Wallace.

responsibility: 700 1 |aWallace, Grace,|cLady,|dd. 1878.

date: 008/06-14 r19781867

date: 008/06-14 s1970

form: LDR/06 a{alpha-numeric notation}

language: 008/35-37 eng

language: 041 1 |aengger

language: 240 10|lEnglish

e-no: e00761

other e-no: e02843

linked w-no: w02826

linked w-no: w02827

linked w-no: w05920

linked w-no: w05921

LCCN: 010 |ar 64001252

LCCN: 010 |ar 64001253

title: 245 00|aConcerto no. 3, in C minor, for piano and orchestra, op. 37.|bFantasy for piano, chorus, and orchestra, op. 80.

responsibility: 700 1 |aBernstein, Leonard,|d1918-

responsibility: 700 1 |aBernstein, Leonard,|d1918- [from old catalog]

responsibility: 700 1 |aSerkin, Rudolf,|d1903-

responsibility: 700 1 |aSerkin, Rudolf,|d1903- [from old catalog]

responsibility: 710 2 |aPhilharmonic-Symphony Society of New York. [from old catalog]

responsibility: 710 2 |aWestminster Choir. [from old catalog]

date: 008/06-14 n

form: LDR/06 a{alpha-numeric notation}

language: 008/35-37 eng
language: 041 1 |aengund
others: 500 |aDuration : 36 min. and 17 min., 40 sec., respectively.

e-no: e00771
other e-no: e00772
other e-no: e00773
linked w-no: w02838
linked w-no: w02839
linked w-no: w02840
LCCN: 010 |a 99567345
LCCN: 010 |a 99571625
LCCN: 010 |a 2001569575
title: 245 00|aConcerto no. 4 in G major for piano and orchestra, op. 58
title: 245 10|aConcerto no. 4 in G major for piano and orchestra, op. 58
responsibility: 245 00|cBeethoven.
responsibility: 245 10|cBeethoven.
responsibility: 511 0 |aRobert Casadesus, piano ; Philadelphia Orchestra ; Eugene Ormandy, conductor.
responsibility: 511 0 |aRobert Casadesus, piano; The Philadelphia Orchestra; Eugene Ormandy, conductor.
responsibility: 700 1 |aCasadesus, Robert,|d1899-1972.|4prf
responsibility: 700 1 |aOrmandy, Eugene,|d1899-1985.
responsibility: 700 1 |aOrmandy, Eugene,|d1899-1985.|4cnd
responsibility: 710 2 |aPhiladelphia Orchestra.
responsibility: 710 2 |aPhiladelphia Orchestra.|4prf
date: 008/06-14 q19501953
date: 008/06-14 q19501959
date: 008/06-14 s1948
form: LDR/06 j{musical sound}
language: 041 0 |geng
series: 490 0 |aColumbia masterworks

Figure 5-7. Merged records at the *expression* level.

w-no: w02537

other w-no: w02540

other w-no: w02619

other w-no: w02646

other w-no: w02647

other w-no: w02648

other w-no: w03360

other w-no: w03361

other w-no: w03713

other w-no: w04409

LCCN: 010 |a   05007955

LCCN: 010 |a   38011386

LCCN: 010 |a   60003189

LCCN: 010 |a   67077968

LCCN: 010 |a   67082837

LCCN: 010 |a   81216026

LCCN: 010 |a   83072975

LCCN: 010 |a   93180883

LCCN: 010 |a   93248102

LCCN: 010 |aa   48007070

title: 240 10|aCorrespondence.|kSelections.

responsibility: 100 1 |aBeethoven, Ludwig van,|d1770-1827.

subject: 082 |a780.924

subject: 082 |a927.8

subject: 082 00|a780.924

subject: 082 00|a780/.92/4|aB|219

subject: 082 00|a780/.92|220

subject: 082 00|a782/.92|aB|220

subject: 600 10|aBeethoven, Ludwig van,|d1770-1827.

subject: 600 10|aBeethoven, Ludwig van,|d1770-1827|xCorrespondence.

subject: 650 0|aComposers|zAustria|xCorrespondence.

subject: 650 0|aComposers|zGermany|xCorrespondence.

subject: 650 0|aMusicians|xCorrespondence.

Chapter 5 Trial on Creation of Text-level Entity Records from Pre-existing MARC Records 159

---

w-no: w03362
other w-no: w03363
LCCN: 010 |a   52003684
LCCN: 010 |a   52006867
title: 245 00|aLetters, journals, and conversations.
title: 245 10|aLetters, journals, and conversations.
responsibility: 100 1 |aBeethoven, Ludwig van,|d1770-1827.
subject: 082 |a927.8

Figure 5-8. *Work* **level records having relationships with the record in Figure 5-4.**

---

w-no: w02603
other w-no: w03420
other w-no: w03461
other w-no: w03501
other w-no: w03527
...
LCCN: 010 |a   00716864
LCCN: 010 |a   82760619
LCCN: 010 |a   88753513
LCCN: 010 |a   90750737
...
title: 240 10|aQuartets,|mstrings,|nno. 4, op. 18, no. 4,|rC minor.
title: 700 12|tQuartets,|mstrings,|nno. 4, op. 18, no. 4,|rC minor.
responsibility: 100 1 |aBeethoven, Ludwig van,|d1770-1827.
responsibility: 700 12|aBeethoven, Ludwig van,|d1770-1827.
form: 008/18-19 uu
form: 008/18-19 zz
form: LDR/06 j{musical work}
subject: 650 0|aString quartets.

w-no: w10925
other w-no: w10927
LCCN: 010 |a   99391314
LCCN: 010 |a   99470895

title: 700 12|tQuartets,|mstrings,|nno. 4, op. 18, no. 4,|rC minor.|pAllegro, ma non tanto.
responsibility: 700 12|aBeethoven, Ludwig van,|d1770-1827.
form: LDR/06 j{musical work}

w-no: w04311
other w-no: w02894
LCCN: 010 |a 2001576455
LCCN: 010 |a 2002658310
title: 700 12|tQuartets,|mstrings,|nno. 4, op. 18, no. 4,|rC minor.|pMenuetto.
title: 700 1 |tQuartets,|mstrings,|nno. 4, op. 18, no. 4,|rC minor.|pMinueto.
responsibility: 700 12|aBeethoven, Ludwig van,|d1770-1827.
form: LDR/06 j{musical work}

w-no: w02889
LCCN: 010 |a 2002658313
title: 700 1 |tQuartets,|mstrings,|nno. 4, op. 18, no. 4,|rC minor.|kSelections.
responsibility: 700 1 |aBeethoven, Ludwig van,|d1770-1827.
form: LDR/06 j{musical work}

Figure 5-9. *Work* level records having relationships among them.

5.5 Prototype System for Retrieving and Displaying Records

I developed a prototype system for retrieving and displaying records created in accordance with the text-prioritized model through the conversion of MARC records. The aim in the development of the system was to demonstrate the retrieval and display of such records with different structures from existing records, and hence show the usefulness of these records. The system requires functions for proper handling of records at the four different levels—i.e., *work, expression, manifestation*, and *item*—in retrieval, display, and navigation. Specifically, it is necessary (a) to retrieve and display records while differentiating their entity levels and (b) to navigate between records at different levels or at the same level. The system developed provides only functions with a simple interface, being not an OPAC that has a sophisticated interface for users.

All records created through the conversion of MARC records were loaded into a database of MySQL, a relational database management system. The system was built with a CGI program in Perl, a Web browser, and an Apache Web server to access the database.

5.5.1 An Example of System Use

Screen shots of the system follow a typical sequence of actions in a search by a user, which was addressed in Chapter 3 as a scenario for the text-prioritized model:

1) Figure 5-10 demonstrates the search screen with a query "Beethoven and letters" that I specified as an example. The system provides choices on search type and mode; the search types are search by author/creator, title, subject heading, or their combination, while the search mode consists of the standard or extended mode, as will be seen later. In the example in the figure, the search type 'all elements, i.e., anywhere' and the standard mode were selected.

2) The search result for the query is shown in Figures 5-11-1 and 5-11-2—the top and bottom parts of the window, respectively. Two *works* and five *expressions* were matched, each being displayed in a brief form. *Works* and *expressions* can be searched directly in the current system. The first *work* (i.e., w02627) was then selected by a click.

3) The *work* selected is displayed in full detail in Figures 5-12-1, 5-12-2, and 5-12-3—the top, middle, and bottom parts of the window, respectively.

Figure 5-12-1 shows that the *work* was made through merging many records of which LC control numbers are enumerated in a concatenated manner. The *work* is identical to what has been illustrated in Figure 5-4 and of course contains that shown in Figure 5-1.

The *work* contained many titles extracted from tags 240, 245, and 700, two responsibility designations from 100 and 700, and many subjects from 082 and 6XX, as seen in Figures 5-12-1 and 5-12-2. Some of those titles contained the term 'letters' and thus this *work* was matched with the search query. Figure 5-12-2 also shows that twenty-four *expressions* were linked to the *work*, each of the first ten *expressions* being displayed in the brief form. Similarly, Figure 5-12-3 demonstrates that two *works* were linked to the *work* as related—those two related *works* are what have been illustrated in Figure 5-8.

4) Next, one *expression* with e00617 shown in Figure 5-12-3 was selected by clicking and displayed in full detail in Figures 5-13-1 and 5-13-2—the *expression* is identical to what has been illustrated first in Figure 5-7 and of course contains that shown in Figure 5-1. Figures 5-13-1 and 5-13-2 also show that there were two *manifestations* linked to the *expression*. There was, on the other hand, no other related *expressions* linked to the *expression* in this case.

5) And finally, one *manifestation* with m00583 in Figures 5-13-1 and 5-13-2 was selected by clicking and displayed in full detail together with the *item* i00583 in Figures 5-14-1 and 5-14-2, in addition to the *expression* information. In this case, no other *expression* was contained in the *manifestation*, as shown at the bottom of the window.

Additionally, the other *manifestation* with m00584, which was linked to the same *expression*, was displayed in Figure 5-15.

6) If we return to the window shown in Figure 5-12-3 and then select another *expression* with e00619, the *expression* is displayed in full detail as seen in Figure 5-16. Next, if we select one *manifestation* linked to the *expression*, the *manifestation* is displayed with the *expression* information, as seen in Figure 5-17.

7) Alternatively, if we return to the window shown in Figure 5-12-3 and then select a related *work* with w02537, the *work* is displayed in full detail and *expressions* linked to the *work* is displayed in the brief form, as seen in Figures 5-18-1 and 5-18-2.

Chapter 5 Trial on Creation of Text-level Entity Records from Pre-existing MARC Records   163

Figure 5-10. Initial search screen.

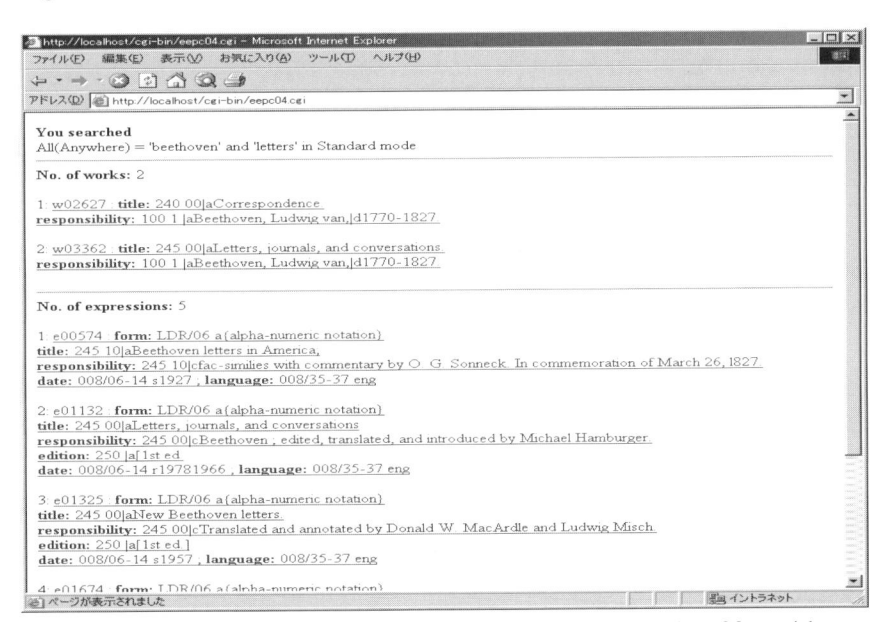

Figure 5-11-1. The result of a search showing hit records in a brief form (the top part).

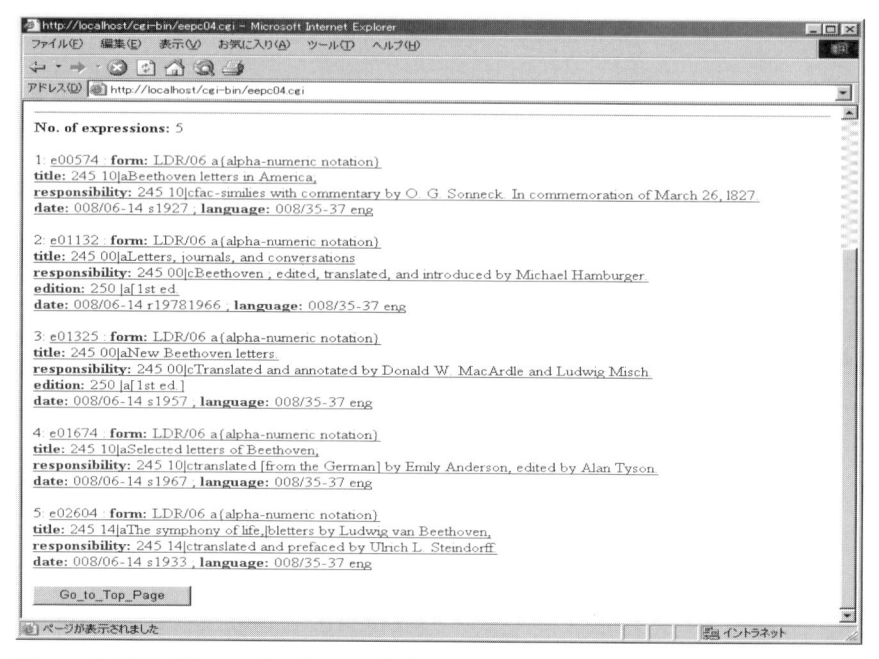

Figure 5-11-2. The result of a search showing hit records in a brief form (the bottom part).

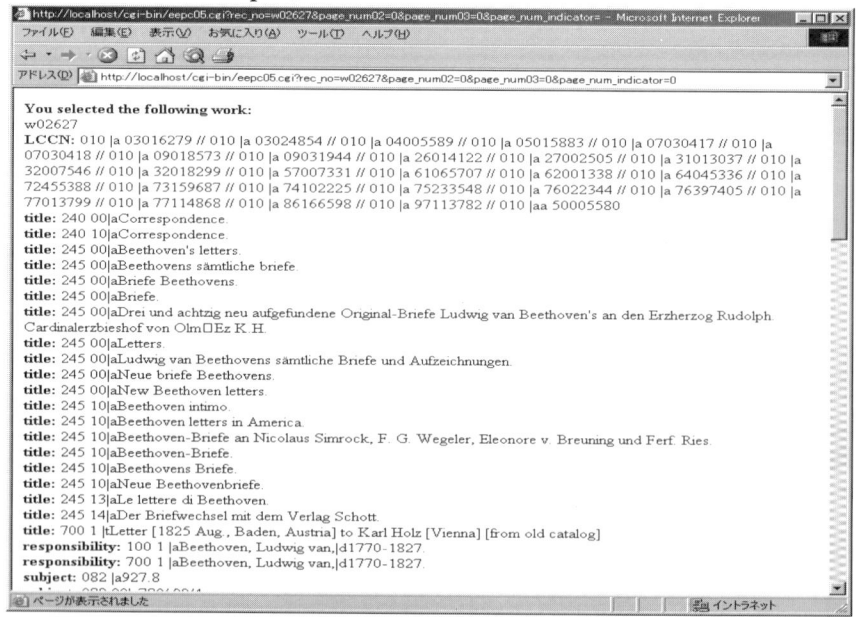

Figure 5-12-1. The screen showing a selected *work* record (the top part).

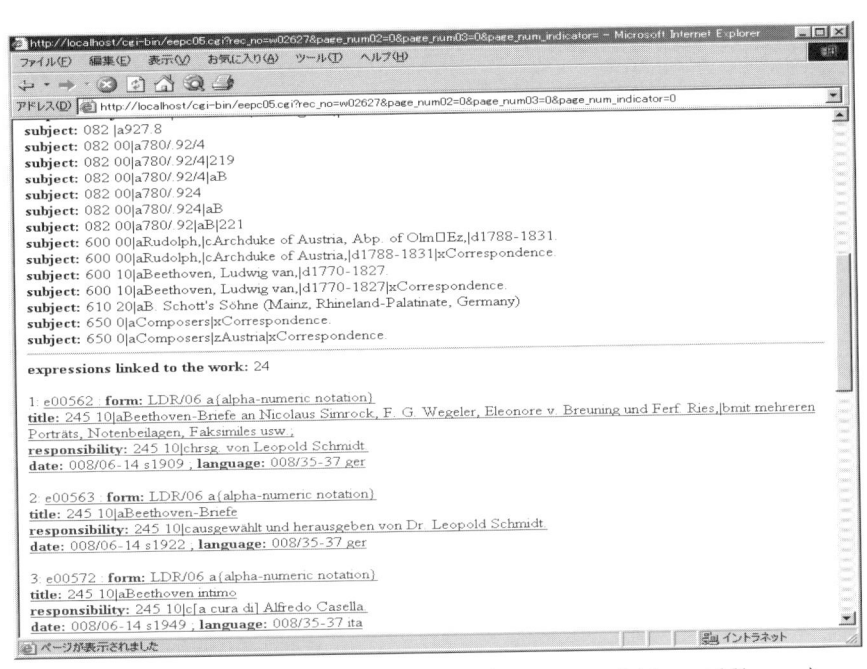

Chapter 5 Trial on Creation of Text-level Entity Records from Pre-existing MARC Records 165

Figure 5-12-2. The screen showing a selected *work* record (the middle part).

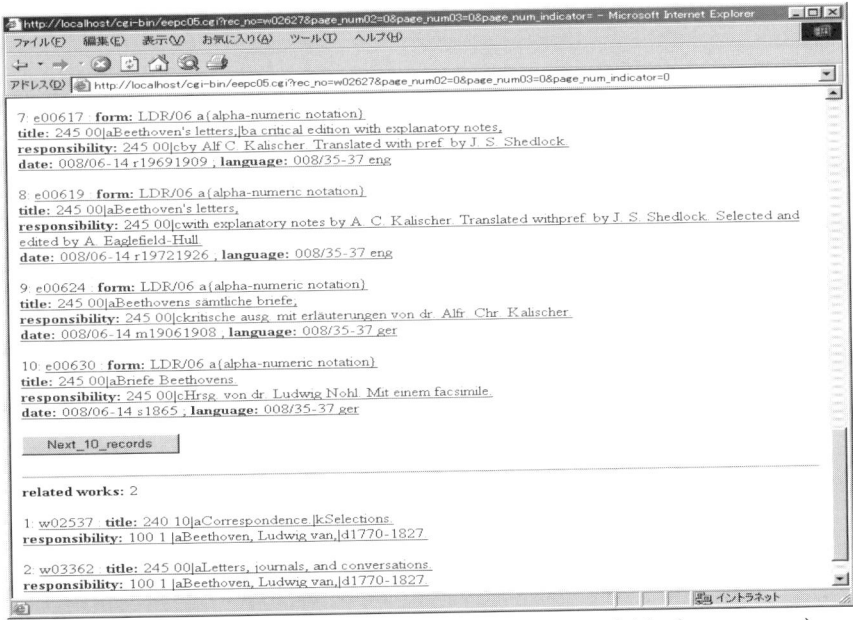

Figure 5-12-3. The screen showing a selected *work* record (the bottom part).

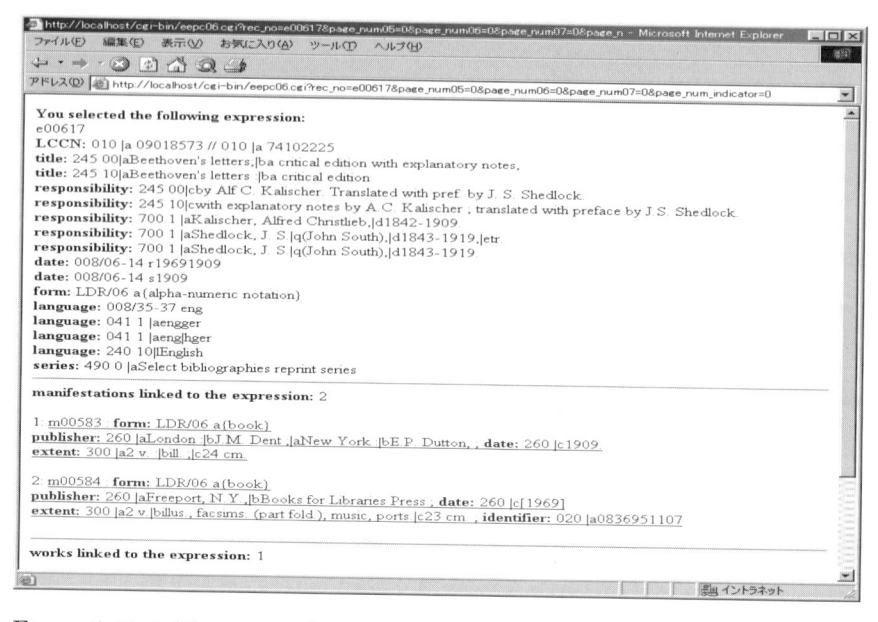

Figure 5-13-1. The screen showing a selected *expression* record (the top part).

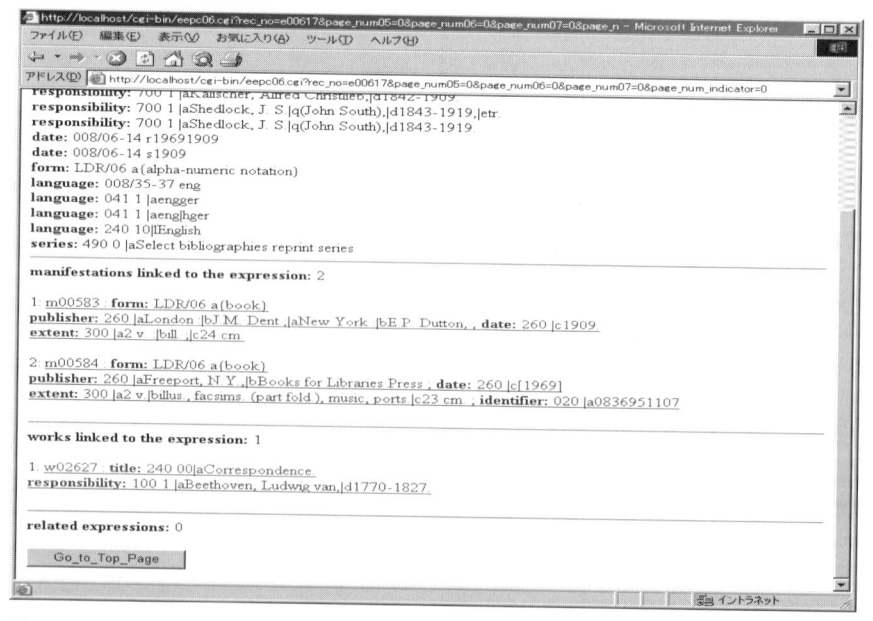

Figure 5-13-2. The screen showing a selected *expression* record (the bottom part).

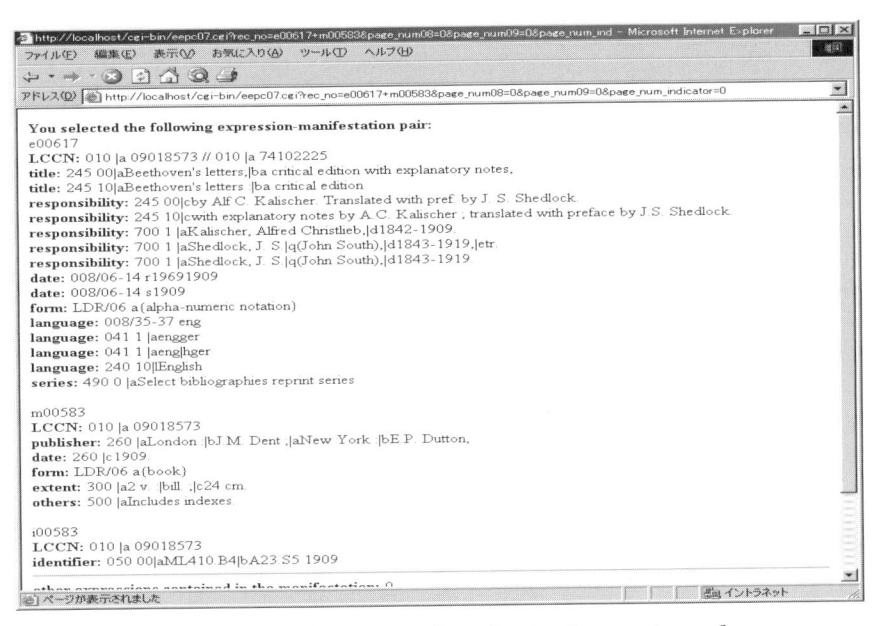

Chapter 5 Trial on Creation of Text-level Entity Records from Pre-existing MARC Records 167

Figure 5-14-1. The screen showing a selected pair of *expression* and *manifestation* records (the top part).

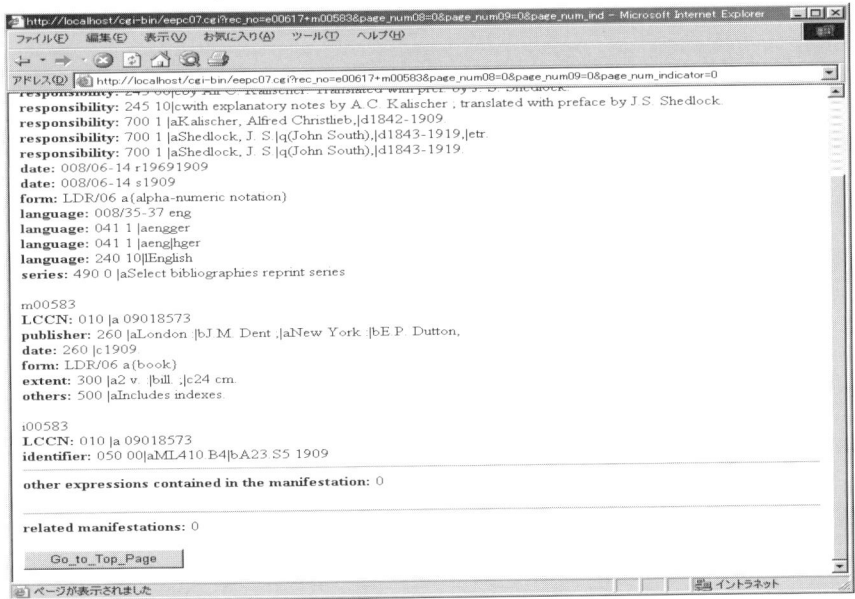

Figure 5-14-2. The screen showing a selected pair of *expression* and *manifestation* records (the bottom part).

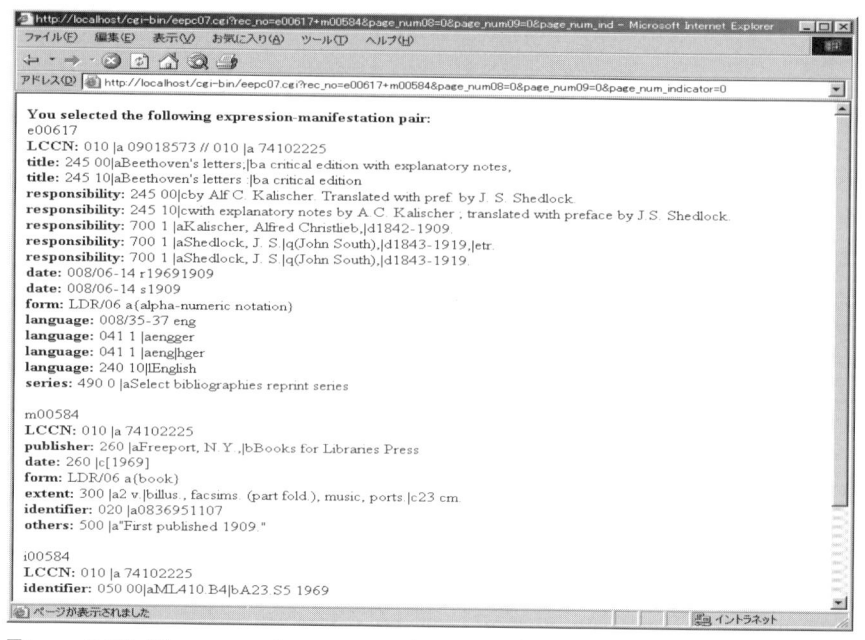

Figure 5-15. The screen showing another pair of *expression* and *manifestation* records.

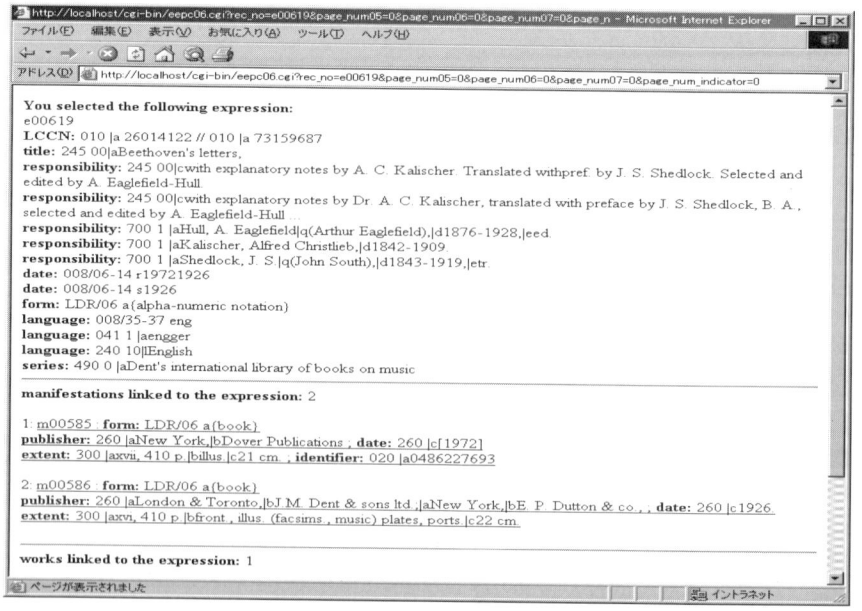

Figure 5-16. The screen showing another *expression* record.

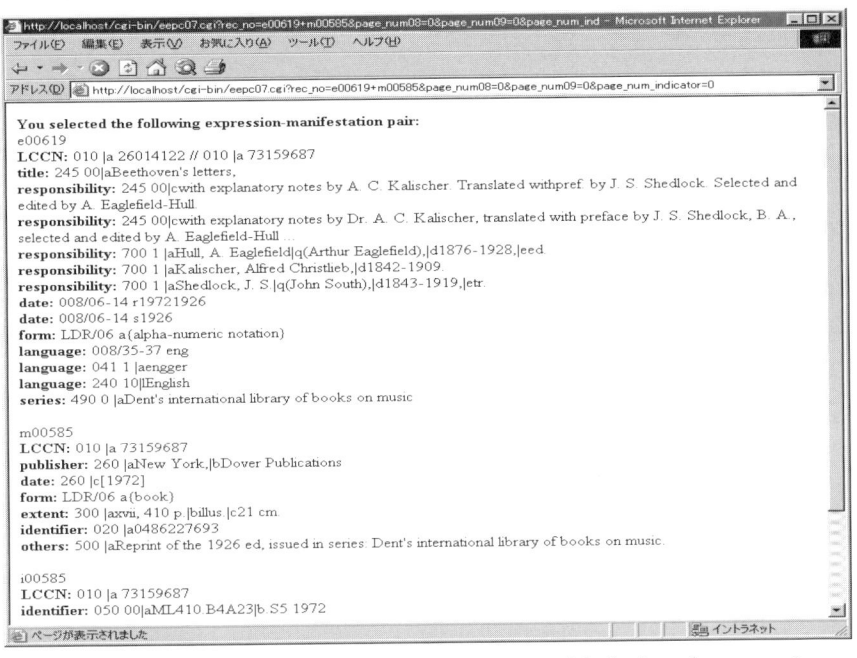

Chapter 5 Trial on Creation of Text-level Entity Records from Pre-existing MARC Records 169

Figure 5-17. The screen showing a *manifestation* record linked to the *expression*.

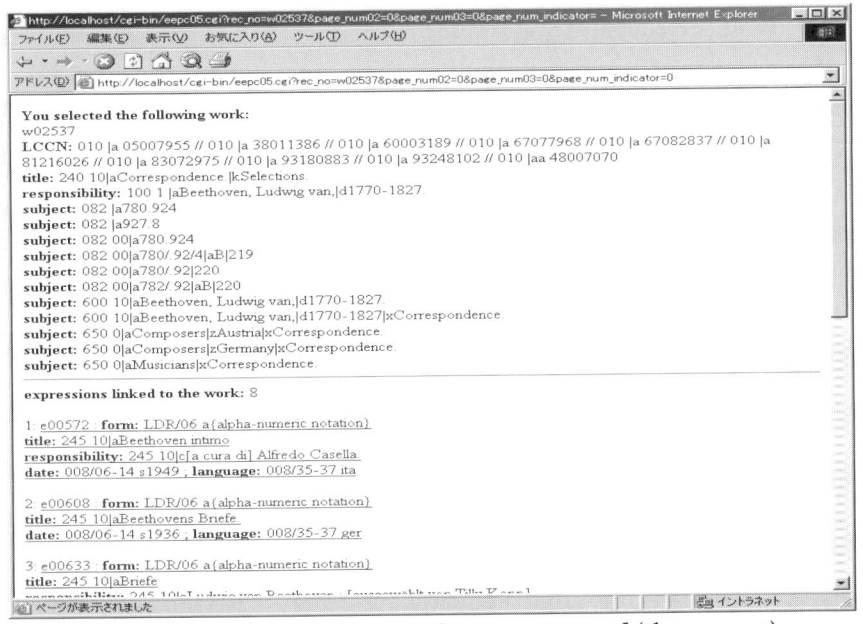

Figure 5-18-1. The screen showing a different *work* record (the top part).

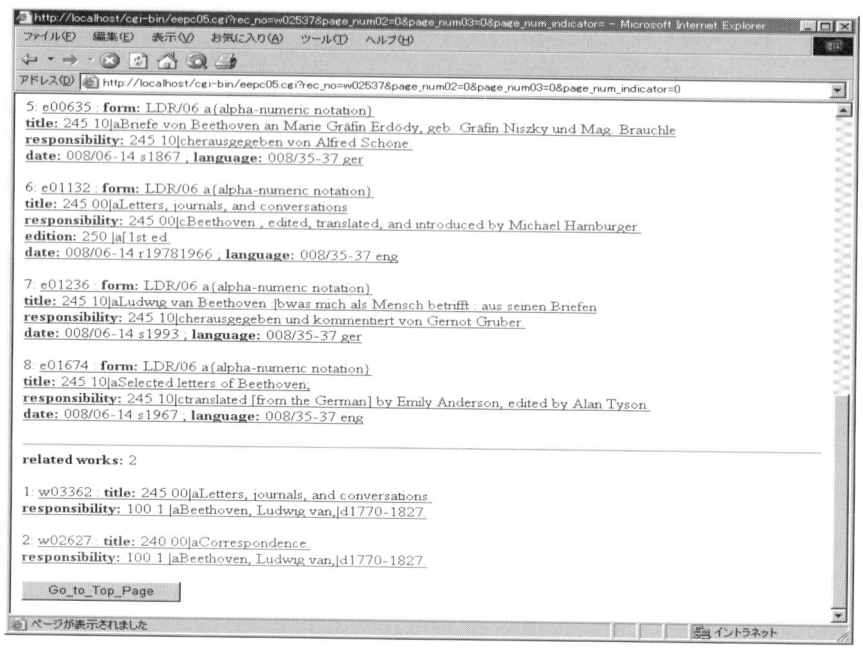

Figure 5-18-2. The screen showing a different *work* record (the bottom part).

5.5.2 Another Example of System Use

The following is another example of a sequence of user actions with the prototype system:

1) In this case, I specified a query "Beethoven and concertos and 4" as an example of musical work searching; the term 'concertos,' not 'concerto,' is used in the current AACR2 as a constituent of uniform titles. The search result for the query is shown in Figures 5-19-1 and 5-19-2—the top and bottom parts of the window, respectively. Four *works* and nine *expressions* were matched, each being displayed in the brief form. The first *work* (i.e., w00460) was then selected by a click.

2) The *work* selected is displayed in full detail as shown in Figures 5-20-1, 5-20-2, 5-20-3, and 5-20-4. The *work* displayed in Figures 5-20-1 and 5-20-2 is identical to what has been illustrated in Figure 5-6. The figures show that sixty-four *expressions* were linked to the *work*, each of the first ten *expressions* being displayed in the brief form. It is also shown that one *work* was linked to the *work* as related.

3) Next, one *expression* with e00771 was selected by clicking and displayed in full detail in Figures 5-21-1 and 5-21-2—the *expression* is equivalent to what has been illustrated in Figure 5-7. These two figures also show that there were three *manifestations* linked to the *expression*. There was, on the other hand, no other related *expressions* linked to the *expression* in this case.

4) And then, one *manifestation* with m00708 was selected by clicking and displayed in full detail in Figures 5-22-1 and 5-22-2 together with the *expression* information. It is also shown that no other *expression* was contained in the *manifestation*.

The other two *manifestations*, which were linked to the same *expression*, were displayed in Figures 5-23 and 5-24.

5) If we return to either the window shown in Figure 5-20-4 or that in Figure 5-19-1 and then select another *work* with w01447, the *work* is displayed in full detail as seen in Figure 5-25.

It may be worth seeing, in passing, a case where a *manifestation* contains more than one *expression*; the case shown in Figure 5-2 is an example. If we come to the first *expression* shown in Figure 5-2, the *expression* is displayed as seen in Figure 5-26. Then, if the *manifestation* linked to the *expression* is selected, the *manifestation* is displayed as seen in Figures 5-27-1 and 5-27-2. Figure 5-27-2 shows that another *expression* (i.e., the second *expression* in Figure 5-2) is contained in the *manifestation*; this is the way that the prototype system deals with such cases. The other *expression* contained in the *manifestation* is displayed in full detail in Figure 5-28.

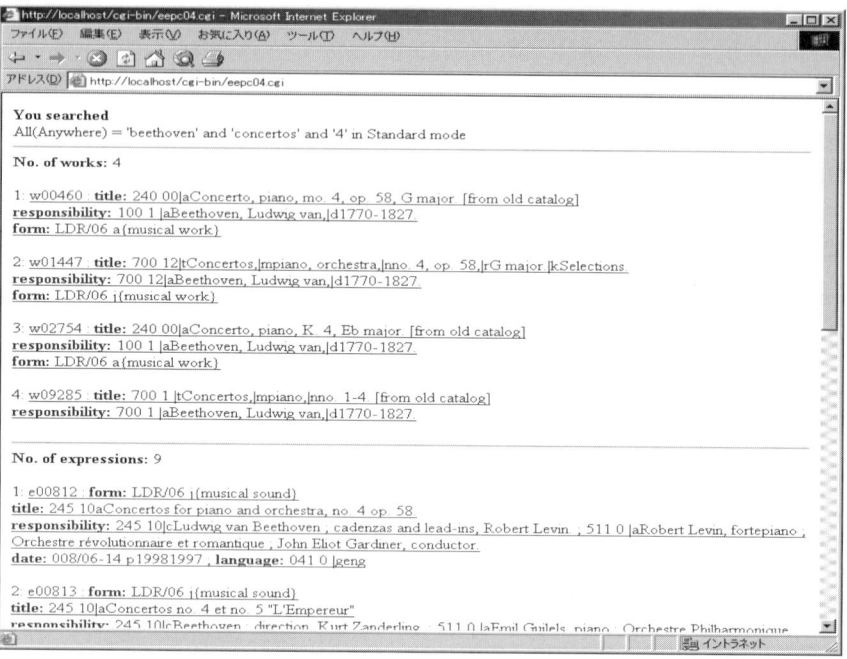

Figure 5-19-1. The result of another search showing hit records (the top part).

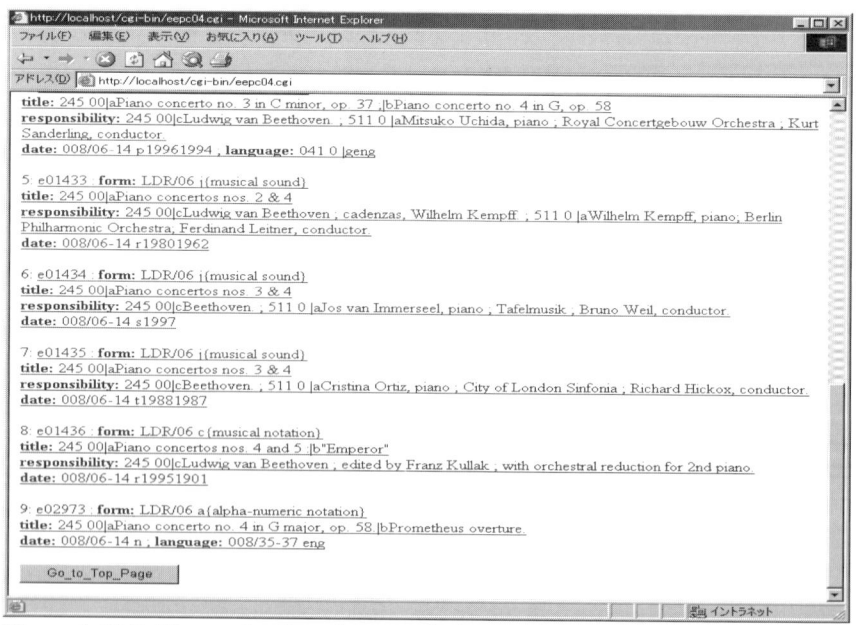

Figure 5-19-2. The result of another search showing hit records (the bottom part).

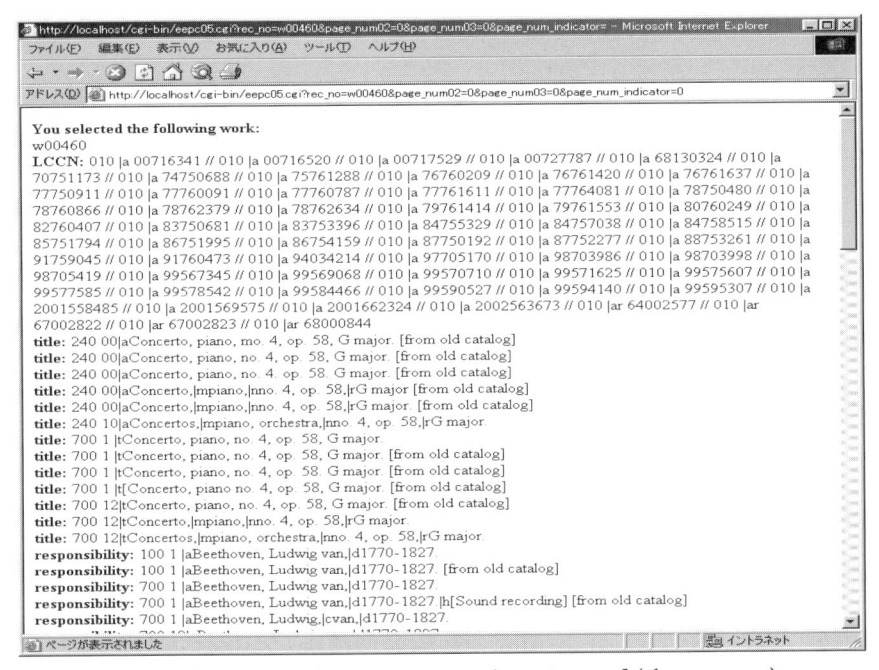

Chapter 5 Trial on Creation of Text-level Entity Records from Pre-existing MARC Records 173

```
You selected the following work:
w00460
LCCN: 010 |a 00716341 // 010 |a 00716520 // 010 |a 00717529 // 010 |a 00727787 // 010 |a 68130324 // 010 |a
70751173 // 010 |a 74750688 // 010 |a 75761288 // 010 |a 76760209 // 010 |a 76761420 // 010 |a 76761637 // 010 |a
77750911 // 010 |a 77760091 // 010 |a 77760787 // 010 |a 77761611 // 010 |a 77764081 // 010 |a 78750480 // 010 |a
78760866 // 010 |a 78762379 // 010 |a 78762634 // 010 |a 79761414 // 010 |a 79761553 // 010 |a 80760249 // 010 |a
82760407 // 010 |a 83750681 // 010 |a 83753396 // 010 |a 84755329 // 010 |a 84757038 // 010 |a 84758515 // 010 |a
85751794 // 010 |a 86751995 // 010 |a 86754159 // 010 |a 87750192 // 010 |a 87752277 // 010 |a 88753261 // 010 |a
91759045 // 010 |a 91760473 // 010 |a 94034214 // 010 |a 97705170 // 010 |a 98703986 // 010 |a 98703998 // 010 |a
98705419 // 010 |a 99567345 // 010 |a 99569068 // 010 |a 99570710 // 010 |a 99571625 // 010 |a 99575607 // 010 |a
99577585 // 010 |a 99578542 // 010 |a 99584466 // 010 |a 99590527 // 010 |a 99594140 // 010 |a 99595307 // 010 |a
2001558485 // 010 |a 2001569575 // 010 |a 2001661362 // 010 |a 2002563673 // 010 |ar 64002577 // 010 |ar
67002822 // 010 |ar 67002823 // 010 |ar 68000844
title: 240 00|aConcerto, piano, no. 4, op. 58, G major. [from old catalog]
title: 240 00|aConcerto, piano, no. 4, op. 58, G major. [from old catalog]
title: 240 00|aConcerto, piano, no. 4, op. 58, G major. [from old catalog]
title: 240 00|aConcerto,|mpiano,|nno. 4, op. 58,|rG major [from old catalog]
title: 240 00|aConcerto,|mpiano,|nno. 4, op. 58,|rG major. [from old catalog]
title: 240 10|aConcertos,|mpiano, orchestra,|nno. 4, op. 58,|rG major.
title: 700 1 |tConcerto, piano, no. 4, op. 58, G major.
title: 700 1 |tConcerto, piano, no. 4, op. 58, G major. [from old catalog]
title: 700 1 |tConcerto, piano, no. 4, op. 58, G major. [from old catalog]
title: 700 1 |t[Concerto, piano no. 4, op. 58, G major. [from old catalog]
title: 700 12|tConcerto, piano, no. 4, op. 58, G major. [from old catalog]
title: 700 12|tConcerto,|mpiano,|nno. 4, op. 58,|rG major.
title: 700 12|tConcertos,|mpiano, orchestra,|nno. 4, op. 58,|rG major.
responsibility: 100 1 |aBeethoven, Ludwig van,|d1770-1827.
responsibility: 100 1 |aBeethoven, Ludwig van,|d1770-1827. [from old catalog]
responsibility: 700 1 |aBeethoven, Ludwig van,|d1770-1827.
responsibility: 700 1 |aBeethoven, Ludwig van,|d1770-1827.|h[Sound recording] [from old catalog]
responsibility: 700 1 |aBeethoven, Ludwig,|cvan,|d1770-1827.
```

Figure 5-20-1. The screen showing a musical *work* record (the top part).

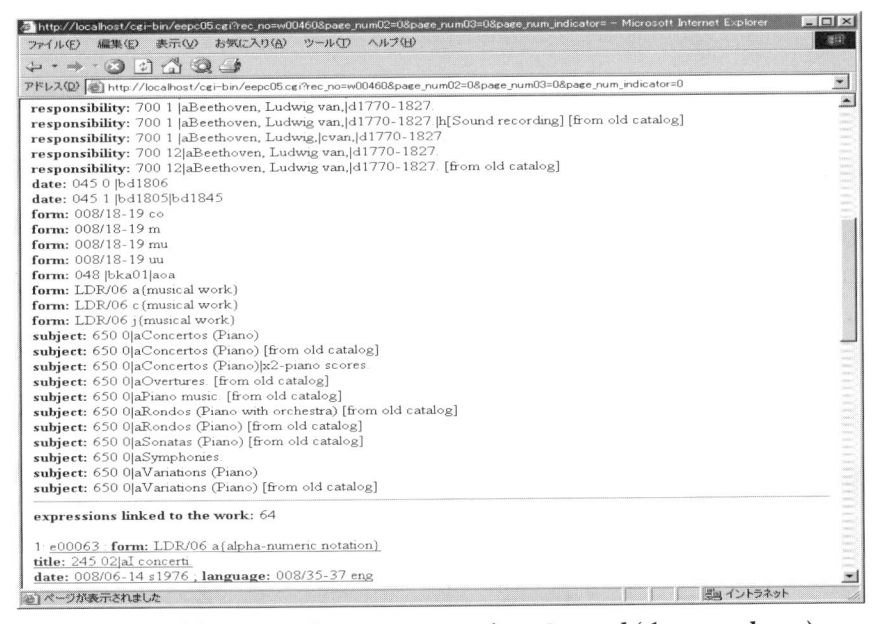

```
responsibility: 700 1 |aBeethoven, Ludwig van,|d1770-1827.
responsibility: 700 1 |aBeethoven, Ludwig van,|d1770-1827.|h[Sound recording] [from old catalog]
responsibility: 700 1 |aBeethoven, Ludwig,|cvan,|d1770-1827.
responsibility: 700 12|aBeethoven, Ludwig van,|d1770-1827.
responsibility: 700 12|aBeethoven, Ludwig van,|d1770-1827. [from old catalog]
date: 045 0 |bd1806
date: 045 1 |bd1805|bd1845
form: 008/18-19 co
form: 008/18-19 m
form: 008/18-19 mu
form: 008/18-19 uu
form: 048 |bka01|aoa
form: LDR/06 a (musical work)
form: LDR/06 c (musical work)
form: LDR/06 j (musical work)
subject: 650 0|aConcertos (Piano)
subject: 650 0|aConcertos (Piano) [from old catalog]
subject: 650 0|aConcertos (Piano)|x2-piano scores.
subject: 650 0|aOvertures. [from old catalog]
subject: 650 0|aPiano music. [from old catalog]
subject: 650 0|aRondos (Piano with orchestra) [from old catalog]
subject: 650 0|aRondos (Piano) [from old catalog]
subject: 650 0|aSonatas [from old catalog]
subject: 650 0|aSymphonies.
subject: 650 0|aVariations (Piano)
subject: 650 0|aVariations (Piano) [from old catalog]

expressions linked to the work: 64

1: e00063 . form: LDR/06 a (alpha-numeric notation)
title: 245 02|aI concerti.
date: 008/06-14 s1976 . language: 008/35-37 eng
```

Figure 5-20-2. The screen showing a musical *work* record (the second part)

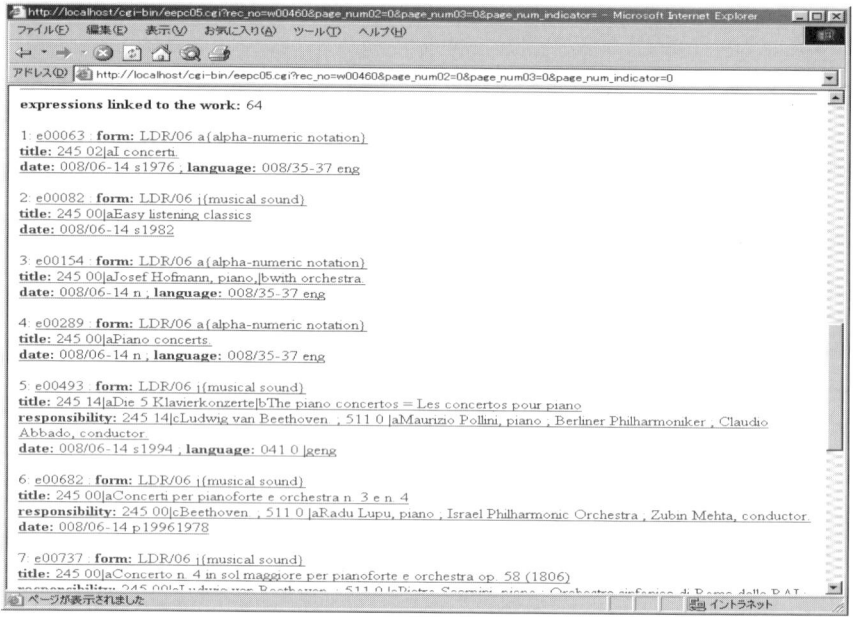

Figure 5-20-3. The screen showing a musical *work* record (the third part).

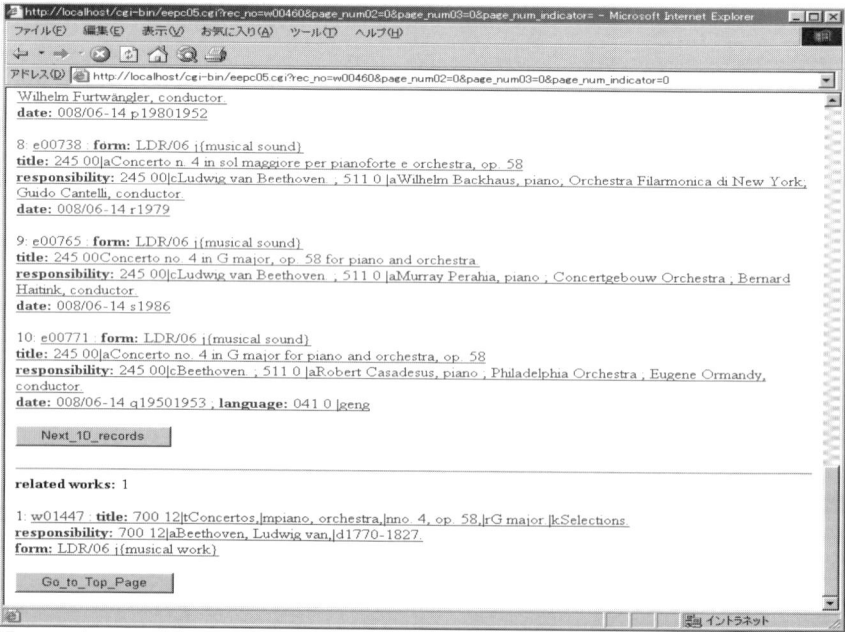

Figure 5-20-4. The screen showing a musical *work* record (the bottom part).

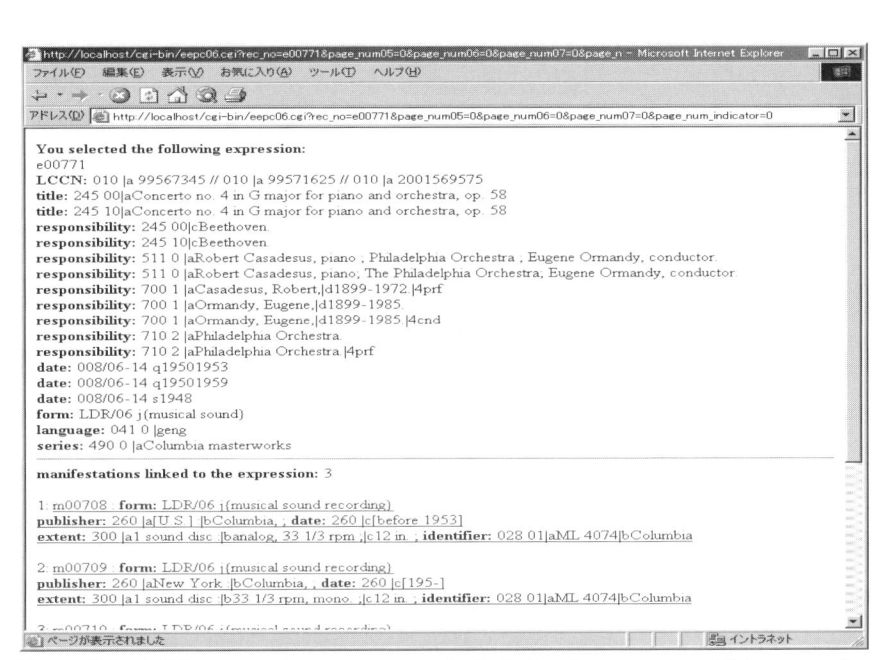

Chapter 5 Trial on Creation of Text-level Entity Records from Pre-existing MARC Records 175

```
You selected the following expression:
e00771
LCCN: 010 |a 99567345 // 010 |a 99571625 // 010 |a 2001569575
title: 245 00|aConcerto no. 4 in G major for piano and orchestra, op. 58
title: 245 10|aConcerto no. 4 in G major for piano and orchestra, op. 58
responsibility: 245 00|cBeethoven.
responsibility: 245 10|cBeethoven.
responsibility: 511 0 |aRobert Casadesus, piano ; Philadelphia Orchestra ; Eugene Ormandy, conductor.
responsibility: 511 0 |aRobert Casadesus, piano; The Philadelphia Orchestra; Eugene Ormandy, conductor.
responsibility: 700 1 |aCasadesus, Robert,|d1899-1972.|4prf
responsibility: 700 1 |aOrmandy, Eugene,|d1899-1985.
responsibility: 700 1 |aOrmandy, Eugene,|d1899-1985.|4cnd
responsibility: 710 2 |aPhiladelphia Orchestra.
responsibility: 710 2 |aPhiladelphia Orchestra.|4prf
date: 008/06-14 q19501953
date: 008/06-14 q19501959
date: 008/06-14 s1948
form: LDR/06 j(musical sound)
language: 041 0 |geng
series: 490 0 |aColumbia masterworks

manifestations linked to the expression: 3

1: m00708 : form: LDR/06 j(musical sound recording)
publisher: 260 |a[U.S.] |bColumbia, , date: 260 |c[before 1953]
extent: 300 |a1 sound disc :|banalog, 33 1/3 rpm ,|c12 in. , identifier: 028 01|aML 4074|bColumbia

2: m00709  form: LDR/06 j(musical sound recording)
publisher: 260 |a[New York] |bColumbia, , date: 260 |c[195-]
extent: 300 |a1 sound disc :|b33 1/3 rpm, mono. ,|c12 in. , identifier: 028 01|aML 4074|bColumbia
```

Figure 5-21-1. The screen showing an *expression* linked to the musical *work* (the top part).

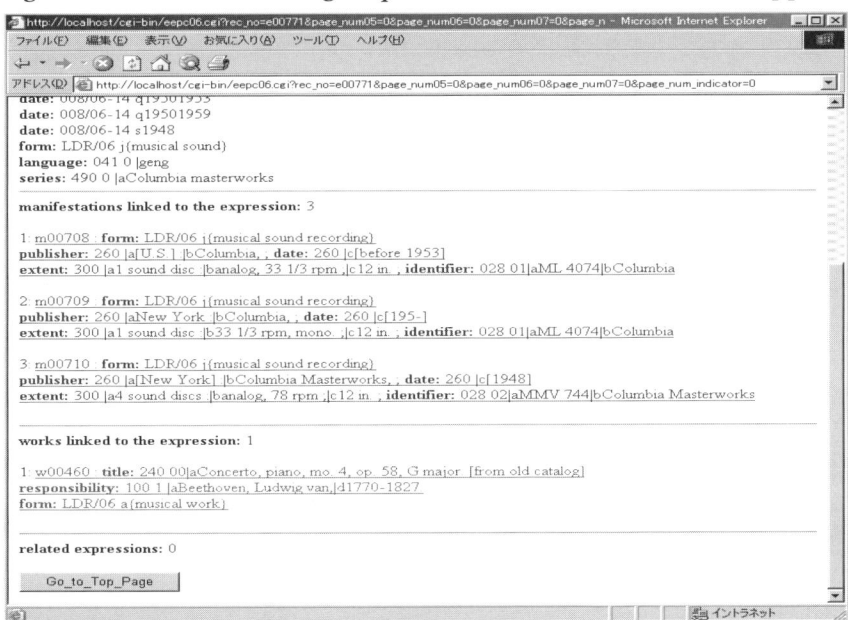

```
date: 008/06-14 q19501953
date: 008/06-14 q19501959
date: 008/06-14 s1948
form: LDR/06 j(musical sound)
language: 041 0 |geng
series: 490 0 |aColumbia masterworks

manifestations linked to the expression: 3

1: m00708 : form: LDR/06 j(musical sound recording)
publisher: 260 |a[U.S.] |bColumbia, , date: 260 |c[before 1953]
extent: 300 |a1 sound disc :|banalog, 33 1/3 rpm ,|c12 in. , identifier: 028 01|aML 4074|bColumbia

2: m00709  form: LDR/06 j(musical sound recording)
publisher: 260 |a[New York] |bColumbia, , date: 260 |c[195-]
extent: 300 |a1 sound disc :|b33 1/3 rpm, mono. ,|c12 in. , identifier: 028 01|aML 4074|bColumbia

3: m00710  form: LDR/06 j(musical sound recording)
publisher: 260 |a[New York] |bColumbia Masterworks, , date: 260 |c[1948]
extent: 300 |a4 sound discs :|banalog, 78 rpm ,|c12 in. , identifier: 028 02|aMMV 744|bColumbia Masterworks

works linked to the expression: 1

1: w00460 : title: 240 00|aConcerto, piano, no. 4, op. 58, G major [from old catalog]
responsibility: 100 1 |aBeethoven, Ludwig van,|d1770-1827.
form: LDR/06 a(musical work)

related expressions: 0

[Go_to_Top_Page]
```

Figure 5-21-2. The screen showing an *expression* linked to the musical *work* (the bottom part).

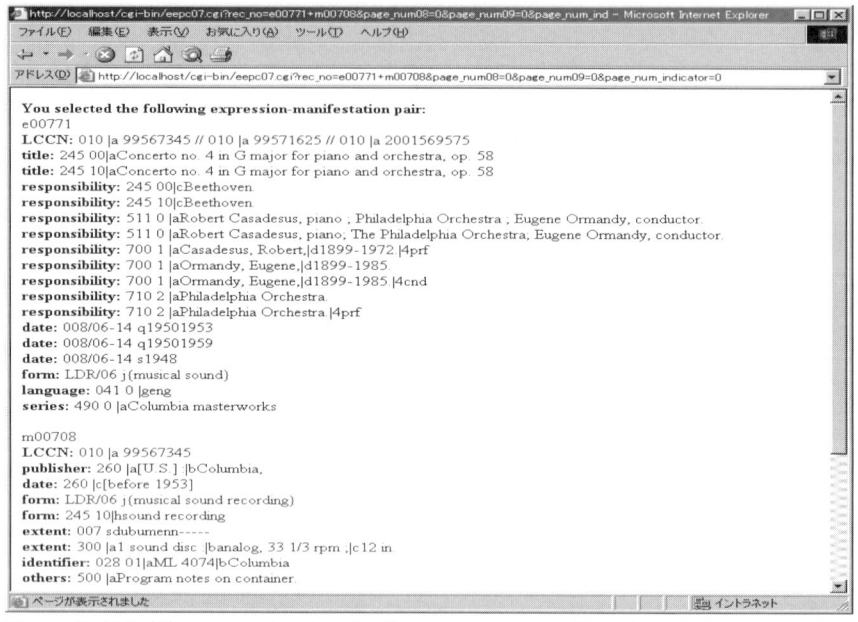

Figure 5-22-1. The screen showing the first *expression-manifestation* pair (the top part).

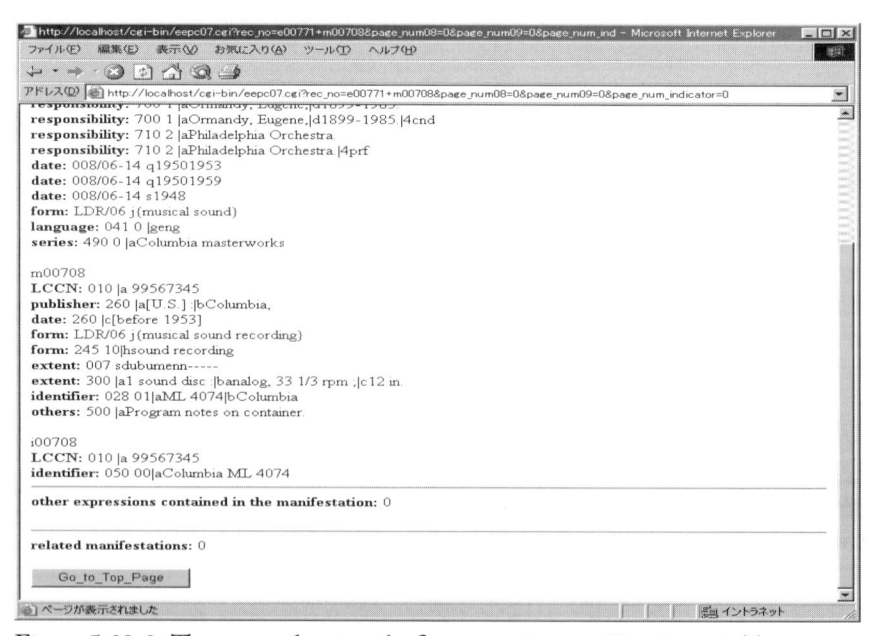

Figure 5-22-2. The screen showing the first *expression-manifestation* pair (the bottom part)

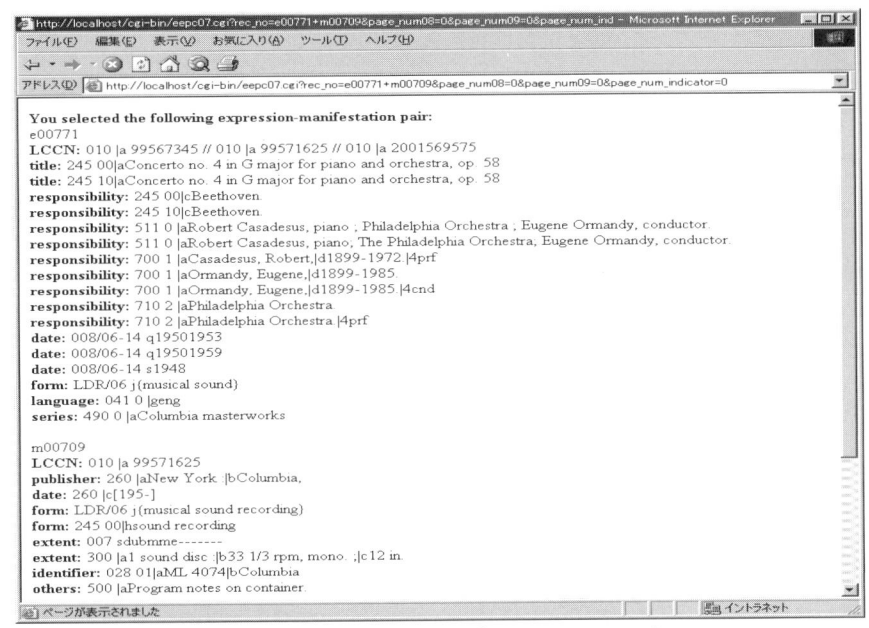

Chapter 5 Trial on Creation of Text-level Entity Records from Pre-existing MARC Records 177

```
You selected the following expression-manifestation pair:
e00771
LCCN: 010 |a 99567345 // 010 |a 99571625 // 010 |a 2001569575
title: 245 00|aConcerto no. 4 in G major for piano and orchestra, op. 58
title: 245 10|aConcerto no. 4 in G major for piano and orchestra, op. 58
responsibility: 245 00|cBeethoven.
responsibility: 245 10|cBeethoven.
responsibility: 511 0 |aRobert Casadesus, piano ; Philadelphia Orchestra ; Eugene Ormandy, conductor.
responsibility: 511 0 |aRobert Casadesus, piano; The Philadelphia Orchestra; Eugene Ormandy, conductor.
responsibility: 700 1 |aCasadesus, Robert,|d1899-1972.|4prf
responsibility: 700 1 |aOrmandy, Eugene,|d1899-1985.
responsibility: 700 1 |aOrmandy, Eugene,|d1899-1985.|4cnd
responsibility: 710 2 |aPhiladelphia Orchestra.
responsibility: 710 2 |aPhiladelphia Orchestra.|4prf
date: 008/06-14 q19501953
date: 008/06-14 q19501959
date: 008/06-14 s1948
form: LDR/06 j (musical sound)
language: 041 0 |geng
series: 490 0 |aColumbia masterworks

m00709
LCCN: 010 |a 99571625
publisher: 260 |a|New York :|bColumbia,
date: 260 |c[195-]
form: LDR/06 j (musical sound recording)
form: 245 00|hsound recording
extent: 007 sdubmmne-------
extent: 300 |a1 sound disc :|b33 1/3 rpm, mono. ;|c 12 in.
identifier: 028 01|aML 4074|bColumbia
others: 500 |aProgram notes on container.
```

Figure 5-23. The screen showing the second *expression-manifestation* pair.

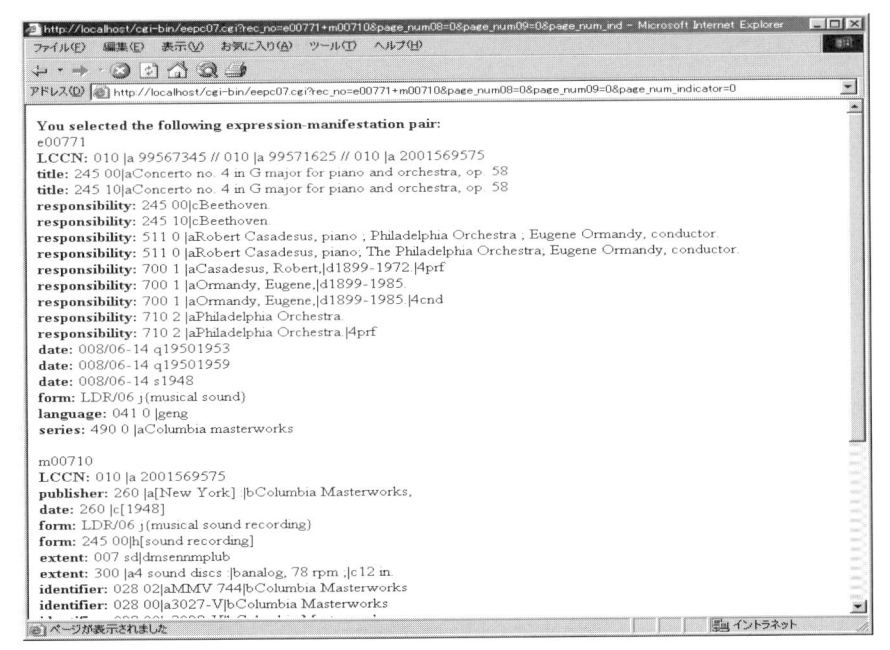

```
You selected the following expression-manifestation pair:
e00771
LCCN: 010 |a 99567345 // 010 |a 99571625 // 010 |a 2001569575
title: 245 00|aConcerto no. 4 in G major for piano and orchestra, op. 58
title: 245 10|aConcerto no. 4 in G major for piano and orchestra, op. 58
responsibility: 245 00|cBeethoven.
responsibility: 245 10|cBeethoven.
responsibility: 511 0 |aRobert Casadesus, piano ; Philadelphia Orchestra ; Eugene Ormandy, conductor.
responsibility: 511 0 |aRobert Casadesus, piano; The Philadelphia Orchestra; Eugene Ormandy, conductor.
responsibility: 700 1 |aCasadesus, Robert,|d1899-1972.|4prf
responsibility: 700 1 |aOrmandy, Eugene,|d1899-1985.
responsibility: 700 1 |aOrmandy, Eugene,|d1899-1985.|4cnd
responsibility: 710 2 |aPhiladelphia Orchestra.
responsibility: 710 2 |aPhiladelphia Orchestra.|4prf
date: 008/06-14 q19501953
date: 008/06-14 q19501959
date: 008/06-14 s1948
form: LDR/06 j (musical sound)
language: 041 0 |geng
series: 490 0 |aColumbia masterworks

m00710
LCCN: 010 |a 2001569575
publisher: 260 |a[New York] :|bColumbia Masterworks,
date: 260 |c[1948]
form: LDR/06 j (musical sound recording)
form: 245 00|h[sound recording]
extent: 007 sd|dmsennrmplub
extent: 300 |a4 sound discs :|banalog, 78 rpm ;|c 12 in.
identifier: 028 02|aMMV 744|bColumbia Masterworks
identifier: 028 00|a3027-V|bColumbia Masterworks
```

Figure 5-24. The screen showing the third *expression-manifestation* pair.

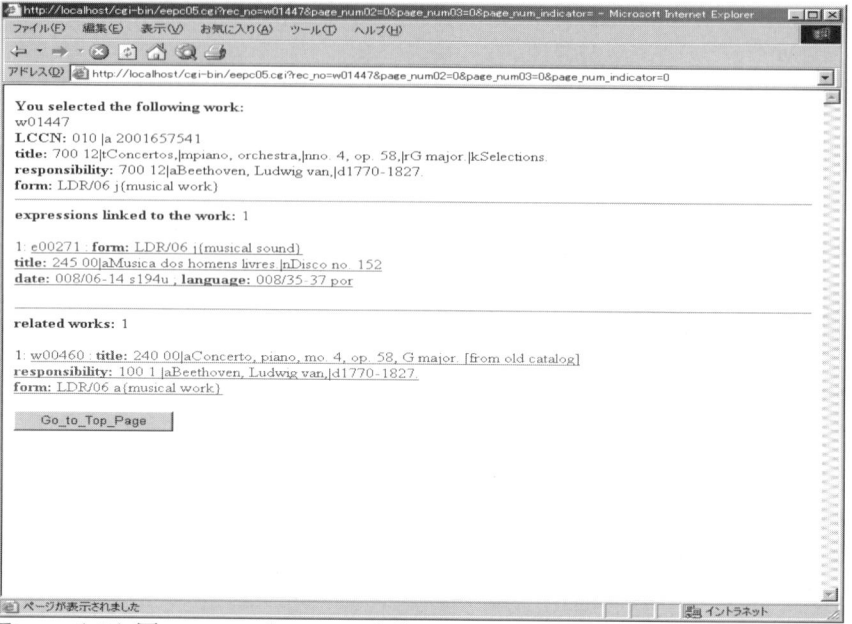

Figure 5-25. The screen showing a different musical *work* record.

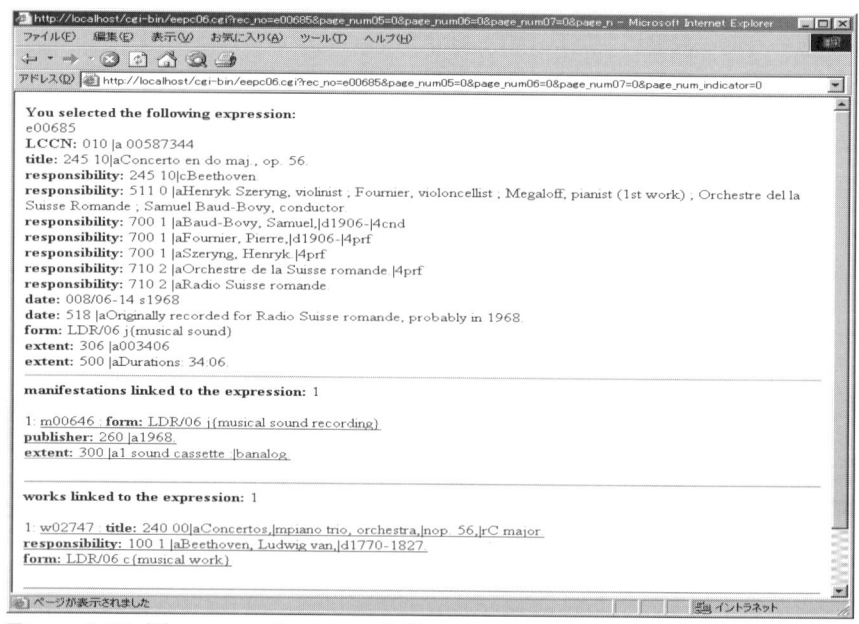

Figure 5-26. The screen showing a different *expression* record.

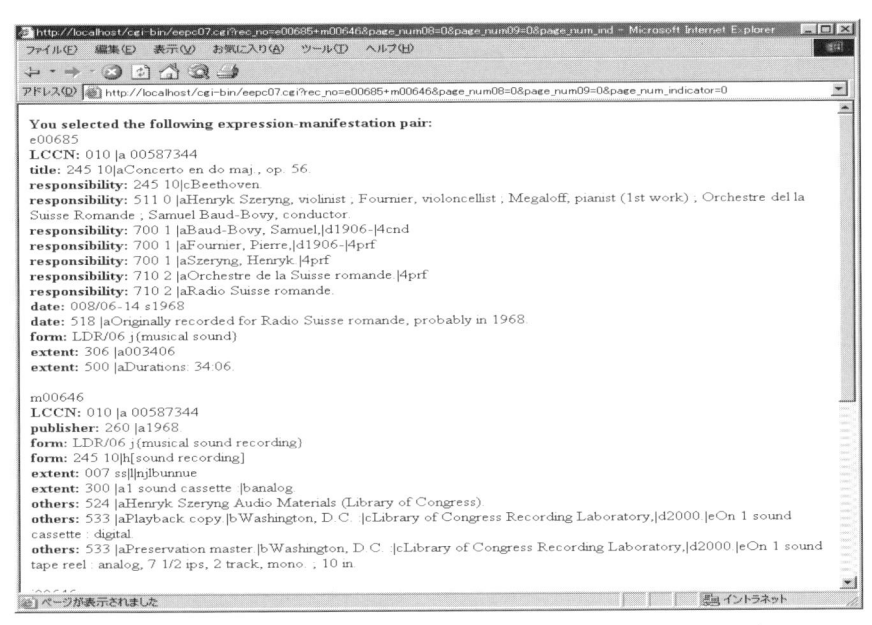

Chapter 5 Trial on Creation of Text-level Entity Records from Pre-existing MARC Records 179

Figure 5-27-1. The screen showing a *manifestation* that contains more than one *expression* (the top part).

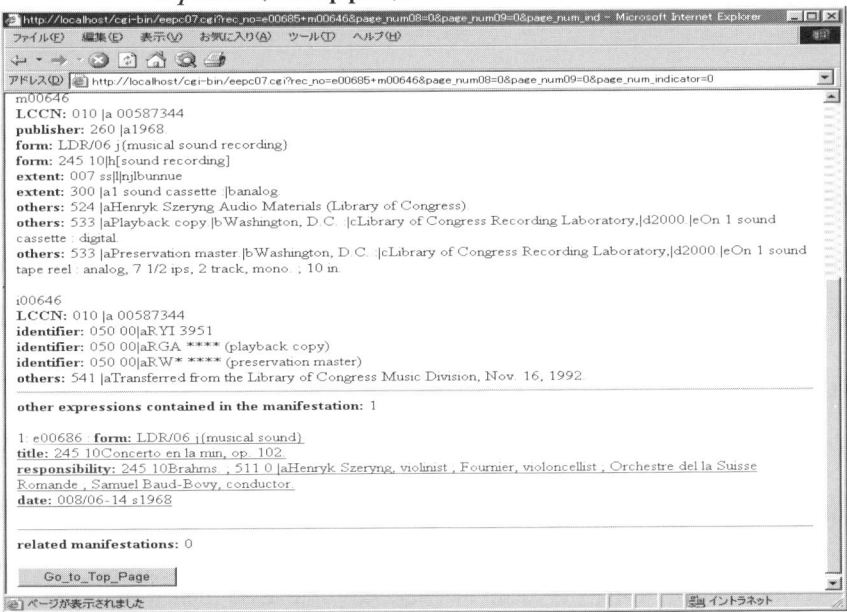

Figure 5-27-2. The screen showing a *manifestation* that contains more than one *expression* (the bottom part).

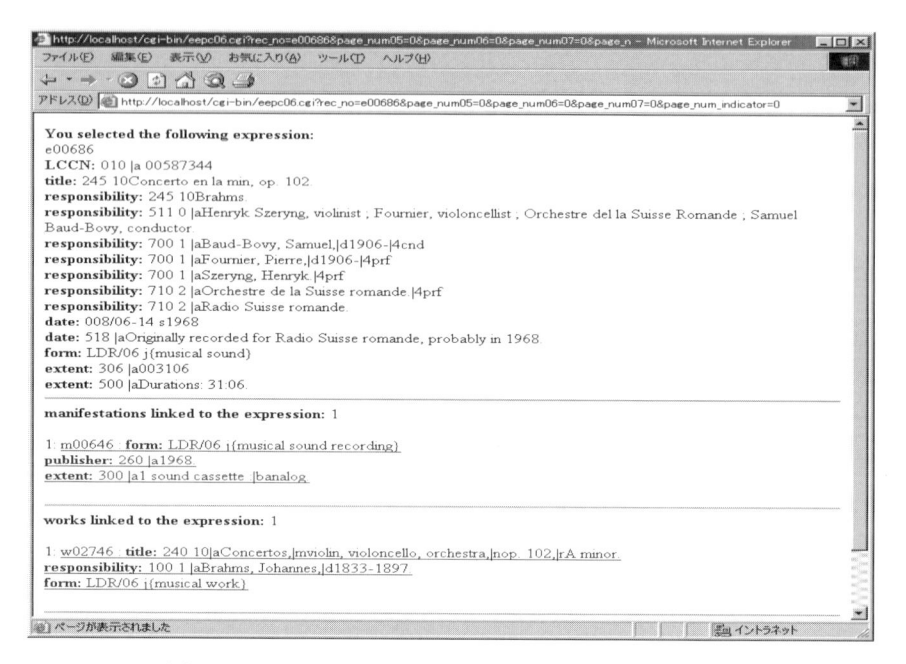

Figure 5-28. The screen showing another *expression* contained in the *manifestation*.

5.5.3 Extended Search Mode

The system at the current stage provides two search modes: standard and extended. The standard mode operates to retrieve records which satisfy by themselves the conditions specified by a query, and the above two examples of a search with the system used this search mode. Figures 5-11 and 5-19 show *works* and *expressions* satisfying the query; i.e., those containing all terms specified.

On the other hand, the extended mode functions as a search to retrieve records with the use of links among the records. For example, when a search query is a combination of author and translator (or that of composer and performer), *expressions* containing only the name of the translator (or performer) are retrieved in the extended mode if they are linked to *works* that contain the author (or composer) name, in addition to the retrieval of *expressions* containing both names.

More formally, using the relational algebra in database theory, this extended search operation can be defined as follows:

Chapter 5 Trial on Creation of Text-level Entity Records from Pre-existing MARC Records

$T_1 \leftarrow \pi_{\{expression\}} (S_{expression} |\times| \sigma_{keyword=term1} (R_{work}))$

$T'_1 \leftarrow \sigma_{keyword=term2} (S_{expression}) \cap T_1$.

R_{work} and $S_{expression}$ denote relations consisting of *works* and *expressions*, respectively. Also, σ, $|\times|$, π and $\cap$ respectively denote the selection, natural join, projection, and set intersection operations. They are defined as:

$\sigma_{keyword=term1} (R_{work}) = \{ work \mid work \in R_{work} \wedge work(keyword) = \text{"}term1\text{"} \}$

$S_{expression} |\times| R'_{work} =$
$\quad \{ (expression, work) \mid expression \in S_{expression} \wedge work \in R'_{work}$
$\quad \wedge expression(linked\text{-}wno) = work(wno) \}$

$\pi_{\{expression\}} (.) = \{ expression \mid expression \in S'_{expression} \wedge work \in R'_{work} \}$,

where *term1*, *keyword*, *wno*, and *linked-wno* are respectively a search term, an attribute of the relation to be matched, *work* ID, and *work* ID to which a given *expression* is linked.

In addition, we need a similar set in which the search terms *term1* and *term2* are transposed:

$T_2 \leftarrow \pi_{\{expression\}} (S_{expression} |\times| \sigma_{keyword=term2} (R_{work}))$

$T'_2 \leftarrow \sigma_{keyword=term1} (S_{expression}) \cap T_2$.

Furthermore, we need another two sets; one is the set intersection of T_1 and T_2 above, i.e., $T_1 \cap T_2$, and the other is:

$T_3 \leftarrow \sigma_{keyword=term1} (S_{expression}) \cap \sigma_{keyword=term2} (S_{expression})$.

Finally, we get combinations of these sets as follows:

$T'_1 \cup T'_2 \cup (T_1 \cap T_2) \cup T_3$.

This can be expanded to cases where more than two terms, i.e., n terms, are specified in a query.

The following are examples of a search carried out in the extended search mode:

1) Figure 5-29 demonstrates the search screen with a query "Beethoven and Szeryng"—the latter search term represents a name of a performer. In this case, the extended search mode was selected. The search result for the query is shown in Figures 5-30-1 and 5-30-2. No *work* was matched, but fourteen *expressions* were matched, each of the first ten *expressions* being displayed in the brief form. One of the *expressions* matched is displayed in full detail in Figure 5-31. The figure shows that this *expression* contains only the names of the performers—'Brahms' is not the composer that I specified—and is linked to two *works*, one of these containing the composer's name that I specified in the query. This is the reason why this *expression* was matched to the query. In contrast, when I chose the standard search mode with the same query, only seven *expressions* that contain both names were matched, as shown in Figure 5-32.

2) Figure 5-33 shows the search result with another query, "Beethoven and Correspondence," in the standard mode. Two *works* were matched but no *expression* was matched. On the other hand, Figure 5-34 shows the search result with the same query but in the extended search mode—thirty *expressions* were matched in addition to the two *works* matched in the standard mode.

We may note, in passing, that the thirty *expressions* of the search result in this case are by chance equivalent to the union of the *expressions* linked to either of the two *works* matched to the query, or to both of the two *works*. Although twenty-four *expressions* are linked to one of the two *works* (i.e., that with w02627) as seen in Figure 5-12-2, and eight *expressions* are linked to the other *work* (i.e., that with w02537) as seen in Figure 5-18-1, only thirty (not thirty-two) *expressions* in total are obtained. This indicates that two *expressions* are linked to both of the *works*. Such a situation happens, since in this trial the record merge at the two different levels (i.e., the *work* and *expression* levels) was carried out independently of each other.

If the extended mode is usually preferable to the standard, it is possible to adopt it as the default search mode. It is also possible to expand this search function to cover the *manifestation* level for retrieving records with attributes at that level, such as the name of publisher, distributor, etc.

Chapter 5 Trial on Creation of Text-level Entity Records from Pre-existing MARC Records   183

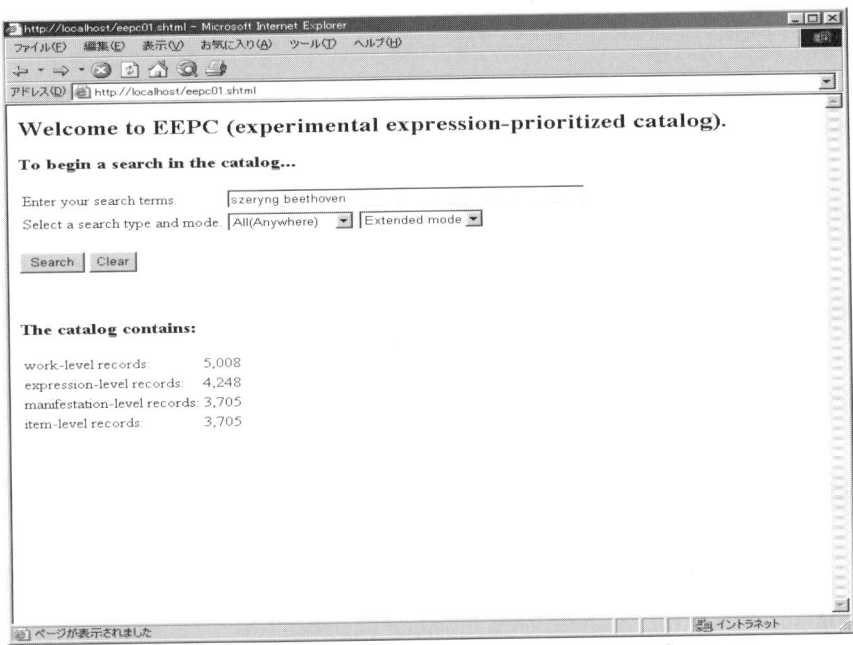

Figure 5-29. The screen showing a search in the extended mode.

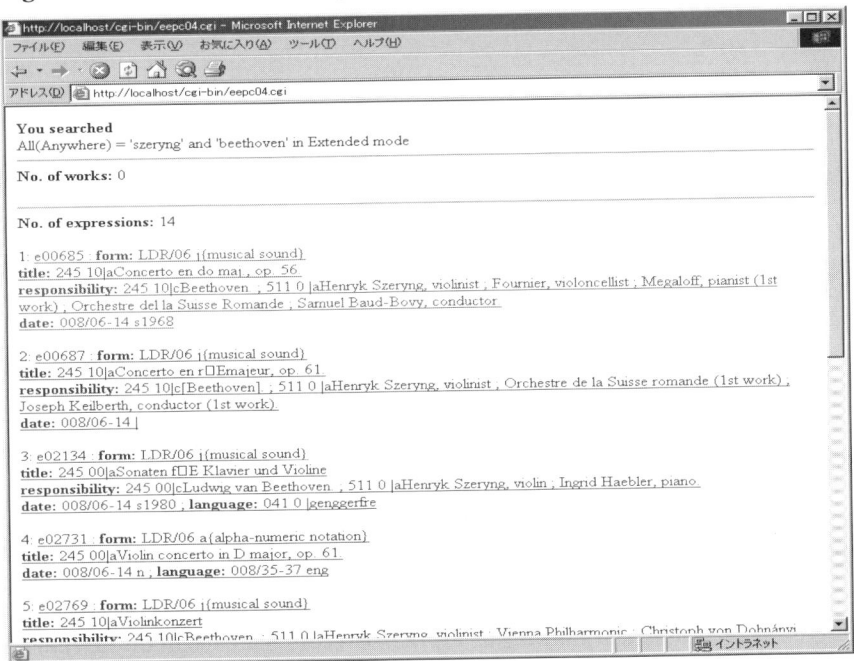

Figure 5-30-1. The result of an extended mode search (the top part).

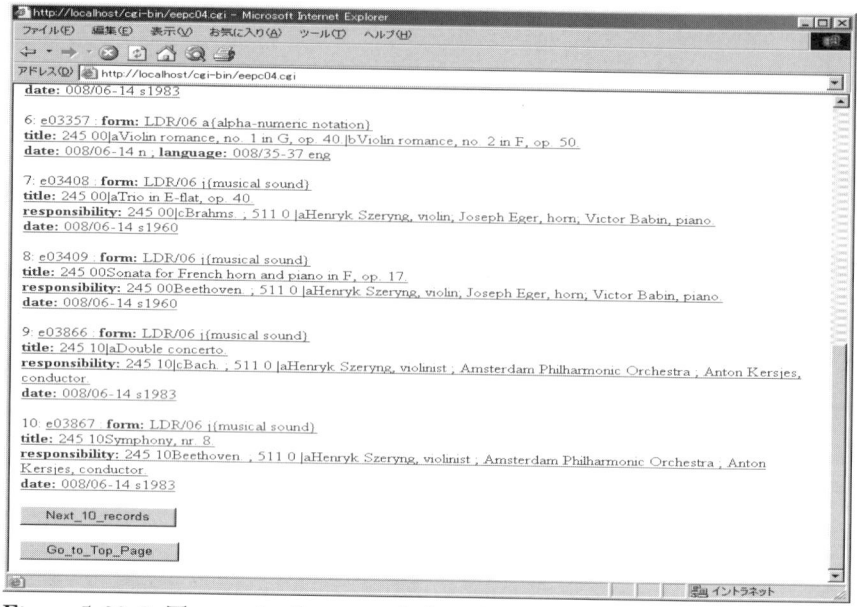

Figure 5-30-2. The result of an extended mode search (the bottom part).

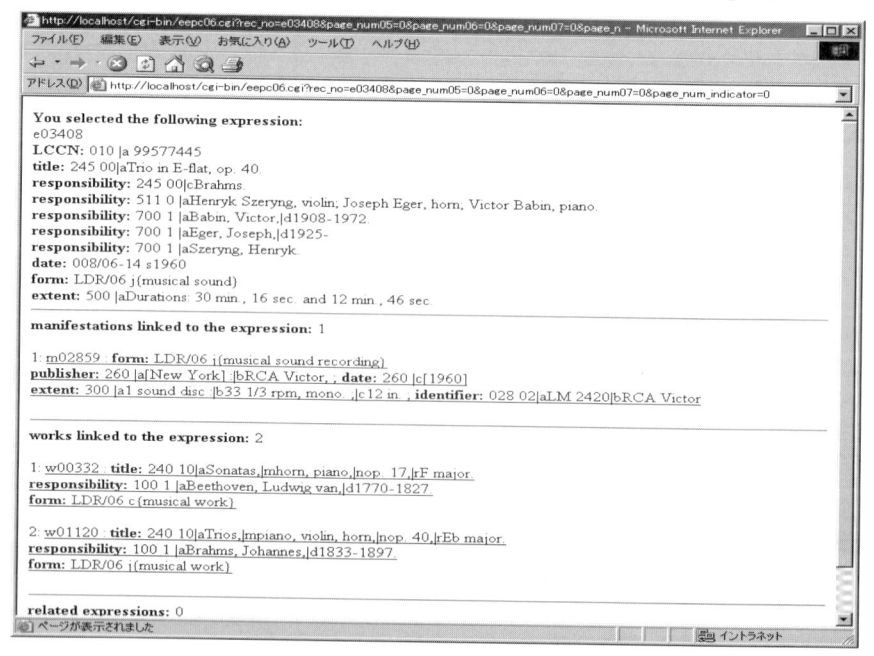

Figure 5-31. The screen showing an *expression* record matched in the extended search mode.

Chapter 5 Trial on Creation of Text-level Entity Records from Pre-existing MARC Records 185

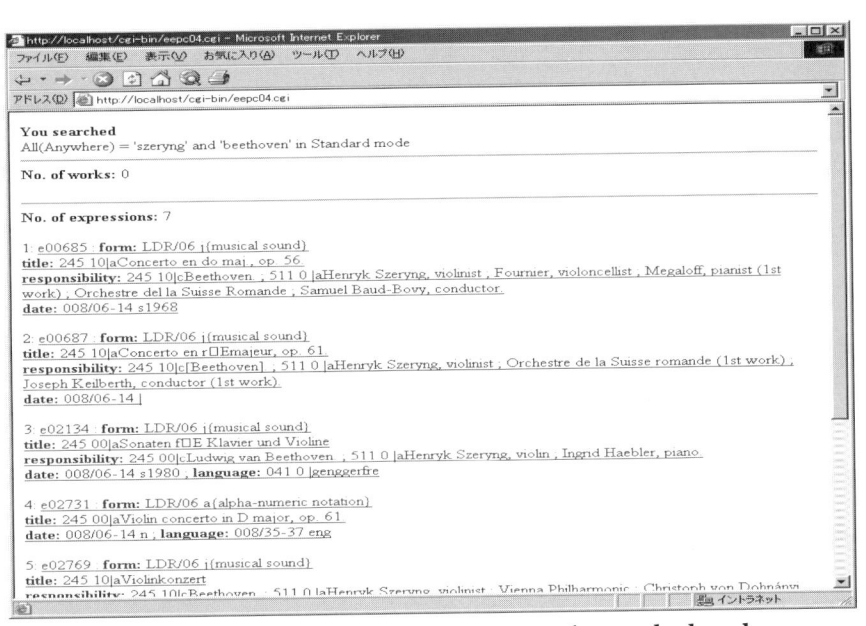

Figure 5-32. A search result with the same query in the standard mode.

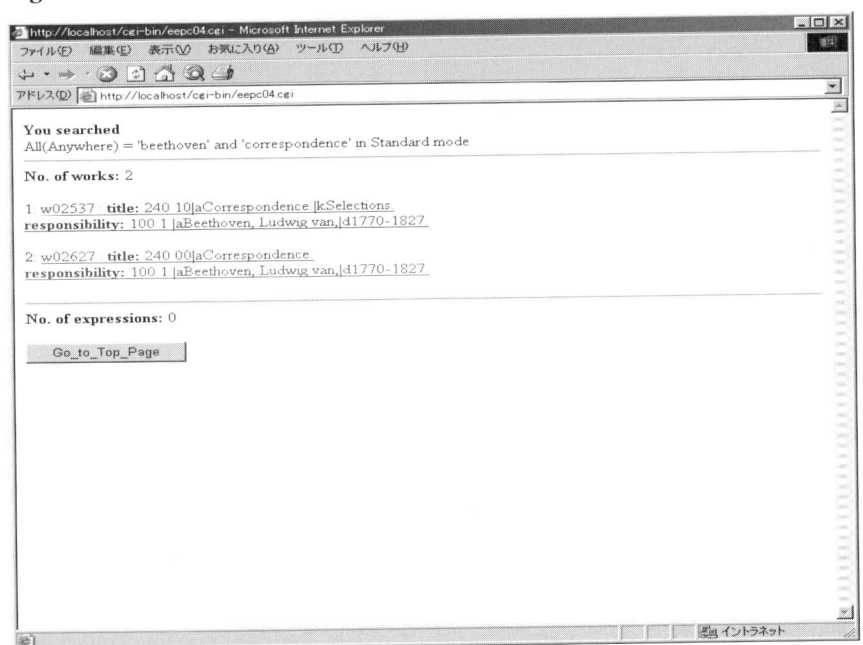

Figure 5-33. The result of another search in the standard mode.

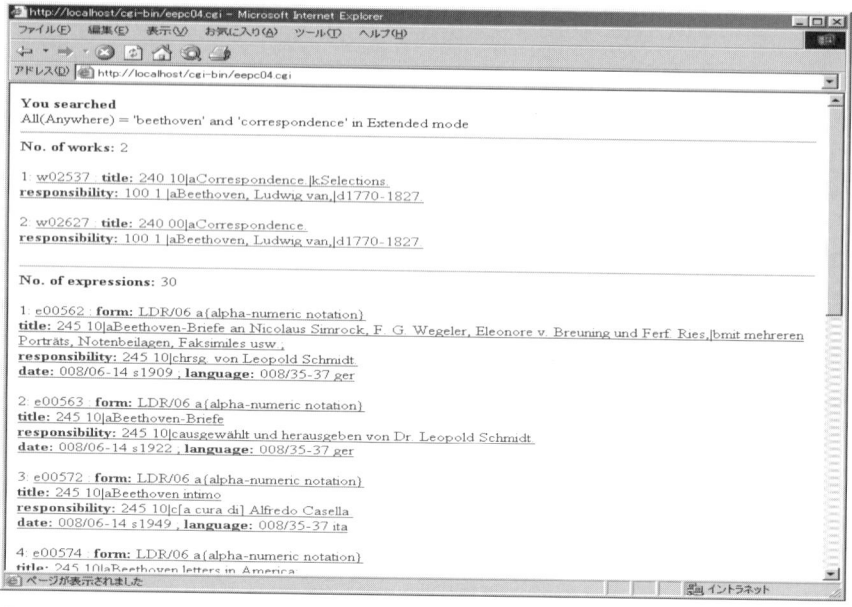

Figure 5-34. A search result with the same query in the extended mode.

5.6 Chapter Conclusion

The feasibility of creating bibliographic records in accordance with the model giving primacy to text-level entity proposed in Chapter 3 was investigated through the conversion of existing MARC records.

1) In terms of the structure under which records are constructed, the methods of creating bibliographic records in accordance with the model were categorized into two approaches: single record approach and hierarchical multiple records approach. These two approaches have their own advantages and disadvantages, but the hierarchical records approach is preferable for showing explicitly the structure of the model on which records are based.

2) Conversion of MARC bibliographic records into those structured under the hierarchical records approach was attempted. The conversion procedure was clarified by (a) identifying steps that need to be carried out by human and (b) identifying possible alternatives in each step of the conversion. The conversion was carried out by developing programs to facilitate it.

3) A prototype system was developed for retrieving and displaying records

created through the conversion of MARC records. Functions necessary in such a system to handle these records were demonstrated, and the usefulness of such records was shown.

Notes

1. Part of this chapter has already been reported as a paper in *Cataloging and Classification Quarterly*. Taniguchi (2004b)
2. Joint Steering Committee for Revision of AACR, Format Variation Working Group (2002b)
3. Joint Steering Committee for Revision of AACR, Format Variation Working Group (2002b)
4. Joint Steering Committee for Revision of AACR, Format Variation Working Group (2002b)
5. Joint Steering Committee for Revision of AACR, Format Variation Working Group (2002b)
6. Aalberg (2002), Hegna and Murtomaa (2002), Hickey et al. (2002), Weinstein (1998), Weinstein and Birmingham (1998)
7. Delsey (2002)
8. Library of Congress (2002)
9. Library of Congress (1999b)
10. Joint Steering Committee for Revision of AACR, Format Variation Working Group (2001)
11. Library of Congress (2002)
12. Program for Cooperative Cataloging (2001)

Chapter 6

Relevant Projects and Discussions

In this section I examine projects and discussions that seem to be relevant to the model giving primacy to text-level entity proposed in Chapter 3. They are (a) what have proposed and adopted different records structures from that under the current way of cataloging with AACR2 and MARC 21—which consists of three sorts of records: uniform title authority, bibliographic, and holdings records—and (b) what have adopted the same records structure as that under the current way but proposed different ways of dealing with resources, e.g., adopting a different unit of bibliographic record creation. Records structures and ways of cataloging are matters belonging to the logical record design level or implementation level, subsequent to the conceptual design level.

I cover such projects and discussions in a loosely chronological order.

1) *Multiple Versions Forum* (1989)

The Multiple Versions Forum was convened in 1989 with the aim of arriving at a consensus on dealing with resources that are the same in text but differ in physical manifestation[1]. The forum rejected the single record approach for handling multiple versions, which the forum called the 'composite record technique,' and thus explored the 'hierarchical records model' and the 'separate record model.'

The 'hierarchical records model' was further divided into two: the two-tier and three-tier models. The two-tier model is "a hierarchical model in which a master record may have holdings records that contain version information linked to it."[2] 'Master record' and 'holdings record' respectively indicate MARC bibliographic and holdings records.

On the other hand, the three-tier model is "a hierarchical model in which a generic description of a work may have linked to records containing version specific information, and these version records may have holdings records (without version information) linked to them."[3] This model is also described as consisting of "a basic bibliographic record (bibliographic entity)," "a version record (physical manifestation)," and "a local holdings record (copy)."[4] We can view this model as similar to the three-layered model that I have proposed since 1990 if we consider that the 'basic bibliographic record' and 'version record' correspond respectively to the text-layer and medium-layer. As mentioned earlier, the three-layered model does not have a layer corresponding to a holdings record. However, it should be noted that all models proposed in the forum, including the three-tier model, were only briefly described and there was no viewpoint given regarding which tier is to be given primacy.

The 'separate record model' indicates the way that separate records would be created for each version, with links among records. This is basically a reflection of the current way of cataloging, with an emphasis on the creation of record links.

Finally, by evaluating each approach against their own criteria, the forum adopted a recommendation to use the two-tier approach. None of the libraries participating in the forum, however, followed through with the recommendation, according to Svenonius[5]. The importance of this forum seems to be that it was the first event providing relatively comprehensive discussions on the multiple versions issue, and also the first trial at proposing alternative approaches to the current way of cataloging, although their examination of such approaches was insufficient.

2) Yee's discussion on the distinction between manifestations and near-equivalents (1994)

Yee closely examined the differences between manifestations and near-equivalents of moving-image resources, and consequently proposed a four- or five-tiered hierarchical technique as a better choice of dealing with such resources[6].

The 'near-equivalent' was used to mean "a copy of the same manifestation of a work that differs from other copies in ways that do not significantly affect the intellectual or artistic content."[7] She emphasized the significance of such a concept in reflecting an abundance of moving-image resources corresponding to the concept.

Instead of the two- or three-tiered hierarchical technique proposed in the Multiple Versions Forum, she examined a four- or five-tiered hierarchical technique to implement the concept of 'near-equivalent.' The four-tier was "work—manifestation—near-equivalent—holding" and the five-tier was "work—

version—manifestation—near-equivalent—holding."[8] The 'version' here was "a manifestation that itself has manifestations, such as the various editions of a particular translation of a work"[9] and thus did not correspond to the text-level but rather to the work-level (or subwork-level). Moreover, near-equivalent-tier records would be created that are dependent and subsidiary to manifestation-tier records only if necessary; the former records would contain information only differing from that recorded in the latter records.

Yee's contribution is significant in trying to refine the manifestation-level and related records structure while focusing on a specific type of resources, i.e., moving-image resources.

3) Bradford OPAC (1995–1997)

Bradford OPAC (BOPAC), developed at the University of Bradford, UK, was an experimental prototype OPAC that contained some new design concepts. One of the prominent features of BOPAC during the first phase of the research project was that, when loading bibliographic records represented in a conventional MARC format into BOPAC, which was constructed on a relational database management system, records are divided and stored in two relation tables: 'manifestation set' and 'manifestation.'[10]

The former table has fields for title (whose data values were extracted from the title proper and a uniform title, if any, of each bibliographic record) and author (whose values were extracted from the name headings of each record). If the data values of these fields are the same between more than one instance (i.e., bibliographic record), these instances are merged into one, being represented with one tuple within the table. On the other hand, the remaining data other than the above fields of a bibliographic record is stored in the latter table, each of whose tuples denotes an individual manifestation and also an item. The two tables are linked; each tuple of the former table is linked to one or more tuples of the latter.

Any initial search on title or author uses the former table within this OPAC. After an initial search is carried out and any of the resulting instances (i.e., tuples) of that table is selected by the user, all instances of the latter table are displayed which are linked to each of the selected instances of the former table. The system at this phase does not use any authority records (i.e., uniform title authority and name authority records), thus the using process is simple.

We may be able, in a sense, to regard an instance of the former table as a text-level record equivalence, whereas there was no recognition of the concept 'text' or 'expression' and the table would rather be viewed as that representing 'works,' as seen in the paper by Ridley[11]. We may also be able to regard this OPAC as an initial version of systems that make use of such a hierarchical records structure. Based on these points, we may say that such records and the BOPAC are a kind of system that implements a text-prioritized model. It is, however, important to recognize that the table is created automatically from bibliographic records made under current cataloging practice, which takes texts into little consideration, and that this OPAC is not sufficient for being viewed as a full implementation of a text-prioritized model.

Most of the results of the first phase were inherited by the second phase, i.e., the BOPAC2 Project. However, the above records structure seemed to be abandoned[12].

4) LS/1 Online Catalog System (1995?–)

This system has been developed at the Kunitachi College of Music Library, Japan, taking into account certain intrinsic characteristics of music resources[13]. It has some interesting features, but only one point closely related to the present study is taken up.

With this system, a conventional bibliographic record is divided into two records—a 'bibliographic record' and a 'medium record' in their terms—and these records are linked to one another. The 'medium record' contains the data elements of ISBD Area 4 (publication, distribution, etc., information), Area 5 (physical description), some elements of Area 7 (notes), and some coded information. Consistent with this, the 'bibliographic record' of this system comprises the remaining part of a conventional bibliographic record: the data elements of ISBD Areas 1, 2, and 3, and some other elements. When we have an item different only in, for example, publication information or physical carrier, from another already cataloged, with this system we need only to make a 'medium record' and link it to the 'bibliographic record' that was created for the other and already stored in the system. This implies that the system intends to make a record corresponding to a text-level entity, being separate from a record corresponding to a manifestation-level entity, although the system does not include any viewpoint regarding which record is to be given primacy.

We should first acknowledge the fact that such a system already exists and is at work, and then examine the limits of this system. Dividing a conventional bibliographic record into these two parts has been mechanically done. Hence, the identity of texts cannot in some cases be reflected in this division. For example, if two items contain identical text but have different data values at one or more data elements associated with the 'bibliographic record,' two different 'bibliographic records' are created and not integrated into one record in the system. This limit seems to be inevitable, since the system should be well operable under the current cataloging environment; it is necessary to efficiently import records created outside the system, and sometimes to export records with a conventional MARC format. Another limit of the system is that the current OPAC developed at that library is unable yet to make sufficient use of this records structure.

5) Howarth's linked four-tier records structure (1997)

This is a new records structure that intends to resolve the 'content versus carrier' issue, including the format variations issue, while requiring only the minimum change from the current records structure so that its implementation would be easy[14]. It refers to the FRBR model, but contains an important difference.

It is a records structure that consists of four sorts of linked records, as its name indicates. They are work-level, authority-level, manifestation-level, and item-level records, which are linked in that order. The authority-level record of this structure equals our conventional authority record like that of a personal or corporate author, or that of a uniform title. If we limit our view to a uniform title authority record, this record corresponds to the work-level entity in the FRBR model and also our text-prioritized model. However, one may notice that this record occupies the second-tier, not the first-tier, of the whole records structure—the reason for which is not clear.

On the other hand, Howarth's work-level record contains "elements which provide a framework of intellectual/artistic or 'content' information common to any work (title, statement of responsibility, series, generic notes about bibliographic or intellectual content)"[15] and access points, including subject headings and class numbers from classification schemes. From this point, one may consider that her work-level record does not correspond to the work-level entity in either the FRBR model or our text-prioritized model. Rather, the work-level record of her model would agree roughly with the text-level entity in the three-layered model and our model, although some elements (e.g., subject headings, class numbers) are dealt with a little differently between her model and the other two; the latter two do not fix the assignment of such elements. I want to emphasize here that her work-level record is different from the work-level entity of other models or the *expression* of the FRBR model.

Similarly, Howarth's manifestation-level record has "descriptions of unique physical properties or of format-specific details,"[16] such as edition statement, publication and distribution information, and physical description. The record is different from the *manifestation* of the FRBR model, but is roughly equivalent to the medium-layer of the three-layered model and, in a sense, to the *manifestation* of our text-prioritized model.

These observations allow us to conclude that there are exclusive relationships among the records at four levels, and thus each constituent of Howarth's records structure is thought to be defined in the parallel way, like the three-layered model. The two models in fact have something in common on the assignment of data elements. It is therefore possible to regard her records structure as a simple implementation of models giving primacy to text-level entity with some limits, although her discussion does not contain any viewpoint regarding which tier is to be given primacy.

6) Weinstein and Birmingham's ontological metadata (1998)

Weinstein and Birmingham developed their model, which is called 'ontological metadata' or 'ontology-based metadata,' within their digital library project[17]. This model was explicitly but partially adapted from FRBR, and consists of "a hierarchy of concepts that loosely models the creation of work."[18] This hierarchy is made up of five 'concepts': conception, expression, manifestation, materialization (digitization), and instance. It relies on bibliographic entities defined in FRBR, but contains some changes: the entity *work* is renamed 'conception'; the entity *item* is renamed 'instance'; and the entity *manifestation* is split into two levels— 'manifestation' and 'materialization (digitization).' In their model, these concepts are defined: "When the EXPRESSION is published, it becomes a MANIFESTATION. The physical embodiment of the MANIFESTATION is a MATERIALIZATION; if digital, the MATERIALIZATION is a DIGITIZATION."[19]

They created 'ontological metadata' in line with their hierarchy of concepts, by generating it from 493 existing MARC bibliographic records. They also developed a Java interface to assist users in finding or selecting resources and navigating relationships among resources. Their conversion procedure from MARC records has something in common with that adopted in our trial reported in Chapter 5. However, there are significant differences between the two trials, since the records and database structures are completely different from each other, reflecting the concerns and implementation environment of each trial.

7) Single record approach and expression-based records/cataloging (1995?–)

The single record approach, already mentioned in Chapter 5, intends "to reduce the creation of separate bibliographic records for multiple manifestations of the same expression by having one bibliographic record serve for more than one manifestation."[20] Several variations on this approach have been proposed using a holdings record or another layer of subrecords.

This approach emanated from discussions on how to deal with, in particular, reproductions and electronic resources. Examples of these are *Guidelines for Bibliographic Description of Reproductions*[21] published in 1995 by ALCTS CCS CC:DA, *ISBD(ER)*[22] published in 1997 by the IFLA, and other guidelines for cataloging electronic resources, such as LC's *Draft Interim Guidelines for Cataloging Electronic Resources*[23], the University of California's *Report to the University of California Heads of Technical Services*[24], and *CONSER Cataloging Manual, Module 31: Remote Access Electronic Serials*[25]. In most of these cases, bibliographic records are made for primary resources (originals for reproductions and print versions for electronic versions) and information on other manifestations are added to the records. In addition, applying this approach is limited to certain types of resources.

Meanwhile, ALCTS CCS CC:DA and also the Joint Steering Committee for Revision of AACR have recently discussed the feasibility of applying the single record approach to any type of resources as a choice to cope with the format variations issue[26]. Their discussion has something in common with that of the present study; for example, creating 'single records' for any type of resources can possibly lead to an implementation of a text-prioritized model. Their investigation, however, appears to cover only the practical aspect of the approach and does not deal with its theoretical aspect. Moreover, they seem finally to have abandoned the approach and adopted a different one.

In their discussion, another name, 'expression-based record/cataloging,' was introduced to cover several other approaches aimed at the same objective, in addition to the single record approach. The other approaches examined were 'expression-level authority records' and 'expression-level citations.' They are obviously neither models giving primacy to *expression*, nor ways of record creation in line with such models, since they create in limited cases 'expression-level authority records' or citations, both of which contain only limited information on texts.

Now, it is worth examining what our text-prioritized model implies when we employ the single record approach. This is a possible implementation of our text-prioritized model, as we have seen at the beginning of Chapter 5. The approach specifies a way in which a single bibliographic record is created that describes both the *expression* and *manifestation* entities so as to keep the whole records structure compatible with that of the current way of cataloging using AACR2 and MARC formats. This consists of three records—a uniform title authority, a bibliographic, and a holdings record. However, at the same time, the question is raised of what is the important difference between our text-prioritized model with the single record approach and current practice with that approach. Based on the discussion pursued in the present study, the answer to that question consists of the following:

1) The unit of bibliographic record creation (and also bibliographic description creation) should in the case of our text-prioritized model be based on the unit of the entity *expression*, not the unit of *manifestation*. In contrast, the current way of cataloging by the single record approach adopts the unit of *manifestation*, resulting in the chance inconsistenly of a bibliographic description which in certain cases involves more than one physical manifestation.

2) The first, second, and third areas of a bibliographic description which are defined in ISBD, AACR2, etc., and which also have a key role in identifying and describing an item, should intend in principle to describe *expression*, if a record is created in line with our model. In other words, those areas must be redefined so as to sufficiently represent the characteristics of the text of an item. This involves an implication that data elements making up those areas should be dealt with so as to cover all *manifestation* instances subordinate to an *expression* in question. In

contrast, it is unclear whether current cataloging practice with the single record approach leads to requesting such changes.

3) Relationships between texts—in particular, relationships that are important for most users—should be indicated in any manner, such as record links between bibliographic records and links between bibliographic records and uniform title authority records, when bibliographic records are created in accordance with our model. The current framework of a bibliographic record, and also the record link structure, must be rearranged in order to implement this. On the other hand, discussions on current cataloging practice with the single record approach have not touched on such a matter, and thus it is unclear whether that method needs such rearrangement or can implement it.

8) *FRBR implementation projects* (1998–)

There have so far been several projects aimed at implementing the FRBR model. Almost all projects inherently aim at implementing FRBR without any alteration of the current way of cataloging. The following are examples:

1) Delsey carried out a comprehensive study, commissioned by LC, of functional analysis of the current MARC21 bibliographic and holdings formats. The study correlates the MARC data elements with the entities specified in FRBR and also his analysis of the logical structure of AACR2. Based on Delsey's study, LC made a specification for displaying bibliographic records for multiple manifestations of the same work in a hierarchical manner, and has also developed a tool to display records in such a manner[27]. I referred to these specifications by Delsey and LC when carrying out the trial reported in Chapter 5.

2) On the other hand, the OCLC Online Computer Library Center has undertaken a series of experiments with algorithms to group existing bibliographic records into works and expressions[28]. However, their studies seem to give up dealing with the *expression* level, since they follow FRBR strictly and at the same time presuppose existing bibliographic records and the current way of cataloging, thus resulting in the problem of identifying texts with very limited clues. Furthermore, they investigate the feasibility of replacing *expressions* with additional attributes of *manifestations*, i.e., enhanced manifestation records where the roles of editors, illustrators, and other contributors are explicitly identified. However, the usefulness of this would be severely limited. Similar experiments have been

carried out by researchers such as Aalberg[29], and Hegna and Murtomaa[30].

3) Another example is the development by several vendors of cataloging systems incorporating FRBR. For example, VTLS's Virtua system allows conventional MARC records and 'FRBR records' to live side-by-side. The latter records are created by splitting the former records into four level records corresponding to the bibliographic entities defined in FRBR. Delsey's mapping of MARC data elements to entities in FRBR was adopted when splitting records.

It should again be noted that all of these projects and studies presuppose the current cataloging framework and practice, and then focus on FRBR—namely, the principal model giving primacy to *manifestation*. That is to say, they do not have any intention of giving primacy to the text-level entity *expression* beyond its treatment in FRBR. Furthermore, the upward pseudo-assignment of attribute values from *manifestation* to *work* and *expression* has not been properly implemented in their systems; all implementations have ignored such upward pseudo-assignment of attribute values.

The other type of FRBR implementation is to aim at partially modifying the current way of cataloging, including revision of the current cataloging rules, to adjust them to FRBR, since the current rules are not necessary perfectly matched with FRBR. Examples of this type are a series of studies by ALCTS CCS CC: DA, and then the Joint Steering Committee for Revision of AACR, Format Variation Working Group, to deal properly with the entity *expression* within the current cataloging framework[31]. However, after investigating some possible approaches and methods, their studies seem to settle for the incorporation of uniform titles corresponding to *expressions*.

Le Boeuf[32], and Zumer and Riesthuis[33], reviewed a considerable number of studies made of FRBR and its implementation, including those covered here. Also, the IFLA Section on Cataloguing, FRBR Review Group, maintains a comprehensive bibliography that lists papers, reports, etc., relating to FRBR[34].

Notes
1   Huthwaite (1994), Multiple Versions Forum (1990)
2   Multiple Versions Forum (1990, p. 5)
3   Multiple Versions Forum (1990, p. 5)

4   Multiple Versions Forum (1990, p. 26)
5   Svenonius (2000, p. 214)
6   Yee (1994a)
7   Yee (1994a, p. 227)
8   Yee (1994a, p. 240)
9   Yee (1994a, p. 240)
10 Ayres, Nielsen, and Ridley (1996, 1997), Ayres, et al. (1995)
11 Ridley (1998, pp. 234-235)
12 Ridley (1998)
13 Matsuura (1996, 1997)
14 Howarth (1998b)
15 Howarth (1998b, p. 154)
16 Howarth (1998b, p. 154)
17 Weinstein (1998), Weinstein and Birmingham (1998)
18 Weinstein and Birmingham (1998, p. 23)
19 Weinstein and Birmingham (1998, p. 23)
20 Joint Steering Committee for Revision of AACR, Format Variation Working Group (2002b)
21 ALCTS CCS CC:DA (1995)
22 IFLA (1997)
23 Library of Congress (1997)
24 University of California Libraries, Task Force on Electronic Resources (1998)
25 Program for Cooperative Cataloging (2002)
26 ALCTS CCS CC:DA (1999, 2000), Joint Steering Committee for Revision of AACR, Format Variation Working Group (2001, 2002a, 2002b)
27 Delsey (2002), Library of Congress (2002, 2003-)
28 Bennett, Lavoie, and O'Neill (2003), Hickey, O'Neill, and Toves (2002), O'Neill (2002)
29 Aalberg (2002)
30 Hegna and Murtomaa (2002)
31 ALCTS CCS CC:DA (1999, 2000), Joint Steering Committee for Revision of AACR, Format Variation Working Group (2001, 2002a, 2002b)
32 Le Boeuf (2001)
33 Zumer and Riesthuis (2002)
34 IFLA Section on Cataloguing, FRBR Review Group (2002-)

Chapter 7

Analysis of Requirements of Cataloging Rules by Use of Orientedness[1]

7.1 What Is 'Orientedness'?

7.1.1 Aim of Introducing a New Concept

The goal of the latter half of this study, i.e., Chapters 7-9, is to propose a method of designing cataloging rules by utilizing conceptual modeling of the cataloging process. We need such a method on the following grounds:

1) Cataloging rules are required on how to create bibliographic record(s) for bibliographic resources(s) in a way that reflects the entities/objects established in a conceptual model of the bibliographic universe, or specifically how to deal with and record each attribute of the entities and each type of relationship between the entities/objects.

2) No conceptual model of the bibliographic universe, which I have pursued in Chapters 3-4, nor any logical design of records based on the conceptual model, which I have dealt with in Chapters 5-6, provides instructions how to create a record, how to deal with each element of the record, and so on.

3) On the other hand, there has been no formalized design methodology for cataloging rules, and thus a more logical and systematic way to design those rules is required.

In order to propose such a method or, to put it more precisely, part of the preliminary phase of the conceptual design of cataloging rules, we need to clarify the requirements to be satisfied by cataloging rules, and also the cataloging process or the output of the process.

Requirements are in general made up of functional requirements, non-functional ones, and others[2]. Functional (or behavioral) requirements are concerned with the fundamental functions of a service or system; functions are specified in terms of inputs, processing, and outputs. Non-functional (or non-behavioral) requirements can be defined as restrictions or constraints placed on a service or system and thus be termed 'quality requirements.'

Attempting to cover both functional and non-functional requirements, I introduce and set up a new concept 'orientedness' that can be used to explain the diversity among cataloging rules and also the difference among possible alternative rules or sets of rules. That concept is a prerequisite for conducting the conceptual design of rules, as well as for deepening our understanding of rules. Of course, the concept is applicable to any rules regardless of models on which rules are based.

First, in this chapter, I present a tentative definition of the new concept. Second, according to its definition, some categories of orientedness are extracted from the general objectives and functions of description and access point/heading indicated in cataloging rules and other documents. Similarly, other categories of orientedness are extracted from other parts of the cataloging rules. Third, the principles (or fundamentals) of description and access point/heading and the elements of bibliographic description and heading established in current cataloging rules are assessed in terms of orientedness. Fourth, the extent to which each individual rule for description, which mainly prescribes methods to transcribe a bibliographic element can be explained is investigated in terms of orientedness with respect to each of the rules contained in *Anglo-American Cataloguing Rules, 2nd ed., 2002 Revision* (AACR2, 2002 revision)[3]. And finally, possible alternatives to each existing rule are shown, along with the difference in orientedness among those alternatives, and a possible set of rules is demonstrated when a given category of orientedness is maximized.

In this chapter, I deal chiefly with rules for bibliographic description and additionally with rules for access points/headings. The rules for bibliographic description are called here 'descriptive rules,' while the rules for choosing access points and building headings—excluding subject and form access points—are called 'access points/headings rules.'

7.1.2 Definition of Orientedness

As the starting point of discussion, I would like to present a tentative definition of 'orientedness.' It is defined as directiveness/inclination of a characteristic toward a certain objective or function. It is a means to bridge an abstract objective/function with various manifestations incorporating the realization of the objective/function. It would seem that the term 'orientation' could be used as an alternative to 'orientedness.' I will not, however, adopt the term 'orientation,' because this term brings to mind firstly the conventional meaning of 'activity of orientating oneself,' such as 'library orientation.' Here, I have chosen the term 'orientedness' in order to convey a specific meaning.

The concept of 'orientedness' has a broader scope than that of 'objectiveness,' which suggests a straight correspondence between an objective/function and its realization. It may be uncertain whether every rule and every factor contained in sets of cataloging rules can be assessed as a rule or factor suitable for the objectives established outside the rule, even if cataloging rules must be constructed as such. If we adopt and apply 'orientedness' as defined above, we can interpret subtle relationships between objectives/functions and a wide variety of manifestations containing their realization even in complicated cases.

In addition to this comparison, we can compare the concept 'orientedness' with other concepts such as 'user tasks' defined in FRBR, or with other objectives and/or principles such as 'objectives for (or principles of) the construction of cataloging codes' described in Chapter 2; this will be tried after the concept is properly set up.

The logical structure of a cataloging code, specifically a set of descriptive rules, can be considered as a multi-phase structure. Ideally objectives of bibliographic description or functions to achieve these objectives are presented first; of course, such objectives/functions must be in compliance with the objectives/functions of catalogs themselves. Several principles (or fundamentals) of bibliographic description to be employed to serve those objectives/functions are then established. The principles concern, for instance, the basic unit of bibliographic record, source of information, organization of description, levels of detail in description, and others. Based on these principles, rules describing in detail the application of the principles in typical cases are developed. These rules are typically those prescribing methods to transcribe a bibliographic element, which is a component of the description. Similar structure would be expected in a set of rules for access points/headings.

It is possible that orientedness is extracted mainly from the first phase of the cataloging code structure and secondarily from the remaining phases. Each principle established in the second phase and each rule in the third phase can be assessed in terms of orientedness.

7.1.3 Orientedness Corresponding to Objectives of Bibliographic Description

Statements on the objectives of bibliographic description can be found in some cataloging rules. For instance, in *Anglo-American Cataloging Rules, North American Text* (AACR1)[4] we find the following:

> The objectives of descriptive cataloging are: 1) to state the significant features of an item with the purpose of distinguishing it from other items and describing its scope, contents, and bibliographic relation to other items: 2) to present these data in an entry which can be integrated with the entries for other items in the catalog and which will respond best to the interests of most users of the catalog[5].

As indicated at the beginning of the passage, this statement manifests the objectives of descriptive cataloging—not just the objectives of bibliographic description itself. This is because the second part of the passage shows the compilation policy of catalogs beyond the description itself. We therefore adopt only the first part of the statement as that of the objectives of bibliographic description.

A statement concerning the objectives of bibliographic description or descriptive cataloging seems to be somehow omitted in the current AACR2. It is possible, however, to find in previous cataloging codes or related documents the same statement or a rough equivalent to that of AACR1, for example, in *Rules for Descriptive Cataloging*[6] and *Studies of Descriptive Cataloging*[7].

The quote from AACR1 actually presents three objectives known and accepted widely: (a) "distinguishing it [i.e., an item] from other items," (b) "describing its scope, contents," and (c) "describing its ... bibliographic relation to other items." We will establish given categories of orientedness corresponding to each of these three objectives, since several practical ways or devices toward the realization of each objective are naturally incorporated in descriptive rules. Thus the directiveness/inclination toward a certain objective in every rule may be observed.

The first objective in AACR1—distinguishing an item from other items—means identifying a given item by describing its significant features and at the same time distinguishing it from all other items with the same description. We must recognize that this objective has in fact a wide range of meanings.

Distinguishing and identifying an item is the principal objective in any bibliographic description. The practical meaning of this objective somewhat depends on the situation where the real achievement of the objective is expected. For example, it may depend on the entire volume of target items to be descriptively cataloged and their characteristics or the expected level of cataloging. It must be remembered that there is, in its real meaning, a great difference between descriptive bibliography and cataloging, which creates bibliographic references/citations for distinguishing and identifying an item. Descriptive bibliography is the detailed physical description and study of books, most often, antiquarian books.

On the basis of the above, I adopted a narrower meaning of the objective in this study—that is, distinguishing and identifying an item suggests the intention of attaining the distinction and identification of an item in each bibliographic element, not in the whole description, as exactly as possible. I call orientedness for this objective 'orientedness toward identity.'

The second objective from AACR1—describing the scope and contents of an item—implies providing any clues of its contents and scope or, in some cases, any clues for judging its quality and confidence. This means providing the description of its contents and scope with some specific bibliographic elements, such as contents note, etc. Orientedness for this objective is called 'orientedness toward contents.'

The third objective from AACR1—describing an item's bibliographic relationships to other items—involves identification of bibliographic relationships related to the item. This may be accomplished in any manner in the description. The ways used to indicate bibliographic relationship categories or types in the description vary according to the set of descriptive cataloging rules[8]. I call orientedness for this objective 'orientedness toward bibliographic relationships.'

Some objectives and functions other than the above three have been pointed out often. A fourth objective is to indicate the conditions to obtain an item or to provide clues for obtaining it. This objective also involves indicating the conditions to access or to use an item held in an institution. Although this objective is often stated in sets of descriptive rules of abstracting-and-indexing (A&I) services, it can also be added as an objective of description in descriptive cataloging. In fact, the bibliographic element 'terms of availability' is connected closely with this objective.

'Terms of availability' can be found in the last bibliographic area of description in ISBD and also AACR2 and other cataloging codes. In addition, elements in the area for publication, distribution, etc. can be regarded as indicators of the conditions to obtain an item. I call orientedness for this objective 'orientedness toward access conditions.'

A fifth objective is to indicate the provenance of an item or the context within which an item was created. Provenance is defined in archival description as, for instance, "The relationship between records and the organizations or individuals that created, accumulated and/or maintained and used them in the conduct of personal or corporate activity"[9]–'records' here mean resources themselves being described—and similar definitions can be found in the field of records management. *ISAD(G): General International Standard Archival Description, 2nd ed.* shows that the objective of archival description is "to identify, manage, locate and explain archival materials and the context and records systems which produced it."[10] Thus the objective of indicating an item's provenance is explicitly stated. It also sets the "context area" in its description; the area is made up of name of creator(s), administrative/biographical history, archival history, and immediate source of acquisition or transfer. Adding the same objective to descriptive cataloging is possible even if the extent to which the objective is required differs from that of archival description. I call orientedness for this objective 'orientedness toward provenance.'

All five objectives, ranging from that indicating the contents and scope of an item to that indicating its provenance and context (and the corresponding orientedness to these objectives), correspond to given bibliographic elements constituting the description.

It is possible to establish other objectives of description by dividing the primary objectives in a way similar to others already reviewed in this study and to define orientedness toward each newly-established objective. I would like to, however, emphasize that these five objectives examined above are possibly applicable to almost all sets of descriptive rules beyond cataloging codes and hence this set of five objectives (and the group of orientedness) are adequate in this research. All of the objectives of description shown in documents on bibliographic description are covered by those already reviewed. Although some such documents add on the objective in which bibliographic description provides the basis for access points that enable us to find or retrieve the description[11], this objective can be ignored in this research since making description to be satisfied with the above five objectives means automatically the satisfaction of this objective.

7.1.4 Other Categories of Orientedness

Turning now to the objectives and functions related to the process of creating a description—not the functions that the created descriptions themselves are expected to perform—two objectives come under this category: consistency and economy.

First, the process should create coherent descriptions in a consistent manner. Compiling rules into a cataloging code represents in itself the effort to make a standard coherent description. Accordingly, practical operations apparently intended to assure consistent description can be found in existing codes, and thus orientedness for this objective can be established and called 'orientedness toward consistency.' Orientedness of this type can theoretically be found in every operation and hence be regarded as the background to each rule. However, I narrowed down orientedness of this type to prescribing the recording order of bibliographic areas and elements, specifying the language and script of description and, in some cases, the terms used in description. This restriction enables clearer comparison with all other types of orientedness.

The second objective of the process of creating a description is to make description in an economical, i.e., cost-effective way. Orientedness for this objective is called 'orientedness toward economy.' Expressions such as 'compactness' and 'cost-effectiveness' are sometimes used to describe this objective. Here, for example, is a passage from *Studies of Descriptive Cataloging*.

EXTENT OF DESCRIPTION   The book is to be described as fully as necessary for the accepted functions, but with an economy of data, words, and expression: no item should be transcribed from the title-page which will duplicate the information of another item, unimportant matter or detail should be curtailed, unnecessary words and phrases omitted, and standard abbreviations used whenever appropriate[12].

There are similar statements in AACR1[13] and *Rules for Descriptive Cataloging*[14].

As indicated in the passage, orientedness for this objective is typically recognized in the process of abridgement or omission of a bibliographic element in creating description. It is reasonable to add restriction of character sets to be used in making description for this category of operation. As also described in the last part of the passage, usage of abbreviations itself is thought to come under the same category of operation, while usage of standard or prescribed abbreviations simultaneously aims at consistency in description. In this study, I have applied a narrower meaning to orientedness toward economy, as in the case of orientedness toward consistency. Accordingly, it does not include, in principle, the operation of transcribing a bibliographic element as shown in an item, although such transcription is sometimes the most cost-effective way among possible ways in recording elements.

7.1.5 Orientedness Involved in Choosing Access Points and Building Headings

In the preceding sections, I dealt with orientedness related to making a bibliographic description. Here, the objectives and functions related to access points and headings should be investigated.

The objectives and functions of access points and headings have been dealt with as being the same as those of a catalog itself, i.e., the finding and collocating objectives, since such objectives of a catalog are attained in principle through access points and headings. The finding and collocating objectives themselves are not suitable for being dealt with as orientedness. If we venture to seek categories of orientedness that have relationship with those objectives, orientedness toward identity and that toward bibliographic relationships might be found as those having such a relationship.

Rather, for access points and headings, a new category of 'orientedness toward ease-of-access' should be set up which refers to the objective of attaining easy access to a record. This category of orientedness indicates that, for example, headings such as names and terms in controlled vocabulary would better if in accord with those that are commonly known, i.e., those that the majority of users prefer. This can be observed in some cataloging codes. An example is found in AACR2, 2002 revision, Chapter 22: Headings for person, 22.1: Choice of name—General rule. The rule 22.1A specifies: "In general, choose, as the basis of the heading for a person, the name by which he or she is commonly known." Another is in Chapter 24: Headings for corporate body, 24.1: General rule. The rule 24.1A says "Determine the name by which a corporate body is commonly identified from items issued by that body in its language ..." This can be traced back to Cutter's code.

Moreover, some of the categories of orientedness extracted from and set up for bibliographic description are also observed in additions to names, and omissions of part of names, in headings for persons and corporate bodies. Additions to names, for example, intend to distinguish a name from all other names and thus orientedness toward identity is easily recognized. Also, if such additions include general designations for expressing the idea of corporate bodies, orientedness toward contents can be recognized.

If we turn to objectives relating to the process of choosing access points and building headings—not the functions that the assigned headings themselves are expected to perform—two objectives come under this category: consistency and economy. These are identical to those in bibliographic description.

The process should choose access points in a consistent manner and build coherent headings. Hence, orientedness toward consistency can obviously be extracted from the process. Orientedness of this type is theoretically found in every operation and thus be regarded as the background to each rule, as I have noted regarding bibliographic description. In the case of building headings, however, I narrowed down this category of orientedness to prescribing the recording order of elements consisting of headings, specifying the language and script of headings, and, in some cases, specifying the terms used in additions to names.

Choosing access points and building headings should also be done in an economical way. Hence, orientedness toward economy is extracted from the process. Orientedness of this type is typically recognized in limiting the scope of adopting access points, and also in abridging or omitting an element while building headings. It is reasonable to add a restriction on character sets to be used in headings for this category of operation.

7.1.6 Relationships Between Orientedness and User Tasks and Between Orientedness and Objectives for Construction of Cataloging Codes

In the preceding sections, I set up the necessary categories of orientedness while closely observing the cataloging codes themselves. On the other hand, the requirements of catalogs have conventionally been discussed only as objectives of catalogs. Recently, however, objectives for (or principles of) the construction of cataloging codes, which are sometimes called 'principles of description and access,' have been realized and discussed as distinct from the general objectives, as mentioned in Chapter 2. This distinction is valid, and both types of objectives should be used as requirements. Moreover, user tasks defined in FRBR may replace the objectives of catalogs. Therefore, we need to examine relationships between orientedness and the user tasks, and between orientedness and the objectives for the construction of cataloging codes—in other words, to examine what relative position orientedness has vis-à-vis the others.

We should first notice that orientedness is the directiveness/inclination of a characteristic toward the objective of making a bibliographic description and choosing and assigning access points/headings. That is to say, orientedness expresses a cataloger's actions and/or intentions, not user needs nor user tasks, although it is true that a cataloger's actions and intentions should correspond, to some extent, to the needs and tasks of users.

It is possible to roughly illustrate relationships between the categories of orientedness and the user tasks as shown in Figure 7-1, although there are ambiguities in determining such relationships.

1) Orientedness toward identity mainly corresponds to the task 'identify,' but there is a gap between them because of differences in the levels that they intend to serve. This category of orientedness might be additionally associated with the task 'find.'

2) Orientedness toward contents corresponds to the task 'select.'

3) Orientedness toward provenance is mapped into the tasks 'identify' and 'select.' This category of orientedness might be additionally associated with the task 'find.'

4) Orientedness toward bibliographic relationships is associated with the tasks 'find,' 'identify,' and 'select.'

5) Orientedness toward access conditions is associated with the tasks 'select' and 'obtain.'

6) Orientedness toward ease-of-access corresponds to the task 'find.'

7) Orientedness toward consistency and economy is not associated with any specific task.

Chapter 7 Analysis of Requirements of Cataloging Rules by Use of Orientedness 211

Consequently, relationships between the categories of orientedness and the user tasks are not clear at the current stage.

categories of orientedness   **user tasks**

orientedness toward identity

orientedness toward contents

find

orientedness toward provenance

identify

orientedness toward bib. relationships

orientedness toward access conditions

select

orientedness toward ease of accese

orientedness toward consistency

obtain

orientedness toward economy

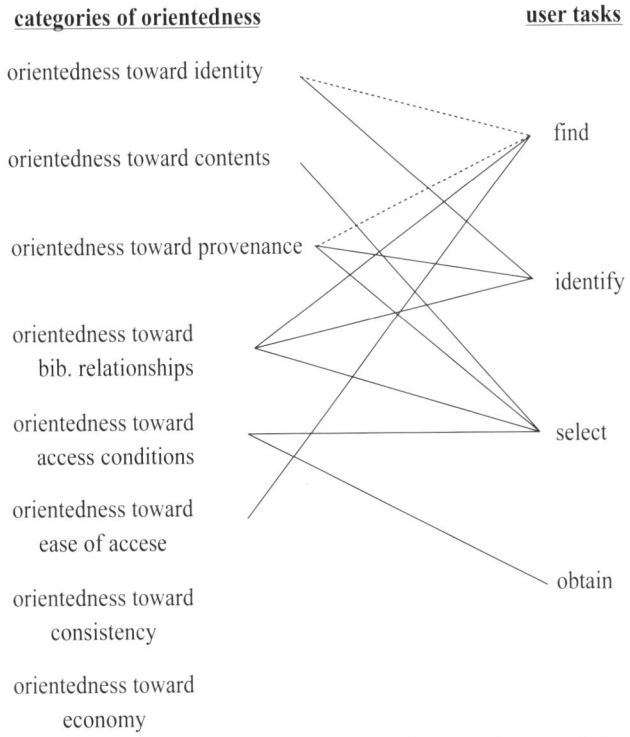

Figure 7-1. Relationships between the categories of orientedness and the user tasks.

Next, relationships between the categories of orientedness and the objectives for the construction of cataloging codes should be examined.

1) An exact (i.e., equivalence) relationship can be identified between orientedness toward ease-of-access and the objective 'common usage' (or its upper level objective 'convenience of the user of the catalogue'). Similar correspondence is pointed out between orientedness toward economy and the objective 'economy.'

2) Orientedness toward consistency corresponds, to some extent, to the objectives 'standardization' or 'integration.' Also, orientedness toward identity is associated with the objective 'accuracy' (or its upper level objective 'representation').

3) I cannot find any relationship between the other categories of orientedness and the other objectives, such as 'sufficiency and necessity' and 'significance.'

Based on these results, I will use orientedness as set up in this study, instead of the user tasks and the objectives for the construction of codes, on the following grounds:

1) The combination of the user tasks and the objectives is too fine to conduct an analysis of existing rules or the conceptual design of rules. On the other hand, orientedness is sufficiently broad.

2) Orientedness can be used to assess an individual rule. In contrast, it would be difficult to properly assess an individual rule in terms of the user tasks and the objectives.

7.2 Assessment of Principles of Description in Terms of Orientedness

7.2.1 Assessment of Description Principles

I have attempted to assess the principles (or fundamentals) of bibliographic description—the principles that should be employed to serve the objectives or functions of description—in terms of orientedness. I will take up each of the principles in order, although what comes under such principles varies to some extent by the given cataloging code.

1) *Basic unit of description.* Defining or selecting the basic unit of description is one of the important issues in sets of rules for description in order to make coherent, standardized description. ISBD, AACR2, and others, however, do not apply rigid definition on the object of description, as some researchers have already pointed out[15].

This issue may be interpreted as treatment principally based on orientedness toward identity (if orientedness of this type is interpreted in a broader sense) and orientedness toward consistency. However, for example, it is impossible to explain the difference among three basic unit concepts within the current cataloging framework—physical unit, bibliographic unit, and work unit—by means of orientedness. The bibliographic unit concept is defined newly and taken in *Nippon Cataloging Rules, 1987 edition* (NCR1987)[16] and its revisions[17]; it views as basic unit an object having a distinctive title of its own. It is also impossible to explain properly most of the prescribed operation related to a specific basic unit in a given rule set in terms of orientedness. Therefore, the concept 'orientedness' is not useful for addressing this issue.

2) *Source of information.* Defining the source of information for description is clearly assessed as the manifestation of orientedness toward identity, since it aims ultimately to prevent producing different descriptions for an identical item or, at least, to minimize the differences in descriptions, by advising the cataloger the source or the range of sources from which one may derive a value.

When we expand the prescription for the source of information to cover cases where an item lacks the prescribed sources or any necessary information is not found in the prescribed sources, other types of orientedness will be incorporated together with that toward identity. For example, AACR2, 2002 revision contains the rule 1.0A2: "Items lacking a chief source of information. If no part of the item supplies data that can be used as the basis of the description, take the necessary information from any available source, whether this be a reference work or the content of the item itself. ..." In this rule, we can identify other intentions, such as indicating the contents or scope of an item, indicating its provenance or context, depending on the category of the bibliographic elements to be sought, in addition to the principal objective, i.e., identifying and distinguishing the item. This implies orientedness toward contents, provenance, etc., exists in such cases.

The prescription for the source of information usually designates the order of preference in adopting the sources for each type of materials, as well as for each area and element of the description. It is recognized as the realization of orientedness toward consistency. Moreover, for some areas and elements of the description, the prescription specifies the recording format or style used for information taken from outside the prescribed sources—for instance, enclosing the information in square brackets and/or supplying the source referred to in the note area. Such prescription is interpreted as adherence to orientedness toward identity.

In this connection, it is possible to explain the difference in description between descriptive bibliography and descriptive cataloging, varying by the difference in the extent of adherence to orientedness toward identity in prescribing the source of information. Descriptive bibliography makes detailed physical description based on rigid transcription of the prescribed sources such as title page, caption title, and running title. Furthermore, it is possible to find the difference in description between A&I services and descriptive cataloging, according to the difference pointed out above. A&I services in general have only lax prescription for the source of information.

3) *Organization of description.* Orientedness incorporated in dividing the description into a number of areas and also dividing each of the areas into a number of elements can be understood well, if we compare this with transcribing all relevant information as shown in the prescribed source such as the title page. Only orientedness toward identity is recognized in the latter. On the other hand, other types of orientedness such as that toward contents, bibliographic relationships, access conditions, and provenance—each of which is involved in certain elements—are found in the former in addition to orientedness toward identity. Defining the areas and elements to be recorded and assigning the recording order to them in the description can be understood from the viewpoint of orientedness toward consistency.

4) *Levels of detail in description.* Orientedness toward economy and that toward consistency are observed in specification of the levels of detail in description. Cataloging codes such as the current AACR2 and NCR1987 adopt three distinct levels of detail. The first level of description consists of elements that are mandatory to be recorded, the second consists of mandatory and semi-mandatory elements, and the third consists of all elements defined in given rule sets. Hence, it is obvious that specifying the levels of detail involves the intention of making consistent description in an efficient manner by taking only mandatory or semi-mandatory elements in case of the first- or second-level of description.

5) *Principle of transcription.* The most fundamental principle in creating description in descriptive cataloging is to transcribe information from the prescribed source of information as it appears there. We have called this 'the principle of transcription.' Obviously, this principle aims at precise identification and distinction of an item and hence is typically identity-oriented. As a matter of fact, subordinate principles and prescriptions follow this principle to relax its fastidious adherence to precision.

6) *Language and script of description.* A given language and script is specified in recording some elements of the description; whereas the areas where transcription from the source is required adopt the language and script represented in the item. Such specification manifests orientedness toward consistency and also orientedness toward economy, since the language and script that the cataloging agency is familiar with and thus easy to handle is eventually chosen.

7) *Abridgements.* In the case of multi-lingual expression, i.e., if information on an element appears in more than one language or script, it is usual to select the expression in the language or script of the title proper or the text contained in the item, with the exception of some elements such as parallel title, parallel series title, and other title information related to these titles. This is thought to represent orientedness toward economy in view of the fact that it prescribes not to record expressions in other languages or scripts. This represents also orientedness toward consistency in that it specifies the language and script to be adopted.

If more than one name, place, etc., or more than the prescribed number of names, places, etc., appear in the source of information, restriction on recording the names, places, etc., is usual in most cataloging codes. For instance, if a single statement of responsibility consists of the names of several persons or corporate bodies performing the same function, all but the first name in each group of such persons or bodies are omitted. Or, if two or more places in which a publisher, distributor, etc., has offices are named in the source, only the first named place is recorded. All of these are understood as the manifestation of orientedness toward economy and in part orientedness toward consistency.

8) *Inaccuracies.* There is a variety of treatment in case of an inaccuracy or a misspelled word in the source as follows: (a) transcribe it as it appears, (b) transcribe it as it appears and supply certain marks indicating inaccuracy or misspelling (e.g., "[sic]" or "[!]"), (c) transcribe it as it appears and add the corrected version enclosed in square brackets, (d) record only the corrected version enclosed in square brackets so as to suggest that correction has been made, (e) record the corrected form as if such inaccuracy did not occur at all.

The difference among these alternatives can be understood from the viewpoint of orientedness involved in each of them. The first alternative is based on orientedness toward identity. The second and the third are also identity-oriented but at the same time contain other types of orientedness like that toward contents, bibliographic relationships, or provenance as secondary orientedness. In the latter group, which one is proper depends on the area and/or element for which one of these alternatives must be implemented. The fourth, as well as the second and the third, contains both orientedness toward identity and others, but the weight of the former and the latter have reversed. The fifth obviously represents orientedness toward contents, bibliographic relationships, or others except orientedness toward identity. ISBD and AACR2 adopt the second and the third; while NCR1987 opts for the fourth. The last is found in A&I services. Hence, we can find the difference in bibliographic description between descriptive cataloging and A&I services in this respect.

9) *Character sets.* The facilities available, like computer systems, restrict the character sets used to record information in the description. In such cases, a character or a symbol that cannot be reproduced has to be replaced with its description or equivalency in appropriate letters or words, or it has to be transliterated into the script used by the facilities. We will face this kind of issues frequently, in particular, in East-Asian languages such as Japanese and Chinese. The restriction of character sets is evaluated as economy-oriented.

10) *Capitalization and numerals.* Capitalization follows the usage of the language and script used in the description in descriptive cataloging, while it is fixed in each area or type of element in most A&I services. Both are consistency-oriented, but the difference between them cannot be properly explained in terms of orientedness.

As for numerals used in the description, roman numerals and numbers expressed as words are substituted with arabic numerals in some areas and elements of the description. This is consistency-oriented.

7.2.2 Assessment of Bibliographic Elements

Orientedness involved in the principle of the organization of description was presented in the last section. This will be followed by an attempt at evaluation of each bibliographic element established in ISBD, AACR2, etc., from the viewpoint of orientedness involved in the element itself. It should be recognized that, in some cases, it is difficult to differentiate inherent orientedness involved in each element from orientedness involved in the procedure of recording the element. In such cases, the former should be interpreted together with the latter.

Titles provide the example. They seem to represent only orientedness toward identity while being transcribed from the source as they appear there. However, they are divided into a certain number of categories of elements: title proper, parallel title, other title information, etc. The title proper is supplied from a source outside the item itself, if no title can be found in any source within the item, or is devised as a brief descriptive title, if no title can be found anywhere. These actions are taken with the intention of providing a clue to the contents, scope, etc., of the item. This allows titles to be contents-oriented as well as identity-oriented.

It is useful to refer to existing cataloging codes such as AACR1, *Rules for Descriptive Cataloging*, and NCR1987 in the course of examining bibliographic elements, since those codes contain relevant descriptions of the objectives in recording certain elements; the current code AACR2, 2002 revision, however, does not contain such descriptions. AACR1, for example, illustrates the imprint, which corresponds to the publication, distribution, etc., area in current codes, as follows:

> The place of publication, of printing, or of copyright, name of the publisher and date of publication, which constitute the imprint of a work, serve both to identify and to characterize the work and sometimes to indicate where it is available. ... The place of publication, particularly if it is not a large publishing center, may suggest a local viewpoint of the author. The publisher's name may also suggest a viewpoint or bias (especially when the publisher is a society or institution) or may be an indication of the quality of the subject matter or the physical make-up of the work. The date generally indicates the timeliness of the subject matter[18]. [The expression 'work' should be replaced with 'item' in accordance with our current usage.]

On the basis of this passage we can judge which orientedness would be involved in the elements, i.e., place of publication, name of publisher, and date of publication. All these elements are primarily identity-oriented as in the case of most elements. The publication place and the publisher's name are secondarily contents-, access-conditions-, and provenance-oriented as well. Likewise, the publication date may be also contents-oriented on the subordinate level.

Figure 7-2 shows the result of the examination of the bibliographic elements established in ISBD, AACR2, etc., from the viewpoint of orientedness.

Title and Statement of Responsibility Area

Title proper, Parallel title, Other title information

→ identity-oriented (main) + contents-oriented (sub)

General material designation

→ access-conditions-oriented

Statement of responsibility

→ identity-oriented (main) + provenance-oriented (sub)

Edition Area

Edition statement, Parallel edition statement, Additional edition statement

→ identity-oriented (main) + bib.-relationships-oriented (sub)

Statements of responsibility relating to the edition, Statements of responsibility following an additional edition statement

→ identity-oriented (main) + provenance-oriented (sub)

Material (or Type of Publication) Specific Area

Publication, Distribution, etc., Area

Place of publication, distribution, etc.

→ identity-oriented (main)

+ contents-, access-conditions-, and provenance-oriented (sub)

Name of publisher, distributor, etc.

→ identity-oriented (main)

+ contents-, access-conditions-, and provenance-oriented (sub)

Statement of function of distributor

→ identity-oriented

Date of publication, distribution, etc.

→ identity-oriented (main) + contents-oriented (sub)

Place of manufacture, Name of manufacturer, Date of manufacture

→ identity-oriented (main) + contents- and provenance-oriented (sub)

Physical Description Area

Specific material designation and extent of item, Other physical details, Dimensions of item, Accompanying material statement

→ identity-oriented

Series Area

Title proper of series or sub-series, Parallel title, Other title information
→ bib.-relationships- and identity-oriented (main) + contents-oriented (sub)

Statements of responsibility relating to the series or sub-series
→ identity-oriented (main) + provenance-oriented (sub)

ISSN of series or sub-series
→ identity-oriented (main) + access-conditions-oriented (sub)

Numbering within series or sub-series
→ identity-oriented

Note Area

Standard Number (or Alternative) and Terms of Availability Area

Standard number (or alternative), Key title
→ identity-oriented (main) + access-conditions-oriented (sub)

Terms of availability and/or price
→ access-conditions-oriented

Qualification
→ access-conditions-oriented (main) + identity-oriented (sub)

Figure 7-2. Orientedness involved in the bibliographic elements in ISBD and AACR2.

7.3 Assessment of Principles of Access Points and Headings in Terms of Orientedness

Next, I have attempted to assess the principles (or fundamentals) of choosing access points and building headings in terms of orientedness. I will address each of the principles in order, although what comes under such principles varies to some extent according to the given cataloging code, as in the case of the principles of bibliographic description.

1) *Scope of access points.* To what extent we should adopt access points and assign them to a record is basically determined by both user convenience and

economy. In general, if we increase the number of access points being adopted, user convenience in searching a record would increase. At the same time, from the viewpoint of economy, such an action requires more labor and cost; that is, orientedness toward economy decreases.

If a cataloging code adopts the main entry system, additional labor and cost is required and thus orientedness toward economy decreases. Orientedness toward consistency is also a key category of orientedness for such a system, since the selection of the main entry heading from among candidates must be done in a consistent manner.

2) *Source of information.* Defining the source of information is applied to determine access points, as well as the name that is the main part of a heading for person and corporate body, or the main part of a uniform title. Examples are found in AACR2, 2002 revision, such as 21.0B "Sources for determining access points," 22.1B "Choice of name. General rule" for headings for persons, 24.2B "Variant names. General rule" for headings for corporate bodies, and so on. Defining the source is clearly assessed as the manifestation of orientedness toward identity, being the same as the case of bibliographic description. It aims at minimizing the differences in determining access points and names by advising the cataloger of the source, or the range of sources, from which one may derive an access point or a name.

The prescription for the source of information usually designates the order of preference in adopting the sources. This is the realization of orientedness toward consistency.

3) *Choice among different names.* Choosing the name by which a person or corporate body is commonly known or identified is a principal rule for headings. Such treatment is widely observed, for example, in AACR2, 2002 revision, rules such as 22.1A, 22.1B, 22.2A1, 24.1A, etc. It is obviously ease-of-access-oriented. This treatment applies to cases involving pseudonyms and change of name.

4) *Choice among different forms of the same name.* Choosing the form of a name among its variants in fullness, language, and spelling, is basically done through identifying the form most commonly found. Examples of such treatment are found in AACR2, 2002 revision. For instance, 22.3A1 prescribes that "If the forms of a name vary in fullness, choose the form most commonly found," while 22.3B1 specifies that "If the name of a person who has used more than one

language appears in different language forms in his or her works, choose the form corresponding to the language of most of the works." This is obviously ease-of-access-oriented.

The prescription for choosing the form of a name includes some additional treatments. The rule 22.3A "<u>Fullness</u>" contains a subrule that "In case of doubt about which is the latest form, choose the fuller or fullest form." This action is understood from the viewpoint of orientedness toward identity, since the fuller or fullest form is more proper for differentiating names.

Likewise, choosing a form in English, i.e., English romanization, for names written in a nonroman script, is understood from the viewpoint of orientedness toward economy as well as that toward ease-of-access; restricting character sets and adopting English romanization are done with the aim of reducing labor and cost and at the same time increasing ease of access by users through their familiar script. Such treatment, however, decreases orientedness toward identity.

The rule 22.3C contains the specification, "Choose the form of name that has become well-established in English-language reference sources for a person entered under given name, etc. ... whose name is in a language written in a nonroman script." Also, the rule 24.1B1 specifies that "If the name of the body is in a language written in a nonroman script, romanize the name according to the table for that language adopted by the cataloging agency."

5) *Entry element.* The entry element is part of the name under which the person or corporate body is entered. Cataloging codes specify the entry element, and also the order of the remaining elements, for several types. For example, AACR2, 2002 revision, contains detailed specifications for personal name headings by dividing cases into 22.5 "<u>Entry under surname</u>," 22.6 "<u>Entry under title of nobility</u>," 22.8 "<u>Entry under given name, etc.</u>," 22.10 "<u>Entry under initials, letters, or numerals</u>," and 22.11 "<u>Entry under phrase</u>." It also contains similar specifications for headings for corporate bodies under the cases of (a) entering a body directly under the name, (b) entering it under the name of a higher or related body, and (c) entering it under the name of a government.

These specifications can be understood as a mixture of orientedness toward consistency and that toward economy; if a cataloging code specifies rigidly divided treatment, orientedness toward consistency would increase with decrease in orientedness toward economy. In addition, orientedness toward ease-of-access would be noticed.

6) *Additions to names.* (a) Titles of nobility and others such as terms of address, (b) persons' dates (birth, death, etc.), and/or (c) fuller forms of person's names, are added as elements of headings for persons under given conditions. Likewise, (a) names of countries, states, provinces, etc., (b) names of institutions, (c) years of founding or inclusive years of existence, and/or (d) appropriate general designations in English, are under certain conditions added to headings for corporate bodies.

These actions are taken chiefly with the intention of distinguishing identical or similar names; thus they are identity-oriented. In some cases, however, orientedness toward contents and provenance would be involved in these additions, since they provide pieces of information on the context and provenance of corporate bodies.

7.4 Investigation of Orientedness in AACR2 Descriptive Rules

I have tried to investigate each descriptive rule, particularly rules prescribing in detail the method of recording individual bibliographic elements, in terms of orientedness, on the basis of results obtained in the previous sections. Let me take AACR2, 2002 revision—a widely-used current cataloging code—and take as examples the rules of 1.4F "Date of publication, distribution, etc." thereof. Before beginning the investigation, it must be noted that orientedness involved in the element 'date of publication' is chiefly orientedness toward identity and secondarily orientedness toward contents, as already verified.

1.4F1. . . . (1) Give dates in Western-style arabic numerals. (2) If the date found in the item is not of Gregorian or Julian calendar, give the date as found and follow it with the year(s) of the Gregorian or Julian calendar. [The subrule number (1) and (2) are added, since the divided treatment of the rule is appropriate in the following discussion; such addition will be made also in other following rules.]

The first subrule specifies the characters to be used to record the dates; this is obviously consistency-oriented. If we consider the possibility that dates could be appear in non-Western-style numerals such as oriental numerical representations, the operation specified in the subrule may be regarded as being economy-oriented. The second subrule is mainly identity-oriented for allowing to give the date as found. It is at the same time somewhat contents-oriented in that the year of the standard calendar is added.

1.4F2. Give the date as found in the item even if it is known to be incorrect. If a date is known to be incorrect, add the correct date. If necessary, explain any discrepancy in a note.

The first sentence holds the principal idea in the rule numbered 1.4F2 and shows orientedness toward identity, as already discussed in the section on the assessment of the principles of description. The second represents orientedness toward contents, since the added correct date provides an indication of the timeliness of the subject matter, as already verified in the section on the assessment of bibliographic elements. The last proposes supplementary operation, which seems to be both identity- and contents-oriented.

1.4F3. Give the date of a named revision of an edition as the date of publication only if the revision is specified in the edition area. In this case, give only the date of the named revision.

This rule is consistency-oriented because it specifies that the date recorded in this area should match the statement in the edition area.

1.4F4. (1) If the publication date differs from the date of distribution, add the date of distribution if it is considered to be significant by the cataloging agency. (2) If the publisher and distributor are different, give the date(s) after the name(s) to which they apply. (3) If the publication and distribution dates are the same, give the date after the last named publisher, distributor, etc.

The first subrule designates orientedness toward identity, since adding the distribution date enhances the power of identifying and distinguishing an item. The second can be considered consistency-oriented if we focus on the point that this subrule specifies the recording position within the area. The last is economy-oriented, specifying not to record the date repeatedly in such a case.

1.4F5. *Optional addition.* Give the latest date of copyright following the publication, distribution, etc., date if the copyright date is different.

Adding the copyright date is interpreted as being contents-oriented, in addition to being identity-oriented, owing to the fact that the copyright date in general has closer relation to the time of the creation or update of the contents.

1.4F6. If the dates of publication, distribution, etc., are unknown, give the copyright date or, in its absence, the date of manufacture (indicated as such) in its place.

This rule contains the same orientedness as the rule 1.4F5. It is mainly contents-oriented in terms of giving the copyright date or the manufacture date, and is also slightly identity-oriented.

1.4F7. (1) If no date of publication, distribution, etc., copyright date, or date of manufacture appears in an item, supply an approximate date of publication. (2) *Optionally*, give an approximate date of publication if it differs significantly from the date(s) specified in 1.4F6.

The first subrule is contents-oriented. It opts most preferably for adopting an approximate date rather than giving "[n.d.]" (stands for "no date"). The second, which is optional, is considered contents-oriented and identity-oriented as well.

1.4F8. Dates for serials, integrating resources, and multipart items. (1) If the first published issue, iteration, or part is available, give the beginning date followed by a hyphen. (2) If the resource has ceased or is complete and the last published issue, iteration, or part is available, give the ending date, preceded by a hyphen. (3) If the first and last published issues, iterations, or parts are available, give the beginning and ending publication dates, separated by a hyphen. (4) If the publication date is the same for all issues, iterations, or parts, give only that date as the single date. (5) For an updating loose-leaf, supply the date of the last update if considered important. (6) If the first and/or last published issue, iteration, or part is not available, do not give the beginning and/or ending date; (7) give information about the beginning and/or ending date in a note if it can be readily ascertained. (8) *Optionally*, supply the beginning and/or ending publication date in the publication, distribution, etc., area if it can be readily ascertained.

The subrules (1)-(4) appear to be mainly consistency-oriented in that they seem to be designed principally for standardization of the style of recording, although they contain orientedness toward identity and that toward contents as well. The fifth subrule, in contrast, is only contents-oriented, since that action provides information on the timeliness of the resource. The sixth avoids improper identification and thus is mainly identity-oriented, whereas the seventh is contents-oriented. The last is obviously contents-oriented; it dares to provide information on date in that area at the risk of improper identification.

1.4F9.(1) Do not record a date for naturally occurring objects that have not been packaged for commercial distribution. (2) For other unpublished items (e.g., manuscripts, . . .), give the date of production (creation, . . .).

The former subrule can be judged as a mixture of orientedness toward economy, contents, and identity. On the other hand, the latter is obviously contents-oriented.

1.4F10. Give the date or inclusive dates of unpublished collections (including those containing published items but not published as collections).

This is a mixture of different types of orientedness such as that toward contents and that toward identity, as in the case of the first subrule of 1.4F9.
Even with a restricted range of examples, such as the rules examined in this section, it is clear that most of the descriptive rules of existing cataloging codes can be properly evaluated and understood extensively from the viewpoint of orientedness.

7.5 Identification of Alternative Rules for AACR2 Descriptive Rules with Their Orientedness

7.5.1 Identification of Possible Alternatives

Possible alternatives for each of existing descriptive rules such as AACR2, 2002 revision rules can be identified and also examined in terms of orientedness in the same way it was applied to existing rules. In order to make this possible, we have to take the following procedures: (a) fixing or somewhat relaxing the condition part of each existing rule, (b) creating possible alternative actions corresponding to the fixed (or slightly relaxed) condition, each then creating an alternative rule in combination with the condition, (c) assessing each alternative rule from the point of view of orientedness. Here, let me take, as the base rules, the 1.4F1-1.4F7 rules of AACR2, 2002 revision already examined in the last section. For the condition of each rule, we can conceive various possible actions including variation in usage of certain punctuation marks such as square brackets and variation in combination of the area (e.g., the publication area or the note area) and the location within the area where a given bibliographic element should be recorded. However, to avoid mixing complicated enumeration with trivialities, only the major alternative actions will be identified, by focusing on the main intention of the base rule and ignoring all possible trivial variations.

1.4F1.(1) [Alternative]: If dates are in non-Western-style arabic numerals (e.g., in roman, oriental numerals, or chronogram), choose either action: (a) give them as they appear in the item, or (b) give them as they appear and follow them with the same dates in Western-style arabic numerals.

The first choice in action obviously assigns priority to orientedness toward identity. On the other hand, the second choice falls in between the first choice and the action taken in the original rule. It is a mixture of orientedness toward identity and that toward consistency; however levels of these categories of orientedness differ from those in the first choice and the original rule.

1.4F1.(2) [Alternative]: If the date found in the item is not of Gregorian or Julian calendar, choose any of the following actions: (a) give the date as found and do not follow it with the date of the Gregorian or Julian calendar, (b) give the equivalent date of the Gregorian or Julian calendar and follow it with the date as found, or (c) give only the equivalent date of the Gregorian or Julian calendar.

The first choice of action is identity-oriented, as is the case in the original action. We can understand that this action is also slightly economy-oriented if we compare this with the original. The second choice instructs change of the recording position of the two dates from the original action—it is more contents-oriented than identity-oriented. The third is contents-oriented.

1.4F2. [Alternative]: If the date as found in the item is known to be incorrect, choose any of the following actions: (a) give the date as found and do not add the corrected date, (b) give the corrected date and add the date as found, or (c) give only the corrected date.

Orientedness involved in each choice is the same as that involved in the alternatives of the rule 1.4F1.(2). Regarding the rule 1.4F3 on date of named revision, there is no major alternative that we identify.

1.4F4.(1) [Alternative]: Even when the publication date differs from the date of distribution, do not add the distribution date.

This is economy-oriented. Incidentally, if the original condition of the rule is relaxed a little, the following alternative rule is obtained: 'Add the date of distribution even if it is the same as the publication date.' This rule is identity-oriented. With regard to the rule 1.4F4.(2), there is no major alternative that we identify.

1.4F4.(3) [Alternative]: Give the publication date after the publisher name and also give the distribution date after the distributor name even if both dates are the same.

This rule is evidently identity-oriented.

1.4F5. [Alternative]: Omit the latest date of copyright, if the copyright date is different from the date of publication, distribution, etc.

This is economy-oriented. Incidentally, if the original condition of the rule is relaxed a little, the following alternative is obtained: 'Give the latest date of copyright following the publication, distribution, etc., date even if the copyright date is the same as the publication, distribution, etc., date.' The rule obtained is more contents-oriented than identity-oriented, because the copyright date seems to be closely associated with the contents of an item.

1.4F6. [Alternative]: If the dates of publication, distribution, etc., are unknown, choose either action: (a) give "[n.d.]", or (b) supply an approximate date of publication.

The former choice is economy-oriented, while the latter is contents-oriented.

1.4F7.(1) [Alternative]: If no date of publication, distribution, etc., copyright date, or date of manufacture appears in an item, choose either action: (a) give "[n.d.]", or (b) give the date taken from a source other than those prescribed (e.g., the preface, introduction, etc.) with proper qualification.

The former is economy-oriented, whereas the latter is identity-oriented.

1.4F7.(2) [Alternative]: Do not provide an approximate date of publication even if it differs significantly from the date(s) specified in the original 1.4F6 rule.

This treatment is simply economy-oriented.

7.5.2 Identification of Possible Sets of Rules

As a next step, possible sets of rules can be identified from the alternative rules examined in the last section. Here, an attempt will be made to demonstrate a set of rules when a given category of orientedness is maximized, that is, a set of rules containing the given orientedness most among possible alternative actions already identified. Let me take the same rules of AACR2, 2002 revision and maximize each type of orientedness in the order of identity, contents, consistency, and economy, since other types of orientedness are not related to the above rules.

First, if we maximize orientedness toward identity without any change in setting of conditions, we can get the following set of rules:

1.4F1.(1) Give dates as they appear in the item even if they are in non-Western-style numerals.
1.4F1.(2) (The same as the original rule, or the following:)
If the date found in the item is not of Gregorian or Julian calendar, give only the date as found.
1.4F2. (The same as the original rule, or the following:)
If the date as found in the item is known to be incorrect, give only the date as found.
1.4F4.(1) (The same as the original rule.)
1.4F4.(3) Give the publication date after the publisher's name and also give the distribution date after the distributor's name even if both dates are the same.
1.4F5. (The same as the original rule.)
1.4F6. (The same as the original rule.)
1.4F7.(1) If no date of publication, distribution, etc., copyright date, or date of manufacture appears in an item, give the date taken from a source other than those prescribed with proper qualification.
1.4F7.(2) (the same as the original rule)

Note that rules 1.4F3 and 1.4F4.(2) are not related to orientedness toward identity.

Second, if we maximize orientedness toward contents, we can get the following set of rules:

1.4F1.(2) If the date found in the item is not of Gregorian or Julian calendar, give only the equivalent date of the Gregorian or Julian calendar.
1.4F2. If the date as found in the item is known to be incorrect, give only the

corrected date.

1.4F5. (The same as the original rule.)

1.4F6. (The same as the original rule, or the following:)
If the dates of publication, distribution, etc., are unknown, supply an approximate date of publication.

1.4F7.(1) (The same as the original rule.)

1.4F7.(2) (The same as the original rule.)

Note that rules 1.4F1.(1), 1.4F3, 1.4F4.(1), 1.4F4.(2), and 1.4F4.(3) are not related to orientedness toward contents.

Third, the set of rules maximizing orientedness toward consistency, which corresponds to rules focusing on the establishment of consistency, is as follows:

1.4F1.(1) (The same as the original rule.)

1.4F3. (The same as the original rule.)

1.4F4.(2) (The same as the original rule.)

1.4F4.(3) (The same as the original rule.)

Note that rules 1.4F1.(2), 1.4F2, 1.4F4.(1), 1.4F5, 1.4F6, 1.4F7.(1), and 1.4F7.(2) are not related to orientedness toward consistency.

Last, I will show the rule set maximizing orientedness toward economy. In this case I will include rules prescribing to transcribe elements as shown in an item, if such transcription would be the most economical way among possible recording actions.

1.4F1.(2) If the date found in the item is not of Gregorian or Julian calendar, give only the date as found.

1.4F2. If the date as found in the item is known to be incorrect, give only the date as found.

1.4F4.(1) Omit the date of distribution even if it differs from the publication date.

1.4F4.(3) (The same as the original rule.)

1.4F5. Omit the latest date of copyright, if the copyright date is different from the date of publication, distribution, etc.

1.4F6. If the dates of publication, distribution, etc., are unknown, give "[n.d.]" only.

1.4F7.(1) If no date of publication, distribution, etc., copyright date, or date of manufacture appears in an item, give "[n.d.]" only.

1.4F7.(2) Do not provide an approximate date of publication even if it differs significantly from the date(s) specified in the original 1.4F6 rule.

Note that rules 1.4F1.(1), 1.4F3, and 1.4F4.(2) are not related to orientedness toward economy.

Table 7-1 shows the results of the above in a summarized manner; but some categories of orientedness involved in the original AACR2 rules are not listed, since the figure was based on the rules identified after maximizing each category of orientedness.

Table 7-1. Summary of possible sets of rules when each category of orientedness is maximized.

	Orientedness toward identity	Orientedness toward contents	Orientedness toward consistency	Orientedness toward economy
1.4F1.(1)	alternative.1	not related	original	not related
1.4F1.(2)	original or alternative.1	alternative.2	not related	alternative.1
1.4F2.	original or alternative.1	alternative.2	not related	alternative.1
1.4F3.	not related	not related	original	not related
1.4F4.(1)	original	not related	not related	alternative.1
1.4F4.(2)	not related	not related	original	not related
1.4F4.(3)	alternative.1	not related	original	original
1.4F5	original (sub)	original (main)	not related	alternative.1
1.4F6	original (sub)	original (main) or alternative.1	not related	alternative.2
1.4F7.(1)	alternative.1	original	not related	alternative.2
1.4F7.(2)	original (sub)	original (main)	not related	alternative.1

7.6 Chapter Conclusion

The new concept 'orientedness' was introduced to analyze cataloging rules from a new viewpoint. As a result of the study conducted in this chapter, the following has been clarified:

1) The set of orientedness established in this chapter would be applicable to a broad range of cataloging codes.

2) Most of the principles (or fundamentals) of description and access points/headings can be assessed in terms of orientedness, with a few exceptions.

3) Bibliographic elements established in sets of rules such as ISBD and AACR2 can be assessed in terms of orientedness. For some elements, the orientedness involved depends on action taken to record those elements.

4) Each rule in existing cataloging codes can be evaluated and understood from the viewpoint of orientedness. Also, each possible alternative to an existing rule can be properly positioned on the basis of orientedness involved in the alternative itself. In other words, the relative position of each alternative rule among all possible alternatives can be understood vis-à-vis the difference in orientedness involved in each alternative.

Notes

1. Part of this chapter has already been reported as a paper in *Journal of the American Society for Information Science*. Taniguchi (1999a)
2. Loucopoulos and Karakostas (1995)
3. Joint Steering Committee for Revision of AACR (2002)
4. American Library Association et al. (1967)
5. American Library Association et al. (1967, p. 189)
6. Library of Congress (1949, p. 7)
7. Library of Congress (1946, pp. 25-26)
8. Tillett (1987, 1991b, 1992a)
9. International Council on Archives (2000, p. 11)
10. International Council on Archives (2000, p. 10)
11. Hagler (1997, p. 43), Rowley (1995, p. 25)
12. Library of Congress (1946, pp. 26-27)

13 American Library Association et al. (1967, p. 189)
14 Library of Congress (1949, p. 7)
15 Gorman (1992), Shinebourne (1979)
16 Japan Library Association (1987)
17 Japan Library Association (1994, 2001)
18 American Library Association et al. (1967, p. 200)

Chapter 8

Design of Cataloging Rules Using Conceptual Modeling of Cataloging Process[1]

8.1 Outline of Conceptual Design Procedure for Cataloging Rules

For conducting the conceptual design of cataloging rules, it would be beneficial to apply conceptual modeling to the cataloging process which is of interest to, and conducted by, catalogers, since cataloging rules should be based on the modeling of the cataloging process. In fact, significant parts of the cataloging process have been specified in and formulated as cataloging rules independent of any situation/system. Applying conceptual modeling to the cataloging process therefore implies utilizing conceptual modeling for re-examination and reformulation of cataloging rules—that is, the design of those rules.

The aim of the present chapter is to propose a method to design cataloging rules by utilizing conceptual modeling of the cataloging process and at the same time applying the concept of 'orientedness' which was introduced in Chapter 7. Another aim is to propose a general model for the cataloging process at the conceptual level. The design method for cataloging rules should be applicable to, consistent in, and scalable for, any situation/system. Also, the general model should be applicable to, and independent of, any situation/system, cataloging code, or conceptual model of the bibliographic universe, in principle. I therefore do not intend to propose a model applicable only to the model giving primacy to text-level bibliographic entity that I proposed in the former part of the present study.

Very few attempts have been made at approaching the cataloging process with conceptual modeling and no conceptual model for the process has ever been developed. To put it more precisely, we have no general models applicable to any situation/system, although there might be models dependent on a specific situation, i.e., operational models for certain cataloging systems.

Conceptual modeling is used at the stage of conceptual design, which precedes detailed design. I propose a step-by-step method to design cataloging rules at the conceptual design stage. The method is made up of the following phases and is illustrated in Figure 8-1.

Phase 0: Specifying requirements to be satisfied with the cataloging process or the output of the process, and defining 'cataloger tasks,' which are generic tasks performed by catalogers when creating a bibliographic record. These should be done before detailed modeling of the cataloging process is performed. They are, of course, independent of any cataloging code.

To specify such requirements, I use the concept of 'orientedness,' which covers both functional and non-functional requirements. Necessary categories of orientedness to specify the requirements should be enumerated at this preliminary phase.

The cataloger tasks, on the other hand, can be defined while referring to some classifications of cataloging rules with respect to the functions they perform. These tasks are the main building blocks of the cataloging process conducted by catalogers; that is, the cataloging process is modeled as a sequence of tasks at a higher level. Necessary tasks are defined at this phase.

Phase 1: Building a core model which demonstrates the basic framework of each individual cataloger task. The core model consists of: (a) basic 'event patterns' that trigger certain actions by catalogers under each individual task, (b) 'action patterns' applicable to each event pattern, and (c) orientedness involved in an event and action pair. At this phase, therefore, specifying basic event and action patterns and assessing categories of orientedness relative to an event-action pair should be carried out. These could be done in this order in step-by-step manner, or done at one time.

The core model covers only events and actions common in principle in all data elements that make up a bibliographic record. It also applies to any cataloging code, except in some tasks. It is thus a general model applicable to any situation/system and independent of any cataloging code.

Phase 2: Propagating the core model to reflect the characteristics of an individual data element and, in some cases, a certain class of materials (i.e., content, carrier, and publication type). Consequently, a comprehensive model containing all event patterns in each individual element, as well as all possible actions against each event, is obtained.

Next, the propagated model is defined by choosing pairs of event and action patterns enumerated in the model in order to match a particular situation. This definition should be done while referring to orientedness indicated in each event-action pair.

This phase is dependent on the data element and the class of materials to reflect their characteristics. Those characteristics are expressed in a cataloging code together with characteristics of the language and script of the cataloging agency. Hence, the resultant model is not a general one independent of any situation/system or cataloging code.

By following these phases, consistent and comprehensive conceptual modeling, i.e., rational conceptual design can be attained. Moreover, a set of event-action pairs reflecting specific requirements through categories of orientedness is obtained.

In a sense, this procedure might be followed, more or less implicitly, within a group of experts or at least inside an expert's mind when designing cataloging rules. However, it is significant to follow the procedure and execute each step in an explicit way to produce more logical and systematic design.

After the conceptual design of cataloging rules is completed, detailed design must be carried out. Transformation will be expected from the event-action pairs identified in the last step of the conceptual design into expressions in natural language to form cataloging rules or others. It is quite possible to convert multiple event-action pairs into one rule expression at the succeeding stage, if such integration makes a rule easier to understand. At this stage, it would be useful also to put rules in the order in which the events covered by the rules might be encountered, that is, the most used rules are provided before those less used, since existing cataloging codes adopt such an order.

Phase 0: Specifying Requirements and Defining Cataloger Tasks
- Orientedness O_1, O_2, ...
- Cataloger task T_1, T_2, ...

Phase 1: Building Core Model
Under Task T_1

  Event E_{1-1} —— Action A_{1-1-1} —— Orientedness O_{1-1-1}
      —— Action A_{1-1-2} —— Orientedness O_{1-1-2}
      —— ...

  Event E_{1-2} —— Action A_{1-2-1} —— Orientedness O_{1-2-1}
      —— Action A_{1-2-2} —— Orientedness O_{1-2-2}
      —— ...

Under Task T_2
 ...

Phase 2

Step 1: Propagating Core Model

Data Element D_1; Under Task T_1

  Event E_{1-1}' —— Action A_{1-1-1}' —— Orientedness O_{1-1-1}
      —— Action $A_{1-1-1'-1}$ —— Orientedness $O_{1-1-1'}$
      —— Action A_{1-1-2}' —— Orientedness O_{1-1-2}
      —— ...

  Event E_{1-2}' —— Action A_{1-2-1}' —— Orientedness O_{1-2-1}
      —— Action A_{1-2-2}' —— Orientedness O_{1-2-2}
      —— ...

...

Data Element D_1; Under Task T_2
 ...

Data Element D_2; Under Task T_1
 ...

Step 2: Defining Propagated Model by Choosing Event-Action Pairs

Data Element D1; Under Task T_1

    Event E_{1-1}' —— Action A_{1-1-1}' —— Orientedness O_{1-1-1}

                  —— Action $A_{1-1-1'-1}$ —— Orientedness $O_{1-1-1'}$

                  —— Action A_{1-1-2}' —— Orientedness O_{1-1-2}

             —— ...

    Event E_{1-2}' —— Action A_{1-2-1}' —— Orientedness O_{1-2-1}

                —— Action A_{1-2-2}' —— Orientedness O_{1-2-2}

           —— ...

...

Data Element D_1; Under Task T_2

...

Data Element D_2; Under Task T_1

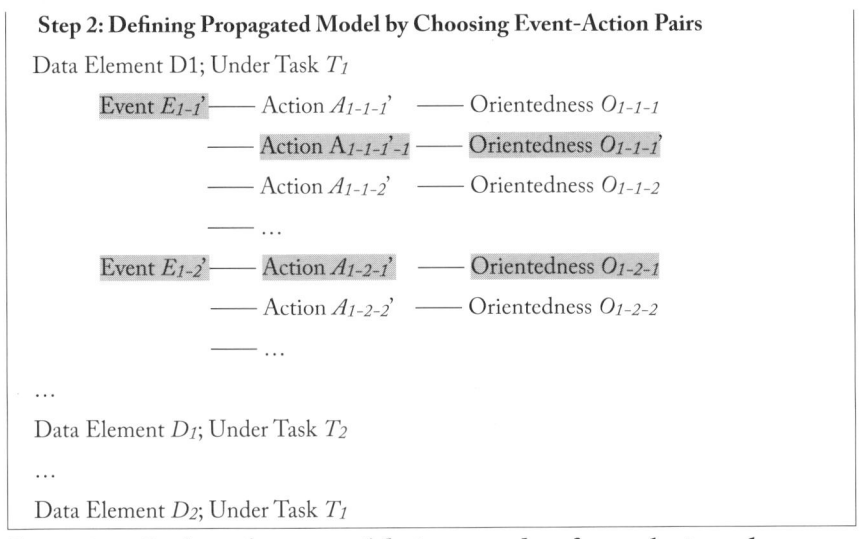

Figure 8-1. Outline of conceptual design procedure for cataloging rules.

8.2 Phase 0: Specifying Requirements and Defining Cataloger Tasks

8.2.1 Specifying Requirements by Use of Orientedness

Attempting to cover both functional and non-functional requirements, I introduced and set up the concept 'orientedness' in Chapter 7. I will use this concept here as what specifies requirements on the cataloging process.

In that chapter, several categories of orientedness corresponding to functional requirements were set up as being extracted from the general objectives and functions of bibliographic description and access points/headings manifested in cataloging codes.

(a) 'Orientedness toward identity,' which corresponds to the objective of attaining the distinction and identification of an item.

(b) 'Orientedness toward contents,' which corresponds to the objective of describing the scope and contents of an item.

Moreover, (c) 'orientedness toward bibliographic relationships,' (d) 'orientedness toward access conditions,' and (e) 'orientedness toward provenance' were also defined. However, we can put together for convenience' sake the above categories (b)-(e) into one category, for instance, orientedness toward contents. I will use orientedness toward contents in the sense that it covers other categories (c)-(e) in the present chapter in order to simplify our discussion.

(f) 'Orientedness toward ease-of-access,' which refers to the objective of attaining easy access to a record.

Other categories of orientedness corresponding to non-functional requirements were also defined, while being referred to other parts of cataloging codes.

(g) 'Orientedness toward consistency,' which indicates the creation of coherent records in a consistent manner.

(h) 'Orientedness toward economy,' which indicates the creation of a record in an economical, i.e., cost-effective way.

Although these two categories of orientedness correspond mainly to the restrictions or constraints on the process of creating a record, they are also secondarily related to cataloging codes themselves which are instructions to create a record. For instance, orientedness toward consistency secondarily indicates consistency in procedures themselves—i.e., standardization or use of a common set of rules—in addition to consistency in a created record. Similarly, orientedness toward economy secondarily indicates simplification of instructions themselves— i.e., simple structure and minimum number of rules—in addition to making a record in a way that requires minimum time and labor.

8.2.2 Defining Cataloger Tasks

The cataloging process contains a wide variety of tasks performed by catalogers from creating a record (and a database) to maintain the record (and the database). For instance, Le Boeuf enumerated several tasks, such as transcribe, describe, make identifiable, link, manage, and convey information relevant to rights management[2].

In the present study, however, I focus on tasks related to creating a bibliographic description and choosing and assigning access points/headings to the description, since those tasks are kernel among a variety of tasks, and are in principle covered and controlled with cataloging codes. It is therefore possible to define tasks while referring to several cataloging codes and also some classifications of cataloging rules developed in previous studies with respect to the functions of the rules. Molto and Svenonius classified rules into source, choice, form, and definition[3]. Fidel and Crandall, using E-R modeling approach, divided rules as specifying content, format, and sources of information; establishing entities, relationships, or attributes; and specifying access points[4]. Still another classification by Jeng is:

definition, description, organization, source of information, identification, and transcription[5]. These classifications are similar to a great extent.

While referring to the classification by Molto and Svenonius, I define necessary tasks related to the creation of a description as follows:

(a) To specify and choose a source from which a value (to be precise, a candidate value) of a data element is to be taken.

(b) To choose a value (i.e., a candidate value) of the data element when more than one, or possibly none, appears in the source.

(c) To form the value chosen in the source into that to be recorded in the data element.

(d) To define a term used in the cataloging process.

The tasks (a)-(c) are performed by catalogers in this sequence. These are called here Specify Source of Values, Choose Values, Establish Form of Values, and Provide Definition, respectively.

In the same way, I define tasks related to the determination of the choice of access points and the form of headings through which a description is accessed, by modifying the classification indicated by Svenonius[6].

(e) To choose persons, corporate bodies, and titles to be used as access points. Such persons, etc., are usually shown in the description.

(f) To specify and choose a source from which a name of the person/corporate body or a name of the work (i.e., a uniform title) chosen in the task (e) is to be taken.

(g) To choose a name of the person/corporate body or the work chosen when more than one, or possibly none, appears in the source.

(h) To form the name chosen in the source into that to be distinctive.

The tasks (f)-(h) are basically similar to those defined against the creation of a description. They are named Choose Access Points, Specify Source of Names, Choose Names, and Establish Form of Names, respectively.

8.3 Phase 1: Building Core Model

A core model which demonstrates the basic framework of each individual cataloger task consists of: (a) basic 'event patterns' that trigger certain actions by catalogers under each individual task, (b) 'action patterns' applicable to each event pattern, and (c) orientedness involved in an event and action pair. In the core model, only events and actions common in principle in all data elements are included. The model is therefore a general one being applicable to any situation/system and independent, in principle, of any cataloging code.

There are many techniques of process modeling and of illustrating the result as a behavioral model; for example, Statecharts, Petri nets, Decision tables and tree, etc[7]. The UML (Unified Modeling Language), by the Object Management Group, uses use-case diagrams, sequence diagrams, statechart diagrams, and activity diagrams for specifying a behavioral model. The modeling method adopted in this study would be a sort of state transition model, in particular, Statecharts[8] and its successor 'statechart diagram' in UML. In such state transition models, any process is recognized as a set of state transitions and then each transition is expressed with an 'event' that triggers the transition, a 'condition' (or 'guard condition') that guards the transition from being taken unless it is true when the event occurs, and an 'action' that is carried out if the transition is taken. The (a) events and (b) actions in the core model are therefore the same as those of state transition models; the 'condition' is incorporated into the (a) events, if necessary. In addition, the modeling method here can inherit the research results on the structural analysis of cataloging rules by, for example, Jeng[9], Molto and Svenonius[10], Taniguchi[11], and others.

On the other hand, any state transition model, of course, does not have a constituent such as orientedness. We need to indicate categories of orientedness involved in each event-action pair so that we can evaluate each individual pair among possible alternatives in terms of orientedness, which reflects requirements of the cataloging process.

8.3.1 Specifying Basic Event and Action Patterns Under Task 'Specify Source of Values'

1) *Basic event patterns*

The task 'Specify Source of Values' is to specify and choose a source from which a data element value is to be taken—this is the case of transcription. In case of describing the characteristics of an item, like the dimensions of an item, the source is an item itself or a part of an item to be described. Other cases such as that indicating general material designation (GMD), a specific source external to an item is dealt with as the source—for instance, in case of GMD, a cataloging code itself. The source (or the range of sources) from which one may derive a data value must be predetermined and prescribed before the cataloging process to start a description/record. Hence, the source(s) is called 'prescribed source(s)' in cataloging codes. The prescription for the source usually designates the order of preference in adopting the sources for each class of materials, as well as for each area and data element of the description.

The basic event patterns are:

(S1) Whether prescribed source(s) can be referred to.
(S1-1) Prescribed source(s) can be referred to.
(S1-2) No prescribed source can be referred to—including cases where an item lacks prescribed sources.
(S2) Whether the prescribed source(s) being referred to is single.
(S2-1) Only one source can be referred to.
(S2-2) More than one source can be referred to.
(S3) Whether other sources outside the prescribed source(s) can be referred to.
(S3-1) Other sources outside those prescribed can be referred to.
(S3-2) No other source outside those prescribed can be referred to.

The event S2 depends completely on S1-1; the former occurs only if the latter occurs. The events S1 and S3 are independent of each other, but S3 is usually taken up when S1-2 occurs—this is an issue in policy.

One could represent event patterns with symbolic logic, including predicate logic[12]. However, the benefit is not clear at the current stage of this study, if we take into account readability and understandability of such representations. Hence I do not pursue representations with symbolic logic.

In *Anglo-American Cataloguing Rules, 2nd ed., 2002 revision* (AACR2, 2002 revision)[13], sources of information are divided into the 'chief source' and others prescribed. If we adapt the basic event patterns above to AACR2, 2002 revision, the patterns are:

(S1') Whether the chief source can be referred to. [AACR2, 2002 revision 1.0A, 1.0A2]

(S2') Whether the chief source being referred to is single. [1.0A1, 1.0H]
(S3') Whether other prescribed source(s) outside the chief source can be referred to. [1.0A1, 1.0A2]
(S4') Whether other prescribed source(s) being referred to is single. [1.0A1]
(S5') Whether sources outside the prescribed source(s) can be referred to. [1.0A2]

2) Action patterns and orientedness

The next step is to enumerate action patterns applicable to each individual event pattern and also to point out categories of orientedness involved in each event-action pair.

First of all, we should examine actions which preexist all events. They are to prescribe source of values for a data element (Action-01), or to not prescribe any source of values for an element (Action-02). Action-01 is prerequisite to all events enumerated above. Several categories of orientedness are involved in each of these alternatives. Action-01 is related to orientedness toward identity and also orientedness toward consistency. Action-02 is related to orientedness toward contents and also economy—orientedness toward contents is used as the representative of some categories of orientedness, like orientedness toward bibliographic relationships, provenance, etc, as mentioned earlier.

Prescribing source of values (Action-01) aims ultimately to prevent producing different descriptions for an identical item or, at least, to minimize the differences in descriptions, by advising the cataloger the source or the range of sources from which one may derive a value. It is therefore identity-oriented, although the degree with which the orientedness is involved in prescribing sources varies by the scope of places to be taken as the sources. It is also consistency-oriented, since the procedure is to be more controlled and the output data will be more consistent as a result. The degree of these categories of orientedness is finally decided after the scope of places to be taken as the sources is specified; it is done at the following phase of the conceptual design.

On the contrary, not prescribing any source (Action-02) is interpreted from two aspects. (a) It is contents-oriented if we seek a data value that is more proper to represent the contents, scope, provenance, or others of an item through several parts of the item and/or outside the item. (b) It is economy-oriented when we make a data value in a way that takes little time and labor; for example, seeking a value from a part that is convenient to see, or if we go so far as to say, making a value without seeking through any source. Action-02 can thus be divided into these two independent actions, if necessary. Moreover, orientedness toward identity and also consistency will decrease when Action-02 is adopted.

Having established this point, we will turn to enumerate action patterns applicable to each event delineated above. All possible actions will be examined beyond existing cataloging codes.

> (S1-1) Prescribed source(s) can be referred to.
> -- (Action-03) Refer to the prescribed source(s).
> ---- (Orientedness) It is identity- and consistency-oriented.

Action-03 is the logical next step following Action-01, i.e., to prescribe sources, and the orientedness involved is the same as that of Action-01. The alternative action "do not refer to the prescribed source(s)" is eventually the same as Action-02.

> (S1-2) No prescribed source can be referred to.
> -- (Action-04) Move to the event S3.
> -- (Action-05) Do not refer to other sources outside those prescribed.
> ---- (Orientedness) It is economy-oriented.

Orientedness involved in Action-05 seems to be obvious since we already saw the case of Action-02. I will not discuss hereafter in principle the interpretation of orientedness involved in each event-action pair, since I already discussed such interpretations in Chapter 7.

> (S2-1) Only one prescribed source can be referred to.
> -- (Action-06 and orientedness) The same as Action-03.
> (S2-2) More than one prescribed source can be referred to.
> -- (Action-07) Refer to all sources; namely, deal with all sources equally.
> ---- (Orientedness) It is contents-oriented and also at lower degree identity- and economy-oriented.

-- (Action-08) Refer to the prescribed sources in order of preference.
---- (Orientedness) It is consistency- and identity-oriented.
(S3-1) Other sources outside those prescribed can be referred to.
-- (Action-09) Refer to other sources outside those prescribed.
---- (Orientedness) It is contents-oriented with decrease in orientedness toward economy.
-- (Action-10 and orientedness) The same as Action-05.
(S3-2) No other source outside those prescribed can be referred to.
-- (Action-11 and orientedness) The same as Action-05.

If the combination of events S1-1 (including S2-1 and S2-2) and S3-1 is dealt with as an independent event, the following patterns are added:

(S4-1) Both the prescribed source(s) and others can be referred to.
-- (Action-12) Refer to both sources prescribed and those not prescribed in order of preference.
---- (Orientedness) It is consistency- and identity-oriented and also at lower degree contents-oriented.
-- (Action-13) Refer to only the prescribed source(s) and do not to others.
---- (Orientedness) It is identity- and consistency-oriented.

Figure 8-2 shows state transitions taken up in the event-action pairs enumerated above (except Action-02 and the event S4-1 and its corresponding Action-12, -13) in an abbreviated manner of the statechart in UML. The diagram expresses both the states that are manifested as the event patterns in the model and the states that the actions bring, as well as transitions between the states. Table 8-1 shows the event-action pairs above with the indication of categories of orientedness and the degree with which orientedness is involved in.

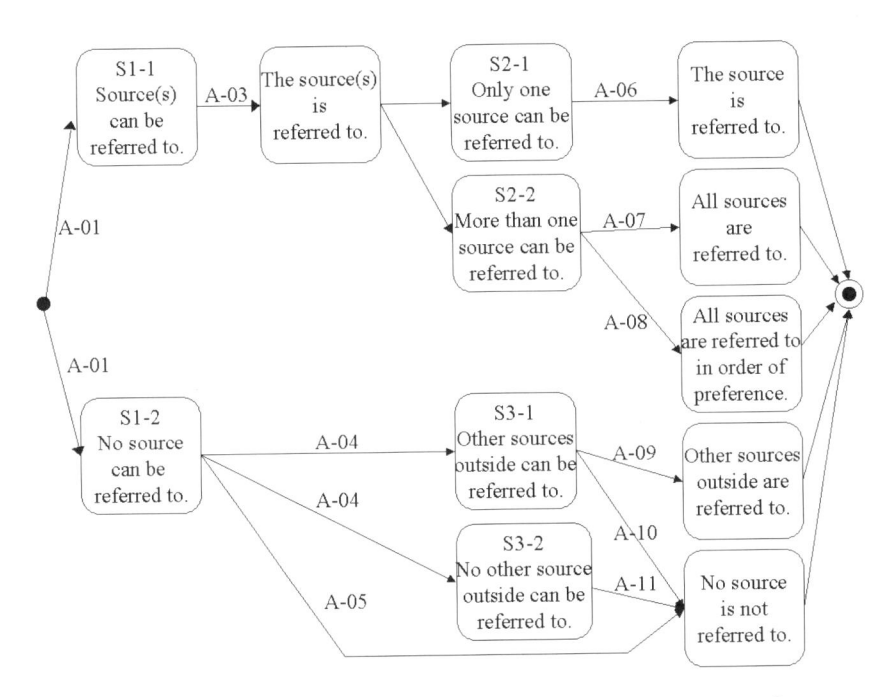

Chapter 8 Design of Cataloging Rules Using Conceptual Modeling of Cataloging Process   247

Figure 8-2. A diagram showing state transitions under the task 'Specify Source of Values.'

Table 8-1. Summary of the categories of orientedness involved in the event-action pairs under the task 'Specify Source of Values.'

Event-action pair	Orientedness toward identity	Orientedness toward contents	Orientedness toward consistency	Orientedness toward economy
Action-01	High/Low	----	High/Low	----
Action-02	Negative	High/Low	Negative	High/Low
(S1-1) Action-03	High/Low	----	High/Low	----
(S1-2) Action-05	----	----	----	High
(S2-1) Action-06	High	----	High	----
(S2-2) Action-07	Low	High	----	Low
(S2-2) Action-08	High	----	High	----
(S3-1) Action-09	Low	High	----	Negative
(S3-1) Action-10	----	----	----	High
(S3-2) Action-11	----	----	----	High
(S4-1) Action-12	High	Low	High	----
(S4-1) Action-13	High	----	High	Low

High: high degree   Low: low degree   Negative: negative degree   ----: not related

8.3.2 Specifying Basic Event and Action Patterns Under Other Tasks

1) *Task 'Choose Values'*

The basic event and action patterns under the task 'Choose Values' are presented in Table 8-2. Action-01 is directly derived from the task Specify Source of Values and does not contain any additional category of orientedness. The alternative action "do not choose the value(s)" is meaningless, since it contradicts the previous task Specify Source of Values.

The event C2 depends completely on C1-1; the former occurs only when the latter occurs. Similarly, the event C3 depends completely on C2-2.

Figure 8-3 and Table 8-3 show the event-action patterns and their orientedness listed in Table 8-2 in the same way as Figure 8-2 and Table 8-1, respectively.

2) *Task 'Establish Form of Values'*

Similarly, the basic event and action patterns under the task 'Establish Form of Values' are presented in Table 8-4. The actions Action-13 to Action-16 are additions that do not have any corresponding event but actually correspond to the results of certain event-action pairs under the tasks Specify Source of Values and Choose Values; for instance, a case where value(s) appears in (or outside) the prescribed sources and is chosen.

In AACR2, 2002 revision, events that are related to abbreviations, and numerals are integral to those events listed in Table 8-4. These are however issues chiefly dependent on the language and script of the cataloging agency and thus they were not added to the basic patterns here.

Figure 8-4 and Table 8-5 show the event-action patterns and their orientedness listed in Table 8-4 in the same way as Figure 8-2 and Table 8-1, respectively; Figure 8-4 however covers only the limited range of event patterns.

3) *Task 'Provide Definition'*

The task 'Provide Definition' has only action patterns—this implies actions always being active and executed without any event or condition. Some examples of such actions are as follows:

-- (Action-01) Make up a description from the following areas: title and statement of responsibility area, edition area, …

-- (Action-02) Make up the title and statement of responsibility area from the following elements: title proper, general material designation, parallel titles, ...

-- (Action-03) Make up the first level of description from the following elements: title proper, first statement of responsibility, ...

These actions can be understood as the mixture of some categories of orientedness, like orientedness toward identity, contents, and consistency. A detailed discussion on this has been provided in Chapter 7.

4) Task 'Choose Access Points'

The basic event patterns under the task 'Choose Access Points' depend completely on a cataloging code and thus it is difficult to show patterns common in cataloging codes. For instance, AACR2, 2002 revision focuses on the choice of a main entry heading and additionally added entry headings, since it adopts the main entry system. In AACR2, 2002 revision, event patterns are considered related to (a) the number of persons/corporate bodies responsible for a work embodied in an item (i.e., shared responsibility), (b) the type of contributions which different persons/bodies have made for a work (i.e., mixed responsibility), (c) the occurrence of a title including a 'collective title' which is an inclusive title for an item containing several works, and (d) the category of a work (e.g., texts, art works, musical works, etc.). Shaw et al. and then Smith et al. illustrated the flow of decisions that must be taken in the procedure of choosing access points in line with AACR2 and its 1988 revision[14]. On the contrary, Nippon Cataloging Rules, 1987 edition and its successors which do not adopt the main entry system consider as necessary event patterns (a) the area of a description where the names of persons/bodies are recorded and (b) the type of contributions that persons/bodies have made for a work/item[15].

The possible actions to be taken for each event under this task are basically restricted to (a) choosing certain person(s), corporate body(-ies), or title(s) as an access point—or, choosing it as either the main or added entry heading in case of the main entry system—and (b) moving to other events. As to orientedness involved in the event-action patterns, it is possible to point out the followings: (a) Orientedness toward economy decreases with increasing complexity in choosing persons/bodies/titles. Also, that category of orientedness decreases as the number of persons/bodies/titles to be chosen increases. (b) Orientedness toward ease-of-access increases in principle as the scope (and the number) of persons/bodies/titles to be chosen becomes wider (and increases).

5) *Tasks 'Specify Source of Names,' 'Choose Names,' and 'Establish Form of Names'*

The basic event-action patterns under the task 'Specify Source of Names' and 'Choose Names' are equivalent to those under Specify Source of Values and Choose Values, respectively. The only addition to the actions under Choose Names is to choose only one value (i.e., name) that is commonly known. This added action is ease-of-access-oriented. Svenonius pointed out the same matter; the process of choosing a name should be guided by the principle of common usage[16].

By contrast, the basic event and action patterns under 'Establish Form of Names' are different from those under Establish Form of Values. Examples of patterns are as follows:

(FN1-1) The name chosen consists of parts/elements; for instance, in case of a corporate body the name consists of several elements in the hierarchy, like the highest, the lowest, and intervening elements.
-- (Action-01) Record all parts/elements consisting of the name.
---- (Orientedness) It is identity-oriented with decrease in orientedness toward economy.
-- (Action-02) Record only some parts/elements of the name and omit the others.
---- (Orientedness) It is economy-oriented with decrease in orientedness toward identity.
(FN2-1) The name chosen contains additions; for example, a title of nobility, terms indicating the type of incorporated entity, and others.
-- (Action-03) Record the name including additions.
---- (Orientedness) It is contents-oriented and also at lower degree identity-oriented. At the same time, orientedness toward economy drops.
-- (Action-04) Omit additions and record only the name part.
---- (Orientedness) It is economy-oriented.

In addition, the following actions can be specified without corresponding specific events.

(Action-05) Add qualifying elements.
-- (Orientedness) It is identity- or contents-oriented with decrease in orientedness toward economy.
(Action-06) Specify the order in which the name—and its additions, if any—is to be recorded.
-- (Orientedness) It is consistency-oriented.

Table 8-2. Basic event and action patterns under the task 'Choose Values.'

Event	Action and orientedness
(C1) Whether value(s) of the data element appears in the source chosen.	
(C1-1) Value(s) of the specific category appears in the source.	**(Action-01)** Choose the value(s). **(Orientedness)** It is identity-oriented.
(C1-2) No value of the specific category appears in the source.	**(Action-02)** Do not adopt any value. **(Orientedness)** It is economy-oriented. **(Action-03)** Supply the value with a presumed/estimated value. **(Orientedness)** It is contents-oriented. **(Action-04)** Supply the value with a note indicating the fact that no value appears. **(Orientedness)** It is identity- and economy-oriented.

(C2) Whether the data value(s) of the specific category that appears in the source is single. **(C2-1)** Only a single value appears in the source.	**(Action-05)** The same as Action-01.

(C2-2) More than one value appears in the source; namely, the values that appear are different from each other.	**(Action-06)** Adopt all values.
	   (Orientedness) It is identity- and contents-oriented, whereas orientedness toward economy decreases in this action.
	(Action-07) Choose one or more values that satisfy the given condition.
	   (Orientedness) It is identity-oriented and also at lower degree contents- and economy-oriented.
	(Action-08) Choose only one value that satisfies the given condition.
	   (Orientedness) It is economy-oriented and also at lower degree identity- and contents-oriented.

(C3) Whether data values that appear in the source are in the same language, script, or notation. **(C3-1)** Values are in the same language, script, or notation.	**(Action-09, -10, -11)** The same as Action-06, -07, and -08.
(C3-2) Values are in two or more languages, scripts, or notations.	**(Action-12, -13, -14)** The same as Action-06, -07, and -08.

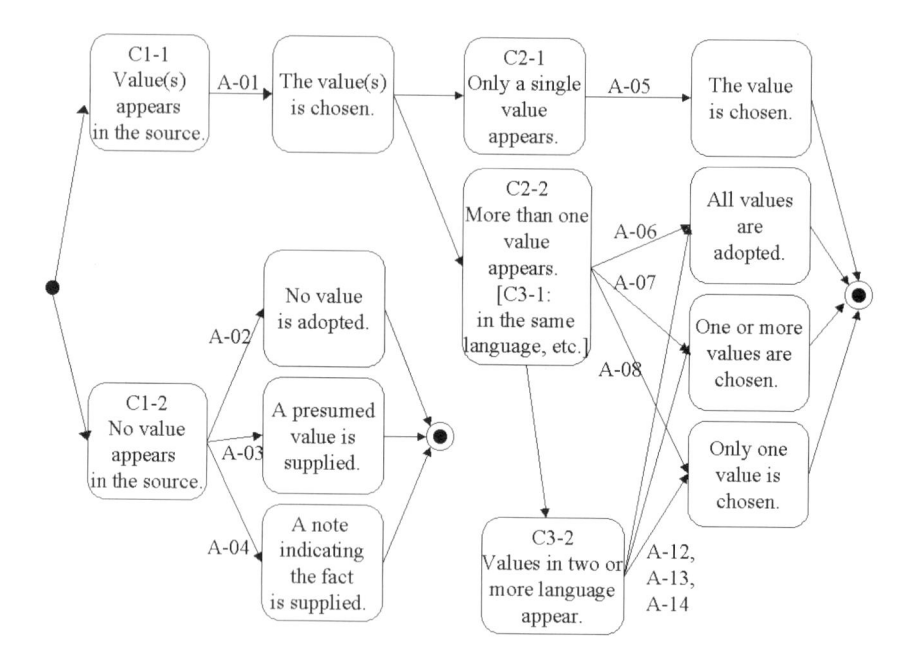

Figure 8-3. A diagram showing state transitions under the task 'ChooseValues.'

Chapter 8 Design of Cataloging Rules Using Conceptual Modeling of Cataloging Process   255

Table 8-3. Summary of the categories of orientedness involved in the event-action pairs under the task 'Choose Values.'

Event-action pair	Orientedness toward identity	Orientedness toward contents	Orientedness toward consistency	Orientedness toward economy
(C1-1) Action-01	High	----	----	----
(C1-2) Action-02	----	----	Low	High
(C1-2) Action-03	----	High	----	----
(C1-2) Action-04	High	----	Low	High
(C2-1) Action-05	High	----	----	----
(C2-2) Action-06	High	High	----	Negative
(C2-2) Action-07	High	Low	----	Low
(C2-2) Action-08	Low	Low	----	High
(C3-1/2) Action-09/12	High	High	----	Negative
(C3-1/2) Action-10/13	High	Low	----	Low
(C3-1/2) Action-11/14	Low	Low	----	High

High: high degree   Low: low degree   Negative: negative degree   ----: not related

Table 8-4. Basic event and action patterns under the task 'Establish Form of Values.'

Event	Action and orientedness
(F0-1) Any of the following events does not occur, i.e., the value chosen does not contain any symbol or other matter that cannot by reproduced by the facilities available, etc.	**(Action-00)** Transcribe the value as it appears. **(Orientedness)** It is identity-oriented and also at lower degree economy-oriented.

(F1-1) The value chosen contains symbols or other matter that cannot be reproduced by the facilities available.	**(Action-01)** Replace them with an explanatory description.
	   (Orientedness) It is identity-oriented.
	(Action-02) Ignore and skip them.
	   (Orientedness) It is economy-oriented.

(F2-1) The value chosen is represented in a script that cannot be dealt with properly.	**(Action-03)** Transliterate them into a form in scripts that can be dealt with properly—usually in roman-alphabet form. **(Orientedness)** It is identity-oriented. **(Action-04)** The same as Action-02.

(F3-1) The value chosen contains inaccuracies or misspelled words.	**(Action-05)** Transcribe the value as it appears.
	   (Orientedness) It is identity- and economy-oriented.
	(Action-06) Transcribe the value as it appears and supply certain marks indicating inaccuracy or misspelling (e.g., "[sic]" or "[!]").
	   (Orientedness) It is identity-oriented.
	(Action-07) Transcribe the value as it appears and add the corrected version.
	   (Orientedness) It is identity- and contents-oriented.
	(Action-08) Give only the corrected form.
	   (Orientedness) It is contents- and economy-oriented.

Chapter 8 Design of Cataloging Rules Using Conceptual Modeling of Cataloging Process 257

(F4-1) The value chosen lacks accents and other diacritical marks.	**(Action-09)** The same as Action-05. **(Action-10)** Add accents and other diacritical marks. 　**(Orientedness)** It is consistency-oriented.
(F5-1) The value chosen uses unusual capitalization out of accord with the usage of the language used in the context.	**(Action-11)** The same as Action-05. **(Action-12)** Capitalize the value in accordance with the usage of the language. 　**(Orientedness)** It is consistency-oriented. **(Action-13)** Record the value in the prescribed element (or area). 　**(Orientedness)** It is consistency-oriented. **(Action-14)** Record the value as a note in the note area. 　**(Orientedness)** It is consistency-oriented. **(Action-15)** Record the value as it appears and is found. 　**(Orientedness)** It is identity- and economy-oriented. **(Action-16)** Enclose the value with specific symbols, like square brackets. 　**(Orientedness)** It is identity- and consistency-oriented.

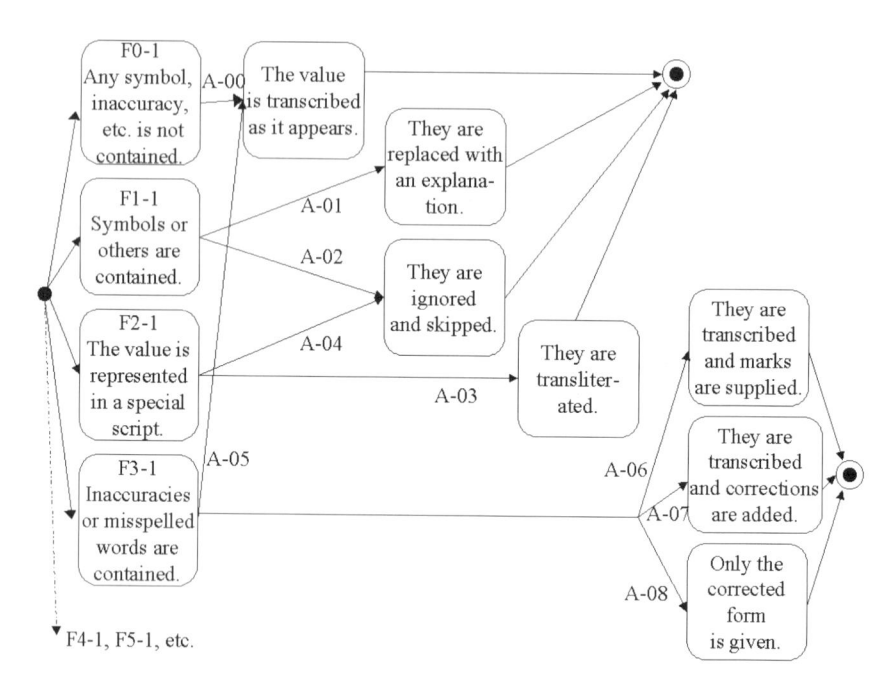

Figure 8-4. A diagram showing state transitions under the task 'Establish Form of Values.'

Chapter 8 Design of Cataloging Rules Using Conceptual Modeling of Cataloging Process 259

Table 8-5. Summary of the categories of orientedness involved in the event-action pairs under the task 'Establish Form of Values.'

Event-action pair	Orientedness toward identity	Orientedness toward contents	Orientedness toward consistency	Orientedness toward economy
(F0-1) Action-00	High	---	---	Low
(F1-1) Action-01	High	---	---	---
(F1-1) Action-02	Negative	---	---	High
(F2-1) Action-03	High	---	---	---
(F2-1) Action-04	Negative	---	---	High
(F3-1) Action-05	High	---	---	High
(F3-1) Action-06	High	---	---	Low
(F3-1) Action-07	High	Low	---	Low
(F3-1) Action-08	Low	High	---	High
(F4-1) Action-09	High	---	---	High
(F4-1) Action-10	---	---	High	Low
(F5-1) Action-11	High	---	---	High
(F5-1) Action-12	---	---	High	Low
Action-13	---	---	High	---
Action-14	---	---	High	---
Action-15	High	---	---	Low
Action-16	High	---	High	---

High: high degree   Low: low degree   Negative: negative degree   ---: not related

8.4 Phase 2: Propagating Core Model and Defining Propagated Model by Choosing Event-Action Pairs

8.4.1 Step 1: Propagating Core Model

By propagating the core model to reflect the characteristics of an individual data element and, in some cases, a class of materials (i.e., content, carrier, and publication type), we can obtain a comprehensive model that contains all event patterns in each individual element and also all possible actions against each event. This propagation is outlined below:

Step 1-1: Applying the basic event patterns under each task to an individual element of the description or to a type of access point/heading such as person, corporate body, or title, while also considering the characteristics of a class of materials, if necessary. During the propagation, bibliographic facts and knowledge peculiar to a certain element or class should be referred to; for example, knowledge on the scope and order of patterns applicable to an element or class.

Step 1-2: Applying the action patterns under each basic event to an individual event enumerated in Step 1-1. The indication of orientedness involved in each basic event-action pattern is inherited to propagated patterns.

I will demonstrate a part of the comprehensive model that covers only some data elements and also patterns applicable to any class of materials, while referring chiefly to AACR2, 2002 revision, Chapter 1: General Rules for Description.

1) *Part of the model on the data element 'parallel title'*

According to AACR2, 2002 revision, Chapter 1, the rule 1.1A2 for sources of information for the title and statement of responsibility area, which includes the element 'parallel title,' and the rule group 1.1D for parallel titles specify patterns under the task Specify Source of Values. They are just a simplified version of the basic event patterns shown at Phase 1. Both 1.1A2 and 1.1D specify only two patterns: (a) the chief source of information is available and data is found there, and (b) other sources are available and data is found there. All events and actions for parallel title under the task in AACR2, 2002 revision, Chapter 1 are therefore included in the core model and we can adopt the core model itself as an alternative to those rules in AACR2, 2002 revision, Chapter 1.

The degree with which the orientedness is involved in these event-action pairs, to be precise, depends on the scope of places specified as the chief source of information for each class of materials. However, the chief source is limited to one or more parts of an item itself, except for some classes of materials. Hence, the orientedness involved here is obviously at high degree.

As to the task Choose Values for parallel title, we can obtain the following event patterns if we incorporate events taken up in 1.1D rules into patterns.

(C1') Whether parallel title(s) appears in the chief source of information (CSI). [AACR2, 2002 revision 1.1D1]
(C2') Whether more than one parallel title appears in the CSI. [1.1D2]
(C3') Whether a parallel title is denoted in a given language or script, like English. [1.1D2]
(C4') Whether a parallel title appearing in the CSI is an original title. [1.1D3]
(C5') Whether a parallel title appears before the title proper in the CSI. [1.1D3]
(C6') Whether a parallel title appears outside the CSI. [1.1D4]

In addition, 1.1D rules incorporates other conditions independent of the element; for instance, (a) whether the title proper is in a nonroman script, (b) which level of detail in the description is intended, and (c) whether the item contains all or some of the text in the original language in case of translation or others.

Regarding the task Establish Form of Values, the basic event and action patterns can be applied to the element without any modification. In addition to them, the rule 1.1D2 considers some events on the element by indicating the application of the instructions in 1.1B, which are rules for the title proper.

(F1'-1) A parallel title contains the marks '…' or '[ ]'. [AACR2, 2002 revision 1.1B1]
-- (Action-01) Record the parallel title as it is.
-- (Action-02) Replace the marks by '--' and '( )', respectively.
(F2'-1) A parallel title is long. [1.1B4]
-- (Action-03) Record the parallel title as it is.
-- (Action-04) Abridge the parallel title and indicate omissions by the mark of omission.

(F3'-1) A parallel title includes separate letters or initials without full stops between them. [1.1B6]
-- (Action-05) Record the parallel title as it is.
-- (Action-06) Transcribe such letters with full stops.
(F4'-1) ...

2) *Part of the model on the data element 'date of publication, distribution, etc.'*

Next, let me take the data element 'date of publication, distribution, etc.' The basic event and action patterns under the task Specify Source of Values can be applied to the element without any modification. The rule 1.4A2 for sources of information specifies only events: (a) the chief source of information or any other source prescribed for the element is available and a date is found there, and (b) a source other than those prescribed is available and a date is found.

For the task Choose Values, the patterns listed in Table 8-6 will be obtained if we follow the AACR2, 2002 revision rules. Events and actions related to date of manufacture is omitted here. Independent conditions whether an item being described is an unpublished item and whether it is an unpublished collection are also omitted.

As for the task Establish Form of Values, most of the basic patterns shown earlier cannot be applied to the element, since the characteristics of the element are different from those expected in the basic patterns. Instead, the patterns in Table 8-7, for example, will be enumerated in line with the AACR2, 2002 revision rules.

Table 8-6. Part of propagated event and action patterns on the 'date of publication, distribution, etc.' under the task 'Choose Values.'

Event	Action and orientedness
(C1') Whether date(s) of publication appears in the source. [AACR2, 2002 revision 1.4F1, 1.4F6, 1.4F7] **(C1'-1)** Date(s) of publication appears in the source. **(C1'-2)** No date of publication appears in the source.	**(Action-01)** Adopt the date(s). 　**(Orientedness)** It is identity-oriented. **(Action-02)** Do not adopt any date; i.e., do not record any date. 　**(Orientedness)** It is identity- and economy-oriented. **(Action-03)** Supply an approximate date. 　**(Orientedness)** It is contents-oriented. **(Action-04)** Look for a date of distribution, copyright date, or date of manufacture. 　**(Orientedness)** It is contents-oriented. **(Action-05)** Supply a note indicating the fact that no date of publication appears. 　**(Orientedness)** It is identity-oriented.
(C2') Whether more than one date of publication appears in the source. [1.4F1] **(C2'-1)** Only one date of publication appears in the source. **(C2'-2)** More than one date of publication appears in the source.	**(Action-06)** The same as Action-01. **(Action-07)** Move to C3.

(C3') Whether different dates of publication correspond to different editions of an item. [1.4F1, 1.4F3]
 	
(C3'-1) Different dates of publication correspond to the same edition of an item.
 	
(C3'-2) Different dates of publication correspond to the different edition of an item.
	(Action-08) Choose all dates of publication.
	  (Orientedness) It is identity-oriented.
	(Action-09) Choose one date of publication that satisfies the given condition.
	  (Orientedness) It is economy-oriented and also at lower degree identity-oriented.
	
	(Action-10 and -11) The same as Action-08 and -09.

(C4') Whether the date of publication differs from the date of distribution, when the date of distribution appears in the source. [1.4F4]
 	
(C4'-1) The date of publication differs from the date of distribution.
 	
(C4'-2) The date of publication is the same as the date of distribution.
	(Action-12) Choose both dates as they are different components of the element.
	  (Orientedness) It is identity-oriented.
	(Action-13) Choose only the date of publication.
	  (Orientedness) It is identity-oriented and also at lower degree economy-oriented.
	
	(Action-14 and -15) The same as Action-12 and -13.

Chapter 8 Design of Cataloging Rules Using Conceptual Modeling of Cataloging Process 265

(C5') Whether the latest date of copyright differs from the date of publication or that of distribution, when the copyright date appears in the source. [1.4F5]
 (C5'-1) The copyright date differs from both the date of publication and that of distribution.
	(Action-16) Choose all of the dates as they are different component of the element.
	   (Orientedness) It is identity-oriented.
	 (Action-17) Choose only the date of publication.
	   (Orientedness) It is identity-oriented and also at lower degree economy-oriented.
	 (Action-18) Choose the date of publication and the copyright date.
	   (Orientedness) It is identity- and contents-oriented.

(C5'-2) The copyright date differs from either the date of publication or that of distribution.	**(Action-19)** Choose all of the dates as they are different component of the element.
	   (Orientedness) It is identity-oriented.
	 (Action-20) Choose only different dates among these dates.
	   (Orientedness) It is identity-oriented.
	 (Action-21) Choose only the date of publication.
	   (Orientedness) It is identity-oriented and also at lower degree economy-oriented.
	 (Action-22) Choose the date of publication and the copyright date.
	   (Orientedness) It is identity- and contents-oriented.

(C5'-3) The copyright date is the same as both the date of publication and that of distribution, i.e., all of the dates are the same.	**(Action-23, -24, and -25)** The same as Action-19, -21, and -22.

Table 8-7. Part of propagated event and action patterns on the 'date of publication, distribution, etc.' under the task 'Establish Form of Values.'

Event	Action and orientedness
(F1'-1) The date of publication, distribution, etc. chosen is not of Gregorian or Julian calendar. [AACR2, 2002 revision 1.4F1]	(Action-01) Record the date as it appears. 　(Orientedness) It is identity- and economy-oriented. (Action-02) Record the date as it appears and follow it with the year of the Gregorian or Julian calendar. 　(Orientedness) It is identity- and contents-oriented. (Action-03) Record the equivalent date of the Gregorian or Julian calendar. 　(Orientedness) It is contents-oriented.
(F2'-1) The date of publication, distribution, etc. chosen is in non-Western-style arabic numerals. [1.4F1]	(Action-04) Record the date as it appears. 　(Orientedness) It is identity-oriented. (Action-05) Record the date in Western-style arabic numerals. 　(Orientedness) It is contents- and consistency-oriented.
(F3'-1) The date of publication, distribution, etc. chosen is known to be incorrect. [1.4F2]	(Action-06) Record the date as found. 　(Orientedness) It is identity- and economy-oriented. (Action-07) Record the date as found and add the corrected date. 　(Orientedness) It is identity- and contents-oriented. (Action-08) Record only the corrected date. 　(Orientedness) It is contents-oriented. (Action-09) Record the date as found and supply certain marks indicating inaccuracy. 　(Orientedness) It is identity- and contents-oriented.

(F4'-1) The date chosen is not the date of publication; namely, a date of distribution, a copyright date, etc. [1.4F4, 1.4F5, 1.4F6]	**(Action-10)** Record the date with proper indication/qualification. **(Orientedness)** It is identity-oriented. **(Action-11)** Record the date without any indication/qualification. **(Orientedness)** It is economy-oriented.
(F5'-1) The date is that supplied by catalogers and not found in the source. [1.4F1, 1.4F2, 1.4F5, 1.4F7]	**(Action-12)** Enclose the date with square brackets. **(Orientedness)** It is identity- and consistency-oriented. **(Action-13)** Record the date without any marks. **(Orientedness)** It is economy-oriented.

8.4.2 Step 2: Defining Propagated Model by Choosing Event-Action Pairs

Defining the propagated model by choosing pairs of event and action patterns enumerated in the model is done in the last step of the conceptual design in order to match a particular situation. This definition should be done while referring to orientedness indicated in each event-action pair. For instance, it is possible to identify a set of pairs when a given category of orientedness is maximized, that is, a set of pairs containing the given orientedness most among possible alternatives pairs. As a result, a set of event-action pairs reflecting specific requirements through categories of orientedness is obtained, and consistent design can therefore be attained.

Let me try to identify a set of event-action pairs by maximizing, for example, orientedness toward identity within the patterns for the element 'date of publication, distribution, etc.' enumerated in Tables 8-6 and 8-7. First, under the task Choose Values, we can get the following set of pairs:

C1'-1 and Action-01; C1'-2 and Action-02 or Action-05.
C2'-1 and Action-06.
C3'-1 and Action-08; C3'-2 and Action-10.
C4'-1 and Action-12 or Action-13; C4'-2 and Action-14 or Action-15.
C5'-1 and Action-16, -17, or -18; C5'-2 and Action-19, -20, -21, or -22; C5'-3

and Action-23, -24, or -25.

Second, under the task Establish Form of Values, the following pairs are identified:

F1'-1 and Action-01 or Action-02.
F2'-1 and Action-04.
F3'-1 and Action-06, Action-07, or Action-09.
F4'-1 and Action-10.

The event F5'-1 is skipped, since the preceding pair C1'-1 and Action-03 under Choose Values is not chosen.

Similarly, if we try to identify a set of pairs under these tasks for the same element by maximizing orientedness toward economy, we will obtain the following:

C1'-2 and Action-02.
C3'-1 and Action-09; C3'-2 and Action-11.
C4'-1 and Action-13; C4'-2 and Action-15.
C5'-1 and Action-17; C5'-2 and Action-21; C5'-3 and Action-24.
F1'-1 and Action-01.
F3'-1 and Action-06.
F4'-1 and Action-11.

Instead of Steps 1 and 2 of this phase, it might be possible to build a target model directly from the core model developed in Phase 1. This implies that we may skip the step to build the comprehensive model containing all possible event and action patterns and instead may build a model made up of only necessary event-action pairs while propagating limited patterns from the core model with focusing on certain restricted categories of orientedness, that is, by specifying events and actions corresponding to those restricted categories of orientedness. However, such schemes would not be better, since the most proper pair is identified after all possible patterns are enumerated clearly.

After the conceptual design of cataloging rules is completed, the detailed design stage (or the implementation stage subsequent to the design stage) must be carried out. Transformation will be expected from the event-action pairs identified in the last step of the conceptual design into expressions in natural language to form cataloging rules or others. It is quite possible to convert multiple event-action pairs into one rule expression at the succeeding stage, if such integration makes a rule easier to understand. At this stage, it would be useful also to put rules in the order in which the events covered by the rules might be encountered, that is, the most used rules are provided before those less used, since existing cataloging codes adopt such an order.

8.5 Chapter Conclusion

A method to design cataloging rules was proposed by utilizing conceptual modeling of the cataloging process and at the same time applying the concept of 'orientedness.' A general model for the cataloging process at the conceptual level was also proposed. The method was made up of the following phases:

Phase 0: Specifying functional and non-functional requirements by use of orientedness. Cataloger tasks, which are constituents of the cataloging process, are also defined.

Phase 1: Building a core model, which consists of (a) basic event patterns under each task, (b) action patterns applicable to each event, and (c) orientedness involved in an event and action pair. This core model is a general one, being applicable to any situation and system.

Phase 2: Propagating the core model to reflect the characteristics of an individual data element and also a certain class of materials. Next, the propagated model is defined by choosing pairs of event and action patterns in the model while referring to orientedness indicated in each event-action pair, in order to match a particular situation. As a result, consistent and scalable design can be attained.

Notes

1 Part of this chapter has already been reported as a paper in *Journal of the American Society for Information Science and Technology*. Taniguchi (2004a)
2 Le Boeuf (2001)

3 Molto and Svenonius (1998)
4 Fidel and Crandall (1988)
5 Jeng (1991)
6 Svenonius (2000, pp. 89-94)
7 Davis (1993), Loucopoulos and Karakostas (1995)
8 Harel (1987), Harel et al. (1990)
9 Jeng (1991)
10 Molto and Svenonius (1998)
11 Taniguchi (1996)
12 If we try to represent the above events with predicate logic, we can obtain, for example, the following representation:

$$\forall x \, \text{Item}(x) \equiv$$
$$\forall y \, [\, \text{PartOf}(y, x) \rightarrow (\, \text{PrescribedSource}(y, x) \vee \neg \, \text{PrescribedSource}(y, x) \,) \,]$$
$$\wedge \, \forall y \, [\, \text{PrescribedSource}(y, x)$$
$$\rightarrow (\, \text{SinglePrescribedSource}(y, x) \vee \neg \, \text{SinglePrescribedSource}(y, x) \,) \,]$$
$$\wedge \, \forall z \, [\, (\, \neg \, \text{PrescribedSource}(z, x) \vee (\, \text{Item}(z) \wedge \neg \, \text{Equal}(z, x) \,)$$
$$\rightarrow (\, \text{OtherSource}(z, x) \vee \neg \, \text{OtherSource}(z, x) \,) \,]$$

The predicate Item(x) means here that 'x is an item,' and PartOf(y, x) means that 'y is a part of the item x.' Similarly, PrescribedSource(y, x) means that 'the part y is the prescribed source of the item x' and thus every PartOf(y, x) is either PrescribedSource(y, x) or not; in this representation an additional premise is introduced that the prescribed source is an internal part of an item.
13 Joint Steering Committee for Revision of AACR (2002)
14 Shaw et al. (1980), Smith et al. (1993)
15 Japan Library Association (1987, 1994, 2001)
16 Svenonius (2000, pp. 89-90)

Chapter 9

Application of Proposed Design Method: Issue of Recording Evidence in Bibliographic Records[1]

9.1 Aim of Recording Evidence

In Chapter 8, I proposed a method to design cataloging rules by utilizing conceptual modeling of the cataloging process and applying the concept of 'orientedness.' The method should be applicable to, consistent in, and scalable for any situation/system. I also showed a few examples of applying the method to certain bibliographic elements defined in the current cataloging codes.

In the present chapter, I will try to apply the method to a quite new issue, that is, recording evidence in bibliographic records, with the aim of showing the usefulness and validity of the method for such an issue. Evidence is information about why and how those values are recorded for elements and recording such evidence is beyond the scope of conventional cataloging practice and rules. No studies have ever tried to comprehensively investigate the manners and feasibility of recording evidence in bibliographic records. Only few attempts outside the cataloging field have so far been made at tracing and recording the origins of scientific data and its movement between databases[2].

Bibliographic records that have been made in cataloging contain in general only data values for bibliographic and other data elements. These data values in records could be values extracted from resources themselves or assigned by catalogers. On the other hand, bibliographic records in catalogs have been representative of qualified records; there are many mechanisms to assure record quality, such as elaborate and standardized cataloging rules and communication formats, authority control of headings, and sharing and authentication of records in large databases. Nevertheless, it has still been necessary to make those records more interoperable and long-term endurable, or more reliable.

Therefore it would be worth proposing recording evidence for data values, in addition to the values themselves, in order to indicate why and how those values are recorded for elements—it would finally lead to the improvement of the interoperability, longevity, and reliability of bibliographic records. It would be also worth proposing recording the history of changes in data values, with the aim of reinforcing recorded evidence. Recording of change history results from (a) recording dates of data creation and updating, and (b) retaining all previous pairs of a data value and its associated date when changes in data values occur.

In this chapter, I first define necessary categories of orientedness involved in actions of recording evidence. And, I categorize evidence that can be inserted in records into some classes in order to define basic action patterns under each cataloger task. Assessing orientedness among evidence classes is also tried. Second, the subsequent design phase is addressed, namely, propagating the core model that contains the actions of recording evidence and then defining the propagated model by choosing pairs of event and action patterns while referring to orientedness involved in the pairs. And third, some examples of records with notes of evidence are demonstrated.

9.2 Phase 0: Specifying Requirements in Terms of Orientedness Involved in Recording Evidence

Phase 0 is the preliminary phase of designing rules and consists of (a) specifying requirements in terms of orientedness and (b) defining cataloger tasks. We need to confirm necessary categories of orientedness and, if necessary, define a new category related to recording evidence.

The significance of recording evidence is to improve the expressiveness and reliability of records. For record creators, the improvement manifests itself as the ability to (a) identify different records for an identical resource with more confidence, (b) distinguish records for different resources from each other with more confidence, (c) enable recording of more than one value for an individual element (namely, to allow multiple occurrences of an element) in a record without any confusion, and (d) in some cases to transform a recorded value into another. For users, the improvement offers similar advantages to those for record creators; namely, items (a) and (b) above are also appropriate for users.

These lead to the point that items (a) and (b) above correspond obviously to orientedness toward identity. On the other hand, the other items (c) and (d) are beyond that category of orientedness; they cannot be explained with that orientedness. Rather, they can be viewed as the result of self-descriptiveness, that is, data elements and/or records describe themselves being understandable or, in other words, contain enough information to explain their properties and values. Thus, I set up the new category 'orientedness toward self-descriptiveness' in this meaning.

Likewise, the significance of recording the change history of data values is also to improve the expressiveness and reliability of records. Recording change history is useful and effective for continuing resources like serials and integrating resources (e.g., updating Web sites, databases, and loose-leafs). This can be explained with orientedness toward identity, not self-descriptiveness.

For the cataloger tasks, those defined in Chapter 8 are sufficient and we need not any additional task related to recording evidence but need only to position such an action under each general task. Necessary general tasks were defined in Chapter 8 related to the creation of a bibliographic description and the determination of the choice of access points and the form of headings. They are Specify Source of Values, Choose Values, Establish Form of Values, Provide Definition, Choose Access Points, Specify Source of Names, Choose Names, and Establish Form of Names.

9.3 Phase 1: Modifying Core Model by Adding Actions of Recording Evidence

9.3.1 Enumerating Action Patterns Based on Classes of Evidence

Phase 1 of the conceptual design procedure is to build the core model which demonstrates the basic framework of each individual cataloger task. Specifying basic event and action patterns and assessing categories of orientedness involved in an event-action pair should be carried out in this phase.

For each cataloger task except Provide Definition, an action pattern 'to record evidence' can be added, since that action is applicable to any of the general tasks. Furthermore, that action pattern can be divided into sub-patterns based on classes or categories of evidence—I call them 'classes' here.

Evidence that can be recorded with data values in records is categorized into three classes: (a) identifiers of actions adopted under tasks, (b) action descriptions of tasks, and (c) input and output data of tasks.

(Class 1) Identifiers of actions that are adopted under given tasks can be used as evidence, if each individual task has its own identifier. For this class of evidence, the action pattern to be specified in the model is 'to record action identifier(s).'

(Class 2) Action descriptions of tasks are expressions of the actions themselves that tasks specify. For this class of evidence, the action pattern to be specified is 'to record action description of task(s).'

All action patterns under each task shown in Chapter 8 are action descriptions of the tasks in natural language as they stand. Alternative representations are those structured with 'rule markup languages,' like XRML[3] and RuleML[4], or those in symbolic logic, including predicate logic. All of these can be used as evidence.

(Class 3) Input and output data of tasks is the third category of evidence to be recorded. For this class of evidence, the action pattern to be specified is 'to record input and/or output data of task(s),' or, more specifically, 'to record input data of task(s)' and 'to record output data of task(s).'

Each task has input data to it and output data from it. If we focus on the tasks Specify Source of Values, Choose Values, and Establish Form of Values, the input and output data of each task is as follows:

(3-a) Input data to the task Specify Source of Values is all sources that are prescribed for a data element in question (or the entire record) and also can be referred to in a given resource to be described. Output data from the task, on the other hand, is the source(s) chosen as the source of the data element.

(3-b) Input data to the task Choose Values is all values of a certain data type that appear in the chosen source(s). Output data is the chosen value(s).

(3-c) Input data to the task Establish Form of Values is the same as the output data from the task Choose Values. The output data of this task is the value finally recorded in the element in question; to date, it is usual for this output data alone to be recorded.

In the discussion about task analysis, Schreiber et al. illustrates a general framework of task description[5]. The framework is made up of: task identifier and name, organization, goal and value, dependency and flow, objects handled, timing and control, agents, knowledge and competence, resources, and quality and performance. The 'organization' defined in the framework "indicate[s] the business process this task is a part of...," and the 'resources' here "describe and preferably quantify the various resources consumed by the task (staff time, systems, and equipment...)."

The 'goal and value' corresponds to an action description of a task and the 'objects handled' corresponds to the input and output data of a task. The other items of the framework except the 'task identifier and name' would not be worth recording as evidence, since (a) some of them are in principle external to tasks themselves and rather are relationships to other tasks, and (b) some are intrinsic but not able to be used as clues that allow other record creators or users to assess the records.

(Class 4) To record the change history of data values, we need (a) to record the dates (and also their associated evidence, if any), of updating of values in addition to the values themselves and moreover (b) to retain previous pairs of a value and its associated date when changes in values occur. Hence, dates of creation and updating for a data element (or an entire record) need to be added to evidence classes. For this class of evidence, the action pattern to be specified is 'to record the date(s) of creating and updating of values.'

All action patterns under the pattern 'to record evidence' are applicable in principle to any basic event pattern enumerated in Chapter 8 with some exceptions, since those action patterns are independent of any event pattern and also independent of each other.

9.3.2 Assessing Orientedness among Evidence Classes

It would be possible to point out categories of orientedness involved in each action pattern of recording evidence. Both recording action identifier(s) and recording action description of task(s) are actions of contributing to identify resources and provide information on the data values recorded in an element or a record. Therefore, those actions are identity- and self-descriptiveness-oriented. In contrast, recording input and/or output data of task(s) and recording the date(s) of creating and updating of values are identity-oriented; they do not provide any information to assist in interpreting data values.

Furthermore, it would be possible, to some extent, to assess the degree with which the orientedness is involved in among some action patterns—actions descriptions of tasks (or identifiers of actions) and input/output data of the same tasks, as follows:

1) The output data of the task Specify Source of Values is significant for the identification function and thus recording the output data is obviously identity-oriented. Examples of recording the output data are found in existing records, as will be seen later.

On the other hand, the usefulness of input data to the task would be questionable. Action descriptions of the task would be significant if the task specifies only one source—in such a case, the action description is equivalent in semantics to specification of the output data. Therefore, the degree with which that orientedness is involved in these two evidence classes would be low.

2) Action descriptions of the task Choose Values are important for identifying resources, since they specify the semantic scope of the data value(s) selected by the task—in other words, they serve toward the semantic refinement of data elements. It therefore is identity-oriented.

Input data to the task includes data values that have not been chosen as values for an element in question, and therefore the input data would be useful for identification function but at lower degree. Usefulness would not be expected of the output data from the task, since the output data is equivalent in semantics to the value that has been finally recorded in an element; thus any orientedness is not expected.

3) Action descriptions of the task Establish Form of Values, i.e., specification of data values' syntax, are useful for understanding the data values. It is mainly self-descriptiveness-oriented and additionally identity-oriented. Input data to the task is the same as output data from the task Choose Values, and usefulness would thus not be expected.

Consequently, we can get the following basic action patterns (and specific patterns under given tasks) and their orientedness:

(Action-x1) Record action identifier(s).
  (Orientedness) It is identity- and self-descriptiveness-oriented.
(Action-x2) Record action description of task(s).
  (Orientedness) It is identity- and self-descriptiveness-oriented.
    (Action-x2-1) Record action description of the task Specify Source of Values.
      (Orientedness) It is self-descriptiveness-oriented and at lower degree identity-oriented.

(Action-x2-2) Record action description of the task Choose Values.
 (Orientedness) It is identity- and self-descriptiveness-oriented.
(Action-x2-3) Record action description of the task Establish Form of Values.
 (Orientedness) It is self-descriptiveness-oriented and at lower degree identity-oriented.
(Action-x3) Record input and/or output data of task(s).
 (Orientedness) It is identity-oriented.
(Action-x3-1) Record the input of the task Specify Source of Values.
 (Orientedness) It is identity-oriented at lower degree.
(Action-x3-2) Record the output of the task Specify Source of Values.
 (Orientedness) It is identity-oriented.
(Action-x3-3) Record the input of the task Choose Values.
 (Orientedness) It is identity-oriented at lower degree.
(Action-x3-4) Record the output of the task Choose Values.
 (Orientedness) There is no orientedness to be expected.
(Action-x3-5) Record the input of the task Establish Form of Values.
 (Orientedness) There is no orientedness to be expected.
(Action-x4) Record the date(s) of creating and updating of values.
 (Orientedness) It is identity-oriented.

9.3.3 Levels to Which Evidence Recording is Applied

There are two ways of applying evidence recording to data elements or records: pre-specification and post-specification. Pre-specification is the way that given tasks, or their actions, which should be used to record a data value in an element (or to create a record), are assigned in advance before the actual process of recording a value (or creating a record) begins. Conversely, post-specification is the way that, at the point of time when a data value is recorded for an element, tasks, or their actions actually adopted, are determined.

At the same time, there are three levels at which evidence recording is applied: record (i.e., an entire record) level, data element level, and data value level. If we examine the combination of these three levels and the two ways of applying evidence recording, we get the following:

1) At the record level, a set of tasks (and their actions) are pre-specified to create a record, but post-specification would be unusual. Only task (and action)

set identifiers are recorded as evidence at record level.

2) For the data element level, tasks and their actions are pre-specified for a data element to be recorded. Therefore, action identifiers and action descriptions of tasks would be applicable to recording evidence at this level.

3) Regarding the data value level, either action identifiers, action descriptions of tasks, or their input and/or output data are applicable to recording evidence associated with a data value being recorded by the post-specification method.

9.3.4 Phase 2: Propagating Core Model and Defining Propagated Model by Choosing Event-Action Pairs

Phase 2 consists of the two steps. In Step 1, by propagating the core model to reflect the characteristics of an individual data element and, in some cases, a class of materials, we can get a comprehensive model that contains all event patterns in each individual element and also all possible actions against each event while being combined with all possible actions of recording evidence.

The important point to note is that all possible action patterns of recording evidence and categories of orientedness involved in those actions, which we have examined in preceding sections, are applicable in principle to any data element and class of materials, since those action patterns are independent of any event pattern and also any data element and class of materials. In other words, those action patterns of recording evidence and their orientedness can be propagated for any data element.

Step 2 of this phase is to define the propagated model by choosing pairs of event and action patterns enumerated in the model while referring in principle to orientedness indicated in each event-action pair. If we choose event-action pairs with orientedness toward identity and/or that toward self-descriptiveness, a set of event-action pairs containing evidence recording is obtained.

After this phase, detailed design of cataloging rules is carried out and finally rules specifying evidence recoding are obtained. Transformation into rule expressions in natural language and putting rules in a more understandable and useful order will be expected in that detailed design phase.

9.4 Examples of Recording Evidence

9.4.1 Examples from Pre-existing Records and Rules

In current bibliographic records and cataloging rules to manage the process of record creation, we can find some but limited examples of recording evidence.

At the record level, an identifier of a cataloging rule set (of course, not a set of tasks and their actions) used to create records has been indicated in the record leader (character position 18, "descriptive cataloging form") of the MARC21 format[6]. The field with tag 005 contains the date and time of the latest transaction and, furthermore, the position 00-05 in tag 008 indicates the date when the record was first entered on file. In addition, the date on which the resource was viewed for description is recorded in the Note area, creating notes like "Description based on contents viewed on Oct. 21, 1999," according to AACR2, 2002 revision, 12.7B23[7].

Regarding the data value level, we can find examples of evidence recording in the current AACR2; in particular, the rules on the Note area.

Notes on 'Source of title proper' (1.7B3), such as "Title from container," and notes on 'Item described' (12.7B23), such as "Description based on: Vol. 1, no. 3 (Aug. 1999)," are cases of recording output data from the task Specify Source of Values.

Notes on 'Variations in title' (1.7B4) and notes on 'Parallel titles and other title information' (1.7B5) can be regarded as recording of data values that have not been adopted for the title proper or other titles in the Title and Statement of Responsibility area. These, therefore, are part of input data to the task Choose Values in each of the title elements. Examples of notes incorporating the source of such titles, like "Cover title: Giovanni da Firenze," are illustrated in AACR2.

Notes on 'Change in title proper' (12.7B4.2), notes on 'Change in statements of responsibility' (12.7B7.2), and others for continuing resources, are examples of recording change history if they contain the date or period of modification, like "Former title: Washington newspapers database (viewed on Oct. 6, 1999)."

Furthermore, authority records, i.e., name and subject headings authority records, are viewed as evidence, since they are sources for headings assigned to bibliographic records. Additionally, the Cataloger's Note area in an authority record contains "notes on sources consulted in establishing the heading, references to specific rules applied, ..., notes justifying the choice of form of name, etc.," according to *Guidelines for Authority Records and References*, 2nd ed. by the IFLA[8]. The field 670 in MARC21 authority format is 'Source data found' to record a source in which information is found about the heading[9]. Such notes are obviously evidence recording for the authorized heading in an authority record.

9.4.2 Examples of Recording Evidence in Bibliographic Records

The following attempts to illustrate some examples of bibliographic records with evidence recording. All examples are those for recording evidence at the data value level, which post-specifies evidence for an individual value.

1) *Example 1: a bibliographic record for loose-leaf resource*

The first example is a MARC bibliographic record for an integrating resource 'AACR2, 2002 revision,' which is a loose-leaf printed resource. Figure 9-1 shows the bibliographic record—its LC Control Number (i.e., tag 010) 2002073596—but omitting local usage fields with tags 9XX. The figure also demonstrates comprehensive evidence recording for each field or subfield, which I have added to the original record. The fields 245 and 260 are shown after dividing into subfields in order to show associated evidence for each subfield. All pieces of evidence are provided by referring to the actual resource being described and also to the rules contained in the resource as a rule set. In this demonstration, evidence is shown on the units of the task Specify Source of Values, Choose Values, and Establish Form of Values. And, for each task, action descriptions of the task and input and output data of the task are shown as much as possible. Additionally, rule identifiers (i.e., rule numbers) in AACR2, 2002 revision are recorded, since all actions but recording evidence are based on AACR2 rules. It is possible to show evidence on the basis of other units, e.g., the unit of field or subfield, without dividing into tasks; however, that method could reduce the clarity and usability of recorded evidence.

1) The record contains three occurrences of the field 020 (ISBN). For all these values, identifiers of the rules used in the task Specify Source of Values are recorded: the rules 12.0B1 and 12.0B3 of AACR2, 2002 revision. Action descriptions of the task are recorded in a brief form; in this case, "Refer to any source." Input and output data of the task are noted as 'any source' and 'verso of title page, and binder,' respectively; the input data is prescribed in the rule

12.0B3. Likewise, rule numbers, action descriptions of the task, and input/output data of the task Choose Values are provided as shown in the figure; it depicts that a limited number of ISBNs have been chosen. Rule numbers and action descriptions of the task Establish Form of Values are noted; however, input and output data of the task are omitted for the reasons mentioned previously.

2) For the subfields '|a' (title proper) and '|c' (statements of responsibility) of the field 245, rule identifiers, action descriptions of the task, and input and output data of the tasks Specify Source of Values, Choose Values, and Establish Form of Values are provided in the same way as for the field 020 above. The recorded evidence indicates that the title proper in this case is the only title appearing on the title page, and part of the statements of responsibility is omitted during the task Establish Form of Values.

3) Likewise, the fields 250, 260, 300, and 504 are shown with their associated evidence on the unit of the task. For the field 260, the subfields '|a' (place of publication, etc.) and '|b' (name of publisher, etc.), and the subfield '|c' (date of publication, etc.), are separately shown.

4) For the fields 050 (LC call number), 082 (Dewey Decimal classification number), and 650 (subject added entry), only input and output data of the task Specify Source of Values and action descriptions of the task Establish Form of Values are provided; they are derived from given classification schedules or subject heading lists. Regarding the field 710 (added entry—corporate name), no evidence is provided in the figure; however, rule numbers used in the tasks Choose Values/Names and Establish Form of Values/Names, e.g., 24.1A (a general rule on headings for corporate bodies), could be provided, if they are worth recording.

If we note only the output data of the task Specify Source of Values, i.e., the source(s) selected, and furthermore limit the data to substantial matters, the following will be added to the original MARC record:

"source: verso of title page, binder" for Field 020,
"source: title page" for Fields 245 and 250,
"source: title page, verso of title page" for Field 260.

Any other choice or combination of evidence classes is applicable; for instance, a combination of rule identifiers of the task Specify Source of Values and input data of the task Choose Values, and so on. In addition, as mentioned above, there is a choice of the unit for recording evidence: unit of record, field, subfield, or task.

We must look more carefully into the issue of which rule identifiers and action descriptions of the task are enough to be recorded as evidence. At the current stage of this study, it is unclear which rules and action descriptions should be recorded; for example, is it necessary to record "Appendix A: Capitalization" of AACR2 as a rule to be referred to for the title and other elements?

2) Example 2: a bibliographic record for electronic journal

The second example is a bibliographic record borrowed from *Maxwell's Handbook for AACR2R* published in 1997[10]. The resource described in the record shown in Figure 9-2 is an electronic journal, and the record is made basically in accordance with AACR2, 1988 revision[11]. Asterisks preceding field tags indicate newly added fields or subfields, which were not contained in the original record.

For an individual field or subfield in the original record, available evidence is provided, such as rule identifiers and action descriptions of the tasks Specify Source of Values, Choose Values, and Establish Form of Values, by referring to AACR2, 1988 revision. The date of recording the values is added as "date: created: 19930000." On the other hand, for a newly added field or subfield, evidence is provided with reference to AACR2, 2002 revision, and the date is recorded as "date: modified: 20031010."

Some changes in the resource itself have occurred after the original record was created. Also, the rules managing the cataloging operation have changed.

1) The subfield '|h' (General material designation) of the field 245 has been changed in accordance with the change in AACR2. In its 1988 revision, the term 'computer file' was adopted; the 2002 revision uses the term 'electronic resource' instead. Therefore, "245 00 |h [electronic resource]" is newly added by the recoding of rule numbers in the 2002 revision. The original value and its associated evidence are retained with the aim of recording the change history.

2) Changes of data values have also occurred in fields 260 and 856. The subfield '|b' (name of publisher, etc.) of field 260 has changed to "American Statistical Association" from "s.n." (i.e., unknown). Likewise, the subfield '|u' (URL) of field 856 has changed. Such change history should be recorded in the Note area if we follow AACR2; however, I adopted a method of repeating fields.

3) The subfield '|b' (other title information) of field 245 is newly added, referring to the current home page of the journal. Its associated evidence, including the source from which the data value is extracted, is noted.

---

000 01293cam 2200277 a 450

001 12821746

005 20021125095344.0

008 020618m20029999onc b 001 0 eng

010 __ |a 2002073596

020 __ |a 083893529X (loose-leaf with binder)

020 __ |a 0838935303 (loose-leaf without binder)

020 __ |a 0838935311 (binder only)

source: ruleID: AACR2-2002rev.-12.0B1, 12.0B3

source: action: Refer to any source.

source: input: any source

source: output: verso of title page, binder

choice: ruleID: 12.8B1/1.8B1, 1.8B2

choice: action: Choose more than one ISBN assigned to the resource and add their qualifications.

choice: input (in verso of title pate): CANADIAN LIBRARY ASSOCIATION, ISBN 0-88802-299-9 (text only), ISBN 0-88802-300-6 (text with binder); CHARTERED INSTITUTE OF LIBRARY AND INFORMATION PROFESSIONALS, ISBN 0-85604-469-6 (text only), ISBN 0-85604-470-X (binder only); AMERICAN LIBRARY ASSOCIATION, ISBN 0-8389-3529-X (text with binder), ISBN 0-8389-3530-3 (text only)

choice: input (in binder): ISBN 0-8389-3531-1

choice: output: ISBN 0-8389-3529-X (text with binder), ISBN 0-8389-3530-3 (text only), 0-8389-3531-1

form: ruleID: 12.8B1/1.8B1

form: action: Record the ISBNs with the agreed abbreviation and with the standard spacing and hyphenation. Add a brief qualification after each number.

040 __ |a DLC |c DLC |d DLC

050 00 |a Z694.15.A56

source: input/output: Library of Congress Classification.

form: action: Follow Library of Congress Classification.

082 00 |a 025.3/2 |2 21

source: input/output: Dewey Decimal Classification and Relative Index, 21st ed.

form: action: Follow Dewey Decimal Classification and Relative Index, 21st ed.

245 00 |a Anglo-American cataloguing rules

source: ruleID: AACR2-2002rev.-12.0B1, 12.0B3

source: action: Refer to the title page of the resource.

source: input: title page

source: output: title page

choice: ruleID: 12.1B1/1.1B1

choice: action: Choose a title appearing the source.

choice: input: ANGLO-AMERICAN CATALOGUING RULES

choice: output: [the same as the input]

form: ruleID: 12.1B1/1.1B1

form: action: Transcribe the title exactly as to wording, order, and spelling, but not necessary as to punctuation and capitalization.

245 00 / |c prepared under the direction of the Joint Steering Committee for Revision of AACR, a committee of the American Library Association ... [et al.].

source: ruleID: AACR2-2002rev.-12.0B1, 12.0B3

source: action: Refer to the title page of the resource.

source: input: title page

source: output: title page

choice: ruleID: 12.1F1/1.1F1, 1.1F5

choice: Choose statements of responsibility appearing the source.

choice: input: prepared under the direction of THE JOINT STEERING COMMITTEE FOR REVISION OF AACR; a committee of: the American Library Association, The Australian Committee on Cataloguing, The British Library, The Canadian Committee on Cataloguing, Chartered Institute of Library and Information Professionals, The Library of Congress

choice: output: [the same as the input]

form: ruleID: 12.1A1, 12.1F1/1.1F1, 1.1F5

form: action: Transcribe the statements of responsibility in the form in which they appear, but omit all but the first of each group of corporate bodies performing the same function. Indicate the omission by the mark of omission and add 'et al.' in square brackets.

250 _ |a 2nd ed., 2002 revision.

source: ruleID: AACR2-2002rev.-12.0B1, 12.0B3

source: action: Refer to the title page, other preliminaries, and colophon of the resource.

source: input: title page, other preliminaries, colophon

source: output: title page

choice: ruleID: 12.2B1/1.2B1, 12.2D1/1.2D1

choice: action: Choose an edition statement and a statement relating to a named revision of the edition.

choice: input: Second Edition, 2002 Revision

choice: output: [the same as the input]

form: ruleID: 12.2A1, 12.2B1/1.2B1, 12.2D1/1.2D1

form: action: Transcribe the edition statement and the statement relating to the named revision of the edition as found on the source, but use abbreviations and numerals as instructed.

260 _ |a Ottawa : |b Canadian Library Association ; |a Chicago : |b American Library Association,

source: ruleID: AACR2-2002rev.-12.0B1, 12.0B3

source: action: Refer to the whole resource.

source: input: the whole resource

source: output: title page

choice: ruleID: 12.4B1, 1.4B3, 12.4C1/1.4C1, 12.4D1/1.4D1, 1.4D4

choice: action: Choose the first named publisher and the corresponding place. Add the subsequently named publisher in the home country of the cataloging agency and its corresponding place.

choice: input: CANADIAN LIBRARY ASSOCIATION / Ottawa; CHARTERED INSTITUTE OF LIBRARY AND INFORMATION PROFESSIONALS / London; AMERICAN LIBRARY ASSOCIATION / Chicago

choice: output: CANADIAN LIBRARY ASSOCIATION / Ottawa; AMERICAN LIBRARY ASSOCIATION / Chicago

form: ruleID: 12.4A1, 1.4B3, 12.4C1/1.4C1, 12.4D1/1.4D1

form: action: Transcribe the places of publication in the form in which they appear in the source. Transcribe the name of each publisher following the place to which it relates.

260 _ |c 2002-

source: ruleID: AACR2-2002rev.-12.0B1, 12.0B3

source: action: Refer to the whole resource.

source: input: the whole resource

source: output: verso of title page

choice: ruleID: 12.4F1/1.4F1, 1.4F8

choice: Choose the date of the first published iteration of the revision named in the edition area.

choice: input: Published 2002; Copyright 2002

choice: output: 2002

form: ruleID: 12.4A1, 12.4F1/1.4F1, 1.4F8

form: action: Record the date (i.e., year) followed by a hyphen.

300 _ |a 1 v. (loose-leaf) ; 30 cm.

source: ruleID: AACR2-2002rev.-12.0B1, 12.0B3

source: action: Refer to the whole resource.

source: input: the whole resource

source: output: the whole resource

choice: ruleID: 12.5B1, 12.5D1/2.5D1

choice: action: Specify the number of binder. Specify the height of the binder.

choice: input: 1 v.; 29.5 com

choice: output: [the same as the input]

form: ruleID: 12.5A1, 12.5D1/2.5D1

form: action: Record the number of binder in arabic numerals followed by 'v.' Record the height of the binder in centimeters, to the next whole centimeter up.

504 _ |a Includes bibliographical references and index.
source: ruleID: AACR2-2002rev.-12.0B1, 12.0B3
source: action: Refer to any resource.
source: input: any source
source: output: resource itself
choice: ruleID: 12.7B17
choice: action: Make a note on the presence and nature of the index in the resource.
choice: input: p. index-1--index-43
choice: output: [the same as the input]
form: ruleID: 1.7A3
form: action: Record the note employing a standard form of words.

650 _0 |a Descriptive cataloging |v Rules.
source: input/output: Library of Congress Subject Headings.
form: action: Follow Library of Congress Subject Headings.

710 2_ |a Joint Steering Committee for Revision of AACR.
710 2_ |a American Library Association.

Figure 9-1. An example of recording evidence in a bibliographic record.

022 0 |a 1069-1898
source: ruleID: AACR2-1988rev.-12.0B2, 9.0B1, 9.0B2
source: action: Refer to any source.
choice: ruleID: 12.8B1
choice: action: Choose ISSN assigned to the resource.
form: ruleID: 12.8B1
form: action: Record the ISSN with the standard spacing and hyphenation.
date: created: 19930000

245 00 |a Journal of statistics education
500 |a Title from title screen of vol. 1, no. 1.
source: ruleID: AACR2-1988rev.-12.0B2, 9.0B1, 9.0B2

source: action: Refer to the home page of the resource.

choice: ruleID: 12.1B1/1.1B1, 12.7B3

choice: action: Choose a title appearing the source. Make notes on the source of the title proper.

form: ruleID: 12.1B1/1.1B1

form: action: Transcribe the title exactly as to wording, order, and spelling, but not necessary as to punctuation and capitalization.

date: created: 19930000

245 00 |h [computer file]

source: ruleID: AACR2-1988rev.-12.1C1/1.1C1, 9.1C1

source: action: Refer to the list of GMD.

choice: ruleID: 12.1C1/1.1C1, 9.1C1

choice: action: Choose terms from the list.

form: ruleID: 12.1C1/1.1C1

form: action: Record the term chosen. Enclose it in square brackets.

date: created: 19930000

*245 00 |h [electronic resource]

source: ruleID: AACR2-2002rev.-12.1C1/1.1C1, 9.1C1

source: action: Refer to the list of GMD.

choice: ruleID: 12.1C1/1.1C1, 9.1C1

choice: action: Choose terms from the list.

form: ruleID: 12.1C1/1.1C1

form: action: Record the term chosen. Enclose it in square brackets.

date: modified: 20031010

*245 |b an international journal on the teaching and learning of statistics

source: ruleID: AACR2-2002rev.-12.0B1, 12.0B2, 12.0B3, 9.0B1, 9.0B2

source: action: Refer to the home page of the resource.

source: output: title screen of the home page

choice: ruleID: 12.1E1/1.1E1

choice: action: Choose titles other than the title proper appearing the source.

form: ruleID: 12.1E1/1.1E1

form: action: Transcribe the title exactly as to wording, order, and spelling, but not necessary as to punctuation and capitalization.

date: modified: 20031010

246 1 |i Also known as: |a JSE

source: ruleID: AACR2-1988rev.-12.0B2, 9.0B1, 9.0B2

source: action: Refer to the home page of the resource.

choice: ruleID: 12.7B4

choice: action: Choose titles by which the resource is commonly known.

form: ruleID: 12.1B1/1.1B1

form: action: Transcribe the title following the introductory wording. Transcribe the title exactly as to wording, order, and spelling, but not necessary as to punctuation and capitalization.

date: created: 19930000

256 |a Computer data.

source: ruleID: AACR2-1988rev.-12.0B2, 9.0B1, 9.0B2

source: action: Refer to any source.

choice: ruleID: 9.3B1

choice: action: Choose terms from the list.

form: ruleID: 9.3B1

form: action: Record the term chosen.

date: created: 19930000

260 |a [s.l. : |b s.n.]

source: ruleID: AACR2-1988rev.-12.0B2, 9.0B1, 9.0B2

source: action: Refer to the home page of the resource.

choice: ruleID: 12.4C1, 1.4C6, 12.4D1, 1.4D7

choice: action: Give s.l. when no place or probable palace can be given. Give s.n. when the name of the publisher, etc., is unknown.

form: ruleID: 12.4A1, 12.4C1, 1.4C6, 12.4D1, 1.4D7

form: action: Record the term specified. Enclose such a term in square brackets.

date: created: 19930000

*260 |b American Statistical Association

source: ruleID: AACR2-2002rev.-12.0B1, 12.0B2, 12.0B3, 9.0B1, 9.0B2

source: action: Refer to the home page of the resource.

source: output: title screen of the home page

choice: ruleID: 12.4D1

choice: action: Choose the name of the publisher, etc., appearing the source.

form: ruleID: 12.4D1/1.4D1

form: action: Transcribe the name of the publisher, etc., in the shortest form in which it can be understood and identified internationally.

date: modified: 20031010

260 |c 1993-

source: ruleID: AACR2-1988rev.-12.0B2, 9.0B1, 9.0B2

source: action: Refer to the home page of the resource.

choice: ruleID: 12.4F1/1.4F1, 1.4F8

choice: action: Give the beginning date of publication, etc.

form: ruleID: 12.4A1, 12.4F1/1.4F1, 1.4F8

form: action: Record the beginning date followed by a hyphen.

date: created: 19930000

310 |a Quarterly

source: ruleID: AACR2-1988rev.-12.0B2, 9.0B1, 9.0B2

source: action: Refer to the home page of the resource.

choice: ruleID: 12.7B1

choice: action: Give the frequency of the serial.

form: ruleID: 12.7B1

form: action: Record an expression of the frequency.

date: created: 19930000

362 0 |a Vol. 1, no. 1(July 1993)-

source: ruleID: AACR2-1988rev.-12.0B2, 9.0B1, 9.0B2

source: action: Refer to the home page of the resource.

choice: ruleID: 12.3B1

choice: action: Give the numeric designation of the first issue of the serial as given in that issue. Give the chronological designation of that issue in the terms used in the issue.

form: ruleID: 12.3A1, 12.3B1

form: action: Record the numeric designation by using specified abbreviations. Enclose the date following the numeric designation in parentheses. Follow them by a hyphen.

date: created: 19930000

538 |a Mode of access: Internet.

source: ruleID: AACR2-1988rev.-12.0B2, 9.0B1, 9.0B2

source: action: Refer to any source.

choice: ruleID: 9.7B1

choice: action: Specify the mode of access to the resource.

form: ruleID: 9.7B1

form: action: Record the mode of access following the introductory wording.

date: created: 19930000

856 7 |u http://www2.ncsu.edu/ncsu/pams/stat/info/jse/homepage.html |2 http

date: created: 19930000

*856 7 |u http://www.amstat.org/publications/jse/ |2 http

date: modified: 20031010

Figure 9-2. Another example of recording evidence in a bibliographic record.

9.5 Possible Usage of Recorded Evidence

At the beginning of this chapter, I pointed out the objectives and significance of recording evidence. In this section, I focus on some possible ways of using recorded evidence.

9.5.1 Identification and Distinction of Resources

Recorded evidence can be used, first of all, (a) for more confidently identifying different records for an identical resource and (b) for more confidently distinguishing from each other records for different resources. It leads to increasing the degree of orientedness toward identity.

The former case occurs when data values of different records are identical and (a) instances of evidence associated with the values are also the same among the records or (b) one instance of recorded evidence is included in another—the inclusion relationship in semantics among instances of recorded evidence. In such a case, confidence in identifying records for an identical resource is consequently increased. An example is a case where the evidence class noted is output data of the task Specify Source of Values and the recorded evidence of a record is 'title page,' but that of the other record is 'title page and its preliminaries.' Also, if data values of different records are identical but the overlap of recorded evidence is not void (except in cases of subset relations), it would be effective in increasing confidence a little.

These points imply that it is possible to judge the inclusion relationship among recorded evidence from the viewpoint of semantic coverage of those instances. This judgment is applied to some evidence classes: action descriptions of tasks and input and output data of tasks, with exceptions such as the task Establish Form of Values which is not related to semantics. As to action identifiers, such judgment is applicable to them if we take into account the semantic scope of each action with the identifier.

The latter case, that of more confidently distinguishing records for different resources, occurs when data values of different records are different and instances of evidence associated with the values also differ from each other. Consequently, confidence in distinguishing records increases. In particular, when the evidence class used is identical among records but the recorded evidence is unconnected, then confidence is highest—e.g., a case where the evidence class is output data of the task Specify Source of Values and one instance of recorded evidence of a record is 'title page' but that for another record is 'cover.' In the case of an instance where evidence for one is included in another, confidence would increase. In these cases, it could be said that the power of recorded evidence is the opposite of the former case requiring identification/discrimination.

If dates of recording of evidence are noted in addition to the actual evidence, the period of validity of data values and their associated evidence must be incorporated into the judgment of identification and discrimination of resources; in particular, serials and integrating resources, including Web sites.

9.5.2 Transformation of Data Values

Next, I discuss another usage of recorded evidence. This is the transformation of data values into others differing in semantics and/or syntax, by utilizing recorded evidence. It is based on orientedness toward self-descriptiveness.

It is applicable to limited cases where sufficient and necessary evidence to determine a value in an element is recorded with the value. We should notice that it is not related to the issue of identifying and distinguishing the resources that records describe, since the transformation is a matter within a record.

1) When action descriptions of the task Establish Form of Values (i.e., the syntax of values) are recorded (or easily inferred from the values recorded) and input data to the task is also recorded, it is possible to transform the value currently adopted into another in a different syntax. For example, the value '10/10/2003' of the element 'date' could be converted into '20031010,' 'Oct. 10, 2003,' and so on, if the syntax of the original value is noted like 'MM/DD/YYYY.'

2) When action descriptions of the task Choose Values are recorded and input data to the task (i.e., all values of a given data type that appear in the source(s) chosen) is also recorded, we are able to transform the value adopted into another within the semantic scope of a data element; that is, to choose another value recorded as input data. For example, the value '2003' of the element 'date' could be converted into 'c2002.' In other words, the latter value could be selected instead of the former if the task being noted is to choose a date of publication, not a copyright date, and both values are recorded as input data to the task.

3) Regarding the task Specify Source of Values, even if action descriptions of the task and input data to the task (i.e., all sources that are prescribed for a data element in question and also can be referred to in a resource to be described) are recorded, it is impossible to transform the value adopted into another, since values appearing in the sources not selected are not usually recorded. However, if the source specified by the task Specify Source of Values is the entire resource being described, input data to the task Choose Values is all candidate values appearing in the resource. Moreover, in such a case, if all candidate values are recorded as evidence, transformation into any value appearing in the resource would be possible.

9.6 Chapter Conclusion

Applying the conceptual design method proposed in Chapter 8 to the new issue of recording evidence in bibliographic records was tried, which is beyond the scope of conventional cataloging practice and rules. Rules for recording evidence for data values in elements were designed at the conceptual level following the proposed design method. Rules for recording the history of changes in data values were also designed based on the design method. As a result, the following has been clarified:

1) Necessary categories of orientedness that are related to the actions of recording evidence are identified; they are orientedness toward identity and that toward self-descriptiveness. Recorded evidence is useful in some cases (a) to more confidently identify different records for an identical resource, (b) to more confidently distinguish records for different resources from each other, and (c) to transform recorded data values into others differing in semantics and/or syntax. Of course, evidence recording enables the recording of more than one value for an individual element (namely, to allow multiple occurrences of an element) in a record, without any confusion.

2) Evidence that can be recorded is categorized into classes: identifiers of actions, action descriptions of tasks, and input and output data of tasks. Dates of recording values and evidence are an additional class. These evidence classes are applicable to any of the cataloger tasks as action patterns in the core model.

3) Propagating the core model that contains the actions of recording evidence and then defining the propagated model by choosing pairs of event and action patterns while referring to orientedness toward identity and that toward self-descriptiveness can be conducted without any problem. As a result, proper rules for recording evidence will be obtained.

Notes

1 Part of this chapter has already been reported as a paper in *Journal of the American Society for Information Science and Technology*. Taniguchi (2005)
2 Buneman, Khanna, and Tan (2000, 2001).
3 Lee and Sohn (2003)

4 Boley and Tabet (2001)
5 Schreiber et al. (2000, pp. 46-47)
6 Library of Congress (1999b)
7 Joint Steering Committee for Revision of AACR (2002)
8 IFLA (2001, p. 20)
9 Library of Congress (1999a)
10 Maxwell and Maxwell (1997)
11 Joint Steering Committee for Revision of AACR (1988)

Chapter 10

Conclusion

In the former half of this study, a conceptual model which gives primacy to text-level bibliographic entity was proposed.

1) A new viewpoint on whether a text-level entity is given primacy among bibliographic ones in a conceptual model was introduced, to examine the role and function of that entity in each model. As a result, it was found that almost all models, including the FRBR model but with a few exceptions such as the three-layered model, do not treat a text-level entity as predominant.

2) A new model giving primacy to text-level entity was proposed, chiefly by indicating differences from the FRBR model. The text-level entity, its main attributes, and relationships between instances of the entity, were examined in particular. As a result, for example, the following matters were clarified on the implications of giving primacy to text-level entity:

2-a) An instance of the text-level entity must be created for every item.

2-b) Bibliographic records must be created based on the unit of the text-level entity when adopting the policy of creating each record based on a bibliographic entity.

2-c) Titles, statements of responsibility, and others that appear in an item (excluding some exceptions), must be associated with the text-level entity. Other attributes (and also data elements) fully characterizing the entity must be associated with it as well. Important relationships between instances of the entity must be identified and represented in any manner.

2-d) User tasks related to the text-level entity are accomplished using the attributes associated with the entity itself and the relationships between instances of the entity.

2-e) A scenario showing the whole process conducted by users begins in most cases with a task related to the text-level entity (i.e., 'find' that level entity). Also, instances of the entity are necessarily 'identified' or 'selected' in the process shown in the scenario.

3) The FRBR model and the text-prioritized model were examined from the viewpoint of modeling component parts of resources. Examination was conducted in terms of two types of component parts—a content part and a document part—to compare the structure resulting from modeling a component part with that from a resource at the integral unit level in each model. Consequently, it was found that in the text-prioritized model any type of resource is modeled in basically the same manner and, in contrast, in the FRBR model it is not.

4) As an investigation of the feasibility of creating bibliographic records in accordance with the text-prioritized model, conversion of MARC bibliographic records into those structured under the hierarchical records approach was attempted. The conversion procedure was clarified by (a) identifying steps that need to be carried out by human and (b) identifying possible alternatives in each step of the conversion. The conversion was carried out by developing programs to facilitate it; but it would still need to elaborate the programs.

5) A prototype system was developed for retrieving and displaying records created through the conversion of MARC records. Functions necessary in such a system to handle those hierarchical records were demonstrated, and the usefulness of such records was shown.

It follows from what has been investigated that (a) the text-prioritized model would provide a solution to issues such as the 'format variations' or 'multiple versions' issue and the 'content versus carrier' issue, including cases of component parts; (b) the model would become a solid basis to provide detailed information on the text (and work) of a resource and on relationships among texts, which are related to the intellectual/artistic aspect of a resource; and thus (c) users would be able to access and use resources in a more consistent and intelligible manner by means of records in line with the model.

In the latter half of the study, a method was proposed of designing cataloging rules by utilizing conceptual modeling of the cataloging process.

1) A new concept, 'orientedness,' was introduced to analyze cataloging rules and thus to represent functional and non-functional requirements in the cataloging process. As a result, the following has been clarified: (a) most of the principles (or fundamentals) of description and access points/headings can be assessed in terms of orientedness, with a few exceptions, and (b) each rule in existing cataloging

codes, and also each possible alternative to the rule, can be properly evaluated and understood from the viewpoint of orientedness.

2) A method of designing cataloging rules was proposed by utilizing conceptual modeling of the cataloging process and at the same time applying the concept of 'orientedness.' A general model for the cataloging process at the conceptual level was also proposed as part of the design method. The method was made up of the following phases:

Phase 0: Specifying functional and non-functional requirements by use of orientedness, and defining cataloger tasks constituting the cataloging process.

Phase 1: Building a core model, which consists of (a) basic event patterns under each task, (b) action patterns applicable to each event, and (c) orientedness involved in an event and action pair. This core model is a general one, being applicable to any situation and system.

Phase 2: Propagating the core model to reflect the characteristics of an individual data element and also a certain class of materials. Next, the propagated model is defined by choosing pairs of event and action patterns in the model while referring to orientedness indicated in each event-action pair, in order to match a particular situation.

3) Applying the conceptual design method to a new issue of recording evidence in bibliographic records was tried, which is beyond the scope of the conventional cataloging practice and rules. Rules for recording evidence for data values in elements were properly designed at the conceptual level, by following the proposed design method.

I may, therefore, reasonably conclude that the proposed concept of 'orientedness' and the proposed design method are positively validated and shown to be useful for designing cataloging rules, since (a) by following the method, consistent and scalable design can be attained, and (b) the method is applicable to, and deals properly with, even an issue beyond the scope of conventional cataloging practice and rules.

Suggestions for future research

The following itemized listing offers several suggested topics for future research.

1) Regarding conceptual modeling for catalogs, verification of the usefulness of the proposed text-prioritized model for electronic resources deserves further

serious research. The model proposed in this study can easily be applied to electronic resources. However, it might be possible and better to further adapt the model for such resources, with some modifications or extensions, with the aim of improving its expressiveness and interoperability.

If we examine the discussions on metadata (in particular, descriptive metadata), it is realized that most models for metadata have so far been deficient in failing to grasp an electronic resource as being a structure that consists of more than one constituent like an entity. It would be valuable to incorporate such a viewpoint and model into discussions on metadata.

2) In-depth investigations of the usefulness of the proposed model, and of records based on the model having different structures from existing records, would be another prospective research topic. However, we do not have any general methodology applicable to an assessment of a model and/or a record by users, i.e., user evaluation. We must develop such methodology itself, as well as conduct those investigations.

3) For conceptual modeling of cataloging rules, it would be worth conducting verification of the interpretation of orientedness involved in rules, i.e., event-action patterns. Different interpretations of orientedness involved in event and action patterns may be obtained if other experts try to interpret orientedness involved in those patterns. It therefore would be necessary to conduct this investigation with more than one expert, and also necessary to try to explore a method to minimize the differences (if any) in interpretation.

4) Verification of the usefulness of representing the conceptual model with symbolic logic such as predicate logic could be another topic to be pursued. Event and action patterns, and knowledge peculiar to a certain data element or class of materials, might be represented with predicate logic. The usefulness is not clear at the current stage. It may, however, be worth investigating the benefit and feasibility of representation with predicate logic, if we take into account its possible future use to develop a system for automating a part of modeling, such as propagation of the core model.

References

Aalberg, T. (2002). "Navigating in bibliographic catalogues." *Research and Advanced Technology for Digital Technology: 6th European Conference, ECDL 2002, Rome, Italy, September 16-18, 2002: Proceedings.* Agosti, M. and Thanos, C., ed. Berlin, Springer, pp. 238-250.

ALCTS CCS CC:DA. (1995). *Guidelines for Bibliographic Description of Reproductions.* Chicago, American Library Association.

ALCTS CCS CC:DA. (1999). *Overview and Recommendations Concerning Revision of Rule 0.24.* (online), available from <http://www.ala.org/alcts/organization/ccs/ccda/tf-024h.pdf>, (accessed 2004-01-19).

ALCTS CCS CC:DA. Task Force on Recommendation 2 in 4JSC/ALA/30. (2000). *Task Force Report.* (online), available from <http://www.ala.org/alcts/organization/ccs/ccda/tf-rec2.html>, (accessed 2004-01-19).

American Library Association et al. (1967). *Anglo-American Cataloging Rules. North American Text.* Chicago, American Library Association.

American Library Association et al. (1974). *Anglo-American Cataloging Rules. Chapter 6: Separately Published Monographs, North American Text.* Chicago, American Library Association.

American Library Association et al. (1978). *Anglo-American Cataloguing Rules. 2nd ed.* Chicago, American Library Association.

Ayres, F.H., Nielsen, L.P.S., and Ridley, M.J. (1996). Bibliographic management: a new approach using the manifestations concept and the Bradford OPAC. *Cataloging & Classification Quarterly.* vol. 22, no. 1, pp. 3-28.

Ayres, F.H., Nielsen, L.P.S., and Ridley, M.J. (1997). Design and display issues for a manifestation-based catalogue at Bradford. *Program.* vol. 31, no. 2, pp. 95-113.

Ayres, F.H., Nielsen, L.P.S., Ridley, M.J., and Torsun, I.S. (1995). *The Bradford OPAC: A New Concept in Bibliographic Control.* London, British Library Research and Development Department, British Library R & D report, 6183.

Bennett, R., Lavoie, B.F., and O'Neill, E.T. (2003). The concept of a work in WorldCat: an application of FRBR. *Library Collections, Acquisitions, & Technical Services.* vol. 27, no. 1, pp. 45-59.

Boley, H. and Tabet, S. (2001). "Design rational of RuleML: a markup language for semantic web rules." *Proceedings of the 2001 International Semantic Working Symposium (ISWWS)*. (online), available from <http://www.semanticweb.org/SWWS/program/full/paper20.pdf>, (accessed 2004-01-19).

Buneman, P., Khanna, S., and Tan, W.C. (2000). "Data provenance: some basic issues." *Foundations of Software Technology and Theoretical Computer Science: Proceedings of the 20th Conference (FST TCS 2000), New Delhi, India, December 13-15, 2000*. Kapoor, S. and Prasad, S., ed. Berlin, Springer, pp. 87-93. (Lecture Notes in Computer Science, 1974)

Buneman, P., Khanna, S., and Tan, W.C. (2001). "Why and where: a characterization of data provenance." *Database Theory: Proceedings of the 8th International Conference (ICDT 2001), London, UK, January 4-6, 2001*. van den Bussche, J. and Vianu, V., ed. Berlin, Springer, pp. 316-330. (Lecture Notes in Computer Science, 1973)

Carpenter, M. (1981). *Corporate Authorship: its Role in Library Cataloging*. Westport, CT, Greenwood Press.

Cockshutt, M.E., Cook, C.D., and Schabas, A.H. (1983). Decision logic for Anglo-American Cataloguing Rules, Chapter 21: 'choice of access points.' *Library Resources & Technical Services*. vol. 27, no. 4, pp. 371-390.

Cutter, C.A. (1904). *Rules for a Dictionary Catalog. 4th ed., rewritten*. Washington, DC, Government Printing Office.

Davis, A.M. (1993). *Software Requirements: Objects, Functions, and States. Revised ed.* Upper Saddle River, NJ, Prentice Hall.

Delsey, T. (1998a). "Modeling the logic of AACR." *The Principles and Future of AACR: Proceedings of the International Conference on the Principles and Future Development of AACR, Toronto, Canada, October 23-25, 1997*. Weihs, J., ed. Chicago, American Library Association, pp. 1-16.

Delsey, T. (1998b). *The Logical Structure of the Anglo-American Cataloguing Rules. Part I.* (online), available from <http://www.nlc-bnc.ca/jsc/aacr.pdf>, (accessed 2004-01-19).

Delsey, T. (1999). *The Logical Structure of the Anglo-American Cataloguing Rules. Part II.* (online), available from <http://www.nlc-bnc.ca/jsc/aacr2pdf>, (accessed 2004-01-19).

Delsey, T. (2002). *Functional Analysis of the MARC21 Bibliographic and Holdings Formats*. Washington, DC, Library of Congress. (online), available from <http://www.loc.gov/marc/marc-functional-analysis/home.html>, (accessed 2004-01-19).

Domanovszky, A. (1975). "6. The second function: the recording of 'works'." *Functions and Objects of Author and Title Cataloguing*. München, Verlag Dokumentation, pp. 87-110.

Fidel, R. and Crandall, M. (1988). The AACR2 as design schema for bibliographic databases. *Library Quarterly*. vol. 58, no. 2, pp. 123-142.

Goossens, P. and Mazur-Rzesos, E. (1982). "Hierarchical relationships in bibliographic descriptions: problem analysis." *Hierarchical Relationships in Bibliographic Descriptions: INTERMARC Software-Subgroup Seminar 4*. Helal, A.H. and Weiss, J.W., ed. Essen, Gesamthochschulbibliothek, pp. 13-128.

Gorman, M. (1992). "After AACR2R: the future of the Anglo-American cataloguing rules." *Origins, Content, and Future of AACR2 Revised*. Smiraglia, R.P., ed. Chicago, American Library Association, pp. 89-94.

Green, R. (1996). The design of a relational database for large-scale bibliographic retrieval. *Information Technology and Libraries*. vol. 15, no. 4, pp. 207-221.

Hagler, R. (1991). *The Bibliographic Record and Information Technology*. 2nd ed. Chicago, American Library Association.

Hagler, R. (1997). *The Bibliographic Record and Information Technology*. 3rd ed. Chicago, American Library Association.

Harel, D. (1987). Statecharts: a visual formalism for complex systems. *Science of Computer Programming*. vol. 8, pp. 231-274.

Harel, D. et al. (1990). Statemate: a working environment for development of complex reactive systems. *IEEE Transactions on Software Engineering*. vol. 16, no. 4, pp. 403-414.

Heaney, M. (1995). Object-oriented cataloging. *Information Technology and Libraries*. vol. 14, no. 3, pp. 135-153.

Hegna, K. and Murtomaa, E. (2002). *Data Mining MARC to Find: FRBR?* (online), available from <http://folk.uio.no/knuthe/dok/frbr/datamining.pdf>, (accessed 2004-01-19).

Hickey, T.B., O'Neill, E.T., and Toves, J. (2002). Experiments with the IFLA Functional Requirements for Bibliographic Records (FRBR). *D-Lib Magazine*. vol. 8, no. 9. (online), available from <http://www.dlib.org/dlib/september02/hickey/09hickey.html>, (accessed 2004-01-19).

Hjerppe, R. and Olander, B. (1989). Cataloging and expert systems: AACR2 as a knowledge base. *Journal of the American Society for Information Science*. vol. 40, no. 1, pp. 27-44.

Hoffman, H.H. (1981). A structure code for machine readable library catalog record formats. *Journal of Library Automation*. vol. 14, no. 2, pp. 112-116.

Howarth, L.C. (1998a). "Key lessons of history: revising the foundations of AACR." *The Future of the Descriptive Cataloging Rules*. Schottlaender, B.E.C., ed. Chicago, American Library Association, pp. 6-18.

Howarth, L.C. (1998b). "Content versus carrier." *The Principles and Future of AACR: Proceedings of the International Conference on the Principles and Future Development of AACR, Toronto, Canada, October 23-25, 1997.* Weihs, J., ed. Chicago, American Library Association, pp. 148-156.

Huthwaite, A. (1994). Multiple Versions Forum and models. *Cataloguing Australia.* vol. 20, no. 1, pp. 7-12.

IFLA. (1988). *Guidelines for the Application of the ISBDs to the Description of Component Parts.* London, IFLA UBCIM Programme.

IFLA. (1997). *ISBD(ER): International Standard Bibliographic Description for Ectronic Resources.* München, K.G. Saur. Also available online from <http://www.ifla.org/VII/s13/pubs/isbd.htm>, (accessed 2004-01-19).

IFLA. (2001). *Guidelines for Authority Records and References. 2nd ed.* München, K.G. Saur.

IFLA Meeting of Experts on an International Cataloguing Code. (2004). "Statement of International Cataloguing Principles." *SCAT News: Newsletter of the Standing Committee of the IFLA Cataloguing Section.* no. 20, pp. 2-7.

IFLA Section on Cataloguing, FRBR Review Group, comp. (2002-). *FRBR Bibliography.* (online), available from <http://www.ifla.org/VII/s13/wgfrbr/bibliography.htm>, (accessed 2004-01-19).

IFLA Study Group on the Functional Requirements for Bibliographic Records. (1996). *Functional Requirements for Bibliographic Records: Draft Report for World-Wide Review.* Frankfurt, IFLA UBCIM Programme.

IFLA Study Group on the Functional Requirements for Bibliographic Records. (1997). *Functional Requirements for Bibliographic Records: Final Report.* Frankfurt, IFLA UBCIM Programme. Also published as: München, K.G. Saur, 1998. Also available online from<http://www.ifla.org/VII/s13/frbr/frbr.pdf>, (accessed 2004-01-19).

IFLA Working Group on Content Designators. (1977). *UNIMARC: Universal MARC Format.* London, IFLA International Office for UBC.

IFLA Working Group on Content Designators. (1980). *UNIMARC: Universal MARC Format. 2nd ed., revised.* London, IFLA International Office for UBC.

International Conference on Cataloguing Principles. (1963). *Report: Proceedings of the Conference, Paris, 9th-18th, October, 1961.* Chaplin, A.H. and Anderson, D., ed. London, Organizing Committee of the Conference.

International Council on Archives. (2000). *ISAD(G): General International Standard Archival Description. 2nd ed.* Ottawa, ICA. (online), available from <http://www.ica.org/biblio/cds/isad_g_2e.pdf>, (accessed 2004-01-19).

ISO/IEC 2382-17 (1999). *Information Technology—Vocabulary—Part 17: Databases.* Geneva, ISO.

ISO/IEC 2382-20 (1990). *Information Technology—Vocabulary—Part 20: System development.* Geneva, ISO.

Japan Library Association. (1987). *Nippon Cataloging Rules. 1987 ed.* Tokyo, Japan Library Association.

Japan Library Association. (1994). *Nippon Cataloging Rules. 1987 ed., 1994 revision.* Tokyo, Japan Library Association.

Japan Library Association. (2001). *Nippon Cataloging Rules. 1987 ed., 2001 revision.* Tokyo, Japan Library Association.

Jeng, L.H. (1991). The structure of a knowledge base for cataloging rules. *Information Processing & Management.* vol. 27, no. 1, pp. 97-110.

Joint Steering Committee for Revision of AACR. (1988). *Anglo-American Cataloguing Rules. 2nd ed., 1988 revision.* Chicago, American Library Association.

Joint Steering Committee for Revision of AACR. (2002). *Anglo-American Cataloguing Rules. 2nd ed., 2002 revision.* Chicago, American Library Association.

Joint Steering Committee for Revision of AACR, Format Variation Working Group. (2001). *Interim Report.* (online), available from <http://www.nlc-bnc.ca/jsc/forvarwg3.pdf>, (accessed 2004-01-19).

Joint Steering Committee for Revision of AACR, Format Variation Working Group. (2002a). *Third Interim Report.* (online), available from <http://www.nlc-bnc.ca/jsc/forvarwg3rep3.pdf>, (accessed 2004-01-19).

Joint Steering Committee for Revision of AACR, Format Variation Working Group. (2002b). *Dealing with FRBR Expressions in MARC21.* Washington, DC, Library of Congress. (MARBI Discussion Paper, No. 2002-DP08) (online), available from <http://www.loc.gov/marc/marbi/2002/2002-dp08.html>, (accessed 2004-01-19).

Jolley, L. J. (1963). "The function of the main entry in the alphabetical catalogue: a study of the views put forward by Lubetzky and Verona." *Report: Proceedings of the International Conference on Cataloguing Principles, Paris, 9th-18th, October, 1961.* Chaplin, A.H. and Anderson, D., ed. London, Organizing Committee of the Conference, pp. 159-163.

Jones, B. and Kastner, A. (1983). Duplicate records in the bibliographic utilities: a historical review of the printing versus edition problem. *Library Resources & Technical Services.* vol. 27, no. 2, pp. 211-220.

Jonsson, G. (2002). *The Basis for a Record in Major Cataloguing Codes and the Relation to FRBR.* (online), available from <http://www.ifla.org/IV/ifla68/papers/052-133e.pdf>, (accessed 2004-01-19).

Le Boeuf, P. (2001). FRBR and further. *Cataloging & Classification Quarterly.* vol. 32, no. 4, pp. 15-52.

Leazer, G.H. (1993). *A conceptual plan for the description and control of bibliographic works.* Columbia University, Ph.D. thesis.

Leazer, G.H. and Smiraglia, R.P. (1996). "Toward the bibliographic control of works:

derivative bibliographic relationships in an online union catalog." *Proceedings of the 1st ACM International Conference on Digital Libraries, March 20-23, 1996, Bethesda, Maryland.* New York, ACM Press, pp. 36-43.

Leazer, G.H. and Smiraglia, R.P. (1999). Bibliographic families in library catalog: a qualitative analysis and grounded theory. *Library Resources & Technical Services.* vol. 43, no. 4, pp. 191-212.

Lee, J.K. and Sohn, M.M. (2003). The extensible rule markup language. *Communications of the ACM.* vol. 46, no. 5, pp. 59-64.

Library of Congress. (1946). *Studies of Descriptive Cataloging.* Washington, DC, US Government Printing Office.

Library of Congress. (1949). *Rules for Descriptive Cataloging in the Library of Congress.* Washington, DC, Library of Congress.

Library of Congress. (1997). *Draft Interim Guidelines for cataloging Electronic Resources.* Washington, DC, Library of Congress. (online), available from <http://lcweb.loc.gov/catdir/cpso/dcmb19_4.> (accessed 2004-01-19).

Library of Congress. (1999a). *MARC21 Format for Authority Data: Including Guidelines for Content Designation.* Washington, DC, Library of Congress.

Library of Congress. (1999b). *MARC21 Format for Bibliographic Data: Including Guidelines for Content Designation.* Washington, DC, Library of Congress.

Library of Congress. (2002). *Displays for Multiple Versions from MARC21 and FRBR.* (online), available from <http://www.loc.gov/marc/marc-functional-analysis/home.html>, (accessed 2004-01-19).

Library of Congress. (2003-). *FRBR Display Tool.* (online), available from <http://www.loc.gov/marc/marc-functional-analysis/tool.html> (accessed 2004-01-19).

Loucopoulos, P. and Karakostas, V. (1995). *System Requirements Engineering.* London, McGraw-Hill.

Lubetzky, S. (1960). *Code of Cataloging Rules: Author and Title Entry.* (An unpublished draft). Chicago, American Library Association.

Lubetzky, S. (1963). "The function of the main entry in the alphabetical catalogue: one approach." *Report: Proceedings of the International Conference on Cataloguing Principles, Paris, 9th-18th, October, 1961.* Chaplin, A.H. and Anderson, D., ed. London, Organizing Committee of the Conference, pp. 139-143.

Lubetzky, S. (1969). *Principles of Cataloging: Final Report. Phase I: Descriptive Cataloging.* Los Angels, University of California, Los Angels, Institute of Library Research.

Matsuura, J. (1996). KOPAC: Kunitachi College of Music Library Online Public Access Catalog. *Joho Kanri: Journal of Information Processing and Management.* vol. 39, no. 1, pp. 22-39. [in Japanese]

Matsuura, J. (1997). "Significance of authority control in online public access." *Electronic Information Environment and Academic Libraries*. Matsushita, H., ed. Tokyo, Kinokuniya, pp. 199-213.

Maxwell, R.L. and Maxwell, F.M. (1997). *Maxwell's Handbook for AACR2R*. Chicago, American Library Association.

Molto, M. and Svenonius, E. (1998). An electronic interface to AACR2. *Cataloging & Classification Quarterly*. vol. 26, no. 1, pp. 3-24.

Multiple Versions Forum. (1990). *Multiple Versions Forum Report: Report from a Meeting Held Dec. 6-8, 1989, Airlie, Virginia*. Washington, DC, Library of Congress.

O'Neil, E.T. (2002). FRBR: Functional Requirements for Bibliographic Records: application of the entity-relationship model to Humphry Clinker. *Library Resources & Technical Services*. vol. 46, no. 4, pp. 150-159.

O'Neil, E.T. and Visine-Goetz, D. (1989). "Bibliographic relationships: implications for the function of the catalog." *The Conceptual Foundations of Descriptive Cataloging*. Svenonius, E., ed. San Diego, Academic Press, pp. 167-179.

Program for Cooperative Cataloging. (2001). *Authority File Comparison Rules: NACO Normalization*. Washington, DC, Library of Congress. (online), available from <http://www.loc.gov/catdir/pcc/naco/normrule.html>, (accessed 2004-01-19).

Program for Cooperative Cataloging. (2002). *CONSER Cataloging Manual, Module 31: Remote Access Electronic Serials*. Washington, DC, Library of Congress. (online), available from <http://www.loc.gov/acq/conser/Module31.pdf>, (accessed 2004-01-19).

Ridley, M. (1998). "Beyond MARC." *The Principles and Future of AACR: Proceedings of the International Conference on the Principles and Future Development of AACR, Toronto, Canada, October 23-25, 1997*. Weihs, J., ed. Chicago, American Library Association, pp. 229-239.

Rolland, C. and Prakash, N. (2000). From conceptual modelling to requirements engineering. *Annals of Software Engineering*. vol. 10, pp. 151-176.

Rowley, J.E. (1995). *Organizing Knowledge*. 2nd ed. Aldershot, UK, Gower.

Schreiber, G. et al. (2000). *Knowledge Engineering and Management: The CommonKADS Methodology*. Cambridge, MA, MIT Press.

Shaw, M., Dent, B., Evans, D., and Smith, D. (1980). *Using AACR2: A Step-by-step Algorithmic Approach to Part II of the Anglo-American Cataloguing Rules*. London, Library Association.

Shelly, G.B., Cashman, T.J., and Rosenblatt, H.J. (2001). *Systems Analysis and Design*. 4th ed. Boston, Course Technology.

Shinebourne, J.A. (1979). A critique of AACR2. *Libri*. vol. 29, no. 3, pp. 231-259.

Smiraglia, R.P. (1992). *Authority control and the extent of derivative bibliographic relationships*.

University of Chicago, Ph.D. thesis.

Smiraglia, R.P. (2002). Bridget's Revelations, William of Ockham's Tractatus, and Doctrine and Covenants: qualitative analysis and epistemological perspectives on theological works. *Cataloging & Classification Quarterly*. vol. 33, no. 3/4, pp. 225-251.

Smiraglia, R.P. and Leazer, G.H. (1999). Derivative bibliographic relationships: the work relationship in a global bibliographic database. *Journal of the American Society for Information Science*. vol. 50, no. 6, pp. 493-504.

Smith, D., Evans, D., Poulter, A., and Shaw, M. (1993). *Using the New AACR2: An Expert Systems Approach to Choice of Access Points*. London, Library Association Publishing.

Svenonius, E. (1992). "Bibliographic entities and their uses." *Seminar on Bibliographic Records: Proceedings of the Seminar held in Stockholm, 15-16 August 1990*. Bourne, R. ed. München, K.G. Saur, pp. 3-18.

Svenonius, E. (2000). *The Intellectual Foundation of Information Organization*. Cambridge, MA, MIT Press.

Taniguchi, S. (1990). A three-layered conceptual model for descriptive cataloging. *Annals of Japan Society of Library Science*. vol. 36, no. 4. pp. 149-166. [in Japanese]

Taniguchi, S. (1992). A comparative study of bibliographic description between descriptive cataloging and abstracting-and-indexing services. *Annals of Japan Society of Library Science*. vol. 38, no. 2. pp. 69-86. [in Japanese]

Taniguchi, S. (1993a). A response to criticism on the three-layered model in descriptive cataloging. *Annals of Japan Society of Library Science*. vol. 39, no. 2, pp. 85-93. [in Japanese]

Taniguchi, S. (1993b). A comparative study of bibliographic descriptions between descriptive cataloging and abstracting-and-indexing services based on the three-layered conceptual model. *Annals of Japan Society of Library Science*. vol. 39, no. 3, pp. 97-118. [in Japanese]

Taniguchi, S. (1993c). Re-examination of the collocating function of catalogs. Presented in the 1993 Spring Research Conference of Japan Society of Library Science, May 1993. [in Japanese]

Taniguchi, S. (1995). A system for analyzing cataloging rules: expansion of an inter-rule relationship analysis. *Annals of Japan Society of Library Science*. vol. 41, no. 3/4, pp. 111-129. [in Japanese]

Taniguchi, S. (1996). A system for analyzing cataloging rules: a feasibility study. *Journal of the American Society for Information Science*. vol. 47, no. 5, pp. 338-356.

Taniguchi, S. (1997a). Revaluation of the three-layered model in descriptive cataloging. *Annals of Japan Society of Library Science*. vol. 43, no. 1, pp. 1-18. [in Japanese]

Taniguchi, S. (1997b). An analysis of oriented-ness in cataloging rules. *Annals of Japan*

Society of Library Science. vol. 43, no. 3, pp. 129-144. [in Japanese]

Taniguchi, S. (1999a). An analysis of orientedness in cataloging rules. *Journal of the American Society for Information Science*. vol. 50, no. 5, pp. 448-460.

Taniguchi, S. (1999b). Two ways to construct a bibliographic entity in conceptual modeling: re-examination of the three-layered model and the IFLA FRBR model. *Journal of Japan Society of Library and Information Science*. vol. 45, no. 2, pp. 45-60. [in Japanese]

Taniguchi, S. (2001). A method for illustrating bibliographic records in line with conceptual models in cataloging: toward the creation of bibliographic records based on a text-level entity. *TP&D Forum Series: Technical Processing & Documentation Forum Series*. no. 10, pp. 5-17. [in Japanese]

Taniguchi, S. (2002a). A conceptual model giving primacy to expression-level bibliographic entity in cataloging. *Journal of Documentation*. vol. 58, no. 4, pp. 363-382.

Taniguchi, S. (2002b). "A conceptual model for cataloging process." *Proceedings of the 65th American Society for Information Science and Technology Annual Meeting, November 18-21, 2002, Philadelphia*. Medford, NJ, Information Today, pp. 569-570.

Taniguchi, S. (2003a). Conceptual modeling of component parts of bibliographic resources in cataloging. *Journal of Documentation*. vol. 59, no. 6, pp. 692-708.

Taniguchi, S. (2003b). *A Conceptual Model Giving Primacy to Text-level Bibliographic Entity in Cataloging: A Detailed Discussion*. Report of Research Project, Grant-in-aid for Scientific Research, 2002. (online), available from <http://www.slis.tsukuba.ac.jp/~taniguch/report200301.pdf>, (accessed 2004-01-19).

Taniguchi, S. (2004a). Design of cataloging rules using conceptual modeling of cataloging process. *Journal of the American Society for Information Science and Technology*. vol. 55, no. 6, pp. 498-512.

Taniguchi, S. (2004b). Expression-level bibliographic entity records: a trial on creation from pre-existing MARC records. *Cataloging & Classification Quarterly*. vol. 38, no. 2, pp. 33-59.

Taniguchi, S. (2005). Recording evidence in bibliographic records and descriptive metadata. *Journal of the American Society for Information Science and Technology*. vol. 56, no. 8, pp. 872-882.

Teory, T.J. (1999). *Database Modelling & Design*. 3rd ed. San Francisco, Morgan Kaufmann.

Thayer, R.H. and Thayer, M.C. (1990). "Glossary." *System and Software Requirements Engineering*. Los Alamitos, CA, IEEE Computer Society Press, pp. 605-676.

Tillett, B.B. (1987). *Bibliographic relationships: toward a conceptual structure of bibliographic information used in cataloging*. University of California, Los Angeles, Ph.D. thesis.

Tillett, B.B. (1991a). A taxonomy of bibliographic relationships. *Library Resources & Technical Services*. vol. 35, no. 2, pp. 150-158.

Tillett, B.B. (1991b). A summary of the treatment of bibliographic relationships in cataloging rules. *Library Resources & Technical Services.* vol. 35, no. 4, pp. 393-405.

Tillett, B.B. (1992a). The history of linking devices. *Library Resources & Technical Services.* vol. 36, no. 1, pp. 23-36.

Tillett, B.B. (1992b). Bibliographic relationships: an empirical study of the LC machine-readable records. *Library Resources & Technical Services.* vol. 36, no. 2, pp. 162-188.

Tillett, B.B. (2001a). "Bibliographic Relationships." *Relationships in the Organization of Knowledge.* Bean, C.A. and Green, R., ed. Dordrecht, Kluwer, pp. 19-35.

Tillett, B.B. (2001b). *Principles of AACR.* (A discussion paper to Joint Steering Committee for Revision of AACR, 4JSC/Chair/74). (online), available from <http://www.nlc-bnc.ca/jsc/prin.html>, (accessed 2004-01-19).

University of California Libraries, Task Force on Electronic Resources. (1998). *Report to the University of California Heads of Technical Services.* (online), available from <http://tpot.ucsd.edu/Cataloging/HotsElectronic/tfer.html>, (accessed 2004-01-19).

Valacich, J.S., George, J.F., and Hoffer, J.A. (2001). *Essentials of Systems Analysis and Design.* Upper Saddle River, NJ, Prentice Hall.

Vellucci, S.L. (1995). *Bibliographic relationships among musical bibliographic entities : a conceptual analysis of music represented in a library catalog with a taxonomy of the relationships discovered.* Columbia University, Ph.D. thesis.

Vellucci, S.L. (1997). *Bibliographic Relationships in Music Catalogs.* Lanham, MD, Scarecrow Press.

Vellucci, S.L. (1998). "Bibliographic relationships." *The Principles and Future of AACR: Proceedings of the International Conference on the Principles and Future Development of AACR, Toronto, Canada, October 23-25, 1997.* Weihs, J., ed. Chicago, American Library Association, pp. 105-146.

Verona, E. (1959). Literary unit versus bibliographic unit. *Libri.* vol. 9, no. 2, pp. 79-104.

Verona, E. (1963). "The function of the main entry in the alphabetical catalogue: a second approach." *Report: Proceedings of the International Conference on Cataloguing Principles, Paris, 9th-18th, October, 1961.* Chaplin, A.H. and Anderson, D., ed. London, Organizing Committee of the Conference., pp. 145-157.

Wanninger, P.D. (1982). Is the OCLC database too large? a study of the effect of duplicate records in the OCLC system. *Library Resources & Technical Services.* vol. 26, no. 4, pp. 353-361.

Weinstein, P.C. (1998). "Ontology-based metadata: transforming the MARC legacy." *Proceedings of the 3rd ACM International Conference on Digital Libraries, June 23-26, 1998, Pittsburgh.* New York, ACM Press, pp. 254-263.

Weinstein, P.C. and Birmingham, W.P. (1998). Creating ontological metadata for digital library content and services. *International Journal on Digital Libraries.* vol. 2, no. 1, pp. 20-37.

Whittington, R.P. (1988). *Database Systems Engineering.* Oxford, Clarendon Press.

Wilson, P. (1968). *Two Kinds of Power: An Essay on Bibliographic Control.* Berkeley, University of California Press.

Wilson, P. (1983). The catalog as access mechanism: background and concept. *Library Resources & Technical Services.* vol. 27, no. 1, pp. 4-17.

Wilson, P. (1989a). Interpreting the second objective of the catalog. *Library Quarterly.* vol. 59, no. 4, pp. 339-353.

Wilson, P. (1989b). "The second objective." *The Conceptual Foundations of Descriptive Cataloging.* Svenonius, E., ed. San Diego, Academic Press, pp. 5-16.

Yee, M.M. (1994a). Manifestations and near-equivalents of moving image works: a research project. *Library Resources & Technical Services.* vol. 38, no. 4, pp. 355-372.

Yee, M.M. (1994b). What is a work?: part 1, the user and the objects of the catalog. *Cataloging & Classification Quarterly.* vol. 19, no. 1, pp. 9-27.

Yee, M.M. (1994c). What is a work?: part 2, the Anglo-American cataloging codes. *Cataloging & Classification Quarterly.* vol. 19, no. 2, pp. 5-22.

Yee, M.M. (1995a). What is a work?: part 3, the Anglo-American cataloging codes. *Cataloging & Classification Quarterly.* vol. 20, no. 1, pp. 25-46.

Yee, M.M. (1995b). What is a work?: part 4, cataloging theorists and a definition. *Cataloging & Classification Quarterly.* vol. 20, no. 2, pp. 3-24.

Yee, M.M. (1998). "What is a work?" *The Principles and Future of AACR: Proceedings of the International Conference on the Principles and Future Development of AACR, Toronto, Canada, October 23-25, 1997.* Weihs, J., ed. Chicago, American Library Association, pp. 62-104.

Young, H., ed. (1983). *The ALA Glossary of Library and Information Science.* Chicago, American Library Association.

Zumer, M. and Riesthuis, G.J.A. (2002). Consequences of implementing FRBR: are we ready to open Pandra's box?" *Knowledge Organization.* vol. 29, no. 2, pp. 78-86.

Index

a

A&I (abstracting-and-indexing) services 205, 213, 216
AACR (Anglo-American Cataloguing Rules) 17, 44
AACR1 45, 204-205, 207, 217
AACR2 26-27, 32, 37, 42-46, 59, 63, 65, 110, 197, Chapter 7, 243-244, 249, 250, 260-262, 279-282
Aalberg, T. 198
access points. *see also* headings
  additions to names 222
  definition of 2
  entry element of names 221
  objectives of 208
  principles of 30-31, 210, 219-222
  scope of 219-220
  source of information 220
access points/headings rules 202-203, 250-252
aggregate resources 124-128
ALCTS CCS CC:DA 40, 49, 195, 198
ANSI/SPARC three-level database architecture 5
attribute
  definition of 7

b

bibliographic description
  definition of 1
  language and script of 214
  levels of detail in 214
  objectives of 203-207
  organization of 214-216
  principles of 30-31, 210, 212-216, 223
  rules for. *see* descriptive rules
  source of information 213, 242-246, 260-261
  unit of 212
bibliographic entities 18-27, Chapter 3, Chapter 4
bibliographic relationships 27-30, Chapter 3, Chapter 4
Birmingham, W.P. 194-195
Bradford OPAC 191-192

c

cardinality 43, 47-49, 51, 54-55, 58-60
Carpenter, M. 16
cataloger tasks 32, 236, 240-241, 272-273
cataloging codes. *see also* cataloging rules
  logical structure of 203
  objectives of 30-31, 203, 210
cataloging process
  general model for 235
  modeling of 8, 32-33, 201, 235-236
cataloging rules. *see also* cataloging codes
  classification of 32, 236, 240
  design process of 8, 235-237
  detailed design of 8, 237, 268-269
cataloging system vendors 198
catalogs
  definition of 1
  design process of 8
  objectives/functions of 8, 13-15
class of materials 236-237, 243, 260-261, 278
Cockshutt, M.E. 37, 45
collocating objective 13-16, 208
component parts Chapter 4
conceptual data modeling 6
conceptual design
  characteristics of 5
  definition of 4

conceptual modeling
  characteristics of 5
  definition of 4
  language of 5, 7
conceptual schema 5
connectivity 43
content parts 108-111, 113-114, 116-122, 128
content versus carrier 130, 193
  see also work versus book
copy
  concept of 23, 46, 52-54
Crandall, M. 32, 240
Cutter, C.A. 14, 16, 209

d

database design 5-6, 8, 14, 21, 23
database life cycle 7
Delsey, T. 26, 42-43, 45, 63, 65, 83, 94, 108, 110, 112, 134-135, 144, 147, 197-198
descriptive bibliography 205, 213
descriptive rules 202-206, 222-231, 242-249
document parts 108, 110, 112-113, 115, 122-125, 128
Domanovszky, A. 17

e

electronic resources 41, 57, 99-103, 195
entity
  definition of 7
E-R (entity-relationship) model/modeling 7, 19, 23-24, 26, 32, 40, 64, 66
evidence
  classes of 273-275
  definition of 271
evidence recording Chapter 9
  orientedness in 272-273, 275-277
expression. *see also* text
  cardinality of 48
  concept of 25, Chapter 3, Chapter 4

existence of 48
title of 65-66
user tasks for 67, 77-78
ways of definition 54-55
expression-based record/cataloging 196
expression-level authority records 196
expression-level citation 196
external consistency of models 128

f

Fidel, R. 32, 240
finding objective 13-14, 208
five-tier hierarchical technique 190
formality 5
format variations 40, 130, 193, 195
four-tier hierarchical technique 190
FRBR implementation 134-135, 197-198
FRBR model 3, 14, 20, 24, Chapter 3, Chapter 4, 135, 144-145, 193-194, 197-198, 203, 210
functional requirements 201-202, 239-240
Functional Requirements for Bibliographic Records. *see* FRBR

g

GARE (Guidelines for Authority and Reference Entries) 25, 65
GARR (Guidelines for Authority Records and References) 280
Goossens, P. 28
Green, R. 14, 23, 28, 61-62
GSARE (Guidelines for Subject Authority and Reference Entries) 25
Guidelines for Bibliographic Description of Reproductions 40
Guidelines for the Application of the ISBDs to the Description of Component Parts 108

h

Hagler, R. 16
headings. *see also* access points
   definition of 2
   objectives of 208
headings rules. *see* access points/headings rules
Heaney, M. 22, 61-62
Hegna, K. 198
hierarchical multiple records approach 131-133, 189-190
hierarchical records model 189-190
hierarchical way of defining entites 25, 42-63
Hjerppe, R. 2
Hoffman, H.H. 16
Howarth, L.C. 45, 193-194

i

IFLA Section on Cataloguing, FRBR Review Group 198
inheritance of attributes 22, 43, 48, 66
implementation independence 5
internal consistency of models 128
International Conference on Cataloging Principles 13, 16-17, 41
ISAD(G) (General International Standard Archival Desctiption) 206
ISBD (International Standard Bibliographic Description) 25, 43, 65, 192, 195, 206, 212, 216-219
ISO/IEC 2382-20 4
item
   concept of 17, 19, 21, 25-26, Chapter 3, Chapter 4
   item level records 81-103, Chapter 5

j

Jeng, L.H. 32, 240, 242
Joint Steering Committee for Revision of AACR 15, 31, 49, 195, 198

Jolley, L.J. 41
Jones, B. 17-18
Jonsson, G. 46

k

Karakostas, V. 4, 5, 128
Kastner, A. 17-18
Kunitachi College of Music Library 192-193

l

Le Boeuf, P. 26, 32, 57, 198, 240
Leazer, G.H. 21, 30, 61-62
Library of Congress 134-135, 144, 147, 197
linked four-tier records structure 193-194
Loucopoulos, P. 4, 5, 128
Lubetzky, S. 14, 16, 41

m

main entry system 16, 250
manifestation
   concept of Chapter 3, Chapter 4
   manifestation level records 81-103, Chapter 5
mapping of data elements to entities 80-83, 94, 134-137, 144, 147, 197
MARC format 21-22, 43
MARC21 format 83, 134-137, 197, 279-280
Mazur-Rzesos, E. 28
model giving primacy to text-level entity 21, Chapter 3, Chapter 4, 194, 235
   implementation of Chapter 5, 192, 194-197
Molto, M. 32, 240-242
multiple manifestations 132, 135, 195, 197
multiple versions 40, 130, 189
Multiple Versions Forum 40, 189-190

multiplicity 43
Murtomaa, E. 198
musical works 110, 135, 143, 145, 149, 170

n

NACO Authority File Comparison Rules 148
navigation objective 15
NCR (Nippon Cataloging Rules) 212, 214, 216-217, 250
non-functional requirements 201-202, 239-240

o

objectiveness 203
object-oriented models/modeling 6-7, 22, 40, 42, 64, 66
OCLC 197
Olander, B. 2
O'Neil, E.T. 18, 61-62
online catalogs 2
OPAC 2, 40, 76-77, 79, 160, 191-193
orientedness Chapter 7, Chapter 8, 272-273, 275-278, 292-293
  categories of 204-209
  definition of 202-203

p

parallel way of defining entites 42-63, 194
Paris Principles. *see* International Conference on Cataloging Principles
Prakash, N. 4
principles of access. *see* access points, principles of
principles of description. *see* bibliographic description, principles of
process modeling 6

r

record conversion 133-160, 195

record design 8, 80, 189
record division 134-147
record exchange 132-133
record merge 148-150
record sharing 132-133
records structures 39, 131-133, Chapter 6
relationship
  definition of 7
requirements analysis and determination 5-8, 201-202, 239-240
Riesthuis, G.J.A. 198
Rolland, C. 4
rule markup languages 274
Rules for Descriptive Cataloging 204, 207, 217

s

scenario of usage 75-80
Schreiber, G. 274
SDLC (systems development life cycle) 5-6
segmental parts 72, 112
separate record model 190
Shaw, M. 250
Shelly, G.B. 6
single record approach 131-133, 195-197
Smiraglia, R.P. 29-30
Smith, D. 250
sound recording 93-99, 110
state transition model 242, 246
Statement of International Cataloguing Principles 15, 31
Studies of Descriptive Cataloging 204, 207
Svenonius, E. 15, 19, 27, 31-32, 61-62, 75, 190, 240-242, 251

t

task description 274-275
Teory, T.J. 7
text. *see also* expression

attributes of   20, 65-72
cardinality of   51, 54-55, 58
concept of   17-20, 22, 24, Chapter 3, Chapter 4
existence of   55
identifier for   57
identity of   56, 133
relationships of   21, 72-75, 197
unit of   51, 55-56, 110, 132-133, 145, 196
user tasks for   67, 69, 77-79
ways of definition   54-55
whole-part relationships of   72, 74, 111-112, 114, 117, 120, 122, 125
text level records   81-103, Chapter 5
text-prioritized model. *see* model giving primacy to text-level entity
Thayer, M.C.   4
Thayer, R.H.   4
three-layered model   19, 42, 50-52, 55, 58, 63, 68, 83, 190, 194
three-tier model   189-190
Tillett, B.B.   15, 21-22, 25, 29-30, 75
two-tier model   189

U

UML (Unified Modeling Language)   7, 42, 60, 75, 242, 246
UNIMARC format   28-29
upward pseudo-assignment of attribute values   66-67, 77-78, 109, 111-112, 125, 198
user scenario. *see* scenario of usage
user tasks   14-15, 25, 64-71, 75-80, 203, 210

V

Valacich, J.S.   6
Vellucci, S.L.   29, 46
Verona, E.   16, 41
Visine-Goetz, D.   18, 61-62

W

Wanninger, P.D.   18
Weinstein, P.C.   194-195
Whittington, R.P.   6
Wilson, P.   16-18, 20, 37-38, 51
work
  concept of   17-27, Chapter 3, Chapter 4
  existence of   59
work level records   81-103, Chapter 5
work versus book   16-17, 44
  see also content versus carrier

Z

Zumer, M.   198

【著者紹介】
谷口祥一（たにぐち　しょういち）
1958年　日立市生まれ
1985年　図書館情報大学卒業
1988―2002年　図書館情報大学 教員
2002年―現在　筑波大学大学院図書館情報メディア研究科
　　　　　　　教員

博士（図書館・情報学）（慶應義塾大学より）

【主な著書】
『図書館情報学における数学的方法』（共著. 日外アソシエーツ, 1994）,『図書館情報学ハンドブック』（第2版, 共著. 丸善, 1999）,『新訂情報検索演習』（共著. 東京書籍, 2004）,『図書館目録とメタデータ』（共著. 勉誠出版, 2004）,『知識資源のメタデータ』（共著. 勁草書房, 2007印刷中）, など

A Conceptual Modeling Approach to Design of Catalogs and Cataloging Rules

発行	2007年2月20日　初版1刷
定価	17000円＋税
著者	© 谷口祥一
発行者	松本　功
印刷所	三美印刷株式会社
製本所	田中製本印刷株式会社
発行所	株式会社 ひつじ書房

〒112-0002 東京都文京区小石川 5-21-5
Tel.03-5684-6871 Fax.03-5684-6872
郵便振替 00120-8-142852
toiawase@hituzi.co.jp　http://www.hituzi.co.jp/

ISBN978-4-89476-332-6　C3000

造本には充分注意しておりますが、落丁・乱丁などがございましたら、小社かお買上げ書店にておとりかえいたします。ご意見、ご感想など、小社までお寄せ下されば幸いです。

既刊書ご案内
進化する図書館へ　進化する図書館の会編　630円
税金を使う図書館から税金を作る図書館へ　松本功著　945円
都立図書館は進化する有機体である　ライブラリーマネジメント研究会編著
　　1050円
情報収集・問題解決のための図書館ナレッジガイドブック　東京都立中央図書館
　　編　2940円

刊行予定書ご案内
ビジネスを支援する図書館　Maxine Bleiweis著　松本功訳
学校図書館ハンドブック　足立正治・井上靖代・庭井史絵著
アメリカの学校図書館　川真田恭子著